THE
ISRAELI-PALESTINIAN
LEGAL
WAR

This Land is Ours

By: Joel M. Margolis

The Israeli-Palestinian Legal War:
This Land is Ours

Copyright © 2021 by Joel M. Margolis

For permissions, contact: authorjoelmargolis@gmail.com

Edited by A.R. Caingles
Cover by Achilles Mina
Book Layout Design Publication Assistance by Grace Perral (GP Digital)

ISBN: **978-0-578-94898-0** (paperback)

PREFACE

Media coverage of the Israeli-Palestinian conflict can be confusing. News reports often use legal terms of art without defining them or explaining their implications. You may have read some of these legal words. "Self-determination." "The British Mandate for Palestine." "Occupation." "The Green Line." "Resolution 242." "Illegal settlements." "The Oslo Accords." "Right of return." "Collective punishment."

Pro-Israeli and pro-Palestinian advocates use the same jargon to shoot off opinions like weapons fire. But what does it all mean? What legal arguments are the parties trying to advance, and who makes the better case?

The Search for Legal Answers

In my 36 years of practice in telecommunications and internet law, I have encountered many controversies where an interpretation of a word or two threatened to change the outcome of a proceeding. I have worked in both the public and private sectors, handling a mix of domestic and international proceedings. Some of these disputes were readily resolved, thanks to a strategic concession or breakthrough in understanding. Other matters remained in limbo despite abundant lawyering. The more emotional the issue, the harder it was to resolve.

During my upbringing, I became aware of an unusually impassioned legal logjam: the Israeli-Palestinian conflict. The following events helped focus my interest in the subject, and ultimately, my desire to write this book.

My maternal and paternal grandparents joined the early 20ᵗʰ Century wave of Jewish immigration to America. They escaped the scourge of European anti-Semitism before it mushroomed into the Holocaust. At the time, Americans tolerated Jews, but only up to a point.

The so-called respectable universities, professions, neighborhoods, and social groups erected tacit obstacles to Jews or excluded them overtly. Through the 1930s, it was perfectly acceptable for Father Charles Coughlin, a precursor of today's televangelists, to punctuate his weekly radio broadcasts with anti-Semitic rants. Jews had to climb out of poverty without the benefit of equal protection laws, government safety net programs, or political calls for "inclusiveness."

I once asked my mom's mother what it was like to reach Ellis Island at age 14. I said, "Grandma, you had no housing, no means of support, no protection from the xenophobic hatred of Jews, and no ability to speak English. Weren't you terrified?" She laughed and said, in her sing-song Yiddish voice, "Moshe, I knew if I could make it to America, everything would be fine."

My parents enjoyed an easier life but still felt the sting of discrimination. My father hoped his straight-A grades and other resume distinctions would qualify him for Brown University. They didn't. During the admissions interview, the questioner quickly focused on my dad's Jewish roots and then told him he'd probably feel more comfortable at another school.

By the 1960's and '70's, when I grew up, American Jews had fully assimilated. I can't recall a single instance during my life in the richly diverse community of Worcester, Massachusetts when I was disadvantaged or even insulted based on ethnicity. Through the mid-

20th Century, Jews allied with other minorities, especially African Americans, to expand civil rights.

But anti-Semitism still simmered in the U.S. and abroad. Among the worst offenders was the Soviet Union. As the communist authorities gradually permitted Jews to emigrate from that closed country, many resettled in Israel and the U.S. with the help of families like mine. My parents hosted a Soviet Jewish family at our house and helped them adapt to life in America. The adults in the room conversed in Yiddish, a language almost entirely unknown to my brother, my sister and me.

It wasn't until 2001, when the 9/11 attack grabbed the worlds' attention, that I began to wonder about militant Islam. I asked the same question raised at the Nuremburg trials: "What would drive members of one ethnic group to mass-murder other ethnic groups?" The horror of 9/11 was not an isolated event. Like-minded fundamentalist groups carried out bombings, shootings, and stabbings from Canada to Western Europe, Russia, India, Nigeria, Indonesia, Australia, and elsewhere.

The extremist movement, whatever its cause, spread far beyond the Middle East. Many of the affected governments sought advice on counterterrorism from Israel. That was no surprise. Israel had been losing civilians to a similar campaign of violence for over a century. There, the target of Muslim grievance was my own people. I wanted to know why.

I had little interest in the religious differences between Muslims and Jews. I already knew that spiritually; the two tribes were remarkably alike. My legal instincts urged me to learn which party in the Israeli-Palestinian conflict was right as a matter of law. I searched for a book that would objectively explain the opposing legal positions. But sadly, I couldn't find one.

Most legal works on the subject championed one side or the other. Some of the writings analyzed only one issue in the dispute without addressing the conflict as a whole. Still others offered theoretical constructs that fascinated scholars but offered scant practical value. What I needed was a complete, neutral, plain-talk presentation of the two opposing legal views. Eventually, I realized the only way to find such a book would be to write it myself.

You Be the Judge

The Israeli-Palestinian Legal War summarizes the major arguments on the major issues in the Israeli-Palestinian legal debate. They are the topics formally designated by the parties themselves as the ones most essential to achieving a "permanent status," or peace treaty.

All the pro-and-con contentions are made comprehensible to lawyers and non-lawyers alike.

The book's first chapter is the introduction, which provides a snapshot of the Israeli-Palestinian conflict and explains the methodology of my legal analysis. Chapter 2 summarizes the laws that govern the conflict. The third chapter gives a timeline of the legally significant events in the conflict from ancient times to today.

Chapter 4 is the heart of the book. It divides the Israeli-Palestinian legal fight into seven topics, covered in Subchapters 4.1 to 4.7. Each subchapter starts with an **Author's Prologue**, which outlines the factual and legal background for the given topic. Following this is a section explaining the Palestinian arguments on the topic ("**The Palestinian Arguments**"). The next section then discusses the Israeli arguments ("**The Israeli Arguments**").

The footnotes attribute each legal point to the particular advocate(s) who raised it. The hyperlinks lead to the texts of the advocates' work so readers can study the legal opinions in their original form and dig deeper into the debate.

In the final chapter, we consider how a two-sided understanding of the Israeli-Palestinian legal debate may help solve the long-running crisis. Nowhere does the book declare a winner of the legal war. By the end of the litigious process, readers should know enough to reach their own conclusions.

The Benefit of the Legal Approach

Why should we examine the Israeli-Palestinian conflict through a legal lens? First of all, there is no global legislature authorized to enact international law. The laws are made ad hoc by different collections of states, usually by treaty, depending only on their willingness to cooperate. Secondly, interpretations of international standards vary widely among legal scholars. There is no reliably independent judiciary to resolve the divergent views. Finally, the general absence of an enforcement mechanism leaves many international duties ignored. Some of the world's most aggressive offenders of human rights commit their crimes with scarcely a word of reproach from the UN.

The record of success of international law is uneven. For every legal initiative that helps to resolve a world conflict (e.g. the UN Security Council resolution authorizing an international force to reverse Iraq's invasion of Kuwait in 1990-1991), many more measures fail to achieve peace (e.g. the UN pronouncements meant to prevent the Rwandan genocide of 1994 and the Sudanese genocide/ethnic cleansing of 2003-2008).

And yet, the world still looks increasingly to global rules to solve every imaginable problem – from territorial disputes to trade friction, crime control, environmental protection, and human rights. Transnational enemies continue to plead their cases as quarrels of international law.

The Israeli-Palestinian dispute is no exception. Each constituency attributes the origin of the conflict to a breach of international law. Each sincerely believes the violation can and should be cured by compliance with international law. At least two of Israel's enemies – Egypt and Jordan – made peace with Israel through negotiated treaties, which are instruments of international law. The only mutually accepted plan to date that promises to resolve the Israeli-Palestinian conflict is the Oslo Accords, also an international contract. Admittedly, the Accords have not yet stopped the recurring bouts of Israeli-Palestinian bloodshed. Nevertheless, they have facilitated progress in key respects. They established interim safeguards against violence, framed the issues in dispute, and established a process to resolve them. Ultimately, only the law can provide what both parties crave the most: legitimacy.

Journey with me as I review the legal claims in the Israeli-Palestinian conflict. Then decide for yourself which party deserves what form of relief.

This Land is Ours

As we take the rugged tour of Israeli and Palestinian legal arguments, consider the larger question: "Why does it matter which ethnic groups occupy which plots of ground?" The dirt under our feet has no ethnicity. People of the same racial, religious or linguistic heritage can share their lifestyles without claiming sovereignty over a defined set of borders.

In the Internet age, close bonds of all kinds are formed among individuals who never physically meet.

And yet, despite the trend of globalization, ethnic majorities still actively hold sway over their states and defend their boundaries by force. The tendency runs in democracies and non-democracies alike. Once an ethnic group associates itself with a certain patch of earth, whether due to historic landmarks, access to waterways and agricultural resources, or the security of some natural barrier, the attachment is difficult to break. The words, "This land is ours" is not just a territorial claim. It is an expression of identity.

TABLE OF CONTENTS

GLOSSARY

Barrier	The structure built by Israel starting in 2002 to separate its population in Israel, East Jerusalem and the West Bank from the Palestinian population in the West Bank
Blockade	The security system installed by Israel starting in 2007 to separate its population from the Palestinian population in Gaza.
BMP	British Mandate for Palestine. The BMP was the treaty-like pronouncement of the League of Nations that authorized Great Britain as an administrator, or "mandatory," to establish a certain portion of the former Ottoman Empire as "a national home for the Jewish people" without prejudicing "the civil and religious rights" of the area's non-Jews.
	The BMP territory consisted of present-day Israel (including all of Jerusalem), Gaza, and the West Bank.
Green Line	The armistice (cease-fire) line between Israel and its neighboring Arab states (Egypt, Lebanon, Syria, and Jordan) at the end of the 1947-1948 War. By that stage of the war, the Arab armies had captured Gaza, East Jerusalem, and the West Bank, which together amounted to 27% of the

territory reserved for the Jewish people by the BMP.[1]

ICRC	International Committee of the Red Cross
IDF	Israel Defense Forces
IHL	International Humanitarian Law
League	League of Nations
Mandatory Palestine	Present-day Israel, Jordan and the Territories as governed by Great Britain from 1923 to 1948
NGO	Non-governmental organization
Oslo I	The 1993 Declaration of Principles (the first of the Oslo Accords)
Oslo II	The 1995 West Bank-Gaza Strip Agreement (one of the Oslo Accords)
PA	Palestinian Authority. The interim Palestinian government authorized by the Oslo Accords to control the major Palestinian population centers of the Territories pending negotiation with Israel of the "permanent status" issues in the parties' dispute.
PLO	Palestinian Liberation Organization
Territories	The Gaza Strip, East Jerusalem, and the West Bank
UN	United Nations
UNRWA	UN Relief and Works Agency for Palestine Refugees

---

[1] To compare the square mileage of sovereign Israel, Gaza, and the West Bank, *see* Bernard Wasserstein, *The Partition of Palestine*, Foreign Policy Research Institute (Dec. 9, 2014), https://www.fpri.org/article/2014/12/the-partition-of-palestine/.

CHAPTER 1:
INTRODUCTION

Palestine has been a holy ground and battle ground for thousands of years. On one level, the Israeli-Palestinian conflict is a fight over three sections of Palestine: the Gaza Strip, East Jerusalem, and the West Bank (collectively, the "Territories"). Beneath this layer lies a clash of two national movements.[2]

The Gaza Strip encompasses 140 square miles (363 square kilometers). It is about the size of Raleigh, N.C. East Jerusalem, meanwhile, covers 27 square miles (70 square kilometers), a space somewhat larger than Manhattan. The West Bank, on the other hand, is 2,180 square miles (5,650 square kilometers) – an area that would fit within Delaware. The whole of Israel is just 8,019 square miles (20,330 kilometers), or just a bit smaller than New Jersey.

A. Israelis and Palestinians both claim sovereign rights to the Territories

Palestinians assert a sovereign claim to the Territories based primarily on a core principle of international law, which is the "right to self-

---

[2] ALAN DOWTY, ISRAEL / PALESTINE 4-12 (2012) [hereinafter DOWTY].

determination." Their self-determination has been wrongly thwarted, they contend, by the movement of Jewish nationalism (Zionism), which displaced Arab Palestinians through aggressive immigration and property acquisition, nation-building, expulsions of Palestinians, military occupation, and annexation.

Israel's claim to the Territories is based primarily on the 1920 San Remo Resolution and the related 1922 British Mandate for Palestine. According to Israelis, Arabs have violated these instruments of international law by rejecting Israel's right to exist and striving to destroy the Jewish state through an endless series of wars, terrorist attacks, political pressure, and economic boycotts.

B. The Israeli-Palestinian peace talks failed to bring peace

To resolve their dispute, Israel and the Palestinians have engaged in numerous rounds of peace negotiations over many decades. The talks produced a set of agreements in the 1990's collectively called the Oslo Accords. It seemed that the Oslo Accords had succeeded in setting the belligerents on a path to peace. Sadly, the Accords remain only partially observed even today. Attempts to complete the Oslo-arranged "permanent status negotiations" have repeatedly failed. Since 1947, Arabs and Jews in the area have fought as many as 12 destructive wars that have claimed tens of thousands of lives.

Conditions between the wars have included countless sporadic eruptions of violence. The tactics on both sides have grown more sophisticated over time, with the death rate rising and falling unpredictably.

Israel is opposed by more than one militant group. A fluid mix of anti-Israel militias with different chains of command, resources, geographic reaches, and methods have either cooperated or competed to overcome their common enemy. The most prominent among these are: the Movement of Islamic Resistance, more commonly known as "Hamas" (whose military wing is known as the Izz ad-Din al-Qassam Brigades); the Palestine Islamic Jihad; and Fatah (whose military wing is the al-Aqsa Martyrs Brigade). Hamas has governed Gaza exclusively since 2007. Hamas and the Palestine Islamic Jihad also coordinate with a Lebanese terrorist group called Hezbollah which dominates Lebanon's government and informally rules the southern region of the country. Together, the group fought two wars with Israel.

In the West Bank, the political and military wings of Fatah hold sway. Fatah, which became the leading faction of the Palestine Liberation Organization (PLO), has conducted anti-Israel terror operations independent of the Gaza-based militants.

Not all the Arab powers dedicated to Israel's destruction in 1947 have remained a military threat. In the Camp David Accords of 1978, Egypt signed a land-for-peace treaty with Israel. The subject land was the Sinai Peninsula, which Israel had captured in the 1967 Six-Day War. In 1994 Israel signed another peace treaty with Jordan.

C. This study summarizes the Israeli-Palestinian legal debate

The legal quarrel between Israelis and Palestinians involves countless arguments, ancillary points, and fallback positions. Any synopsis of the debate requires drastic simplification.

The Israeli-Palestinian Legal War conducts the pruning process with a fierce commitment to neutrality. The study omits extremist legal theories in favor of mainstream views. Moreover, an argument labeled as "Palestinian" does not necessarily mean that the advocate is Palestinian. Some influential adherents to the Palestinian cause happen to be Israeli Jews. Likewise, certain pro-Israeli arguments have been advanced by non-Israelis.

Chapter 2 shows the legal framework of the Israeli-Palestinian debate. The laws include the Oslo Accords, a set of peace agreements signed by Israel and the Palestine Liberation Organization in the 1990's. Other guidelines are found in the treaties of international humanitarian law, human rights, law, and United Nations (UN) pronouncements.

Chapter 3 adds a legal timeline of the Holy Land rivalry from antiquity to today. Readers will see how today's legal antagonisms were foreshadowed by thousands of years of conflict. The timeline cites to several numbered maps, which are shown in numerical order in the appendix. The maps illustrate how the disputed land was administered over the centuries.

Chapter 4 contains the substance of the Israeli-Palestinian legal debate. The sections of this chapter examine the legal issues designated by the parties as the ones most instrumental to achieving a "permanent status," or peace treaty.[3] The first three sections outline the

---

[3] The instant legal analysis ignores a related struggle over land outside the Territories. In the 1967 Six-Day War, Israel captured a part of Syria called the Golan Heights. Since then, Israel

disagreement over where the parties should mark their borders. Specifically, these pages review the opposing arguments on the following questions: (a) have the Palestinians already established a sovereign state with borders encompassing the disputed territory; (b) does Israel have a sovereign claim to the same geography; and (c) should their mutual border be the 1949 "Green Line?" The subsequent section examines competing views on which party should govern Jerusalem. This is followed by the section on whether Israel may keep settlements in the disputed area. A later section exhibits the pro and con opinions on whether Palestinian refugees have a right of return to Israel. In the last section, the parties dispute the appropriate security parameters needed to maintain peace.[4]

Chapter 5, the Conclusion, assesses the implications of airing both sides of the Israeli-Palestinian legal debate. It invites the reader to consider the two perspectives on the conflict and decide for themselves how it should be resolved. Finally, it expresses the author's hope that a good faith dialogue between Israelis and Palestinians, strongly anchored on international law, will help resolve their differences.

D. **This study employs neutral terminology**

---

has annexed the Golan, but Syria never relinquished its sovereign claim. Attempts to negotiate the standoff have been fruitless. But that territorial deadlock does not necessarily affect the interplay of rights and responsibilities between Israel and the Palestinians.

[4] The parties' formal list of permanent status issues includes two more topics: "relations with neighboring states" and "other issues of common concern". But those matters seem too open-ended and political for a proper legal analysis. Therefore, they are excluded from this study.

In the Israeli-Palestinian debate, some legal issues are so contentious that the antagonists disagree over the words used to describe them. This study attempts to avoid controversy by using the following terms.

The Territories:

Palestinians refer to the Territories as "the occupied Palestinian territories" or "the State of Palestine." Israelis call the Territories "disputed" lands under "military administration." This study opts for the neutral term "Territories."

The West Bank:

The largest portion of the Territories is the West Bank. Israel knows the area by its two historic names, "Judea" (a word that referred to the Jews) and "Samaria." The UN once used the same terms.[5] However, when Jordan conquered those lands in the 1947-1948 war, it began to call them "the West Bank." It was an attempt to portray the area as the west side of the Jordan River, and by implication, the west side of Jordan. Since then the area has become most widely known by its Jordanian name. Therefore, that newer name is used herein.

Settlement:

The term "settlement" is considered pejorative by some pro-Israel stalwarts. To them, the expression makes Israeli communities in East

---

[5] In 1947, when UN Resolution 181 (III) proposed to partition Palestine into Arab and Jewish states, the world body described the land west of the Jordan River as "the hill country of Samaria and Judea." G.A. Res. 181 (III), U.N. Doc. A/RES/181(III) (Nov. 29, 1947) [hereinafter UN Partition Plan].

Jerusalem and the West Bank sound like the footholds of foreign colonial rule. The word "settlement" has no more legal significance than "community," "city," or "town." Nevertheless, Israel has formally accepted the word for purposes of the Oslo Accords, described further below. In fact, one of the core issues to be negotiated pursuant to the Accords is "settlements."[6] Therefore, the same word with the same meaning is used here.

The Barrier:

A combination of walls and fences separate Israel from the Territories. The array of structures is alternatively referred to as the "security fence," "separation barrier," "segregation wall," "annexation wall," and "apartheid wall." This study uses the non-connotative term "barrier."

Palestinians:

In the instant discussion, the Arab citizens of Israel are referred to as "Arab Israelis," while the Arab residents of the Territories are called "Palestinians." These terms track the legal distinction between the two groups, even though a small number of Arab Israelis identify themselves as "Palestinian."[7]

---

[6] Oslo 1, Article V.3.

[7] Noah Slepkov, Professor Camil Fuchs, Shmuel Rosner, *2020 Pluralism Index*, Jewish People Policy Institute (April 23, 2020), http://jppi.org.il/new/en/article/index2020/#_ftnref6. According to this report, 51% of the non-Jews living in Israel regard their "main identity" as "Arab Israeli," 23% of the non-Jewish individuals consider themselves "Israelis," 15% call

Terrorism:

One term used repeatedly in this study that has the potential of becoming a flashpoint is the word "terrorism." There is no universally accepted definition of terrorism.[8] Still, various treaties define the term for purposes of combating specific types of terrorist activity.[9] One such treaty, the Terrorist Financing Convention of 1999, is considered particularly authoritative because it was ratified by as many as 187 states.[10] The Convention defines "terrorism" as an act:

> intended to cause death or serious bodily injury to a civilian, or to any other person not taking an active part

---

themselves "Arabs," and seven percent say they are "Palestinian." The Jewish People Policy Institute describes itself as "an independent [non-profit] think tank" dedicated to the survival of the Jewish people.

[8] MALCOLM N. SHAW, *INTERNATIONAL LAW* 841-42 (2014) [hereinafter SHAW]. Professor Shaw is Senior Fellow at the Lauterpacht Centre for International Law at the University of Cambridge and a Trustee of the British Institute of International and Comparative Law. Previously, he taught international law and human rights law at the University of Leicester. He has advised the UK government and various other governments on matters of international law. He has also appeared before the ICJ, the European Court of Justice, and the European Court of Human Rights. His treatise on international law is a widely-cited textbook. His "International Law" has become a standard textbook for law school courses on the subject.

[9] *International Instruments Related to the Prevention and Suppression of International Terrorism*, ISBN 978-92-1-133777-8, United Nations publication Sales No. E.08.V.2, https://www.unodc.org/documents/terrorism/Publications /Int_Instruments_Prevention_and_Suppression_Int_Terrorism/Publication_-_English_-_08-25503_text.pdf.

[10] *See International Convention for the Suppression of the Financing of Terrorism*, G.A. Res. 54/109, U.N. Doc. A/RES/54/109 (Dec. 9, 1999) [hereinafter *Terrorist Financing Convention*], http://www.un.org/law/cod/finterr.htm.

in the hostilities in a situation of armed conflict, when the purpose of such act, by its nature or context, is to intimidate a population, or to compel a government or international organization to do or abstain from doing any act.[11]

Some Palestinians reject the word "terrorism." They view attacks on Israelis as acts of "resistance" to the Israeli "occupation." However, "resistance" has no legal meaning. Even more controversial, the word ascribes a political justification for the attack – as if the violence were confronting political oppression.

The rules of war apply equally to all combatants, regardless of political motive, and protect all civilians, regardless of political status. Therefore, the word for such acts should also be color-blind. Hence, the more agnostic word "terrorism" is more appropriate for a legal analysis.

E. The attached maps were chosen for accuracy, not advocacy

Any dispute involving a complex evolution of territorial claims cannot be understood without maps. However, a map maker may draw a border, emphasize a landmark, or add a caption in a way that favors an interested party.[12] Some maps in this study may reflect shades of political bias. But the items were chosen for their cartographic, historical, and socio-political accuracy, not to endorse any political

---

[11] *Terrorist Financing Convention*, Article 2(1)(b).

[12] For a good analysis of how maps convey ideologies, see Jeremy W. Crampton and John Krygier, *An Introduction to Critical Cartography*, 4.1 *ACME: An International Journal for Critical Geographies*, 11-33 (2005).

views. They are reproduced in this book as is to protect the rights of the copyright holders.

CHAPTER 2:
LAWS GOVERNING THE
ISRAELI-PALESTINIAN DISPUTE

Any analysis of the competing claims in the Israeli-Palestinian dispute requires an understanding of the relevant legal framework.

A. The parties agreed to seek peace through the Oslo Accords

Multiple sources of international law arguably apply to the Israeli-Palestinian dispute. Perhaps the most important source is the one negotiated by the disputants themselves. Between 1993 and 1999 Israel and the Palestine Liberation Organization (PLO) signed the Oslo Accords, a set of six agreements that gave Palestinians autonomy (but not a state), provisionally addressed the Israeli-Palestinian diplomatic impasse with an "interim" arrangement, and began a five-year process to negotiate a "permanent status" agreement.

The six Oslo Accords are: (1) the Declaration of Principles of 1993 (Oslo I);[13] (2) the Gaza-Jericho Agreement of 1994;[14] (3) the Israeli-Palestinian

---

[13] *Declaration of Principles on Interim Self-Government Arrangements*, Sept. 13, 1993, Israel – P.L.O., 32 I.L.M. 1525 [hereinafter Oslo I].

[14] *Agreement on the Gaza Strip and Jericho Area*, May 4, 1994, Israel – P.L.O., 33 I.L.M. 622.

Interim Agreement on the West Bank-Gaza Strip of 1995 (Oslo II);[15] (4) the Hebron Protocol of 1997;[16] (5) the Wye River Memorandum of 1998;[17] and (6) the Sharm el-Sheik Memorandum of 1999.[18]

Along with the Oslo Accords, Israel and the PLO also signed a companion agreement called the Paris Protocol of 1994 to establish interim terms of economic cooperation.[19] This was incorporated into the Israeli-Palestinian Interim Agreement on the West Bank-Gaza Strip of 1995 (Oslo 2). The Paris Protocol established a "customs union" designed to facilitate borderless trade between the parties. The arrangement essentially preserved economic relations already in effect at the time.

---

[15] *Interim Agreement on the West Bank and the Gaza Strip*, Sept. 28, 1995, Israel – P.L.O., 36 I.L.M. 551 [hereinafter Oslo 2].

[16] *Protocol Regarding the Redeployment in Hebron*, Jan. 17, 1997, Israel – P.L.O., 36 I.L.M. 650.

[17] *Wye River Memorandum*, Oct. 23, 1998, Israel – P.L.O., 37 I.L.M. 1251.

[18] *Sharm-el-Sheikh Memorandum on Implementation of Timeline of Outstanding Commitments of Agreements Signed and the Resumption of Permanent Status Negotiations*, Sept. 4, 1999, Israel – P.L.O., 38 I.L.M. 1465, http://mfa.gov.il/MFA/ForeignPolicy/MFADocuments/Pages/Treaties%20and%20Agreements.aspx.

[19] *Gaza-Jericho Agreement*, Annex IV, *Protocol on Economic Relations between the Government of the State of Israel and the P.L.O., representing the Palestinian People*, April 29, 1994 [hereinafter Paris Protocol], https://mfa.gov.il/MFA/ForeignPolicy/Peace/Guide/Pages/Gaza-Jericho%20Agreement%20Annex%20IV%20-%20Economic%20Protoco.aspx .

Various joint statements by the parties fleshed out further details of the Oslo arrangement between 1994 and 1999.[20] The Accords also created the Palestinian Authority (PA), an administrative body charged with the temporary governance of the major Palestinian population centers in the Territories pending negotiation of the permanent status agreement. The permanent status negotiations have been repeatedly stalled due to eruptions of hostilities and political mistrust.

The Oslo Accords are not treaties. Treaties are agreements between or among states,[21] and the Palestinian signatory in the Accords was the PLO, not a state.[22] However, the signatories of the Accords, as well as legal scholars, believe the Accords constitute a non-treaty agreement

---

[20] *See Agreement on Temporary International Presence in Hebron of 1994*, Joint Communique of 1996 (after the first round of permanent status negotiations), Protocol Concerning the Redeployment in Hebron of 1997, Note for the Record of 1997 (prepared by the US Special Middle East Coordinator to confirm agreements on issues unrelated to Hebron), Trilateral Statement of 2000 (concluding a round of final status negotiations at Camp David and outlining principles to guide future talks), and Joint Statement of 2001 (after final status negotiations in Taba, Egypt).

[21] *Vienna Convention on the Law of Treaties*, art. 2.1 (signed May 23, 1969, entered into force Jan. 27, 1980) [hereinafter *Vienna Convention*], http://www.oas.org/legal/english/docs/Vienna%20Convention%20Treaties.htm.

[22] GEOFFREY R. WATSON, *THE OSLO ACCORDS: INTERNATIONAL LAW AND THE ISRAELI-PALESTINIAN PEACE AGREEMENTS* 57-74 (2000) [hereinafter WATSON]. Professor Watson is the Director, Comparative and International Law Institute Professor of Law at Catholic University's Columbus School of Law. Previously he served as an attorney-advisor in the Office of the Legal Adviser of the US State Department, specializing in international criminal law and US policy in the Middle East. His book, The Oslo Accords, was the first comprehensive analysis of the agreements, and it remains a widely-cited reference work on the topic.

between Israel, a state, and the PLO, a non-state entity, but nevertheless a "subject [under the authority] of international law."[23]

B. IHL governs parties engaged in armed conflicts or occupations

The body of international law that protects against undue harm in the context of war and military occupations is known as international humanitarian law (IHL). IHL is expressed in a set of global treaties. The oldest IHL treaties are the 1899 and 1907 Hague Regulations.[24] The 1907 Hague Regulations superseded the 1899 version. Formal interpretations of IHL are issued by the International Committee of the Red Cross (the "ICRC"), a component of the International Red Cross and Red Crescent Movement.[25] The ICRC is a major voice in the Israeli-Palestinian legal debate due its mission of monitoring compliance with IHL.

---

[23] Vienna Convention, art. 3; WATSON, *supra* at 91-102.

[24] *Hague Convention (2) Respecting the Laws and Customs of War on Land* and its *Annex: Regulation Concerning the Laws and Customs of War on Land,* July 29, 1899, arts. 23, 42-42, 187 Consol. T.S. 429; *Hague Convention (4) Respecting the Laws and Customs of War on Land and its Annex: Regulations Concerning the Laws and Customs of War on Land,* Oct. 18, 1907, 36 Stat. 2277, 1 Bevans 631, 205 Consol. T.S. 277 [hereinafter the *Hague Regulations*], https://ihl-databases.icrc.org/ihl/INTRO/195.

[25] *Statutes of the International Red Cross and Red Crescent Movement,* art. 4, para. 2(g). The ICRC is authorized, among other things, "to work for the understanding and dissemination of knowledge of international humanitarian law applicable in armed conflicts and to prepare any development thereof . . . "

Although Israel is not a party to the Hague Regulations, which were adopted long before Israel was declared a state, Israel's Supreme Court has accepted their precepts as binding "customary international law"[26] and incorporated them into its domestic law.[27] A "binding" law is one that is legally enforceable. Treaties, for example, are binding laws, whereas U.N. General Assembly resolutions are merely advisory political statements. Customary international laws are unwritten tenets considered so basic to universal notions of justice that they bind all states and non-state actors, even those that never signed the treaty-codified versions of the laws. A standard of conduct becomes customary international law if it is a widespread and uniform practice of nations, and if nations follow the practice out of a sense of legal obligation (called *opinio juris*).[28] Unfortunately, different states frequently debate which standards meet these criteria.[29] The important point is that a customary international law is binding (i.e. legally enforceable) on *all* international actors, even those that do not consent to it.

Israel's acceptance of customary international law influences its administration of the Territories. When the Israeli Supreme Court

---

[26] Keren Greenblatt, *Gate of the Sun: Applying Human Rights Law in the Occupied Palestinian Territories in Light of Non-Violent Resistance and Normalization*, Nw. 12 UJ Int'l Hum. Rts. 152, 167-68 (2014) [hereinafter Greenblatt].

[27] *Head of Deir Samit Village Council v. Commander of the IDF Forces in the West Bank and Commander of the Hebron Brigade*, HCJ 3969/06 (October 22, 2009) [hereinafter *Deir Samit Village Council*], para 10.

[28] Jack Landman Goldsmith III, Eric A. Posner, *A Theory of Customary International Law*, University of Chicago Law School, John M. Olin Law & Economics Working Paper 63, 5 (1998), https://core.ac.uk/download/pdf/234136256.pdf .

[29] *Id.* at 4.

reviews the actions of the military commander in the Territories, the customary provisions of IHL are included in the applicable law.[30]

The Palestinians have not signed the Hague Regulations but are considered subject to them by force of customary law.

In 1949, the world community signed a set of four more IHL treaties known collectively as the Geneva Conventions. The post-world war Conventions emerged to protect certain classes of individuals not involved in fighting during a war.[31] The first three Conventions protected soldiers who were wounded, sick, shipwrecked, or held as prisoners during times of war.[32] The Fourth Geneva Convention extended similar wartime protection to civilians.[33]

Israel ratified (signed) and acceded to (became subject to) the Fourth Convention in 1951. But the Jewish state does not believe the Fourth Convention applies to its administration of the Territories. It contends, based on the Convention's inaugural provisions, that occupation law applies only where a combatant seizes the territory of a sovereign government, and that Israel took the Territories from two countries

---

[30] *Yesh Din v. IDF Commander in the West Bank*, HCJ 2690/09 (March 17, 2010) at para. 6.

[31] The Geneva Conventions of 1949 and their Additional Protocols, ICRC (Oct. 29, 2010), https://www.icrc.org/eng/war-and-law/treaties-customary-law/geneva-conventions/overview-geneva-conventions.htm.

[32] *Id.*

[33] *Id. See Geneva Convention Relative to the Protection of Civilian Persons in Time of War*, Aug. 12, 1949, arts. 2-3, 6, 75 U.N.T.S. 287] [hereinafter the Fourth Convention], https://ihl-databases.icrc.org/applic/ihl/ihl.nsf/Treaty.xsp?documentId=AE2D398352C5B028C12563CD002D6B5C&action=openDocument.

(Egypt and Jordan) that never acquired sovereignty in those lands.[34] In practice, however, Israel has pledged to respect the treaty's "humanitarian provisions" on a *de facto* (in practice) basis despite their lack of *de jure* (in law) applicability.[35] Israel has not enumerated the specific provisions that it considers as 'humanitarian.'[36]

Israel's Supreme Court asserted jurisdiction over the nation's military authorities.[37] But because the state never incorporated the Geneva Conventions into its domestic law, the Supreme Court found itself jurisdictionally barred from interpreting the Fourth Convention provision that determines whether there is an occupation in the Territories.[38] On the other hand, as the Court reviewed IDF activities in the Territories, the judges reasoned that certain humanitarian portions of the Fourth Convention applied to the Territories on a *de jure* basis as

---

[34] Greenblatt, *supra* at 167. Israel's occupation law position is explained more fully at Chapter 4.5.B.ii.

[35] Kretzmer Supreme Court, *supra* at 208-210.

[36] Greenblatt, *supra* at 167. Israel implements the humanitarian provisions of occupation law through its military code. In fact, the first military commander of the Territories unilaterally incorporated the Fourth Convention in the military code at the outset of the alleged occupation in 1967, before the government's political and judicial branches had analyzed whether an occupation had legally occurred. DAVID KRETZMER, *THE OCCUPATION OF JUSTICE* 32 (2002) [hereinafter KRETZMER *OCCUPATION*].

[37] *Id.* Technically speaking, Israel's Supreme Court sits as the "High Court of Justice" when adjudicating matters such as petitions from Palestinians, which do not fall under the jurisdiction of any other Israeli court. *The High Court of Justice*, the High Court of Justice Website, https://knesset.gov.il/lexicon/eng/bagatz_eng.htm (last viewed September 30, 2017).

[38] KRETZMER *SUPREME COURT*, *supra* at 212-213.

customary law.[39] The Court has made its customary law determinations on a case-by-case basis.[40] Where these provisions of humanitarian law prove inadequate to address a case, the Court may supplement its analysis with guidance from human rights law.[41] Meanwhile, the Court has followed the English law approach to international law by enforcing customary international laws only to the extent that they can be reconciled with Israel's domestic laws.[42]

In sum, while Israel does not consider itself an occupying power in the Territories, it administers those lands under an evolving but unlisted mix of nonbinding (humanitarian) and binding (customary) provisions of occupation law. The binding provisions are those found in The Hague Regulations and certain humanitarian clauses of the Fourth Convention. The binding elements are enforced to the extent found consistent with domestic law.

Outside Israel, the state's interpretation of the Fourth Convention has been universally rejected.[43] The ICRC, UN Security Council, and UN General Assembly have all opined that the entire Fourth Convention binds Israel as customary law in all situations of armed conflict and

---

[39] Greenblatt, *supra* at 167-70. *See also Yesh Din et. al. v IDF Commander in the West Bank*, HCJ 2690/09 (March 28, 2010) at para. 6.

[40] *Id.*

[41] *Head of Deir Samit Village Council v Commander of IDF Forces in the West Bank*, HCJ 3969/06 (Oct. 22, 2009) at para. 10.

[42] KRETZMER *SUPREME COURT*, *supra* at 211-212.

[43] Hiba B'irat, *International Law Position on the Israeli Separation Wall 2*, Palestinian American Community Center (May 10, 2017), https://www.paccusa.org/blog/international-law-position-on-the-israeli-separation-wall-2 .

occupation, including its control of the Territories. Joining this position was the International Court of Justice, or ICJ. The ICJ is the component of the UN that adjudicates legal disputes submitted to it by states and delivers advisory opinions on questions raised by the other UN departments.

In 2012, when the UN General Assembly named "Palestine" a non-member observer state, Palestinians applied for membership as a state in several international treaties. On this basis, in 2014 Palestine ratified and acceded to the Fourth Convention.

After enacting the Fourth Convention, the international community elaborated on IHL via three more instruments called "protocols." Most relevant to the protection of civilians in wartime were the 1977 Additional Protocols I and II.[44] Israel has not become a party to the Additional Protocols. Neither Protocol, as a whole, is considered international customary law. On the other hand, Israel's Supreme Court has ruled that at least some provisions of Additional Protocol I are customary and therefore binding on Israel.[45]

---

[44] *Protocol Additional to the Geneva Conventions of 12 August 1949, and relating to the Protection of Victims of International Armed Conflicts*, 8 June 1977, 1125 UNTS 3 [hereinafter Protocol 1], https://ihl-databases.icrc.org/applic/ihl/ihl.nsf/Treaty.xsp?documentId=D9E6B6264D7723C3C12563CD002D6CE4&action=openDocument; *Protocol Additional to the Geneva Conventions of 12 August 1949, and relating to the Protection of Victims of Non-International Armed Conflicts*, 8 June 1977, 1125 UNTS 609 [hereinafter Protocol 2], https://ihl-databases.icrc.org/applic/ihl/ihl.nsf/Treaty.xsp?documentId=AA0C5BCBAB5C4A85C12563CD002D6D09&action=openDocument.

[45] Deir Samit Village Council, *supra* at para. 10; *Beit Iksa Local Council v Minister of Defense*, HCJ 281/11 (September 6, 2011) at para. 25.

The State of Palestine, represented by the PLO, ratified and acceded to Additional Protocol I in 2014 and to Additional Protocol II in 2015.

If a nation is bound by a source of IHL (whether through ratification and accession or via customary law), and one of its citizens (e.g. a military commander) commits a "grave" (extreme) breach of that law, that person is said to have committed a "war crime." A war crime may be prosecuted in any nation's courts. Alternatively, the trial may be held in an ad hoc international tribunal, if a tribunal is established for such purpose. If no other forum is available, the case may be brought before the International Criminal Court (ICC), if that court has jurisdiction.

Backstopping the enforcement of IHL is the 2002 Rome Statute, which founded the ICC.[46] The purpose of the ICC is to prosecute the most serious international crimes when there are no other venues for prosecution. The list of ICC-level crimes includes genocide, crimes against humanity (including ethnic cleansing and apartheid), war crimes, and the crime of aggression.

Although most states have ratified and acceded to the Rome Statute, there are many significant exceptions, including the US, Russia, China, India, most of the Arab Middle East, and Israel. The objectors feared, among other things, that their enemies might politicize the ICC and

---

[46] International Criminal Court, *Rome Statute of the International Criminal Court*, U.N. Doc. A/CONF.183/9 (1998) [hereinafter *Rome Statute*], http://undocs.org/A/CONF.183/9.

wield it as a weapon against their leaders.[47] The Statute is not considered customary law.

The State of Palestine has ratified and acceded to the Rome Statute.[48] Whether the accession was valid depends on whether Palestine is a state. That issue is addressed in Chapter 4.

C. The parties are also bound by human rights law

IHL is a subset of human rights law.[49] Both bodies of law protect human life, health, and dignity.[50] Human rights law outlines the obligations of governments towards their inhabitants.[51] Its purpose is to guarantee rights such as freedom of speech, freedom of assembly, freedom of religion, freedom of movement, health, education, and self-determination.[52] By comparison, the purpose of IHL is to balance considerations of military necessity against risks of harm to non-combatants in times of armed conflict and military occupations.[53] More

---

[47] *See, e.g. U.S. Announces Intent Not to Ratify International Criminal Court Treaty,* American Society of International Law, (May 11, 2002), https://www.asil.org/insights/volume/7/issue/7/us-announces-intent-not-ratify-international-criminal-court-treaty.

[48] *International Criminal Court Welcomes Palestine as State Party to the Rome Statute,* UN News Centre (April 1, 2015), http://www.un.org/apps/news/story.asp?NewsID=50477#.WclutsiGNRY .

[49] Greenblatt, *supra,* at 153-54.

[50] *Id.*

[51] *Id.*

[52] See *Id.*

[53] See *Id.*

specifically, the IHL precepts of the Fourth Convention require that during a battle or occupation, combatants must pursue their military objectives in a manner that minimizes civilian harm.

IHL and human rights law address some of the same topics, including the arbitrary or unlawful deprivation of life, the right to a fair trial, torture, and the abuse of women and children. The regulatory overlap sometimes causes confusion over which set of laws should apply. Some legal experts view IHL as the *lex specialis* (superseding body of law) that supersedes human rights law during armed conflicts and military occupations.[54] Human rights must yield to those emergency demands, the thinking goes, or a combatant may risk its own security.[55] Other experts apply human rights law and IHL as co-equal legal regimes.[56]

The three main treaties of human rights law are the 1948 Universal Declaration of Human Rights,[57] the 1966 International Covenant on

---

[54] Greenblatt, *supra* at 157.

[55] EYAL BENVENISTI, *THE INTERNATIONAL LAW OF OCCUPATION* 75 (2d. ed., Kindle Edition 2012) [hereinafter BENVENISTI]. Professor Benvenisti is Whewell Professor of International Law, University of Cambridge. He serves on the editorial boards of the British Yearbook of International Law and the American Journal of International Law. He was previously a professor of human rights at Tel Aviv University and a member of the Global Law faculty at New York University School of Law. His supremely analytical survey of post-World War II occupations, "The International Law of Occupation," revived interest in a long-neglected body of law.

[56] Greenblatt, *supra*, at 157.

[57] *Universal Declaration of Human Rights* (Dec. 10, 1948) [hereinafter *Universal Declaration of Human Rights*], http://www.un.org/en/universal-declaration-human-rights/.

Civil and Political Rights,[58] and the 1966 International Covenant on Economic, Social and Cultural Rights.[59] Another human rights treaty, one of particular relevance to the Israeli-Palestinian dispute, is the 1951 Convention Relating to the Status of Refugees.[60] The Refugee Convention figures in debates over the rights of Palestinians who claimed refugee status after the 1947-1948 War of Independence, when the State of Israel was founded.

Various other treaties give human rights further elaboration. For the following reasons, only select issues of human rights law are addressed in this analysis.

Just as the ICRC monitors international compliance with IHL, the UN Human Rights Council (UNHRC) oversees the observance of human rights law. The UNHRC is the UN agency responsible for examining and issuing pronouncements on human rights offenses worldwide. However, the Council cannot track human rights in the Territories because no party reports on those matters. Israel does not file such reports for four reasons: 1) the Knesset never adopted the human rights treaties into Israel's domestic law, [61] 2) Israel does not consider itself

---

[58] *International Covenant on Civil and Political Rights* (Dec. 16, 1966), http://www.ohchr.org/en/professionalinterest/pages/ccpr.aspx.

[59] *International Covenant on Economic, Social and Cultural Rights* (Dec. 16, 1966), http://www.ohchr.org/EN/ProfessionalInterest/Pages/CESCR.aspx.

[60] Office of the High Commissioner for Human Rights, *Convention Relating to the Status of Refugees* (July 28, 1951) [hereinafter the *Refugee Convention*], http://www.ohchr.org/EN/ProfessionalInterest/Pages/StatusOfRefugees.aspx.

[61] Greenblatt, *supra* at 173-74.

41

responsible for human rights beyond its recognized borders, [62] 3) the nation points to the Palestinian governments as the parties responsible for human rights in the Palestinian-controlled reaches of the Territories,[63] and 4) the government says IHL supersedes human rights law as the *lex specialis* in the Territories.[64]

The UNHRC rejects Israel's human rights analysis.[65] The agency holds Israel responsible for human rights in the Territories based on the theory that the properties fall within Israel's effective control.[66]

The two Palestinian governments – Hamas in the Gaza Strip and the Palestinian Authority (PA) in the West Bank – avoid the Council's purview on the grounds that neither represents a UN member state.

The Oslo Accords require both Israel and the Palestinians to perform their contractual obligations "with due regard to internationally-accepted norms and principles of human rights ..."[67] However, the Accords do not state which party is responsible for human rights in which parts of the Territories. The legal terms merely assign to the PA

---

[62] *Id.*

[63] *Id. See also Implementation of the International Covenant on Economic, Social and Cultural Rights – Second Periodic Report*, State of Israel, UN Doc. E/1990/6/Add.32 (August 3, 2001), paras. 5-8, http://undocs.org/E/1990/6/Add.32 .

[64] Greenblatt, *supra* at 173-74.

[65] Office of the High Commissioner for Human Rights, *Concluding Observations on the Fourth Periodic Report of Israel*, CCPR/C/ISR/CO/4 (Nov. 20, 2014), http://undocs.org/CCPR/C/ISR/CO/4 .

[66] *Id.*

[67] Oslo II, art. XIX.

control of the major Palestinian population centers of the Territories (Area A), preserve Israel's control of the outer reaches of the Territories (Area C), and give the parties shared control of the spaces in between (Area B). As a practical matter, neither party takes any particular steps to implement the unelaborated provision in the Territories.[68] Instead, each accuses the other of human rights violations without limiting their complaints to certain Oslo-assigned zones.

The present inquiry mentions the above-named human rights conventions as needed to address the Israeli-Palestinian controversy over refugee rights. Beyond that, human rights laws will not be explored. They do not directly govern any other Oslo-defined "permanent status" issue in the dispute. Given the unsettled relationship between human rights law and IHL, it is unclear whether and how human rights norms apply to the dispute. And without Israeli or Palestinian cooperation with the Human Rights Council, there is no reliable human rights record in the Territories to analyze.

D. The conflict has been addressed by countless UN resolutions

The Israeli-Palestinian conflict has been addressed by countless UN resolutions, with numerous Muslim UN member states voting against Israel.[69] When resolutions are adopted by the 193-member UN General Assembly, they are merely political statements, not binding (i.e. legally

---

[68] WATSON, *supra*, at 168-69 (2000).

[69] Greenblatt, *supra* at 175.

enforceable) rulings like those of a court, because the Assembly has only the power of recommendation.[70] Also, the political pronouncements are not constrained by international law. If a General Assembly resolution claims a state action is "illegal," the action may or may not actually be illegal. Despite these limitations, General Assembly resolutions passed by a wide margin of votes can provide important expressions of global opinion.

When a resolution is passed by the 15-member UN Security Council, it is not always clear whether the communication is binding or merely advisory.[71] If the Council acts under the remit of UN Charter Chapter VI, the resolution is advisory.[72] If the Council acts under Chapter VII, lawyers look to other indicia to determine whether the measure is binding. If the text lacks an enforcement mechanism (i.e. economic or military sanctions), and the language is not expressly binding, the message is thought to be advisory.[73] Under these circumstances, international lawyers have generally not argued that any Security Council resolutions addressing the Israeli-Palestinian dispute are binding.

The most important UN pronouncement on Israeli-Palestinian affairs was UN Security Council Resolution 242, adopted after the 1967 Six-

---

[70] UN Charter, art. 10.

[71] Security Council Report (June 23, 2008), *Special Research Report: Security Council Action under Chapter VII*, http://www.securitycouncilreport.org/atf/cf/%7B65BFCF9B-6D27-4E9C-8CD3-CF6E4FF96FF9%7D/Research%20Report%20Chapter%20VII%2023%20June%2008.pdf.

[72] *Id.*

[73] *Id.*

Day War and reaffirmed in Resolution 338 after the 1973 Yom Kippur War.[74] These Resolutions directed Israel and its neighboring Arab states to resolve their dispute through negotiation.

E. Legal judgments are shaped by equitable considerations

International lawyers, like their domestic counterparts, interpret legal standards against a backdrop of equitable concerns.[75] An equitable argument is a notion of fairness rooted in non-legal sources such as politics, economics, philosophy, and the sciences.[76] For example, Palestinians and Israelis both claim historic ties to the land. Both sides regard some or all the Territories as spiritually sacred. And throughout the violent conflict, both have lost many lives. This discussion highlights the major equities in their dispute to the extent those concerns are raised by their advocates.

---

[74] UN Security Council, S.C. Res. 242, U.N. Doc. S/RES/242 (Nov. 22, 1967) [hereinafter Resolution 242], https://digitallibrary.un.org/record/90717?ln=en ; S.C. Res. 338, U.N. Doc. S/RES/338 (Oct. 22, 1973) [hereinafter Res. 338], https://digitallibrary.un.org/record/93466?ln=en .

[75] *See* SHAW, *supra* at 31-48.

[76] *Id.* at 40.

CHAPTER 3:
LEGAL TIMELINE OF THE
ISRAELI-PALESTINIAN DISPUTE

The eastern Mediterranean region, traditionally known as the Levant, is one of the cradles of civilization (see Map 1, Prehistoric: The Levant).

MAP 1
THE LEVANT(PREHISTORIC)

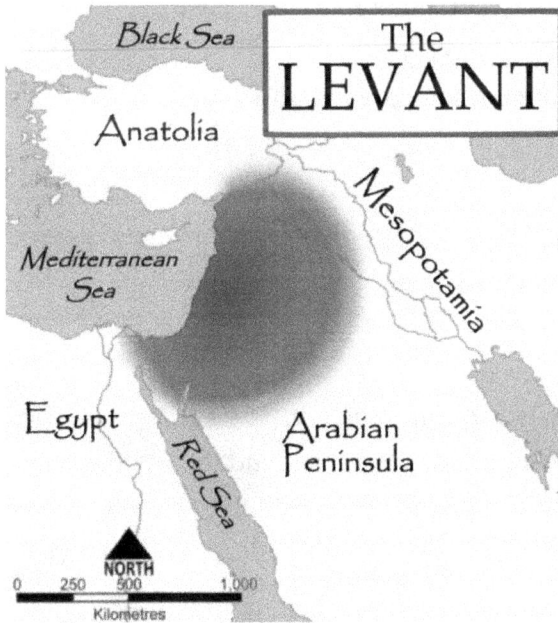

Source: No machine-readable author provided. MapMaster assumed (based on copyright claims). - No machine-readable source provided. Own work assumed (based on copyright claims). https://bit.ly/ajm-map1, CC BY-SA 3.0,

Note: To see this map in its original color version (with a zoom-in feature for more detailed viewing), download the PDF in the Appendix.

On the shore of Israel's Lake Tiberius (also called the Sea of Galilee or Lake Kinneret) near the northern tip of present-day Israel, archeologists found evidence of a society dating back 20,000 years.[77] Biblical scholars attribute a uniquely seminal role to one Levantine figure: Abraham. They report that between 2100 and 1800 B.C.E. Abraham lived near the town of Hebron, in the region known today as the West Bank, and founded the Jewish religion.

Although historians debate whether and how the Biblical account of Abraham matches the secular evidence known to date, Judaism spread throughout the Levant and beyond. Some of its core precepts appeared in later faiths, most prominently Christianity and Islam. Followers of all three religions, plus many others, laid claim to territory in the region. The conflicts frequently exploded into wars.

One of the current Levantine conflicts is a struggle for sovereignty in the Territories. Assessing the dispute from a legal perspective requires a historical review. The following timeline summarizes the relevant events from ancient times to today.

1206 B.C.E. Early Israelite Society. The earliest historical reference to the Israelites (the self-claimed descendants of the Biblical patriarchs Abraham, Isaac and Jacob) appears in the 1206 B.C.E. Merneptah Stele, a stone monument inscribed by Egyptian Pharaoh Merneptah, son of

---

[77] Jordan Valley Eco-Center (last viewed Nov. 27, 2016), *Neolithic Jericho and the Origins of Civilization*, http://www.aujaecocenter.org/index.php/the-story-of-the-valley/neolithic-jericho-and-the-origins-of-civilization.

Ramesses II.[78] Archaeologists have uncovered additional evidence of an Israelite tribe in the central hill country north and south of Jerusalem and the lower Galilee.[79]

ca. 1020 B.C.E. Jewish Rule. The Israelite tribes organize the Kingdom of Israel, first under the rule of King Saul in 1020 B.C.E. and then King David. The Kingdom corresponds to present-day Israel, the Territories, much of Jordan, and portions of Lebanon and Syria (see Map 2, The Ancient Kingdom of Israel, ca. 1020 BCE).

---

[78] William Dever, *Archeology of the Hebrew Bible*, Nova, PBS.org, November 18, 2008, http://www.pbs.org/wgbh/nova/ancient/archeology-hebrew-bible.html.

[79] *Id.*

MAP 2,
THE ANCIENT KINGDOM
OF ISRAEL (C. 1020 B.C.)

By Regno di Davide.svg: RobertoReggi12 Tribes of Israel Map.svg:
Richardprins12_tribus_de_Israel.svg: Translated by Kordas12 staemme israels
heb.svg: by user:12⬤⬤⬤⬤ staemme israels.png: by user:Janzderivative work:
Richardprins (talk) - Regno di Davide.svg12 Tribes of Israel
Map.svg12_tribus_de_Israel.svg12 staemme israels heb.svg12 staemme israels.png,
CC BY-SA 3.0, https://bit.ly/ajm-map2

*Note: To see this map in its original color version (with a zoom-in feature for more
detailed viewing), download the PDF in the Appendix.*

On or about 1006 B.C.E. Jerusalem becomes the Kingdom's political, spiritual, and cultural center. David is succeeded by his son Solomon, who orders the construction of a Jewish Temple on the Temple Mount, an elevated site in the city's center.[80] This temple, more popularly known at that time as *Solomon's Temple* – and later as the *First Temple* – becomes the holiest place in Judaism.

ca. 722 B.C.E. Assyrian Rule. The Assyrians overthrow the Kingdom of Israel.

586 B.C.E. Babylonian Rule. Babylonian invaders destroy the First Temple and drive the Jews into exile. Jewish liturgy incorporates a prayer of devotion to "Eretz Yisrael" (the Land of Israel)[81] and Jews adopt the practice of facing Jerusalem when they worship.

538-515 B.C.E. Persian Rule. The next group of foreigners to invade the Land of Israel are the Persians, who defeat the Babylonian Empire. A Persian policy of religious toleration permits Jews to regain autonomy in their homeland. They build a second temple on the site of the First Temple. However, Jewish autonomy is lost to subsequent invasions, first by Alexander the Great and later by the Seleucids.

167 B.C.E. The Jewish Hasmonean Kingdom. Led by Judah Maccabee, the Jews rebel against the Seleucids and re-establish an independent nation, known as the Hasmonean Kingdom, in the portion of the Land of Israel known as Judea, the southern region of the present-day West Bank.

---

[80] PAUL JOHNSON, *A HISTORY OF THE JEWS* 11 (1988).

[81] *Id.* at 374.

63 B.C.E. Roman Rule. The Land of Israel becomes a vassal state of the Roman Empire. Rome grants the Jews autonomy. The Second Temple is expanded, as the Jewish population grows to between five and seven million.

66-70 C.E. The Great Rebellion. The Jewish population rebels to win their independence from the Roman Empire. In retaliation, the Romans destroy much of Jerusalem, and with it, the Second Temple.

132-135 C.E. The Bar Kochba Revolt. Increasing Roman restrictions on Jewish life motivate the Jews to organize an uprising known as the Bar Kochba Revolt. The Romans crush the movement by slaughtering and exiling most Jews from the area. They further attempt to erase Jewish history by renaming the Jewish homeland "Syria Palaestina." The term "Syria" misidentifies the Land of Israel as a southern district of Syria. The word "Palaestina" was a deliberate act on the part of Rome to misrepresent the Jewish inhabitants there as Philistines. Rome succeeds to some extent and the area disappears as a political unit until the advent of Mandatory Palestine in 1922.[82]

313-636 C.E. Byzantine Rule. Jews come under the rule of the Byzantine Empire, which proclaims Christianity as the official religion. To the Jews, the unrecognized and borderless territory named Syria Palaestina is still called the Land of Israel. But devout Christians, recalling the rise of Christianity, refer to the undefined area as "Palestine."

---

[82] *See* DOWTY, *supra* at 19.

614 C.E. Persian Rule. The Persians briefly retake the Land of Israel/Palestine. Previously exiled Jews return to the area, join the community of Jews who never left, and regain autonomy in Jerusalem under the tolerant government. Three years later, the Byzantines return and again drive Jews into exile.

636 C.E. Arab Rule. The Prophet Muhammad introduces Islam in present-day Saudi Arabia. He and a subsequent Islamic ruler banish the Christians and Jews from the country, and the refugees flee to the Land of Israel/ Palestine. The Islamic army, meanwhile, launches a campaign of international conquest and proselytization. Peoples in conquered territories were encouraged or coerced to convert to Islam. The invading forces spread throughout the Middle East, including the Land of Israel/Palestine, and conquer Jerusalem in 636. By 750, the Islamic World stretches from India to Spain (see Map 3, 750 C.E., Arab Muslim Empire).

MAP 3
ARAB MUSLIM EMPIRE, 750 A.D.

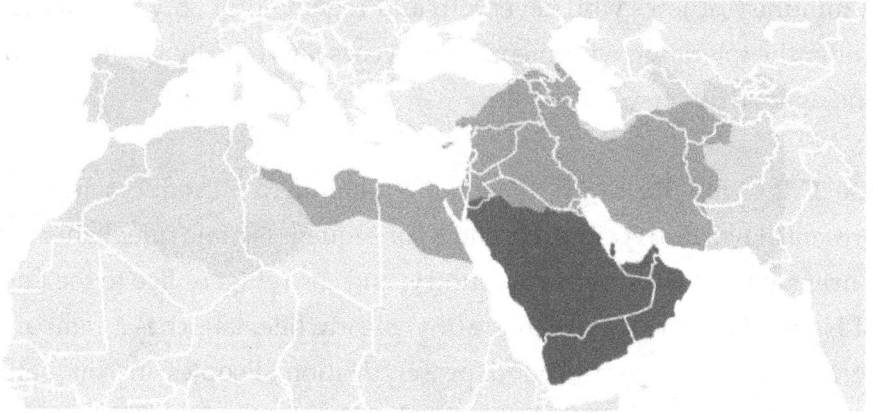

Age of the Caliphs ● Expansion under the Prophet Mohammad, 622-632
● Expansion during the Patriarchal Caliphate, 632-661 ● Expansion during the
Umayyad Caliphate, 661-750

By DieBuche [Public domain], via Wikimedia Commons

*Note: To see this map in its original color version (with a zoom-in feature for more
detailed viewing), download the PDF in the Appendix.*

The Arab Muslim rulers govern Christians and Jews as "dhimmi" – a second-class population bound by religious restrictions, forced to pay uniquely high taxes, and sometimes subjected to violent abuse.[83] The persecution gradually drives Christians and Jews to leave or convert to Islam (see Map 4, 636-1880: Jews under Foreign Rule).

---

[83] JOHNSON, *supra* at 174-175. See also *Dhimmi, Jewish Legal Status under Muslim Rule* , Katz Center - University of Pennsylvania, available at https://katz.sas.upenn.edu/resources/blog/what-do-you-know-dhimmi-jewish-legal-status-under-muslim-rule.

MAP 4
JEWS UNDER FOREIGN RULE: 636-1880 A.D.

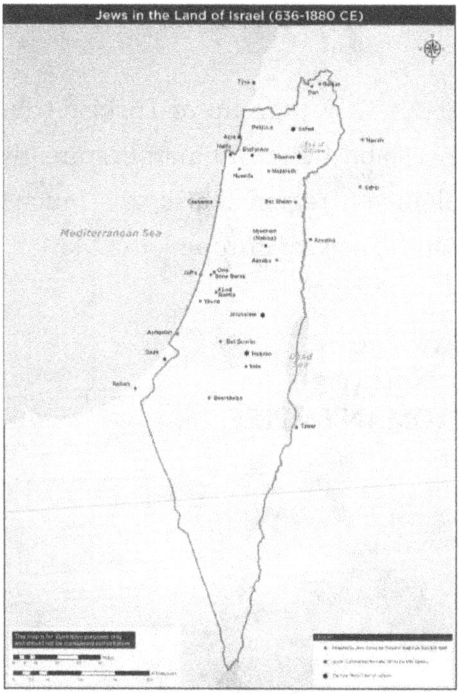

Source: Israel Ministry of Foreign Affairs website

Note: To see this map in its original color version (with a zoom-in feature for more detailed viewing), download the PDF in the Appendix.

Arab Muslims build two Islamic shrines – the Al-Aqsa Mosque and the Dome of the Rock – on the ruins of the two Jewish temples in Jerusalem.

1099: Crusader Rule. European crusaders invade the Land of Israel/Palestine in a quest to reclaim the "Holy Land" for Christianity. They massacre non-Christians, including Muslims and Jews. Both of the targeted communities are devastated, though remnants survive. Jews gradually return from their diaspora to resettle in the land. In 1187, the Kurdish Muslim Saladin of Damascus leads an army that drives the Crusaders out of Jerusalem and from much of the region.

55

1260: Mameluk Rule. A Muslim military clan rules the Land of Israel/Palestine from a base in Cairo, Egypt. Throughout the Middle Ages, various European nations expel Jews from their territories.

1517: Ottoman Rule. On or about 1299, a group of Turkish tribes in a portion of modern-day Turkey establish the Ottoman Empire. By 1517, the Ottomans invade and colonize a region that spans much of the Middle East, North Africa, and Eastern Europe (see Map 5, 1683: Ottoman Empire).

MAP 5
THE OTTOMAN EMPIRE: 1683

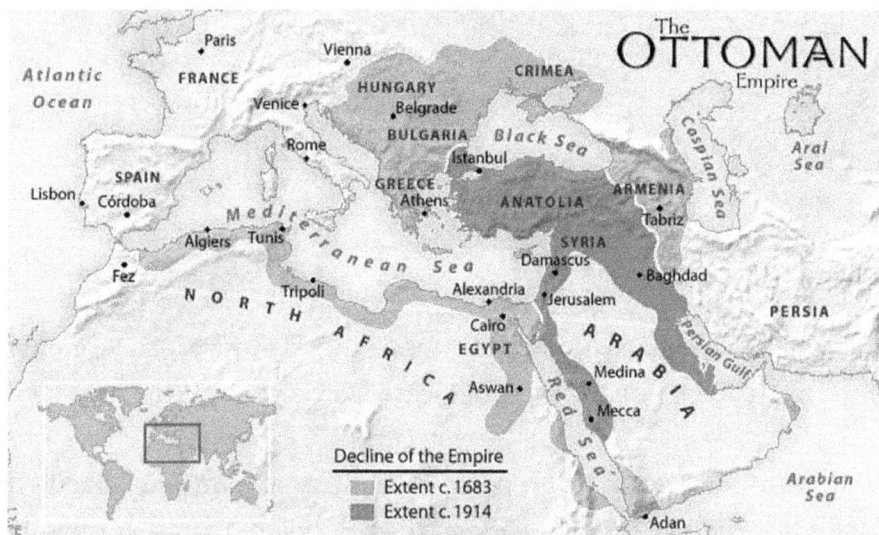

Reprinted from faculty.polytechnic.org, https://bit.ly/ajm-map5

Note: To see this map in its original color version (with a zoom-in feature for more detailed viewing), download the PDF in the Appendix.

During Ottoman rule, the Land of Israel/Palestine is governed as four political subdivisions of southern Syria: the Vilayet (province) of Beirut, the Sanjaq (District) of Jerusalem, the Sanjaq of Ajlun, and the Sanjaq of Maan (see Map 6, 1683-1917: The Ottoman Levant).[84]

MAP 6
THE OTTOMAN LEVANT: 1683-1917

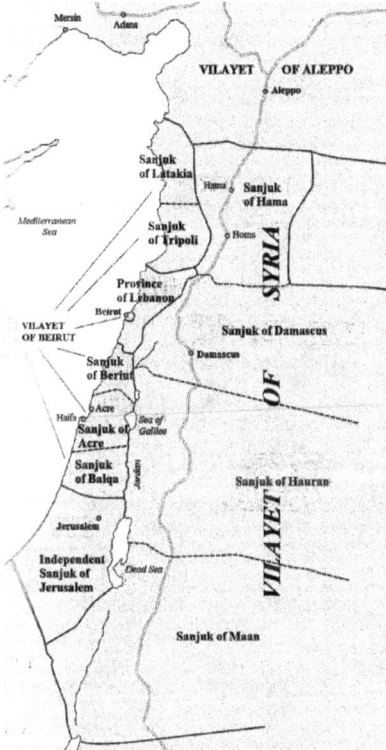

Source: By Tallicfan20 - based off of Efraim Karsh's Palestine Betrayed, Public Domain, https://bit.ly/ajm-map6

Note: To see this map in its original color version (with a zoom-in feature for more detailed viewing), download the PDF in the Appendix.

---

[84] MARK TESSLER, *A HISTORY OF THE ISRAELI-PALESTINIAN CONFLICT* 159-64 (1994) [hereinafter TESSLER]. Professor Tessler is Samuel J. Eldersveld Collegiate Professor in the Department of Political Science, University of Michigan. His previous positions at the University include: Vice Provost for International Affairs and Director, International Institute. He has served on the editorial boards for Middle East Law and Governance, Israel Studies, and Journal of North African Studies. His "A History of the Israeli-Palestinian Conflict" is an authoritative account of the passionately-debated subject.

A degree of religious tolerance in the Empire allows Muslims, Christians and Jews to flourish. More Jews migrate from Europe to the Land of Israel/Palestine.

1827: Jewish Immigration to the Land of Israel/Palestine. At the start of the 19th Century, in the Ottoman subdivisions that Jews and Christians continue to call the Land of Israel and Palestine, the population is roughly 275,000 to 300,000.[85] The vast majority are Arab Muslims. Only seven to ten thousand are Jews.[86]

Starting in 1827, a small wave of European Jews migrate to the Land of Israel/Palestine. The immigrants call the land "Zion," the Old Testament name for Jerusalem, and by extension, the Land of Israel.[87] The "Zionists" join Jews who have lived in various components of the Jewish homeland – including Gaza, Ashkelon, Galilee, Hebron, and Jerusalem – since ancient times.[88]

1839: The Tanzimat Reforms. In 1839, the Ottoman Empire passes a series of laws, titled the Tanzimat Reforms, inviting foreign investment

---

[85] BENNY MORRIS, *RIGHTEOUS VICTIMS: A HISTORY OF THE ZIONIST-ARAB CONFLICT*, 1881-2001 4 (Kindle Edition 2001) [hereinafter MORRIS RIGHTEOUS VICTIMS]. Professor Morris is a professor of history in the Middle East Studies Department at Israel's Ben Gurion University. Known as one of Israel's "New Historians," he analyzed previously unexposed archival records of the 1947-1948 war, and based on those materials, revised the traditional Zionist view of Israeli history.

[86] *Id.*

[87] JOHNSON, *supra* at 321.

[88] JOAN PETERS, *FROM TIME IMMEMORIAL* 80-85 (1984) [hereinafter PETERS].

to revive the Empire's crumbling economy.[89] The Tanzimat Reforms grant all religions equal status and permit foreigners to purchase Ottoman land.[90] The regulations revolutionize systems of land ownership, taxation, and general administration after decades of governmental corruption and neglect.[91] To Jewish immigrants, the new laws are a welcome change. Through the rest of the 19th Century, immigration to the Land of Israel/Palestine/Zion from Europe and surrounding Arab countries grows significantly, transforming the area from a ghost town to a teeming carnival of ethnicities.[92]

In the mid-19th Century, despite sporadic interethnic clashes, social relations in the Land of Israel/Palestine/Zion are good.[93] Meanwhile, Jewish identification with the land evolves into a nationalist movement to restore their ancient state.[94] Decades later, this particular expression of Jewish nationalism came to be called "Zionism."[95]

In 1881, the swelling population of the Land of Israel/Palestine/Zion includes 450,000 Arabs – about 90% Muslim and 10% Christian – and

---

[89] AMY DOCKSER MARCUS, *JERUSALEM 1913: THE ORIGINS OF THE ARAB-ISRAELI CONFLICT* 42 (Kobo Books Edition 2007) [hereinafter MARCUS].

[90] *Id.*

[91] BARUCH KIMMERLING AND JOEL S. MIGDAL, *PALESTINIANS: THE MAKING OF A PEOPLE* 15 and 38 (1993) [hereinafter KIMMERLING].

[92] *See* MARCUS, *supra* at 41-42.

[93] MARCUS, *supra* at 44-46.

[94] JOHNSON, *supra* at 374-376.

[95] *Id.* at 398. The Oxford English Dictionary defines Zionism as "[a] movement for (originally) the reestablishment and (now) the development and protection of a Jewish nation in what is now Israel. English, Oxford Living Dictionaries, http://www.oxforddictionaries.com /us/definition/american_english/zionism.

25,000 Jews.[96] From the initial Jewish immigrations in 1827 up to 1881, the Jewish segment of the area's total population doubles (from 2.5% to 5.3%), but remains a small minority. Politically, Arabs support the Ottoman Empire[97] and continue to regard the Land of Israel/Palestine/Zion as a southern portion of Syria. Jewish immigrants buy agricultural plots, typically from Arab landlords, in desolate, barren, sparsely populated fields.[98] The strategy is to settle in places avoided by Arabs.[99] They call their embryonic community the "Yishuv." (See MAP 7, 1881-1914: Major Arab and Jewish Settlements)

---

[96] BENNY MORRIS, *1948: A HISTORY OF THE FIRST ARAB–ISRAELI WAR 2 (Kobo Books Edition 2008)* [hereinafter MORRIS *1948*].

[97] *Id.* at 10.

[98] ARI SHAVIT, *MY PROMISED LAND* 36 and 49-50 (2013) [hereinafter SHAVIT].

[99] JOHNSON, *supra* at 645.

MAP 7
MAJOR ARAB TOWNS AND
JEWISH SETTLEMENTS, 1880 - 1914

Major Arab Towns and Jewish Settlements in Palestine, 1881-1914

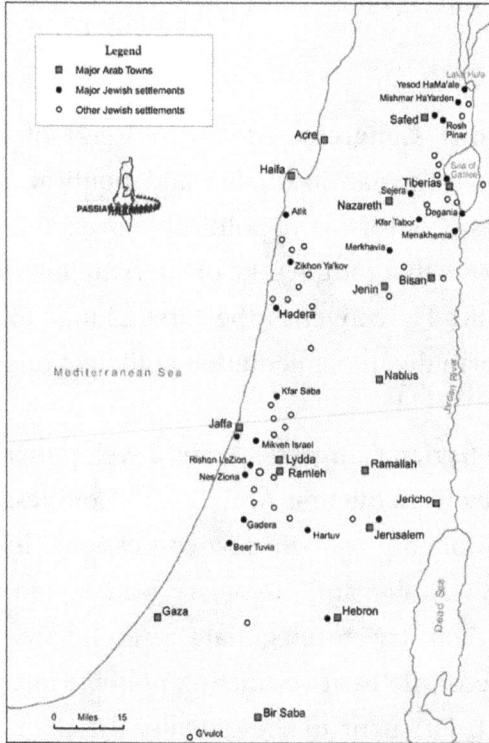

Legend
■ Major Arab Towns
● Major Jewish settlements
○ Other Jewish settlements

Adapted from: Sachar, H.W. *A History of Israel: From the Rise of Zionism to Our Time.* New York: Knopf, 1981

**Palestinian Academic Society for the Study of International Affairs
(PASSIA)**

Source: PASSIA

*Note: To see this map in its original color version (with a zoom-in feature for
more detailed viewing), download the PDF in the Appendix.*

1891: Repeal of the Tanzimat Reforms. Ottoman Arabs feel threatened
by the burgeoning influx of Jews, with their non-Islamic beliefs,
Western culture, consolidation of land, transformative economic power,
growing autonomy and nationalist aspirations. A delegation of Arab
community leaders persuades the Ottoman Sultan to repeal the

61

Tanzimat laws.[100] The Sultan goes further. He disqualifies Jews from buying property, curbs Jewish immigration, and begins to deport them.[101] Relations between Arabs and Jews break down.[102] Increasingly frequent Arab killings of Jews compel the Yishuv to form a paramilitary group.[103]

1897: First Zionist Congress. Amidst a trend of anti-Semitism in Europe, Austro-Hungarian journalist and political activist Theodore Herzl formalizes Zionism as a political movement. His book, "The Jewish State," avers that for the sake of survival Jews must reconstitute their ancient state. He convenes the First Zionist Congress in Basel, Switzerland to plan the implementation of the nationalist dream.

1913: First Arab Syrian Congress. Arabs develop their own concept of nationalism. They form the first Arab Syrian Congress and petition the Ottomans for autonomy but win few concessions. In the wake of the disappointment, Arab and Zionist leaders in the Land of Israel/Palestine/Zion try to negotiate peaceful co-existence.[104] The parties cannot reconcile their conflicting political interests but manage to avoid conflict. Pursuant to the detente, the chairman of the Arab nationalist Cairo Committee issues a formal statement pledging to

---

[100] MARCUS, *supra* at 43.

[101] Mim Kemal Oke, *The Ottoman Empire, Zionism and the Question of Palestine (1880 – 1908)* 14(3) INTERNATIONAL JOURNAL OF MIDDLE EAST STUDIES 329, 333-338 (1982).

[102] MARCUS, *supra* at 44-46.

[103] *Id.* at 108-109.

[104] MARCUS, *supra* at 124-133.

"protect Jewish national rights" in consideration of "the valuable assistance" Jews can offer the local economy.[105]

By 1914, the area population expands to 731,000 Arabs and 60,000 Jews.[106] The Arab expansion, which continues through future decades, is substantially embodied by job-seeking immigrants from Syria, Jordan, and Egypt. The rising tide of Jews during the same period flows from the anti-Semitic regimes of Europe. The growing Jewish population increasingly alarms the Arab majority.

1914-1918: World War I. Two geopolitical alliances spark a world war involving over 100 countries. In World War I, Germany, Austria-Hungary, and Bulgaria unite as the "Central Powers," while Great Britain, France, Italy, Japan and the U.S. form the "Principle Allied Powers." The Ottoman Empire joins the Central Powers. After two years of fighting, the Ottoman leaders sense impending defeat. They blame Arabs and Jews and vent their anger through violent attacks on both groups.[107]

---

[105] HOWARD M. SACHAR, *HISTORY OF ISRAEL FROM THE RISE OF ZIONISM TO OUR TIME* 165 (2007) [hereinafter SACHAR]. Professor Sachar is Professor Emeritus of History and International Affairs at George Washington University in Washington. He has authored 14 works of history focusing mainly on Israel and the Middle East. His thoroughly detailed "History of Israel from the Rise of Zionism to our Time" is a definitive history of the nation.
[106] ProCon/Encyclopaedia Britannica, *Israeli-Palestinian Conflict, Population Statistics*, ProCon.org (Sept. 17, 2010), http://israelipalestinian.procon.org/view.resource .php?resourceID=000636.
[107] MARCUS, *supra* at 143-146.

1915: The Hussein-McMahon Correspondence. During World War I, Sir Henry McMahon, British High Commissioner of Egypt, writes a letter to Hussein Ibn Ali, the Sherif of Mecca, promising that if the Arabs help Britain defeat the Ottoman Empire, Britain will reward the Arabs with political independence in some vaguely described Arab-inhabited region of the Empire. The letter becomes known as the Hussein-McMahon Correspondence.[108] The promise of statehood might be interpreted to include the region Arabs call southern Syria (present-day Israel, Jordan, and the Territories). But Hussein later admits the wording of the message is so noncommittal that it accomplishes nothing.[109]

1916: The Sykes-Picot Agreement. Anticipating the overthrow of the Ottoman Empire, Great Britain and France hold secret talks to plan the post-war dismemberment and reallocation of the Ottoman territories into zones of influence that suit their strategic interests. The western powers cannot decide who should control the Land of Israel/Palestine/Zion, so they agree to leave it under a loosely outlined regime of international administration. After Russia joins the talks, a piece of the Empire is earmarked for their control. The resulting pact is known as the Sykes-Picot Agreement.[110]

---

[108] The World War I Document Archive, *Hussein–McMahon Correspondence*, https://wwi.lib.byu.edu/index.php/Letters_between_Hussein_Ibn_Ali_and_Sir_Henry_Mcma hon.

[109] DAVID FROMKIN, *A PEACE TO END ALL PEACE* 181-85, 528 (1989) [hereinafter FROMKIN].

[110] Sykes-Picot Agreement, United Kingdom - France, 19 May 1916, http://avalon.law.yale .edu/20th_century/sykes.asp.

Three years later, when word of the Sykes-Picot Agreement leaks to the public, Arabs are outraged because the plan ignores their expectations for the post-war order. The Allied powers modify the planned Sykes-Picot borders in hopes of placating Arab opinion. The new configuration blueprints the territorial dimensions of states founded after the war and implicitly reassures Arabs that they would not be subjected to new colonial masters but achieve genuine independence. Meanwhile, European Jews lobby to convert the Land of Israel, with its growing population of indigenous Jews and Jewish immigrants, into a state for the Jewish people.

1917: The Balfour Declaration. The British government, represented by Foreign Secretary Arthur James Balfour, pens a letter to leaders of Britain's Jewish community addressing their growing demand to reconstitute their ancient homeland. The letter becomes known as the Balfour Declaration.[111] The Balfour Declaration pledges to "favor the establishment in Palestine of a national home for the Jewish people," subject to the condition that "nothing shall be done which may prejudice the civil or religious rights of existing non-Jewish communities in Palestine ..."[112]

The British leadership supports the Zionist movement for many reasons: they believe the Jews deserve the opportunity to reestablish self-rule in their ancestral homeland;[113] their Christian faith inspires

---

[111] Balfour Declaration, United Kingdom, 2 Nov. 1917, http://avalon.law.yale.edu/20th_century/balfour.asp.

[112] *Id.*

[113] FROMKIN, *supra* at 293 (1989).

them to restore the Jews to their biblical "Promised Land";[114] developing the land into a client state would complete transportation routes connecting British possessions from Africa to Asia;[115] and the strategic initiative would restrain France's competing imperial ambitions.[116]

Arabs oppose the Balfour Declaration because it anticipates a state for Jews, including a multitude of Jewish European immigrants, in an area inhabited overwhelmingly by Arab Muslims. To them, Zionism is a European colonial implantation.[117]

1918: British Control. The Allied victory over the Central Powers in November of 1918 defeats the German Empire, the Austro-Hungarian Empire, and the Ottoman Empire. Great Britain and France impose military rule over the vanquished territories of the Middle East, with the British controlling the Land of Israel/Palestine/Zion.

1919 (January): The Faisal-Weizmann Agreement. Leaders of the Arab nationalist movement, as opposed to the Arabs of Palestine, support collaboration with Zionists for the sake of mutual economic development.[118] A meeting is held between the heads of the two movements. Representing the Arab nation is Royal Emir Faisal I bin al-Hussein, who later becomes king of Iraq. Speaking for the Zionists is Dr. Chaim Weizmann, who later becomes Israel's first president. The

---

[114] *Id.* at 268-69 and 274.

[115] *Id.* at 269 and 281.

[116] *Id.* at 269.

[117] JOHN QUIGLEY, *THE CASE FOR PALESTINE*, 31 (2005) [hereinafter QUIGLEY *CASE FOR PALESTINE*].

[118] TESSLER, *supra* at 141-45.

leaders forge an Agreement of Understanding and Cooperation, later known as the Faisal-Weizmann Agreement.[119]

The Faisal-Weizmann Agreement celebrates the common Middle East ancestry of Arabs and Jews. The pact authorizes the creation of two companion states: an "Arab State" for Arabs and "Palestine" for the Jews.[120] Subsequent provisions encourage Jewish immigration to Palestine "on a large scale" and promote improved conditions for Arab peasant farmers.[121]

Emir Faisal conditions his contractual commitment to Dr. Weizmann on Great Britain's promise to give Arabs independence, with Faisal as king of Syria. When the Emir loses faith in the British, he voids his deal with Weizmann. Faisal, his followers, and the Arabs in Palestine then resolve to establish a Syrian state that would include Palestine.[122]

1919 (January): Founding of the League of Nations. After World War I, the Principal Allied Powers, along with delegates from 27 other nations, meet at the Paris Peace Conference to negotiate the Treaty of Versailles, the peace treaty that formally ends the war and charts the post-war political order. Among other things, the Treaty forms the League of Nations (the "League"), the first international organization dedicated to world peace, and authorizes the world body to transition

---

[119] Faisal-Weizmann Agreement (January 3, 1919),

https://mfa.gov.il/mfa/foreignpolicy/peace/mfadocuments/pages/the%20weizmann-feisal%20agreement%203-jan-1919.aspx .

[120] *Id.*, arts. I and II.

[121] *Id.*, art. IV.

[122] CONOR CRUISE O'BRIEN, *THE SIEGE* 144-45 (1986) [hereinafter CRUISE O'BRIEN].

the defeated empires to new spheres of sovereignty.[123] The transition process, called the "mandate system," is outlined in a section of the Treaty known as the League of Nations Covenant.[124] The Covenant pledges to assist the political independence of different ethnic "peoples" that were "not yet able to stand by themselves."[125]

1919 (July): Resolutions of the General Syrian Congress. The Syrian Congress adopts a resolution appealing to the US – the most powerful non-member of the League of Nations – to recognize the independence of their desired pan-Arab state.[126] In the Syrian Resolutions, the Arabs name the proposed state "Greater Syria," a reference to Syria in ancient times. The state's borders would include present-day Lebanon, Syria, Iraq, Jordan, Israel and the Territories. A provision in the Resolutions protests the mandate system set forth in the League Covenant.[127] Referring to Palestine as the "southern part of Syria," the document declares: "We reject the claims of Zionists for the establishment of a Jewish commonwealth in that part of southern Syria which is known as Palestine and we are opposed to Jewish immigration into any part of the country."[128]

---

[123] The US was not a member of the League of Nations.

[124] *Treaty of Versailles*, Part I, Art. 22 (1919) [hereinafter LON Covenant], http://avalon.law. yale.edu/20th_century/leagcov.asp.

[125] *Id.*, art. 22, para. 1.

[126] Resolutions of the General Syrian Congress (1919), https://bcc-cuny.digication.com /MWHreader/Resolutions_of_the_General_Syrian_Congress_1919.

[127] *Id.*

[128] *Id.*

1920 (February): The Nabi Musa Riots: The first major outbreak of violence between Arabs and Jews begins with an Arab armed attack on two Jewish communities in a northern locality of the Land of Israel/Palestine/Zion.[129] Arabs wage a follow-up round of killings two months later during an annual Muslim observance known as the Nabi Musa pilgrimage.[130]

The second stage of the mob violence coincides with the San Remo Resolution (described below) and the Jewish holiday of Passover. Muslim cleric Haj Amin al-Husseini, who eventually leads the Arab Palestinian nationalist movement, instigates the bloodshed with a speech railing against British plans for the area's political future.[131]

1920 (March): Reestablishment of Greater Syria. The Syrian National Congress proclaims Faisal bin al-Hussein King of the Arab Kingdom of "Greater Syria," a concept that includes the Land of Israel/Palestine/Zion.[132] Arabs throughout the new Kingdom cheer the coronation as the fulfillment of their political independence, a restoration of ancient Syria, a rejection of European colonialism, and a retort to Zionism. However, the Kingdom is soon overthrown by the French army.

1920 (April): San Remo Resolution. At a conference in San Remo, Italy, the Allied Powers sign a treaty with Turkey that restructures the former

---

[129] KIMMERLING, *supra* at 77-78.

[130] *Id.*

[131] *Id.*

[132] CRUISE O'BRIEN, *supra* at 145.

Ottoman Empire.[133] The treaty, known as the San Remo Resolution, applies the League Covenant by creating three new political districts and labeling them "Syria," Mesopotamia" (which eventually achieves statehood as "Iraq"), and "Palestine."[134] Echoing the Balfour Declaration, the Resolution entrusts the British government with "the establishment in Palestine of a national home for the Jewish people" while doing nothing to "prejudice the civil and religious rights of existing non-Jewish communities in Palestine."[135] Because the San Remo Resolution is a treaty, it is binding on its signatories, not a mere political statement.[136] The Resolution legally recognizes the Jewish people as a nation, not just a religion, and also recognizes the nation's historic ties to the Land of Israel.[137] However, the Allies use the term "national home … in Palestine," not "State of Palestine," in deference to Great Britain, which wants flexibility to decide how much territory in Mandatory Palestine would ultimately belong to the Jews.[138]

1920 (August): Treaties of Sevres and Lausanne. The 1920 Treaty of Sevres is prepared to formalize Turkey's surrender of the Ottoman

---

[133] San Remo Resolution (April 25, 1920) [hereinafter San Remo Resolution], http://www.cfr.org/israel/san-remo-resolution/p15248.

[134] Bobbette Deborah Abraham, *From Mandate to Mineshaft: The Long Rocky Road to the Modern State of Israel*, 5 Regent J. Int'l L. 147-48 (2007) [hereinafter Abraham].

[135] San Remo Resolution, art. b.

[136] The distinction between binding law and advisory political statements is explained at Chapter 2, Section B.

[137] Evan Gottesman, *Unpacking San Remo, The Centerpiece of Israel's Annexation Narrative*, Israel Policy Forum (April 27, 2020), https://israelpolicyforum.org/2020/04/27/unpacking-san-remo-the-centerpeice-of-israels-annexation-narrative/.

[138] *Id.*

colonies to the Principal Allied Powers.[139] The Turks, in a last gasp of imperial pride, refuse to sign the treaty, but they ultimately relinquish sovereignty in the 1923 Treaty of Lausanne.[140]

1920 (December): Franco-British Boundary Agreements. The French and British governments draw the boundaries of the post-Ottoman mandate territories in a set of agreements called the Franco-British Boundary Agreements.[141] A more detailed version of the plan is produced by an expert commission and approved on March 7, 1923. The boundaries set for Syria cover present-day Syria and Lebanon. The map of Mesopotamia outlines present-day Iraq. And the contours of Palestine include present-day Israel, Jordan and the Territories.

1920 (December): First Palestinian Arab Congress. After French troops crush the inception of Greater Syria, and the San Remo Resolution endorses Jewish self-determination in Palestine, Arabs form a strategy to thwart the western plan. At a 1920 Arab political conference in Haifa, members propose to make Palestine an Arab state with no Jewish national home.[142] The idea inspires the founding of the Palestinian Arab Congress, which elects an Arab Executive in the following year.[143]

---

[139] *Treaty of Sevres* (Aug. 10, 1920) [hereinafter *Treaty of Sevres*], http://www.hri.org/docs/sevres/.

[140] *Treaty of Lausanne*, 1923, https://wwi.lib.byu.edu/index.php/Treaty_of_Lausanne.

[141] *Franco-British Convention on Certain Points Connected with the Mandates for Syria and the Lebanon, Palestine and Mesopotamia*, Vol. 16, Am. J. Int'l L., Supplement: Official Documents (Jul., 1922), pp. 122-126, https://www.jstor.org/stable/2213236?seq=1#page_scan_tab_contents.

[142] SACHAR, *supra* at 169-70.

[143] *Id.*

Although the Congress meets for only eight years and is never recognized by the British "mandatory" (Great Britain serving as the temporary administrator of British Mandate Palestine), its genesis marks the first expression of Arab Palestinian nationalism, the movement to make all of Palestine an Arab state.[144]

1921 (May): Appointment of Haj Amin el-Husseini as *Grand Mufti*. The British appoint Haj Amin el-Husseini as Grand Mufti of Jerusalem and later name him leader of the Supreme Muslim Council, making him head of Palestine's Muslim community. With these appointments, the British bestow on local Muslims a significant degree of self-rule.[145] The Mufti becomes the most powerful Arab leader in Palestine. For decades he galvanizes and directs the violent Arab resistance to Zionism. One of his first initiatives is a 1921 riot that kills Jews and demolishes Jewish property in communities across Palestine.[146] In response, the Jews form a militia group called the *Haganah* (Defense).[147] The British attempt to assuage Arab animosity by temporarily suspending Jewish immigration to Palestine.[148] They also plan to reallocate all of Mandatory Palestine east of the Jordan River for the creation of a new Arab state.

---

[144] *Id.*

[145] KIMMERLING, *supra* at 85.

[146] MARTIN GILBERT, *ISRAEL: A HISTORY* 47-48 (1998). Sir. Martin Gilbert was the British historian best known for the official eight-volume biography of Winston Churchill. He wrote 88 books, most focusing on the world wars, the Holocaust, and the Middle East. He advised a succession of British prime ministers on Middle East affairs and was appointed to the committee that investigated Great Britain's involvement in the Iraq war.

[147] TESSLER, *supra* at 186.

[148] *Id.* at 48.

1922 (June): The Churchill White Paper. To allay Arab fears over the League's disposition of Palestine, the British government issues a policy statement known as the Churchill White Paper.[149] The White Paper clarifies that the planned "Jewish National Home" will not occupy all of Palestine but only emerge "in" Palestine so the Arab community will not be subordinated to the Jewish one.[150] The Paper further states that the Zionist leadership will have no share in the mandatory government. Next, the policy document states that Jewish immigration to Palestine will be limited by the capacity of the economy to absorb them. Lastly, the document asserts that the 1915 Hussein-McMahon Correspondence never intended to earmark Palestine for Arabs.

1922 (July): The British Mandate for Palestine. A unanimous League vote approves the British Mandate for Palestine (the "BMP"), a mandate governing present-day Israel, the Territories and Jordan.[151] (See Map 8: British Mandate for Palestine, 1922).

---

[149] *The Churchill White Paper of June, 1922*, http://avalon.law.yale.edu/20th_century/brwh1922.asp.

[150] SACHAR, *supra* at 127.

[151] The British Mandate for Palestine, 1922 [hereinafter BMP], http://avalon.law.yale.edu/20th_century/palmanda.asp.

MAP 8
BRITISH MANDATE PALESTINE, 1920

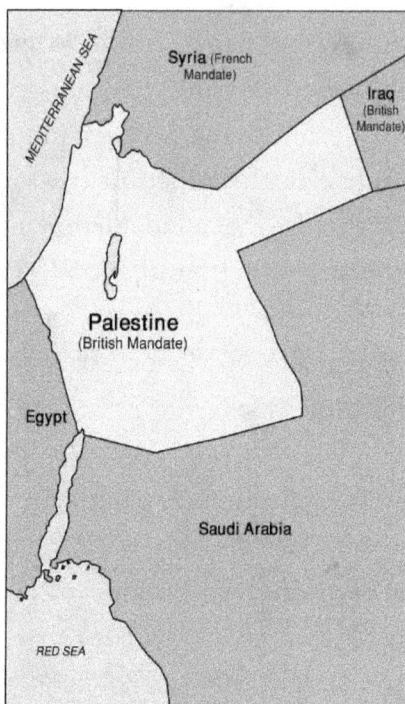

Source: Jewish Virtual Library

Note: *To see this map in its original color version (with a zoom-in feature for more detailed viewing), download the PDF in the Appendix.*

Area Allocated for Jewish National Home
San Remo Conference, 1920

The BMP obligates the British government to "secure the establishment of the Jewish national home... in Palestine" while safeguarding the civil and religious rights of non-Jews.[152] Justifying the territorial award is the "historical connexion of the Jewish people with Palestine and... the grounds for reconstituting their national home in that country."[153] British Mandate Palestine includes present-day Israel (including East

---

[152] BMP, pmbl..

[153] *Id.*

Jerusalem), Gaza, the West Bank, and Jordan.[154] Another BMP clause instructs the British to "facilitate Jewish immigration" to the area and "encourage... close settlement [i.e. dense population] by Jews on the land."[155] To help prepare the national Jewish home for statehood, the BMP authorizes the Jewish government-in-waiting, called the "Jewish Agency," to assist the British governance of the district. The BMP, as a promulgating instrument of the San Remo Resolution, shares the Resolution's binding status.

A last-minute edit to the BMP gives the British discretion to reapportion the eastern 77% of Palestine (present-day Jordan) to create an Arab state.[156] The goal is to reduce Arab antipathy towards the creation of a Jewish state in western Palestine (present-day Israel and the Territories).[157]

Upon inception of Mandatory Palestine, the British administrators register all residents of the district as "Palestinians." Resident Jews welcome the designation as a precursor of citizenship in a future Jewish state. Local Arabs abhor the label as a foreign denial of Arab self-determination.

1923: The Birth of Transjordan. Great Britain exercises its BMP discretion to reallocate the eastern 77% of Palestine to form a new state for Arab Palestinians, despite Jewish Palestinian objections.[158] The

---

[154] *See* Chapter 3, subtitle 1920 (December): *Franco-British Boundary Agreements.*

[155] BMP, art. 6.

[156] See BMP, art. 25.

[157] TESSLER, *supra* at 164.

[158] SACHAR, *supra* at 127.

decision creates the Emirate of Transjordan. (See Map 9: Creation of Transjordan, 1922)

MAP 9
CREATION OF TRANSJORDAN, 1922

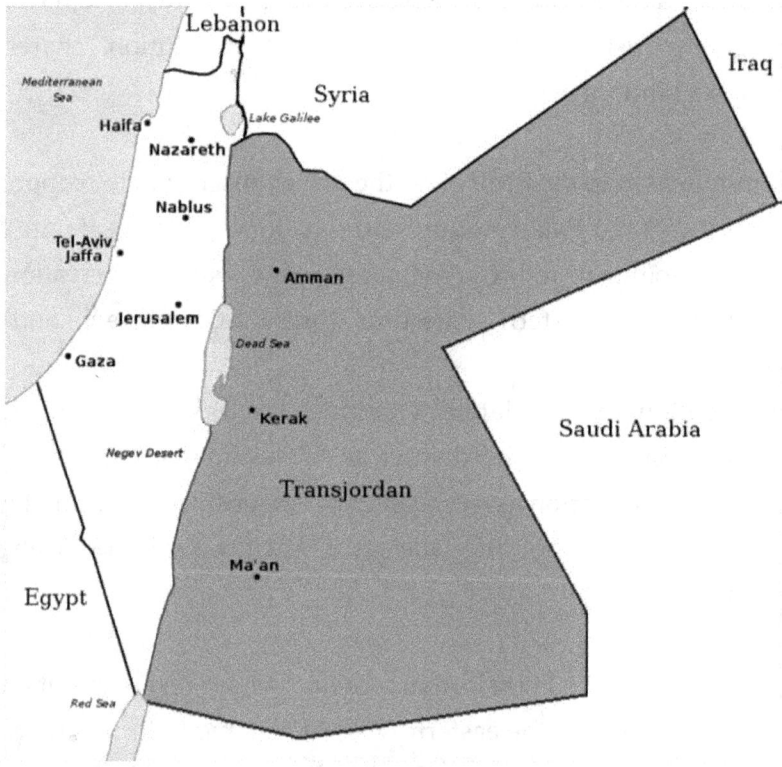

Source: User:Doron - Originally uploaded on the English Wiki (all linking to en.wikipedia):08:13, 8 June 2005 Doron (Talk / contribs) uploaded "Image:PalestineAndTransjordan.png", CC BY-SA 3.0, htps:/bit.ly/ajm-map9

Note: To see this map in its original color version (with a zoom-in feature for more detailed viewing), download the PDF in the Appendix.

The Emirate adopts a nationality law that excludes Jewish Palestinians from citizenship.[159] As a result, most of the land reserved by the San Remo Resolution for the Jewish National Home becomes off-limits to Jews.[160] Western Palestine ("Mandatory Palestine") remains subject to the BMP. The Emirate in eastern Palestine evolves into the Hashemite Kingdom of Transjordan in 1946. It was constitutionally renamed the "Hashemite Kingdom of Jordan" in 1949.

1924: The Anglo-American Convention. Although the US never joined the League, the world power lends its imprimatur to the League-authorized BMP by signing the Anglo-American Convention on the Mandate for Palestine.[161] The Convention incorporates the language of the BMP, including the decision to establish in Palestine "a national home for the Jewish people" based on their "historical connection" to the land.

1929: The Hebron Massacre. The Mufti and fellow agitators in the Old City of Jerusalem instigate a riot against Jews by spreading false rumors that Jews are seizing control of the Al Aqsa Mosque.[162] Enraged Arab mobs wielding knives, axes and iron bars slaughter nearby Orthodox Jews.[163] The crowd then rushes to Hebron, an ancient town holy to Jews

---

[159] See Kingdom of Jordan, Law No. 6 of 1954 on Nationality (last amended 1987), sect. 3, http://www.refworld.org/docid/3ae6b4ea13.html.

[160] PETERS, *supra* at 72-73, and 234-239.

[161] *See* Office for Israeli Constitutional Law, *Justice Now for Israel*, http://www.alliedpowersholocaust.org/wp-content/uploads/2015/03/1924-Anglo-American-Convention.pdf.

[162] SACHAR, *supra* at 173-74.

[163] See *Id.*

and Muslims, and turns its weapons on the Orthodox Jewish community.[164] Eventually the killing spreads to several Jewish agricultural villages in Mandatory Palestine.[165] The surviving Jews of Hebron are forced to relocate, leaving the Jewish holy place devoid of Jews.

1930 (March): The Shaw Commission Report. After the Hebron Massacre, the British government appoints a commission to identify the cause of the riot and recommend a strategy to avoid repetitions of the violence. The resulting Shaw Commission Report finds that the Hebron tragedy was caused by "racial animosity on the part of the Arabs, consequent upon the disappointment of their political and national aspirations and fear for their economic future."[166] To address the Arab concerns, the Report advises the mandatory (Great Britain) to show more consideration for the non-Jewish communities of Mandatory Palestine, constrict (but not completely block) the flow of Jewish immigration, and restrain Jewish land purchases. The British government suspends Jewish immigration to Mandatory Palestine.

1930 (October): The Hope Simpson Report. Following the Shaw Commission Report, another British government inquiry on Mandatory Palestine finds "signs of an economic crisis" and states that Zionist land purchases are causing widespread landlessness and unemployment

---

[164] *Id.*

[165] *Id.*

[166] Report of the Commission on the Palestine Disturbances of August, 1929, excerpts available at: http://ecf.org.il/media_items/1464.

among Arabs.[167] The study, called the Hope Simpson Report, exceeds the advice of the Shaw Commission by recommending a complete cessation of Jewish immigration to the mandatory district.

1930 (October): The Passfield White Paper. Yet another government policy statement released the same day, the Passfield White Paper, further emphasizes the harm to Arab landholding and employment caused by Zionist property acquisition in Mandatory Palestine. The White Paper recommends a halt to Jewish immigration and further restrictions on land sales to Jews. Additional findings downplay the BMP mission of creating a Jewish National Home. Instead, the authors interpret the BMP in a manner that would serve Arab and Jewish Palestinians equally. They also criticize the Jewish Agency and the local Jewish labor unions for hiring policies that discriminate in favor of Jews.

1931: The MacDonald Letter. The two 1930 government reports on Mandatory Palestine comfort Arab Palestinians but outrage British conservative party leaders, representatives of the incumbent Labor party, and Jewish communities worldwide.[168] British Prime Minister Ramsey MacDonald issues a letter to the Jewish Agency that recasts the prior government statements on Mandatory Palestine in a pro-Zionist light.[169] The MacDonald Letter ensures continued Jewish immigration and land purchases in the district. Disdainful Arabs brand the document the "Black Letter."

---

[167] Sir John Simpson, Palestine: *Report on Immigration, Land Settlement and Development*, Jewish Virtual Library, https://www.jewishvirtuallibrary.org/hope-simpson-report.

[168] SACHAR, *supra* at 175-77.

[169] Ramsay MacDonald, *The MacDonald Letter*, 1931, Jewish Virtual Library, http://www.jewishvirtuallibrary.org/jsource/History/MacdonaldText.html.

By 1935, the Arab Palestinian population reaches 960,000.[170] The Jewish Palestinian headcount reaches 500,000.[171]

1936-1939: The Arab Revolt. In the 1930's, the rise of the Nazi party in Germany fuels anti-Semitic persecution across Europe, forcing hundreds of thousands of Jews from their homes. Many escape to Mandatory Palestine. Hitler's anti-Jewish laws are cheered throughout the Arab world,[172] but especially in Mandatory Palestine, where the growing volume of Jewish immigrants and ensuing land acquisitions breed resentment among local Arabs. In this anti-Semitic milieu, the Mufti instigates a wave of terrorist riots known as the Arab Revolt. The rampage kills many Jews, along with their cattle and crops.[173] Also targeted are Britons, who are blamed for conveying "Arab land" to the Jews. The Arab Revolt is more organized, widespread, and virulent than previous Arab attacks.[174]

Gradually, the rebels target their fellow Arabs. The civil war settles scores among rival clans, vents religious hatred of Arab Christians, exacts vengeance against corrupt members of the upper class, and preempts struggles for political power.[175] Militant followers of the Mufti murder or exile hundreds of Arab leaders.[176] A total of 18,000 Arabs flee

---

[170] SACHAR, *supra* at 178.

[171] *Id.*

[172] SACHAR, *supra* at 196 and 211.

[173] SACHAR, *supra* at 200.

[174] SHAVIT, *supra* at 73 and 77.

[175] *See* KIMMERLING, *supra* at 98-122.

[176] SACHAR, *supra* at 212; See TESSLER, *supra* at 241.

to foreign lands.[177] The Mufti himself flees to evade a British arrest warrant and finds refuge in Nazi Germany. Arab Mandatory Palestine is left with a leadership vacuum.[178]

Eventually, British troops suppress the Revolt. A Jewish extremist splinter group called *Irgun* supplements the British force and conducts retaliatory terrorist attacks on Arabs.[179] Starting in 1940, another Jewish terrorist group – *Lehi* – launches equally vicious attacks. Both terror groups exacerbate tensions between the Arab and Jewish communities, despite repeated denunciations of their terror tactics by the Jewish Agency and Haganah.[180]

1937: The Peel Commission Report. Another British government study, known as the *Peel Commission Report*, finds that:

> An irrepressible conflict has arisen between two national communities within the narrow bounds of one small country. About 1,000,000 Arabs are in strife, open or latent, with some 400,000 Jews. There is no common ground between them. The Arab community is predominantly Asiatic in character, the Jewish community predominantly European. They differ in religion and in language. Their cultural and social life,

---

[177] *Id.* at 213.

[178] KIMMERLING, *supra* at 122-23.

[179] SHAVIT, *supra* at 77; TESSLER, *supra* at 207.

[180] GILBERT, *supra*, at 157.

their ways of thought and conduct, are as incompatible as their national aspirations.[181]

The Report proposes to resolve the conflict by splitting Mandatory Palestine into two states. Twenty percent of western Palestine – the Jewish majority portion – would be reserved for a Jewish state. Seventy percent would be Arab ruled. The remaining 10%, essentially including Jerusalem and Bethlehem, would be retained by the British. See Map 10: Peel Commission Partition Plan, 1937

---

[181] The Palestine Royal Commission, The Palestine Royal Commission Report of 1937 [hereinafter Peel Commission Report], Part III, Ch. XX, p. 370, para. 5., available at https://unispal.un.org/pdfs/Cmd5479.pdf.

MAP 10
PEEL COMMISSION PARTITION PLAN, 1937

MAP OF THE ROYAL COMMISSION'S PARTITION PLAN
(REPRODUCED FROM THEIR REPORT) MAP No. 3

(Area outlined in red = proposed Jewish state)
(Area in cross-hatch = proposed to remain under British control)
(Remainder = proposed Arab state

Source: By UK Government (Palestine Partition Committee report 1937) [Public domain], via Wikimedia Commons

Note: To see this map in its original color version (with a zoom-in feature for more detailed viewing), download the PDF in the Appendix.

An exchange of minorities between the two rival populations (i.e. all Jewish Palestinians to be relocated to the Jewish state and all Arab Palestinians to be relocated to the Arab section) would complete the segregation and is thereby hoped to ensure the security of both peoples.

The Jewish Agency, acting as the government of the Jewish Palestinians, reluctantly accepts the proposed two-state solution.[182] The Arab Higher Committee, meanwhile, refuses to recognize Britain's authority to partition Mandatory Palestine.[183] As a result, the partition plan fails to materialize.

1939 (May): The British White Paper of 1939. The British decide the BMP is unworkable. As a political matter, they cannot force Arab Palestinians to be citizens of a Jewish state without provoking more bloodshed. As a strategic matter they cannot upset the Arab nations without jeopardizing a major source of British oil, especially considering the looming threat of another world war.[184] The situation compels the British to adopt a pro-Arab policy.[185] The resulting British White Paper of 1939 announces a sharp curtailment of Jewish immigration and land purchases in the mandated district.

Jews complain the British White Paper eviscerates the purpose of the BMP, which is to reconstitute the Jewish state for world Jewry and encourage Jewish immigration to the mandatory area.[186] Nevertheless, the British turn away Jewish immigrants. Jews who subsequently flee Hitler's "Final Solution" lose their most reliable escape route.[187] They are refused entry by nearly all other nations, including the US.

---

[182] See TESSLER, *supra* at 206.

[183] *Id.* at 244.

[184] SACHAR, *supra* at 225.

[185] The British White Paper of 1939, available at http://avalon.law.yale.edu/20th_century/brwh1939.asp.

[186] SACHAR, *supra* at 224.

[187] *Id.* at 236-44.

The two Jewish Palestinian terror groups, *Irgun* and *Lechi*, contrive to continue Jewish immigration illegally. In the process they attack installations of the mandatory government, despite the outrage of the Zionist leadership. Their acts of sabotage and murder continue into the 1940's. In one particularly lethal attack, Irgun bombs Britain's administrative headquarters in Jerusalem's King David Hotel, killing dozens of British workers.

On the other hand, Arab Palestinians also denounce the White Paper of 1939 because it fails to halt Jewish immigration completely and ignores the Arab demand for Britain to leave Mandatory Palestine.

1939 (September): World War II. Germany's invasion of Poland precipitates World War II. A Nazi program of genocide – later termed the "Holocaust" – herds millions of Jews (plus other perceived undesirables) into "death camps" where they are slaughtered en masse.

Jewish Palestinians suspend their anti-British resentment and join the British army to defend against the Germans. Arab Palestinians ally with Germany. The Mufti relocates to Berlin, coordinates with the Third Reich to broadcast anti-British, anti-Semitic propaganda, recruits Bosnian Muslims to murder Jews, and arranges to extend the Holocaust to the Middle East.[188] But he never assembles the resources to carry out the planned extermination.

---

[188] *Id.* at 227-29.

1945 (September): End of World War II. The liberation of Nazi death camps and discovery of related atrocities spreads awareness that the Holocaust has annihilated 67% of Europe's 8.8 million Jewish residents[189] and a third of the world's 18 million Jews.[190] The publicity broadens support for Zionism among non-Jews, especially in the United States, where the government calls for the immediate admission of Holocaust survivors to Mandatory Palestine.

By this point, Zionist land purchases cover six percent of the mandate territory (see Map 11: Land in Jewish Possession, 1944)

---

[189] JOHNSON, *supra* at 497.

[190] *Id.* at 559-560. For a summary of the Holocaust see JEWISH VIRTUAL LIBRARY, *The Holocaust: an Introductory History*, available at https://www.jewishvirtuallibrary.org/jsource/Holocaust/history.html.

MAP 11
WESTERN PALESTINE LAND
IN JEWISH POSSESSION, 1944

(Blue = Jewish National Fund)
(Green = Jewish company & private)
(Total land in Jewish possession = 6%)

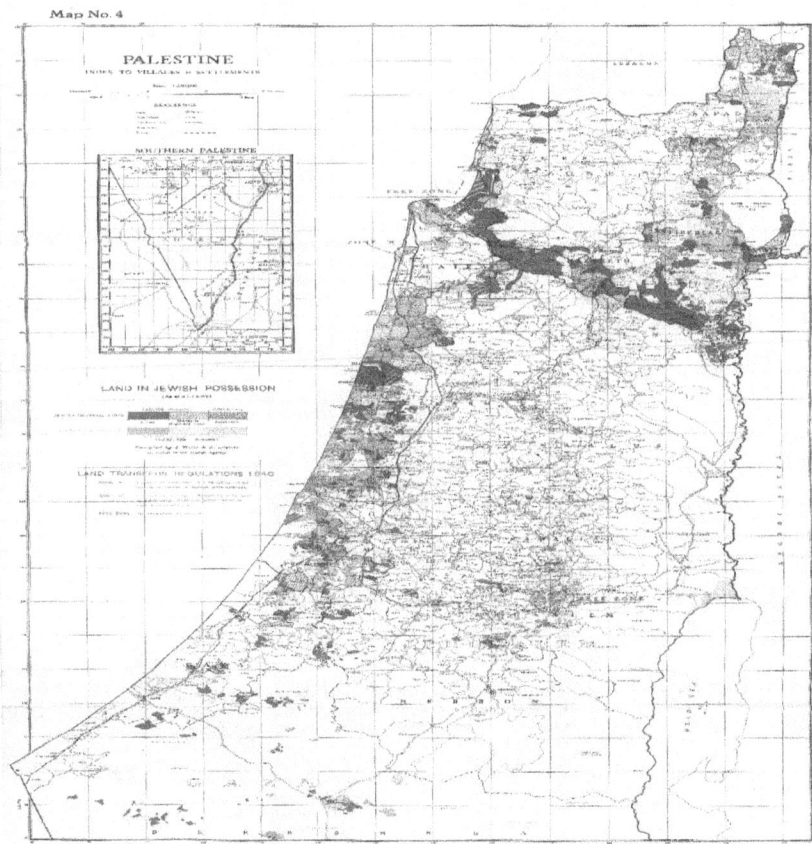

Source: By w:Office of Public Sector Information [Public domain], via Wikimedia
Commons; https://bit.ly/ajm-map11

*Note: To see this map in its original color version (with a zoom-in feature for
more detailed viewing), download the PDF in the Appendix.*

1945 (October): Founding of the United Nations (UN). Representatives
of fifty nations convene in San Francisco and establish a new
international body called the United Nations. The UN Charter commits

its members to a more effective framework of world peace and security. Article 80 of the Charter preserves the national rights created by the League of Nations mandates. The following year the League of Nations transfers its powers to the UN and then disbands.[191]

The number of Jewish Palestinians reaches 630,000 while the Arab Palestinian population rises to 1.3 million.[192]

1947 (November): The UN Partition Plan. Great Britain formally asks the UN to resolve the sectarian impasse in Mandatory Palestine in April of 1947. The UN responds by creating the Special Committee on Palestine (UNSCOP). In November 29, 1947, barely eight months later, a modified version of the UNSCOP majority report is put before the General Assembly for a vote, and UN Resolution 181 is adopted, albeit contentiously – with 33 votes in favor, 13 against, and 10 abstentions. The six Arab nations in the General Assembly stage a dramatic walkout.

The Partition Plan advises the UN Security Council and Great Britain to terminate the BMP and divide Mandatory Palestine. Fifty-six percent of the mandatory realm would be assigned to the Jewish Palestinians, and 42% would go to the Arab Palestinians. The remaining 2% -- consisting of Jerusalem – would bear the special status of *corpus separatum*

---

[191] *See* General Assembly Resolution 24(I), *Transfer of Certain Functions, Activities and Assets of the League of Nations* (February 12, 1946), available at https://undocs.org/en/A/RES/24(I) .

[192] From the 1920s to the mid-1940s, Arabs argued that because they were the majority population of Mandatory Palestine, they held superior rights to the land. Zionists countered that their people had inhabited the land for over a thousand years before the arrival of the first Arabs. However, neither argument was supported by the League Covenant. *See* discussion at Chapter 4.1 (Is Palestine a State in the Territories), Author's Prologue.

(separate land) subject to UN administration. (see Map 12: UN Partition Plan, 1947)

MAP 12
UN PARTITION PLAN, 1947

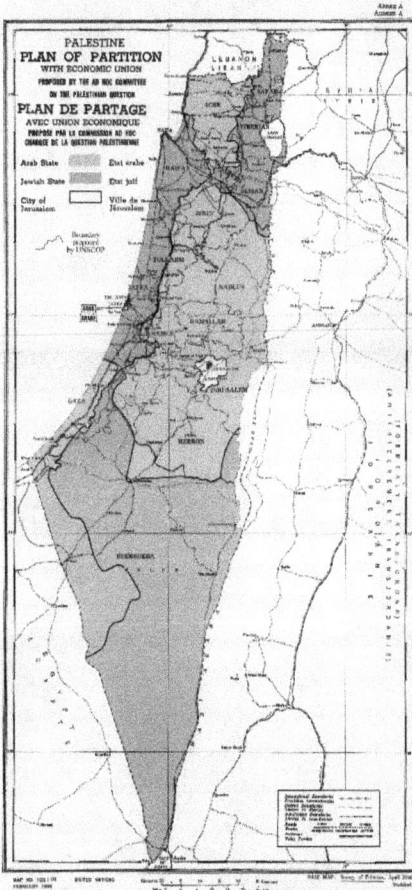

Source: UN Special Commission on Palestine, Report to the General Assembly, September 3, 1947 [Public Domain]
https://bit.ly/ajm-map12

Note: To see this map in its original color version (with a zoom-in feature for more detailed viewing), download the PDF in the Appendix.

The aim is to give each adversary a state in the locality where its population is the majority.[193] Similar partitions have averted political

---

[193] MORRIS 1948, *supra* at 48.

and religious-based warfare in Germany, British-ruled India, and Korea.[194]

Jewish Palestinians reluctantly support the Partition Plan.[195] Arab Palestinians, along with the UN's Muslim voting bloc, oppose it.[196] In their view, the UN lacks authority to transfer Arab land to a non-Arab people.[197] The Arab League, a recently-formed organization representing the Arab World, threatens war if the UN Plan is imposed.[198] During the mandatory period (1922 to 1948), the Arabs had rejected any solution for Palestinian nationhood that included Jews.[199] However, throughout the latter half of that period, the Arab Palestinians lacked a political leadership comparable to the Jewish Agency that could assume the functions of government in Palestine.[200]

Great Britain informs the Security Council it will not endorse the Partition Plan recommendation if it is opposed by the Arabs or Jews. The British want Arab goodwill to ensure their continued access to Arab oil.[201] Middle East oil also becomes a national priority to the US.[202]

---

[194] KIMMERLING, *supra* at 139-140.

[195] SACHAR, *supra* at 284-85.

[196] *Id.* at 294.

[197] TESSLER, *supra* at 259.

[198] SACHAR, *supra* at 285.

[199] SACHAR, *supra* at 309.

[200] *Id.*

[201] SACHAR, *supra* at 285 and 296.

[202] *Id.* at 287-89.

As a result, the Plan fails to win the approval of both Great Britain and the Security Council.

1947 (November): War of Independence. Arab Palestinian militiamen, supplemented by troops from neighboring Arab states, attempt to remove the Jewish Palestinian population by force.[203] The effort backfires, displacing up to a hundred thousand Arab Palestinians from their homes.[204] Most flee to other Arab villages in Mandatory Palestine while others venture to surrounding Arab countries.[205] The violence becomes known as the "civil war" phase of Israel's War of Independence.

Under the auspices of the Arab League, Arab states negotiate to incorporate Palestine in a new Arab confederation modeled on Greater Syria.[206] The talks ignore the Arab Palestinian nationalists, who accuse the states of surreptitiously vying for their own territorial gains.[207]

1948 (May): Proclamation of Independence. Jewish Palestinian leaders form a Provisional State Council, which issues a Proclamation of Independence for the State of Israel.[208] Despite the ongoing war, the Proclamation urges Arab Palestinians to "participate in the upbuilding

---

[203] BENNY MORRIS, *BIRTH OF THE PALESTINIAN REFUGEE PROBLEM REVISITED* 65-66 (2004). [hereinafter MORRIS *BIRTH REVISITED*].

[204] *Id.* at 67.

[205] *Id.*

[206] KIMMERLING, *supra* at 135 and 144.

[207] *Id.*

[208] State of Israel: Proclamation of Independence (May 14, 1948) [hereinafter Israeli Proclamation of Independence], available at: http://avalon.law.yale.edu/20th_century/israel.asp.

of the State on the basis of full and equal citizenship and due representation in all its provisional and permanent institutions."

Israel is soon recognized as a sovereign state by all major powers except Great Britain.

In the coming years, Israel develops a code of "Basic Law" founded on the laws of Great Britain, the US, the Ottoman precedent, the Torah, and the ancient Jewish Talmud.[209]

1948 (May): Internationalization of the War of Independence. On May 14, 1948, the day that the British Mandate over Palestine expires, the Jewish People's Council issues its Declaration of the Establishment of the State of Israel, or Proclamation of Independence. That same day, the Arab League military invades Israel. The invasion begins with an Egyptian aerial bombing of Tel Aviv.[210] Follow-up offensives are launched by the armies of Egypt, Lebanon, Syria, Jordan, and Iraq, assisted by expeditionary forces from Sudan, Yemen, and Saudi Arabia.[211] British forces complete their withdrawal from Mandatory Palestine the following day, though certain British officers remain as commanders of the Arab League maneuvers. The Arab invasion transforms the civil war into an international one.

From 1947 to the early 1950's, several Arab states outside the war zone adopt anti-Semitic policies that unleash violent rampages and/or

---

[209] SACHAR, *supra* at 360-61.

[210] GILBERT, *supra* at 189.

[211] DANIEL GORDIS, ISRAEL: *A CONCISE HISTORY OF A NATION REBORN* 170 (2016) [hereinafter GORDIS].

persecution against their own Jewish populations.[212] The Arab regimes force an exodus of five to six hundred thousand Jews, though some leave voluntarily.[213] The governments confiscate the property abandoned by the fleeing Jews. Most of the Jewish refugees emigrate to Israel.

Israel wins the war. In the process, it captures territory in former Mandatory Palestine beyond the borders proposed for it by the UN Partition Plan. Egypt conquers Gaza. Jordan takes East Jerusalem and the West Bank. Syria grabs a strip of former Mandatory Palestine along the eastern shore of the Sea of Galilee. Israel confiscates the properties abandoned during the war by Arab Palestinian "absentees." Israeli civilians move into the emptied neighborhoods.[214]

1948: Al-Nakba. The 1947-1948 war drives an estimated 700,000 Arab Palestinians from their homes.[215] A general label is given for this phenomenon and alleged wrongdoing – the Arab word *Al-Nakba* (catastrophe). The exact number of affected Palestinians is disputed. According to a UN estimate issued shortly after the war, the total is 711,000.[216] Some Arab sources calculate a total as high as a million, while

---

[212] MORRIS 1948, *supra* at 412-15; GILBERT, *supra* at 154. The Arab states involved in the anti-Semitic hostilities include Morocco, Algeria, Tunisia, Libya, Egypt, Lebanon, Syria, Iraq, and Yemen.

[213] MORRIS 1948, *supra* at 412-15.

[214] GILBERT, *supra* at 163.

[215] MORRIS *BIRTH REVISITED, supra* at 588 and 603-04.

[216] U.N. GAOR, 5th Session, Supplement No. 18, U.N. Doc U.N. A/1367/Rev.1. (23 October 1950), available at https://digitallibrary.un.org/record/704900?ln=en .

Israeli spokesmen say the number is 500,000.[217] Most of the expatriated Palestinians resettle in other parts of former Mandatory Palestine. About 160,000 move to surrounding Arab countries.[218]

Arab Palestinian nationalism after the 1947-1948 war finds new roots in the Arab nations outside former Mandatory Palestine.[219] According to the new generation of Arab Palestinian activists, the wartime Arab displacement within the mandatory district and exodus from the district was a Zionist-planned mass expulsion. "Nakba" would gain popularity in the 1990s when it would become occasion for Arab Palestinian protest marches each year on Israel's Independence Day. Israelis deny the charge of pre-meditated expulsion, claiming most Arabs who moved within the district and outside of it did so to escape the Arab-initiated war.

1948 (December): UN Resolution 194 (III). The wartime exodus of Arab Palestinians from Israel to Arab states, and the offsetting flight of Jews from Arab countries to Israel, produce an exchange of populations. It leaves the Israeli population with 1.3 million Jews and 150,000 Arabs, a drastic reversal of Mandatory Palestine's demographics in 1945, when Arabs outnumbered Jews by 1.3 million to 630,000. Israel grants citizenship to the expelled Jews and resettles them in the month-old

---

[217] TESSLER, *supra* at 279-80; MORRIS BIRTH REVISITED, *supra* at 602.

[218] MORRIS *RIGHTEOUS VICTIMS*, *supra* at 258.

[219] RASHID KHALIDI, *THE IRON CAGE* 136 (2006) [hereinafter RASHID KHALIDI IRON CAGE]. Professor Khalidi is the Edward Said Professor of Modern Arab Studies at Columbia University and editor of the Journal of Palestine Studies. He was President of the Middle East Studies Association, and an advisor to the Palestinian delegation that negotiated the Oslo Accords.

state. The Arab states, on the other hand, refuse to absorb the Arab share of the refugee population. Instead, they plan to regroup their military forces, conquer Israel, and let the displaced Arab Palestinians return home.

The UN General Assembly adopts Resolution 194 (III), which establishes a Conciliation Commission to resolve the outstanding disputes between Arabs and Israelis.[220] Paragraph 11 of the Resolution states that "refugees wishing to return to their homes and live in peace with their neighbors should be permitted to do so at the earliest practicable date ..." The Arab states, however, oppose the Resolution because it would require them to implicitly recognize Israel.

1949 (February to July): The Green Line. At this point, Israel and its Arab enemies are not considering or negotiating any peace treaties because the latter remain implacably opposed to Israel's existence.[221] Instead, the armies of Israel, Egypt, Jordan, Lebanon and Syria sign armistice (truce or cease-fire) agreements.[222] These included the

---

[220] General Assembly Resolution 194 (III)(December 11, 1948), *Palestine-Progress Report of the United Nations Mediator*, available at: https://digitallibrary.un.org/record/210025?ln=en .

[221] GILBERT, *supra*, at 254-55.

[222] See Egyptian-Israeli General Armistice Agreement, Egypt-Isr., Feb. 23, 1949, UN Doc S/1264 ("Egypt-Israel Armistice Agreement"), available at https://undocs.org/en/S/1264 ; *General Armistice Agreement, Leb.-Isr.*, Mar. 22, 1949, UN Doc S/1296 ("Lebanon-Israel Armistice Agreement"), available at https://undocs.org/en/S/1296 ; Armistice Agreement between the Hashemite Kingdom of Jordan and Isr., Jordan-Isr., April 3, 1949, UN Doc S/1302 ("Jordan-Israel Armistice Agreement"), available at https://undocs.org/en/S/1302 ; Armistice Agreement between Isr. and Syria, Syria-Isr., July 20, 1949, UN Doc S/1353 ("Syria-Israel Armistice Agreement"), available at https://undocs.org/en/S/1353 .

definition of demarcation lines which represent the *de facto* borders of Israel at that point in time (see Map 13: Armistice Lines, 1949).

MAP 13
ARMISTICE LINES AFTER
1948 WAR OF INDEPENDENCE

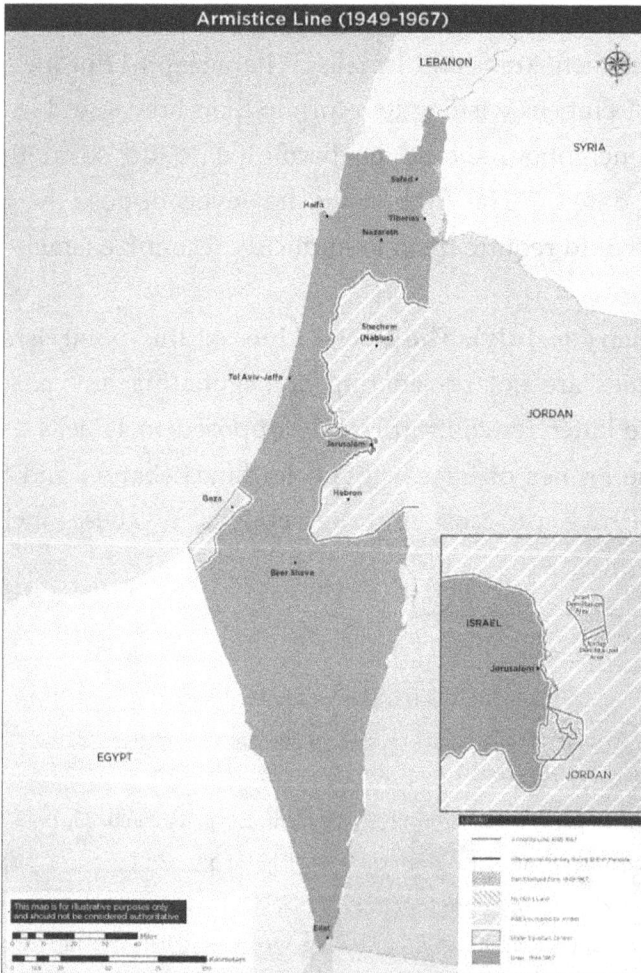

Source: Israel Ministry of Foreign Affairs website

te: To see this map in its original color version (with a zoom-in feature more detailed viewing), download the PDF in the Appendix.

The antagonists do not recognize the cease-fire lines as permanent borders.[223] The cease-fire line between Israel and Egypt, along with the cease-fire line between Israel and Jordan, become known as the "Green Line."

Four months later Israel proposes a peace deal that would convert the Green Line to a border. In addition, Israel offers to repatriate a limited number of Arab Palestinian refugees. The Arab nations decline the offer because it would require them to recognize Israel and resettle most of the refugees in their own countries. Three Arab states propose peace deals that would expand their borders to include much of Israel, and the offers are rejected.[224]

In the wake of the diplomatic standoff, displaced Arabs cannot return to their villages in the Israeli-controlled section of former Mandatory Palestine, i.e. Israel (see Map 14: Depopulated Palestinian Villages, 1948 and 1967), and displaced Jews cannot return to their homes in Arab-controlled parts of former Mandatory Palestine (see Map 15: Jewish Communities Lost in the 1947-1948 War). The segment of the Green Line that divides Jerusalem is uniquely disruptive. That stretch of barbed

---

[223] Egypt-Israeli Armistice Agreement stated at Article V.2.: "The Armistice Demarcation Line is not to be construed in any sense as a political or territorial boundary, and is delineated without prejudice to rights, claims and positions of either Party to the Armistice as regards ultimate settlement of the Palestine question." *See also* Jordan-Israel Armistice Agreement, Art. VI.9; *Syria-Israel Armistice Agreement*, Art. V(a).

[224] Avi Shlaim, *The War of the Historians*, 59:1 Annales 161-67 (January-February 2004), available at: http://users.ox.ac.uk/~ssfc0005/The%20War%20of%20the%20Israeli %20Historians.html.

wire fencing fortifies Jordan's control over the eastern neighborhoods it conquered during the war, while Israel controls the rest of the city (see Map 16: Division of Jerusalem, 1948-1967).

MAP 14
DEPOPULATED PALESTINIAN
VILLAGES IN 1948 AND 1967

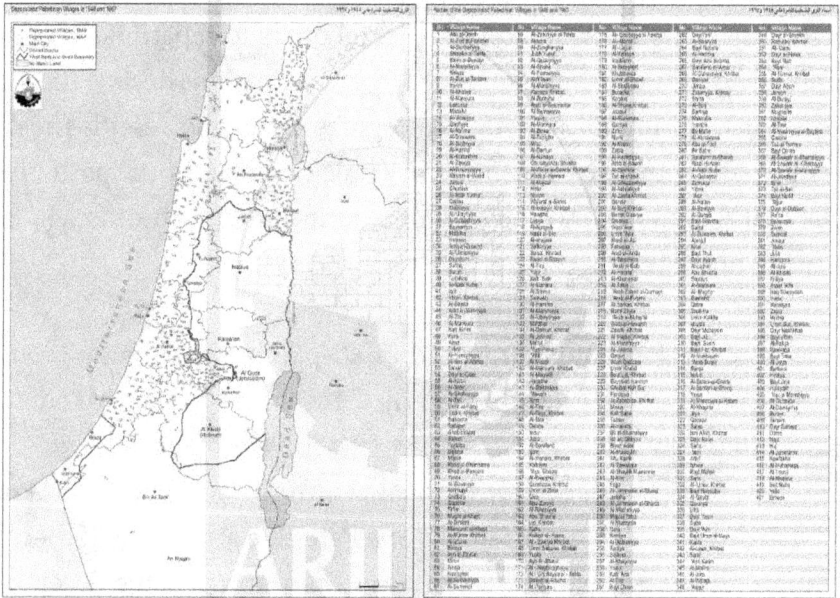

Source: Applied Research Institute -- Jerusalem
https://bit.ly/ajm-map14

Note: To see this map in its original color version (with a zoom-in feature for more detailed viewing), download the PDF in the Appendix.

MAP 15
JEWISH COMMUNITIES LOST
IN THE 1947-1948 WAR

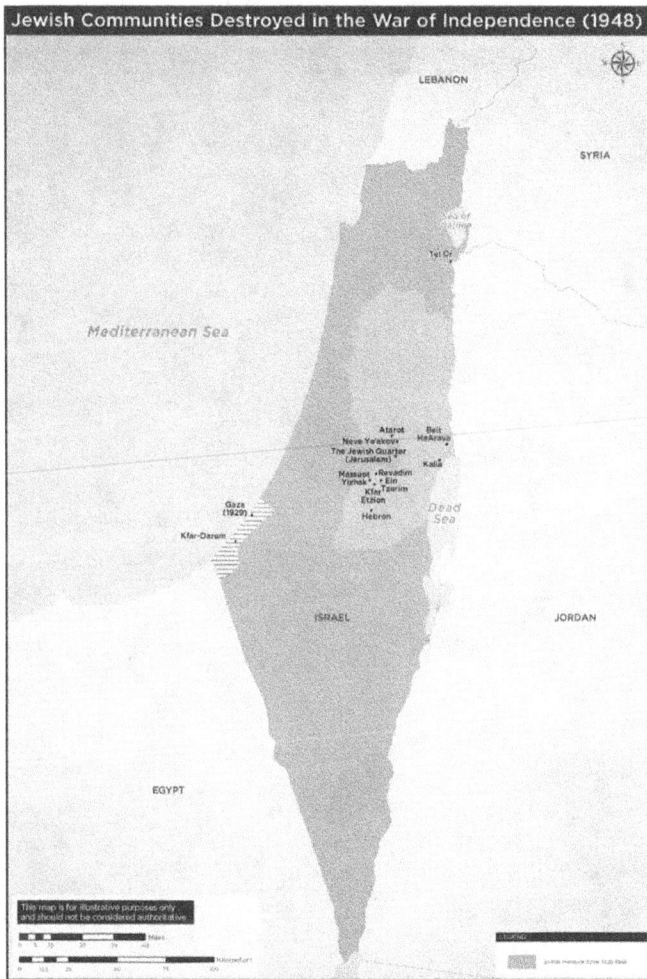

Source: Israel Ministry of Foreign Affairs website

Note: To see this map in its original color version (with a zoom-in feature for more detailed viewing), download the PDF in the Appendix.

MAP 16
DIVISION OF JERUSALEM
(1948 to 1967)

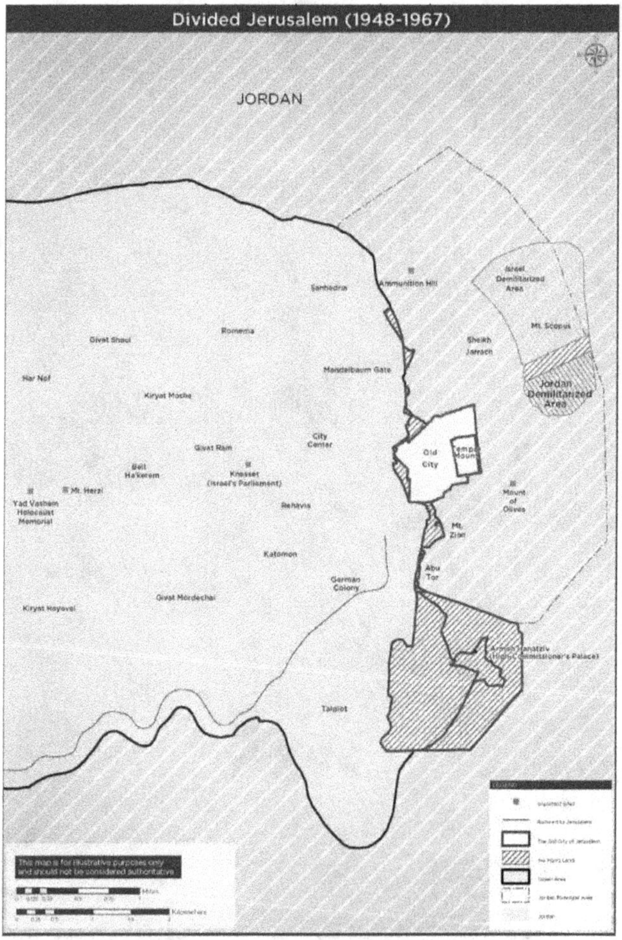

Source: Israel Ministry of Foreign Affairs website

Note: To see this map in its original color version (with a zoom-in feature for more detailed viewing), download the PDF in the Appendix.

1949 (March): Israel Becomes a UN member. After Israel signs armistice agreements with Egypt, Jordan and Lebanon, the UN Security

Council votes to admit Israel as a UN member.[225] Two months later, the UN General Assembly likewise approves Israel's membership.[226] Ninety-four nations officially recognize Israel. Another 25 countries, nearly all Muslim, withhold recognition. Arab Palestinians who remained in Israel during the war become Israeli citizens, subject to post-war national security supervision. They form political parties and elect Arabs to the Israeli Knesset.

The Arab Palestinians of the West Bank, which is now part of Jordan, become citizens of Jordan and comprise the majority population of that country. Arab Palestinians in Gaza are ruled by Egypt but not granted citizenship.

1949 (August): The Geneva Convention. Starting in 1949, the world community signs a series of treaties designed to prevent repetitions of the kind of atrocities witnessed in World War II. The Fourth Geneva Convention prescribes terms of humane treatment of civilians in wartime.

1949 (December): UN Relief and Works Agency for Palestinian Refugees. Lebanon, Syria and Jordan hold the displaced Arab Palestinians in refugee camps pending the planned re-invasion of Israel, hoping the refugees would return to Israel. The camps are supported by a UN humanitarian relief organization called the UN Relief and Works Agency for Palestine Refugees (UNRWA). UNRWA-managed camps

---

[225] SC Resolution 69 [*On Admission of Israel to Membership in the United Nations*], UN Doc S/RES/69(1949) (March 4, 1949), available at https://undocs.org/en/S/RES/69(1949).

[226] General Assembly Resolution 273 (III), *Admission of Israel to Membership in the United Nations*, (May 11, 1949), available at https://undocs.org/en/A/RES/273(III).

are also established in Gaza, East Jerusalem, and the West Bank. Although the arrangement is meant to be temporary, it lasts indefinitely. (see Map 17: Palestinian Refugee Camps, 2003).

MAP 17
PALESTINIAN REFUGEE
CAMPS (2003)

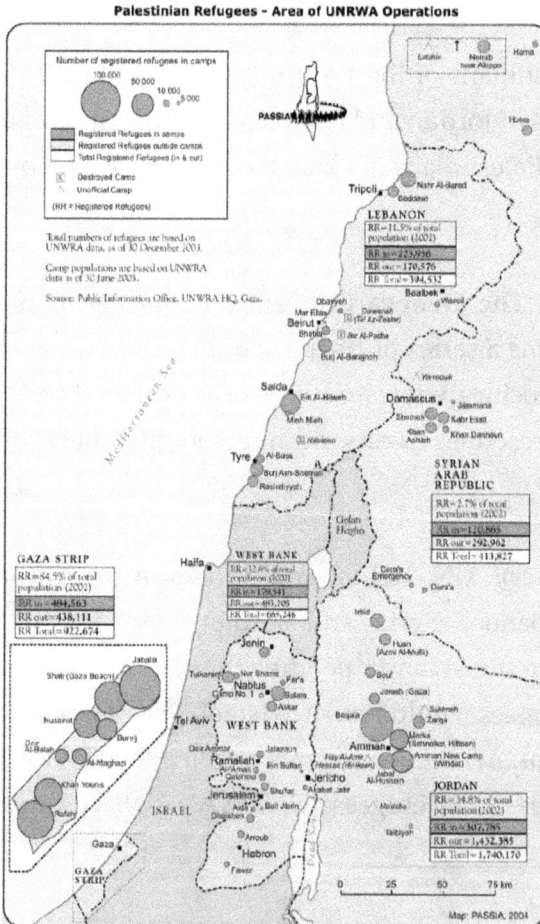

Palestinian Refugees - Area of UNRWA Operations

Reprinted with permission from PASSIA

Note: To see this map in its original color version (with a zoom-in feature for more detailed viewing), download the PDF in the Appendix.

Independent of UNRWA, Egypt builds temporary camps in its territory for over 11,000 Arab Palestinian refugees[227] and then expels as many of them as possible to Gaza and other countries.[228] For the few thousand individuals who manage to evade the expulsion and stay in Egypt, the government converts the camps to villages and leaves the residents without citizenship or government services.[229] The authorities keep the Arab Palestinians of Gaza under military control.

1950: Israeli and Jordanian Territorial Claims. The Israeli Knesset declares Jerusalem the capital of Israel. The UN condemns the announcement. Many nations believe the city should be internationalized, as proposed in the aborted Partition Plan. Most governments that agree to diplomatic relations with Israel locate their embassies in Tel Aviv, while a few place their embassies in Jerusalem.

Jordan claims sovereignty over East Jerusalem and the West Bank. However, the annexation is generally denounced as illegal by the international community, including all seven members of the Arab League except Jordan. Great Britain recognizes Jordanian sovereignty over the West Bank. Pakistan recognizes Jordanian sovereignty over the West Bank and East Jerusalem. West Bank Arabs accept Jordanian citizenship.

---

[227] Oroub El-Abed, *Unprotected Palestinians in Egypt since 1948,* Institute for Palestine Studies and International Development Research Centre, 17 (2009).

[228] *Id.* at 36.

[229] *Egypt's Forgotten Palestinian Refugee Community,* MIDDLE EAST EYE, September 16, 2015, available at http://www.middleeasteye.net/in-depth/features/forgotten-refugee-last-what-left-1948-palestinian-refugees-1735668584.

In violation of its armistice agreement with Israel, Jordan forbids Jews from visiting the Jewish holy sites, including the Mount of Olives and the Western Wall, in Jerusalem's Old City.[230] Jordanians dynamite 34 of the 35 historic East Jerusalem synagogues, desecrate others, ransack the Mount of Olives, and use the Western Wall as a garbage dump.[231]

1951: Israeli Accession to the Geneva Conventions. Israel ratifies the Geneva Conventions. It expresses no reservations from the treaties, including the Fourth Convention, which governs belligerent occupations.

1956: The Suez War. From 1949 to 1956, Egypt orchestrates commando attacks on Israel from Egyptian and Jordanian soil.[232] The armistice violations prompt Israel to launch cross-border reprisal raids.[233] Meanwhile Syria violates its cease-fire pact with Israel by deploying field artillery along the high-ground of the Golan Heights, which overlooks northern Israel, and randomly bombarding the Israeli agricultural villages below.

Egypt develops ties with the Soviet Union and the US, angling to play each side against the other.[234] The deception antagonizes the US, Britain and France, leading to the cancellation of a World Bank loan. Egypt retaliates by nationalizing the British-French owned Suez Canal

---

[230] TESSLER, *supra* at 326-27.

[231] *Id.* at 329.

[232] SACHAR, *supra* at 475 and 488.

[233] *Id.*

[234] SACHAR, *supra* at 485-86.

Company. Without declaring war, it commits acts of war by imposing naval blockades to Israeli shipping at the Suez Canal and Straits of Tiran.

Backed by Britain and France, Israel uses military force to take control of the Canal and reopen the Straits of Tiran. In the process, Israel captures the Gaza Strip and Egypt's Sinai Peninsula. Combined pressure from the US and the Soviet Union halts the anti-Egyptian plan, with Israel withdrawing from the Sinai and Gaza. The UN deploys a peace-keeping force in the Sinai to help separate the Egyptian and Israeli forces. The US guarantees Israel's rights of shipping through the Straits of Tiran.

1964: The PLO Charter. Egyptian President Gamal Abdel Nasser establishes the Palestine Liberation Organization (PLO), a militant organization with both political and military wings, to help organize the Arab Palestinians as a military force. Its manifesto, the 1964 PLO Charter, pledges to eradicate Israel.[235]

According to the PLO Charter, the Arabs of former Mandatory Palestine are "Palestinians," whose nationality is the same as "the rest of the Arab Countries," otherwise known as the "Arab Nation," or Greater Syria.[236] The Charter adds that: (1) "Palestine" has the boundaries of Mandatory Palestine;[237] (2) "the Arab Nation must mobilize its military, spiritual,

---

[235] *Palestinian National Covenant of 1964* [hereinafter *1964 PLO Charter*], available at http://www.jewishvirtuallibrary.org/jsource/Peace/cove1.html.

[236] *Id.*, art. 1.

[237] *Id.*, art. 2.

and material potentialities [for] the liberation of Palestine;"[238] (3) "Jews of Palestinian origin are considered Palestinians if they are willing to live peacefully and loyally in Palestine;"[239] (4) the mandate system is a "fraud" because the Jews lack "historic and spiritual ties" to the disputed area;[240] and (5) the PLO disclaims sovereignty over the Territories, which are occupied by Egypt and Jordan.[241]

Many Palestinian militant groups, including Fatah, unite under the PLO umbrella. After the Six-Day War, the PLO operates independently of Egypt, establishes its own political voice, and gains recognition from 122 nations as the representative of the Palestinian people.

1967 (June): The Six-Day War. Israel develops a modern army but remains surrounded by enemy nations many times its size (see Map 18: Israel, Arab States and Organization of Islamic Cooperation States, pre-1967). After decades of terrorist attacks that fail to extinguish the Jewish state, Egypt, Syria, and Jordan mobilize armed divisions to Israel's borders. (see Map 19: Arab Mobilization before Six-Day War, 1967).

---

[238] *Id.*, art. 14.

[239] *Id.*, art. 7.

[240] *Id.*, art. 18.

[241] *Id.*, art. 24.

MAP 18
ISRAEL, ARAB LEAGUE STATES, AND ORGANIZATION
OF ISLAMIC COOPERATION STATES (Pre- 1967)

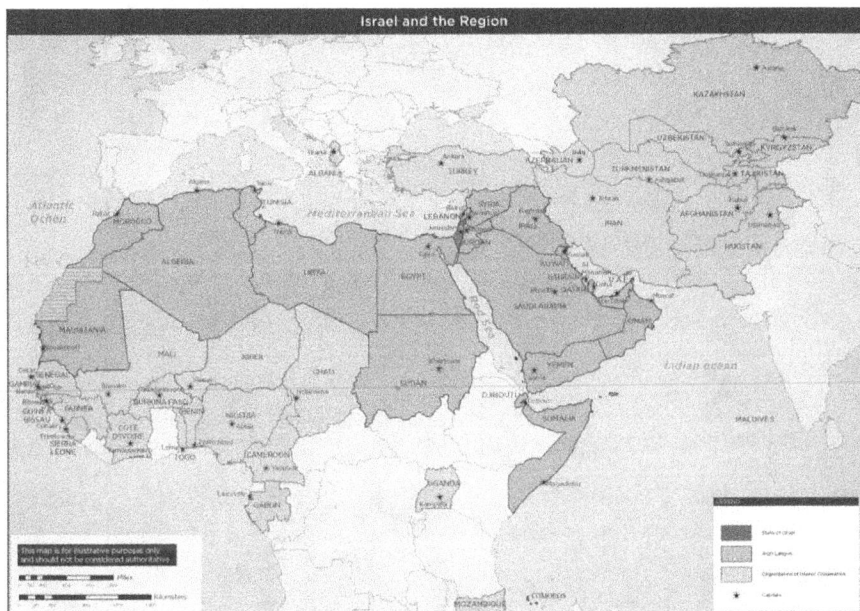

Source: Israel Ministry of Foreign Affairs website

Note: To see this map in its original color version (with a zoom-in feature for more detailed viewing), download the PDF in the Appendix.

MAP 19
ARAB MOBILIZATION BEFORE
SIX-DAY WAR (1967)

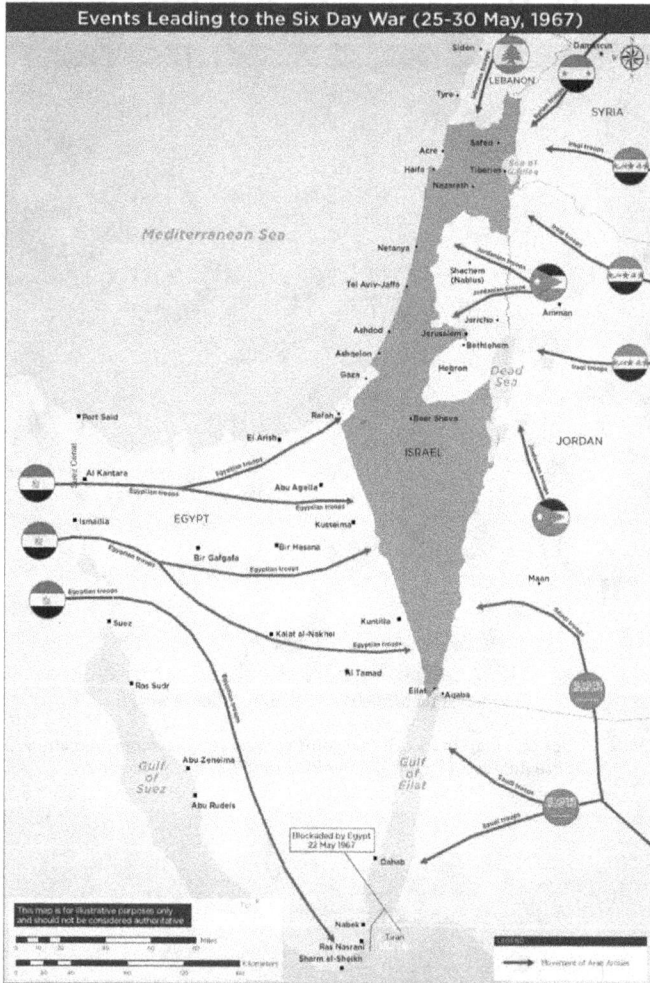

Source: Israel Ministry of Foreign Affairs website

Note: To see this map in its original color version (with a zoom-in feature for more detailed viewing), download the PDF in the Appendix.

Egypt's president and other Arab leaders swear to "wipe Israel off the map."[242] The PLO similarly vows to "throw the Jews into the sea."[243] Egypt blockades the Straits of Tiran to Israeli shipping, repeating the act of war it committed in 1956. It orders the UN peacekeeping troops out of the Sinai, and the UN complies. Instead of fulfilling its promise to ensure Israeli shipping through the Straits of Tiran, the U.S. announces an arms embargo on all involved parties, including Israel. The Soviet Union ferries weapons to the Arab states.

The Israeli military strikes first, using the IDF to destroy Egypt's unlaunched air force on the ground. The Egyptian and Syrian armies respond. Israel urges Jordan to accept a deal of mutual non-aggression, but the Jordanians refuse.[244] Jordanian fighter jets bomb Israel and Jordanian artillery units shell West Jerusalem.[245] Israel defeats the Arab forces in six days, leading observers to dub the conflict "the Six-Day War."

By war's end, Israel captures Gaza and the Sinai Peninsula from Egypt, East Jerusalem and the West Bank from Jordan, and the Golan Heights from Syria (see Map 20: Israel and the Territories after Six-Day War, 1967).

---

[242] TESSLER, *supra* at 393 (quoting the president of Iraq in a statement of May 31, 1967).

[243] *Id.* (quoting a remark by the PLO Chairman Ahmad Shuqari prior to the 1967 Six-Day War).

[244] *Id.* at 401.

[245] *Id.*

MAP 20
ISRAEL AND THE TERRITORIES
AFTER THE SIX-DAY WAR (1967)

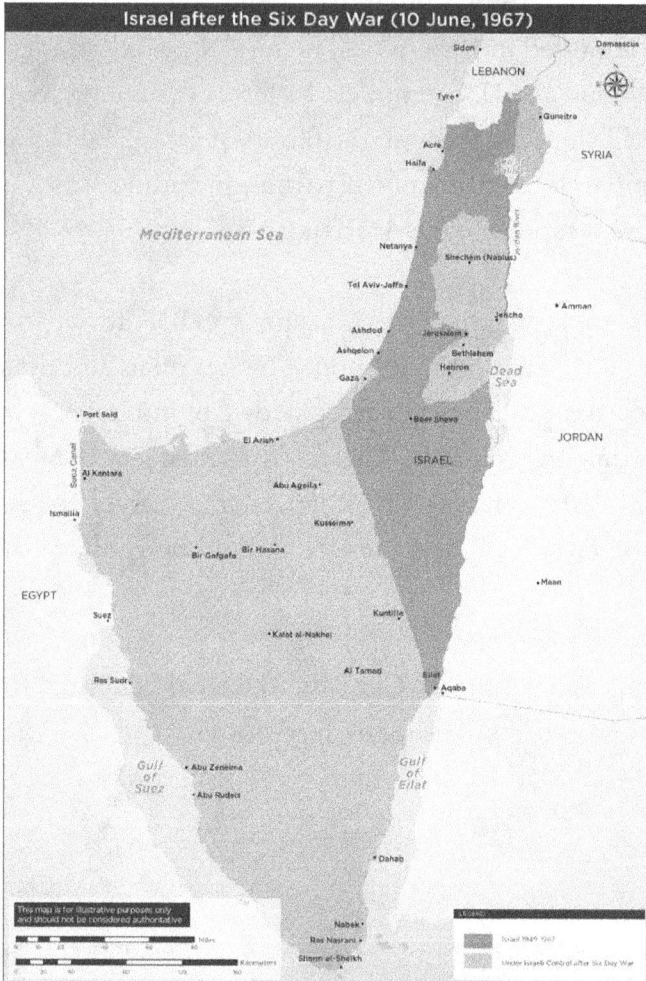

Source: Israel Ministry of Foreign Affairs website

Note: To see this map in its original color version (with a zoom-in feature for more detailed viewing), download the PDF in the Appendix.

Israel accomplishes its military objectives without resorting to expulsions. However, an estimated 250,000 Palestinians flee from the

Territories to Jordan to escape the fighting. Virtually all international authorities view Israel's military control of the Territories as an "occupation."

Mobs in Egypt, Yemen, Lebanon, Tunisia, and Morocco attack their Jewish residents.[246] The targeted individuals are killed, imprisoned, raped, banned from travel, and/or forced to wear identity cards stamped "Jew."[247] Thousands of the victims race to Israel. There is no offsetting flight of Arab Israelis from Israel because they do not encounter Jewish mob violence.

1967 (June): Reunification of Jerusalem. Israel reunifies East and West Jerusalem, removes the barrier that divided the city, and expands the municipal borders. The UN immediately declares the *de facto* annexation invalid.

Israel permits the Arabs of East Jerusalem to convert from Jordanian to Israeli citizenship. The Arabs generally reject the offer. Israel grants them permanent resident status with municipal voting rights pursuant to a legislative package that applies Israeli law to East Jerusalem and effectively declares all of Jerusalem part of Israel.

1967 (September) The Khartoum Resolutions. Israel prepares to negotiate land-for-peace deals with the defeated Arab nations.[248] The Arab League meets in Khartoum, Sudan and issues a revanchist response. Specifically, the organization declares there will be "no peace

---

[246] SACHAR, *supra* at 731-32.

[247] *Id.*

[248] CRUISE O'BRIEN, *supra* at 489-90.

with Israel, no recognition of Israel, no negotiations with it."[249] The Arabs follow up their "Three No's" resolution with continued anti-Israeli terrorist operations.[250]

Israelis and Jews from other nations relocate to the Territories, adding a civilian presence to the military one. They rebuild the communities they had left in the 1948 war.[251] In addition, the Israelis erect military bases and new settlements, including some strategically located along the border with Jordan. Religious Zionists build settlements throughout the West Bank in a messianic[252] quest to reclaim the ancient Land of Israel.[253]

1967 (November): UN Resolution 242. The UN Security Council adopts Resolution 242, which calls for peace negotiations between Israel and its Arab enemies. The Resolution: (1) requires Israel to withdraw its "armed forces" from "territories occupied" in the war; (2) calls for the negotiation of "secure and recognized borders"; (3) orders all states in the conflict to recognize the sovereignty of the others; (4) urges a "just settlement of the refugee problem"; (5) expects a guarantee of territorial integrity and political independence through measures such as "demilitarized zones"; and (6) appoints a "special representative" to

---

[249] *The Khartoum Resolutions*, art. 3, September 1, 1967, *Israel-Arab Peace Process: The Khartoum Resolutions* (September 1, 1967) Jewish Virtual Library [hereinafter the *Khartoum Resolutions*], http://www.jewishvirtuallibrary.org/jsource/Peace/three_noes.html.

[250] TESSLER, *supra* at 408-09.

[251] SHAVIT, *supra* at 204.

[252] In the doctrine of Judaism, the messiah is a descendant of King David who will bring peace and justice to the world at a future date.

[253] GILBERT, *supra* at 406-07.

help the involved states reach agreement on the issues in dispute.[254] The UN resolution does not say which parties hold sovereign claims to the Territories, effectively leaving the ownership issue to the assigned negotiations. The pronouncement is approved by all interested states except Syria.

1968 (May): UN resolutions on Jerusalem. After Israel captures East Jerusalem in the 1967 war it reunifies the east and west sides of the city under its own exclusive governance, all the while ignoring multiple UN General Assembly resolutions announcing that the status of Jerusalem may not be lawfully altered. The UN Security Council adopts similar resolutions. Security Council Resolution 252 deplores Israel's failure to comply with the prior General Assembly resolutions, declares Israel's annexation of Jerusalem "invalid," and orders Israel "to rescind all such measures already taken and to desist forthwith from taking any further action which tends to change the status of Jerusalem."[255] Israel continues to govern Jerusalem undeterred.

1968 (July): Amended PLO Charter. The PLO updates its 1964 Charter.[256] The 1968 PLO Charter reiterates the 1964 statements that "Palestine" is an "indivisible part of the Arab homeland" and "the Palestinian people are an integral part of the Arab nation."[257] However,

---

[254] Resolution 242, paras. 1-4.

[255] S.C. Res. 252, U.N. Doc. S/RES/252 (May 21, 1968), available at https://undocs.org/en/S/RES/252(1968).

[256] *The Palestinian National Charter: Resolutions of the Palestine National Council*, July 1-17, 1968, [hereinafter the *1968 PLO Charter*], Yale Law School, Lillian Goldman Law Library, The Avalon Project, available at http://avalon.law.yale.edu/20th_century/plocov.asp.

[257] 1968 PLO Charter, art. 1.

the new Charter refers to former Mandatory Palestine as a distinct "country."[258] Again differing from the 1964 pronouncement, the 1968 document defines the boundaries of "Palestine" more expansively, claiming they include not only Israel but the Territories.[259] The definition of "Palestinians" is broadened to include those living in the "diaspora" (foreign refugee camps).[260] But the definition now omits the 1964 reference to Jews "willing to live peacefully and loyally in Palestine." Instead, the new concept of nationality includes only Jews who lived in Palestine "before the Zionist invasion" (i.e. before the late 19th Century).[261] "[A]rmed struggle" through "commando action" is still deemed "the only way to liberate Palestine."[262] Finally, all nations are urged to "consider Zionism an illegitimate movement" and "outlaw its existence."[263]

Referring to UN Security Council Resolution 242, the 1968 Charter rejects "all solutions which are substitutes for the total liberation of Palestine."[264] The Charter similarly rejects the BMP and the UN Partition Plan as "entirely illegal."[265]

---

[258] *Id.*, art. 2.

[259] See *Id.* The text refers to the boundaries of Palestine "during the British Mandate." *Id.*

[260] *Id.*, arts. 4 and 5.

[261] *Id.*, art. 6.

[262] *Id.*, arts. 9 and 10.

[263] *Id.*, art. 23.

[264] *Id.*, art. 21. See also Palestinian National Council: Resolutions (June 1974), in THE ISRAEL-ARAB READER, A DOCUMENTARY HISTORY OF THE MIDDLE EAST CONFLICT, 7th ed. (Walter Laqueur and Barry Rubin eds., 2008) at 162-63 (asserting that Resolution 242 "obliterates the patriotic and national rights of our people and treats our national cause as a refugee problem.").

[265] *Id.*, arts. 19 and 20.

1969 - 1970: War of Attrition. The Soviet Union supplies Egypt and other Arab states with massive quantities of armaments and thousands of military advisors.[266] Egypt uses the weapons to wage a low-scale war against Israel called the "War of Attrition." In the War, the Egyptian army attacks Israeli forces in the occupied Sinai with artillery fire and commando raids. After sustaining escalating losses, Israel orders air raids into Egypt. US pressure leads to a cease-fire, but no peace treaty is signed.

1970: The Jordanian-PLO War of 1970 (also known as Black September). The PLO and the Popular Front for the Liberation of Palestine, also known as the "PFLP," exercise increasing governmental authority and military control in parts of Jordan, where the majority population is Palestinian. They form a quasi-state for Palestinians, [267] which they would use as launching pad for terrorist attacks on Israel. Ironically, the PLO becomes a greater threat to Jordan.[268] After a mounting power struggle with the Jordanian government, the PLO launches a war to overthrow Jordan's King Hussein and to rename Jordan "Palestine." Tens of thousands of Jordanian Palestinians flee their homes to escape the fighting. After ten months of fighting, Jordanian forces crush the insurgency and expel the PLO from their country.

The PLO moves its operations to Lebanon. It forms a quasi-state for Palestinians in the southern part of the country and leverages the new

---

[266] SACHAR, *supra* at 689-690.

[267] SACHAR, *supra* at 685.

[268] *Id.*

platform to fire Katyusha rockets at Israel.[269] There are 560 such incidents between 1969 and 1970, all directed at Israeli communities.[270]

1972: The Munich Massacre. Through the late 1960s and early 1970s, Palestinian terrorists kill hundreds of Israeli civilians and soldiers.[271] In addition, they carry out a number of spectacular acts of international terrorism, especially airline hijackings.[272] In one heavily-publicized operation at the 1972 Munich Olympics, they take 11 Israeli athletes hostage and murder them.[273]

1973 (October): The Yom Kippur War. Egypt and Syria launch a surprise attack on Israel during the Jewish holiday of Yom Kippur and make surprising military gains.[274] Jordan and Iraq also send their military personnel and resources. The conflict becomes known as the Yom Kippur War. Israel successfully repulses the invaders but sustains heavy losses. The outcome restores Egypt's sense of honor and shakes Israel's confidence in its military. [275] The UN Security Council adopts UN Resolution 338, which reiterates the need to implement UN Resolution 242.[276]

---

[269] *Id*. at 697.

[270] TESSLER, *supra* at 451.

[271] GILBERT, *supra* at 418.

[272] *Id*.

[273] *Id*. at 419.

[274] GILBERT, *supra* at 426-61.

[275] *Id*. at 460-61.

[276] UN Resolution 338, *supra* at n. 31.

1974 (June): The Phased Plan. At a session of the Palestinian National Council in Cairo, the PLO replaces the prior military strategy of conquering Israel through a single traditional war with a "Phased Plan" to destroy the Jewish state in incremental stages ...[277] The Plan calls for a "union" with a growing alliance of "confrontation countries" dedicated to taking territory in pieces through "armed struggle" until they complete "the liberation of all Palestinian territory."[278]

1974 (October): The Rabat Summit Resolution. The Arab League unanimously recognizes the PLO as "the sole, legitimate representative of the Palestinian people" and agrees that the "Palestinian struggle in the confrontation with the Zionist enemy" should proceed under the PLO's command.[279] The resolution ends Jordan's role as spokesperson for the Palestinian people. However, Jordan continues to regard itself as the legitimate sovereign of East Jerusalem and the West Bank, and the guardian of the Muslim holy places of East Jerusalem.

1974 (November): UN recognition of Palestinian rights. The UN General Assembly adopts two non-binding (i.e. political, not legal) resolutions supporting Palestinian rights. The first, Resolution 3236, recognizes the Palestinian right to "self-determination," "national

---

[277] FreeMiddleEast.com, *The Phased Plan*, 1974, available at: http://www.freemiddleeast.com/blog/free_middle_east/the-phased-plan/21.

[278] *Id.*

[279] League of Arab States, *Seventh Arab League Summit Conference Resolution on Palestine*, Rabat, Morocco, October 28, 1974, https://unispal.un.org/DPA/DPR/unispal.nsf/0/63D9A930E2B428DF852572C0006D06B8.

independence," and "sovereignty."[280] The second statement, Resolution 3237, grants the PLO observer status in UN proceedings.[281]

1975: U.N. Racism Resolution. The UN General Assembly approves Resolution 3379, which states that "Zionism is a form of racism and racial discrimination."[282] Sixteen years later, after the break-up of the Soviet Union creates several new UN members, the UN repeals the pronouncement over the objection of several Muslim states.

1977 (November): Anwar Sadat visits Israel. Egyptian President Anwar Sadat becomes the first Arab leader to visit Israel. He delivers an historic speech to Israel's Knesset that calls for peace. The Israeli public receives him with enthusiasm. The event sets the stage for peace talks at Camp David a year later.

1977: Expansion of Israeli settlements. Israelis elect a right-wing government, which significantly expands the number and size of Israeli settlements in the Territories. The Israeli population in the West Bank increases fivefold in about three years.[283]

---

[280] G.A. Res. 3236, *Question of Palestine*, U.N. Doc. A/RES/3236 (XXIX) (Nov. 22, 1974) [hereinafter Resolution 3236], available at: https://undocs.org/en/A/RES/3236(XXIX).

[281] G.A. Res. 3237(XXIX), *Observer Status for the Palestine Liberation Organization*, U.N. Doc. A/RES/3237(XXIX) (Nov. 22, 1974), available at: https://undocs.org/en/A/RES/3237(XXIX).

[282] G.A. Res. 3379 (XXX), *World Conference to Combat Racism and Racial Discrimination*, U.N. Doc. A/RES/3379(XXX) (Nov. 10, 1975) [hereinafter *UN Racism Resolution*], https://undocs.org/en/A/RES/3379(XXX).

[283] TESSLER, *supra* at 520-21.

1978: Israel invades southern Lebanon. PLO commandos based in southern Lebanon cross the Israeli border intermittently to kill Israeli civilians and troops. Israel responds with retaliatory strikes. After a PLO massacre of Israeli children on a school bus, Israel invades southern Lebanon to clear out the PLO bases and establish a security zone. The UN Security Council compels Israel to withdraw and establishes a UN peacekeeping force in southern Lebanon called the United Nations Interim Force in Lebanon (UNIFIL).[284] UNIFIL is not required to remove the PLO bases in the area. Over time, the PLO expands its bases and military strength and the cross-border hostilities continue.

1978 (September): Camp David Accords (Egyptian-Israeli peace treaty). Implementing UN Resolution 242, Egypt and Israel sign a "framework for peace" called the Camp David Accords, wherein Egypt agrees to recognize Israel's right to exist and Israel agrees to withdraw from the Sinai and return the territory to Egypt.[285] In the process, Israel uproots over 7,000 Israelis from their homes and businesses in the Sinai, removing many of the distraught residents by force. Egypt disclaims any rights to the Gaza Strip. The agreement establishes an 8.7-mile-long security corridor called the Philadelphia Corridor along the southern edge of Gaza to help separate Gaza from Egypt. Six months later the framework ripens into the Egypt-Israeli Peace Treaty. The 1979 treaty established Egypt as the first Arab state to recognize Israel.

---

[284] UNSC Resolution 425 (2074th Meeting, March 19, 1978) and 426 (2074th Meeting, March 19, 1978).

[285] Camp David Accords (1978) [hereinafter Camp David Accords], http://mfa.gov.il/MFA/ForeignPolicy/Peace/Guide/Pages/Camp%20David%20Accords.aspx.

Additional provisions in the peace treaty chart a path of negotiations to end the Israeli-Palestinian dispute. The intended talks contemplate an incremental withdrawal of Israelis from the Territories, a just settlement to the Palestinian refugee dispute, Palestinian autonomy in Gaza and the West Bank, and Arab recognition of Israel's right to exist.[286] The PLO denounces the deal, claiming it would legitimize the alleged occupation rather than create a sovereign Palestinian state.[287]

The Arab League protests the treaty by suspending Egypt's membership in the organization. The punishment lasts for nine years. In 1981 Sadat is assassinated by the Egyptian Islamic Jihad.

1979 (March): UN resolution on settlements in Territories. The UN Security Council issues Resolution 446, addressing all ground occupied by Israel since 1967 (including the Territories, the Sinai Peninsula, and the Golan Heights).[288] The Resolution declares that the Israeli settlements in those areas "have no legal validity" and constitute a "serious obstruction" to achieving a just and lasting peace. It further orders Israel to "abide scrupulously" by its Fourth Convention obligations, rescind its settlement-promoting measures, desist from any action that would alter the legal or material status of the "occupied" territories, and stop transferring its civilian population to those places. Israel continues its settlement building. Two years later, the Israeli

---

[286] TESSLER, *supra* at 512-19.

[287] *Id.* at 518-19.

[288] UNSC Resolution 446, S/RES/446, March 22, 1979, available at https://undocs.org/en/S/RES/446(1979)

government fast-tracks the strategy by subsidizing the widely opposed housing developments.[289]

1980: Israel solidifies its claim to Jerusalem as the nation's capital. Israel amends its Basic Law to state that "Jerusalem, complete and united, is the capital of Israel."[290] The reference to "complete and united" expresses the belief that East and West Jerusalem should not be re-divided. Related provisions of the Law confirm that Jerusalem is Israel's seat of government, reinforce Israel's commitment to protect the Holy Places of the Old City, and provide for Jerusalem's economic development.[291] The UN Security Council unanimously declares the action null and void and urges all nations to relocate their embassies out of Jerusalem.[292] The few nations with embassies in Jerusalem relocate them to Tel Aviv.

1981: Israel adopts Golan Heights Law. Israel attempts to reopen peace negotiations with Syria but Syria reiterates its "Three No's" position. Israel then extends its jurisdiction over the Golan Heights by replacing its military administration with civilian rule. Specifically, the Golan Heights Law states that "[t]he Law, jurisdiction and administration of the state shall apply to the Golan Heights."[293] Druze residents of the

---

[289] TESSLER, *supra* at 547-48.

[290] Basic Law: Jerusalem, Capital of Israel (Aug. 5, 1980), https://www.knesset.gov.il/laws/special/eng/basic10_eng.htm.

[291] *Id.*

[292] UNSC Resolution 478, S/RES/478, August 20, 1980, available at https://undocs.org/en/S/RES/478(1980).

[293] Golan Heights Law (Dec. 14, 1981), http://www.mfa.gov.il/mfa/foreignpolicy/peace/guide/pages/golan%20heights%20law.aspx.

Golan are offered Israeli citizenship, but they decline. Israel assigns them permanent resident status.

Israel's reclassification of the Golan avoids using the term "annexation," the word used by the rest of the world community. In the same vein, Israel notifies the UN that the Golan decision is made without prejudice to future peace talks in which the Golan may be returned to Syria. However, the UN Security Council votes unanimously to condemn Israel's maneuver as an illegal annexation.[294] The resolution demands a repeal of the controversial law and declares the measure "null and void." Some Israelis complain Israel has no right to apply its law to areas such as the Golan that lie beyond the BMP.

1982 (June): Israel-PLO Lebanon War. PLO terrorists in southern Lebanon, despite the presence of co-located UNIFIL forces, attack northern Israel, and Israel launches reprisal raids. A PLO splinter group shoots and nearly assassinates Israel's ambassador to Great Britain. In response, the IDF invades southern Lebanon, defeats the PLO, and occupies the foreign ground as a military "security zone." US and European Union troops supervise the forced departure of the PLO from Lebanon. The PLO moves its headquarters to Tunisia.

1982: The rise of Hezbollah. In response to Israel's invasion of Lebanon, Iran and Syria support the creation of a Shiite Islamic militant group called Hezbollah to oust Israeli forces from Lebanon, end its occupation of the Territories, and vanquish the country.

---

[294] UNSC Resolution 497, S/RES/497 (December 17, 1981), available at https://undocs.org/en/S/RES/497(1981).

1987: The First Intifada: Palestinians demonstrate against Israeli policies in the Territories, including deportations, home demolitions, and curfews. The protests lead to civil disobedience, which in turn detonate spontaneous hostility and then coordinated attacks on Israeli soldiers and civilians. The attacks typically employ Molotov cocktails, other explosives, tire-burning and rock-throwing. In time the uprising is called the *Intifada* (shaking off). The physical attacks are supplemented by an economic boycott of Israeli businesses, a refusal to pay taxes, and a labor strike.

The PLO's Fatah command in Tunis is surprised by the Intifada but manages to control and direct it.[295] In the turmoil, the Palestinians slay 160 Israelis, Israelis kills 1,100 Palestinians, and Palestinians wipe out 1,000 other Palestinians suspected of "collaborating" with Israel.

1988 (July): Jordan renounces claim to the Territories. The PLO asserts national rights to East Jerusalem and the West Bank. In particular, the organization demands that Jordan renounce its claim of sovereignty in those parts of the Territories. Jordan complies. It then revokes the Jordanian citizenship of East Jerusalem and West Bank Palestinians.

1988 (August): The rise of Hamas. An offshoot of Egypt's Muslim Brotherhood inaugurates an anti-Israel organization with both political and military wings. The entity is formally titled the Islamic Resistance Movement but is better known as "Hamas." The Hamas Covenant pledges to "raise the banner of Jihad in the face of the oppressors."[296]

---

[295] SACHAR, *supra* at 964.

[296] *The Covenant of the Islamic Resistance Movement*, Art. 3, August 18, 1988 [hereinafter the Hamas Covenant], http://avalon.law.yale.edu/20th_century/hamas.asp.

Based on ideals of militant Islam, Hamas vows to turn former Mandatory Palestine into an Islamic caliphate.[297]

Hamas wages terrorist attacks on Israel, often with suicide bombings. The militant group is eventually deemed a terrorist organization by Israel, the US, Canada, the European Union, Australia, Japan, and Egypt. It is also banned in Jordan.

1988 (November): Declaration of Palestinian independence. The PLO's legislative branch, called the Palestine National Council, adopts a Declaration of Independence for the State of Palestine with Jerusalem as its capital.[298]

The Declaration asserts "the right of the Palestinian Arab people to sovereignty based on "the conditions of international legitimacy" created by the UN Partition Plan of 1947.[299] The cited Partition Plan was the same proposal that the Palestinians had violently opposed in 1947. By stating that the UN Partition Plan "partitioned Palestine into two states, one Arab and one Jewish,"[300] the Declaration implicitly defines the territory of the new state as the Territories plus the land that the Partition Plan apportioned to the proposed Arab state but was captured by Israel in the 1948 War of Independence. The document adds that the targeted region "is an Arab state," and "an indivisible part of the Arab

---

[297] See *Id.* at art. 27.

[298] *National Council: Declaration of Independence*, November 15, 1988, https://en.wikisource.org/wiki/Palestinian_Declaration_of_Independence.

[299] *Id.*

[300] *Id.*

nation."[301] It further describes the area as "a peace-loving State that rejects terrorism and believes in peaceful coexistence."[302] In conclusion, it praises the "much blessed Intifada" and pledges to continue the "struggle" to "terminate Israel's occupation of the Palestinian territories."[303] The State of Palestine is recognized by over 100 nations.

1988 (December): PLO delegation renamed "Palestine." The UN General Assembly votes to change the name of the PLO's UN delegation from "the Palestine Liberation Organization" to "Palestine"[304] but maintains the entity's observer status.

1991: The Madrid Conference. Spain hosts a peace conference with multilateral and bilateral dimensions to resolve the Israeli-Palestinian dispute. The multilateral exchanges include the US and Soviet Union. On the bilateral level, Israel negotiates with a joint Jordanian-Palestinian delegation, as well as Lebanon and Syria. The meetings lay the groundwork for the Oslo Accords.

1993-1999: The Oslo Accords. Negotiations in Oslo, Norway between Israelis and Palestinians produce a series of bilateral agreements called the Oslo Accords. The deal revives the concept, conceived in the 1978 Camp David Accords, of a transitional Palestinian government.

---

[301] *Id.*

[302] *Id.*

[303] *Id.*

[304] UNGA Resolution A/Res/43/177, *Question of Palestine* (December 15, 1988), available at https://undocs.org/en/A/Res/43/177.

Pursuant to the Oslo Accords, Israel and the PLO exchange letters of mutual recognition.[305] The Accords additionally create self-rule for the Palestinians with an elected government called the Palestinian Authority (the PA). Moreover, the agreement assigns the PA and Israel different degrees of control in different parts of the Territories (see Map 21: Oslo Accords Allocation of West Bank Areas A, B, and C; 1993-1999).

---

[305] Yasser Arafat and Yitzhak Rabin, *Israeli-Palestinian Peace Process: Letters of Mutual Recognition* (Sept. 9, 1993), Jewish Virtual Library [last viewed March 22, 2021], available at https://www.jewishvirtuallibrary.org/israel-palestinian-letters-of-mutual-recognition-september-1993/.

MAP 21
OSLO ACCORDS ASSIGNMENT OF
WEST BANK AREAS A, B AND C (1993-1999)

(Tan = Area A = full Palestinian control)
(Rose = Area B = shared control)
(White = Area C = full Israeli control)

By Wickey-nl - Own work. Adaptation of OCHAoPt Map Centre., Public Domain, https://bit.ly/ajm-map21

Note: To see this map in its original color version (with a zoom-in feature for more detailed viewing), download the PDF in the Appendix.

Israel further agrees to an immediate withdrawal of military forces from Gaza and Jericho in the West Bank as the first stage of a broader withdrawal.

The above terms are considered an "interim" arrangement to be followed by "permanent status" negotiations over the next five years.[306] The permanent status agenda includes the most divisive issues: borders, Jerusalem, security arrangements, settlements, refugees, relations and cooperation with other neighbors, and other issues of common interest.[307] The five-year deadline to complete the final status discussion is May 4, 1999. Pending resolution of the final issues, neither side may "change the status" of the Territories.[308]

The Israeli and Palestinian leaderships encounter angry recriminations from their people when the terms of the Oslo deal are disclosed.[309]

Through the 1990's, Hamas tries to derail the interim agreement with random shootings, stabbings, and bombings that kill Israeli civilians in Gaza and Israel's largest cities.[310] Meanwhile, Hezbollah and Islamic Jihad intensify their rocket attacks on Israel's communities. To suppress the assaults, Israel deports hundreds of Hamas militants.[311] In response, the terror groups escalate their attacks.[312] Israeli terrorists in the West Bank then murder Arabs suspected of involvement in the fighting.[313]

---

[306] Oslo I, *supra* at arts. I, II and V.

[307] *Id.* at art. V.

[308] Oslo II, art. XXXI(7).

[309] SACHAR, *supra* at 993.

[310] SACHAR, *supra* at 989-90, 998, and 1010.

[311] *Id.* at 989-90.

[312] *Id.*

[313] *Id.*

Ultimately, Israel restores security by sealing off Gaza and the West Bank, despite the harm to Israel's own economy.[314]

1994: Israel-Jordan peace treaty. Israel and Jordan, following a mutual declaration terminating the state of war between them at a US-hosted meeting in Washington, D.C., negotiate and sign a peace treaty.[315] Among other things, the principals recognize each other's sovereignty, define their international boundary, pledge to cooperate in defending against terrorism, and agree to help alleviate the regional problem of refugees and displaced persons. Israel surrenders a small amount of territory to Jordan. The parties also sign related protocols governing issues of commerce and trade.

Mid-1990's: Growth of Israeli settlements. More Israeli civilians relocate to East Jerusalem and West Bank Area C, increasing the area's Jewish population and land development. Most of the migrants are secular Jews and moderately religious Jews who believe Israel is entitled to the Territories for legal and historic reasons. A vocal minority of settlers are orthodox Jews devoted to the Territories based on biblical ties. As the settlers start families their numbers swell through natural growth.

In Hebron, the Oslo Accords establish two adjacent premises -- H1 and H2 – where Arabs and Jews live in close proximity. Eighty percent of the town is occupied by 15,000 Palestinians, while the remaining 20

---

[314] *Id.*

[315] *Treaty of Peace between the State of Israel and the Hashemite Kingdom of Jordan*, Isr.-Jordan, October 26, 1994, available at: http://peacemaker.un.org/sites/peacemaker.un.org /files/IL%20JO_941026_PeaceTreatyIsraelJordan.pdf.

percent houses 500 Jews.[316] An IDF contingent of 500 soldiers guards the Jewish minority.[317]

1997: The PA bans the sale of land to Jews. The PA revives a Jordanian law that imposes the death penalty on any Arab who sells land in the Territories to a Jew.[318] Over the next four months, the punishment is imposed on five Arab real estate agents.[319]

2000 (May): Israel withdraws from Lebanon. Israel withdraws from its self-declared security zone in southern Lebanon. UNIFIL resumes its mission in the zone. Hezbollah seizes control of the area and commences a series of anti-Israel terrorist attacks. The organization becomes a "state within a state" in Lebanon. In 2008 it gains representation in Lebanon's unity government.

2000 (July): Camp David Summit. At a summit hosted by US President Bill Clinton in Camp David, Maryland, Israel and the Palestinians engage in permanent status negotiations under the Oslo Accords. The intensive talks fail to produce an agreement.

2000 (September) – 2005: The Second Intifada. In an atmosphere of frustration following the collapse of the Camp David Summit, Israeli political opposition leader Ariel Sharon orchestrates a public appearance at Jerusalem's Temple Mount/Haram, an Old City site holy

---

[316] SACHAR, *supra* at 1019.

[317] *Id.*

[318] GILBERT, *supra* at 601.

[319] *Id.*

to both Muslims and Jews.[320] Palestinians, along with many Arab Israelis, construe the visit as a provocation and begin a violent rampage against Israelis.[321]

The Palestinian violence becomes known as the *Second Intifada*. Deadlier than the First Intifada, the second one deploys suicide bombers in crowded Israeli locations such as a community Passover service, a pizzeria, a commuter bus, and a disco.[322] The attackers use military grade explosives.[323] Meanwhile, Gaza-based members of Hamas fire mortars at nearby Israeli towns. Other radicals use pipe bombs. PA leaders neither orchestrate the bombardments nor restrain them, even as PA-affiliated Fatah party members participate in the attacks. By the time the warfare ends five years later, it claims the lives of approximately 3,000 Palestinians and 1,000 Israelis.

2000 (December). The Clinton Parameters. In a continuing attempt to broker a peace treaty, President Clinton invites Israeli and Palestinian negotiators to the White House to review a proposal known as the "Clinton Parameters." The Parameters propose to bridge the gaps between the opponents as follows:[324]

---

[320] DENNIS ROSS, *THE MISSING PEACE* 728-29 (2004) [hereinafter *ROSS MISSING PEACE*]. Ambassador Ross is counselor and William Davidson Distinguished Fellow at The Washington Institute for Near East Policy. He designed US policy on the Israeli-Palestinian conflict for President George H.W. Bush and later led the team of US negotiators that represented the Clinton administration during the drafting of the Oslo Accords.

[321] *Id.* at 730; SACHAR, *supra* at 1037-39.

[322] SACHAR, *supra* at 1048-54.

[323] *Id.* at 1054.

[324] ROSS *MISSING PIECE, supra* at 748-53.

1. Borders: A Palestinian state would be formed on all of Gaza and
    between 94 and 96% of the West Bank. The remaining four to six
    percent of the West Bank would be annexed to Israel. That
    residual real estate, called "the major settlement blocs," mostly
    surrounds Jerusalem, hugs the Green Line, and contains 80% of
    the Israeli settler population. [325] To offset this territorial change,
    Israel would surrender one to three percent of its pre-1967 land
    to the State of Palestine. A permanent safe passage would
    connect Gaza to the West Bank (see Map 22: The Clinton
    Parameters, 2000).

2. Settlements: Israeli settlers in the major settlement blocs would
    remain in place. The tens of thousands of other Israeli settlers in
    the Territories would relocate to Israel.

3. Jerusalem: The Palestinians would gain sovereignty over the
    Arab neighborhoods while Israel becomes sovereign in the
    Jewish neighborhoods. The Haram/Temple Mount would be
    controlled under one of two alternatives. Either the Palestinians
    would gain sovereignty over the Haram and the Israelis would
    have sovereignty over the Western Wall and symbolic
    ownership of the Holy of Holies (or the holy space of which it is
    a part), or the Palestinians would gain sovereignty over the
    Haram and the Israelis would have sovereignty over the
    Western Wall and the parties would share functional

---

[325] The major settlement blocs have not been officially defined but are commonly thought to
include the communities of Gush Etzion, Ma'aleh Adumim, Givat Ze'ev, Modi'in Illit, and in
the Olmert Peace Plan, Ariel. For a map of the settlement blocs, see *Explained: How Big an
Obstacle Are Israeli Settlements to Peace*, HAARETZ, February 14, 2017,
http://www.haaretz.com/israel-news/.premium-1.771263.

sovereignty over excavation at the site (see Map 23: The Old City of Jerusalem, 2000).

4. Security: An international force would monitor the implementation of the agreement and gradually replace the IDF presence, which would remain in the Jordan Valley for up to six years. In cases of emergency, the IDF could deploy to the Jordan Valley. Israel would retain three early-warning sites in the West Bank with a Palestinian liaison presence for as long as Israel deems necessary. The Palestinian state would be a non-militarized state but maintain an armed force for policing and border security. The State of Palestine would have sovereign control over its airspace but share space for Israeli training and operational needs.

5. Refugees: Refugees would either have a right of return to former Mandatory Palestine or a right to return to their "homeland," where homeland is defined as the State of Palestine and the portions of Israel transferred to the State of Palestine in the proposed land-swap. Any entry to Israel would be in Israel's sole discretion. Remaining details are left unclear.

MAP 22
THE CLINTON PARAMETERS (2000)

Source: Jewish Virtual
Library
https://bit.ly/ajm-map22

Note: To see this map in its
original color version (with
a zoom-in feature for more
detailed viewing), download
the PDF in the Appendix.

MAP 23
THE OLD CITY OF JERUSALEM, 2000

TheCuriousGnome (talk) - Map_of_Jerusalem_-_the_old_city.png, CC BY-SA 3.0,
https://bit.ly/ajm-map23

Note: To see this map in its original color version (with a zoom-in feature for more detailed viewing), download the PDF in the Appendix.

The Clinton Parameters are supported by Egypt, Saudi Arabia and Jordan.[326] Israel accepts the Parameters with minor reservations.[327] The Palestinians raise objections that amount to multiple deal-killers.[328] Specifically, the Palestinian negotiators contend the Clinton Parameters would let Israel retain over nine percent of the West Bank, and in exchange deliver an amount of Israeli land equal to just one percent of the retained real estate.[329] The Palestinians also observe that the Parameters do not address the fate of 40 Israeli settlements, home to 40,000 Israelis, located in the proposed State of Palestine.[330] Next they note that Israel would gain sovereignty over at least one-third of East Jerusalem, as well as the Haram/Temple Mount compound.[331] Finally, they consider the solution for refugees inadequate.

President Clinton leaves office without securing an Israeli-Palestinian peace deal.

2001 (January): The Taba Summit. Amidst the chaos of the Second Intifada and the pressure of an imminent Israeli election, the adversaries

---

[326] *Id.* ROSS MISSING PIECE, *supra* at 763.

[327] *Id.* at 754-55.

[328] *Id.*

[329] *How Generous is Generous, What Happened at Camp David*, Settlement Report, Vol. 10 No. 8, Winter 2000, published in AMERICAN MUSLIMS FOR PALESTINE, http://www.ampalestine.org/palestine-101/history/peace-processes/how-generous-generous-what-happened-at-camp-david.

[330] *Id.*

[331] *Id.*

reconvene in Taba, Egypt. Israeli Prime Minister Ehud Barak presents a peace proposal and the Palestinians respond as follows:[332]

1. Borders: Israel gives the Palestinians 94% of the West Bank. Israel annexes the remaining six percent, which contains the major settlement blocs, and leases from the Palestinians an additional two percent. The eight percent of the West Bank that remains with Israel is offset by an eight percent land-swap from pre-1967 Israel. The particular lands to be included in the annexation and land-swap are undecided. An above-ground highway connects Gaza to the West Bank.

   - The Palestinians seek an annexation limit of 3.6 percent.

2. Settlements: Israeli settlers in the major settlement blocs remain; all other settlers relocate to Israel proper.

3. Jerusalem: Israel keeps the Israeli neighborhoods while Palestinians hold the Palestinian ones. The Old City and Holy Places may be subject to divided sovereignty, international sovereignty, divine sovereignty, or no sovereignty.

   - The Palestinians want the dividing line to be permeable, with no governmental entity supervising the two city halves.

---

[332] David Matz, *Special Report, Trying to Understand the Taba Talks,* PALESTINE-ISRAEL JOURNAL, Vol. 10, No. 3, 2003, http://www.pij.org/details.php?id=32.

4. Security: The State of Palestine would accept military limits. The IDF would retain a presence in the Jordan Valley for an unstated length of time. Control over airspace is left undecided.

   - The Palestinians want no IDF presence in their sovereign state.

5. Refugees: Israel lets an undetermined number of Palestinian refugees return to Israel.

   - The Palestinians believe a six-figure sum of refugees should be permitted to return.

The Taba Summit reaches a stalemate and disbands. Israel elects a new prime minister who opposes his predecessor's concessions. Palestinians continue their terror operations. But the Summit brings the belligerents closer than ever to making peace.[333]

2002 (March) UN endorses two-state solution: UN Security Council Resolution 1397 demands an end to all acts of violence between Israel and the Palestinians, calls on the parties to resume their diplomacy on the issues in dispute, and supports the efforts of the UN Secretary General and other intermediaries to assist the peace process.[334] One of the document's introductory clauses speaks of "[a]ffirming a vision of a region where two States, Israel and Palestine, live side by side within secure and recognized borders."[335] The parlance revives the concept of

---

[333] DOWTY, *supra* at 170.

[334] *SC Res. 1397*, UN Doc S/RES/1397(2002) (March 12, 2002), available at https://undocs. org/en/S/RES/1397(2002).

[335] *Id.*

the 1937 Peel Commission Report and 1947 UN Partition Plan, which proposed a two-state solution for Arab and Jewish Palestinians.

2002 (March) The Arab Peace Initiative. The Arab League proposes a plan for peace with Israel.[336] The Arab Peace Initiative first envisions that Israel will withdraw all troops and settlements from all the Territories. Second, the perimeters of Gaza, East Jerusalem and the West Bank would become the State of Palestine. Third, the Arab world would normalize relations with Israel. Fourth, the "just solution" for Palestinian refugees would permit them to return to their homes in Israel and the Territories or receive monetary compensation. Finally, East Jerusalem would become the capital of the Palestinian State. The Initiative is presented as a take-it-or-leave-it offer not subject to discussion.

The Arab Initiative is accepted by the PA but rejected by Hamas. Israel objects on the grounds that the proposal ignores Israel's needs as defined by UN Resolution 242 and the Oslo Accords. Essentially, Resolution 242 and the Oslo Accords expected the disputing parties to establish permanent borders, safeguard national security for Israel, and resolve the refugee issue through negotiation, whereas the Arab Initiative precluded negotiation.

2002 (March – May): Israel re-invades West Bank Areas A and B. During the Second Intifada combat, the IDF redeploys to West Bank Areas A and B, including all six major West Bank Palestinian cities. The

---

[336] *Arab League Peace Initiative of August 15, 2012*, available at: https://undocs.org/en/S/2002/932.

troops kill hundreds of militants, arrest thousands more, impose curfews, and shatter Palestinian military infrastructure.

2003 (April): Quartet Roadmap for Peace. During the Second Intifada the UN Security Council, along with the US, EU and Russia, try to revive the Israeli-Palestinian peace process by crafting a new two-state solution. The group of four is known as the "Quartet," and the plan is called the "Roadmap for Peace."[337]

The Roadmap for Peace urges Israel and the PA to: (1) satisfy certain preconditions for a Palestinian state, including the implementation of the Oslo Accords; (2) create an independent Palestinian state with temporary borders; and (3) negotiate a permanent status agreement including recognition of a Palestinian state with permanent borders. The first phase of the Roadmap never materializes, in part because both parties attach several conditions to the plan and in part because the Palestinians ignore the recommended preconditions to gain recognition for statehood. Palestinians continue acts of terrorism while Israel continues adding housing units and settlers to the Territories.

2003 (July): The Barrier. Between April 2002 and July 2003 Israel completes the first segment of a separation barrier (the "Barrier") designed to stop the infiltration of terrorists from the West Bank. Several years later the Barrier stretches 436 miles long and up to 26 feet high (see Map 24: Green Line and the Barrier, 2011).

---

[337] U.N. Doc. S/2003/529 (May 7, 2003), *Performance-based Roadmap to a Permanent Two-State Solution to the Israeli-Palestinian Conflict*, available at https://undocs.org/en/S/2003/529 ; endorsed by S.C. Res. 1515, U.N. Doc. S/RES/1515 (Nov. 19, 2003) [hereinafter *Quartet Roadmap for Peace*], available at https://undocs.org/en/S/RES/1515(2003).

MAP 24
GREEN LINE AND THE BARRIER (2011)

The Barrier Route in the West Bank July 2011

By Wickey-nl - Own work.
Adaptation of OCHAoPt
Map Centre., CC BY 3.0,
https://bit.ly/ajm-map24

Note: To see this map in its original color version (with a zoom-in feature for more detailed viewing), download the PDF in the Appendix.

The structure follows a winding path that generally tracks the Green Line but also weaves into the West Bank, at some points protruding into that section of the Territories by as much as nine miles. The detours keep major West Bank settlements on the west side of the fence. Over 95% of

141

the structure consists of a fence, but portions in urban sectors are concrete walls built to block Palestinian snipers. Israel supplements the Barrier with patrol roads, ditches, and electronic surveillance devices.

The Barrier sharply reduces the rate of terror attacks. However, the construction project impedes Palestinian access to their farmland, orchards, schools and other facilities. Checkpoints along the Barrier let Palestinians commute to jobs in Israel, but their movement is substantially slowed.

2004: The ICJ Barrier Opinion. The UN's International Court of Justice issues an opinion that the Barrier violates international law.[338] Essentially, the Court finds that the structure illegally frustrates the Palestinian right to self-determination and is not justified by a right of self-defense. The Court acknowledges that it lacks jurisdiction to issue a binding (legally enforceable) ruling on the Barrier because such jurisdiction would require the consent of both parties in the dispute, and Israel withheld its consent. Nevertheless, the Court proceeds to address the matter on a non-binding "advisory" basis.

2005: Disengagement from Gaza. Israel unilaterally withdraws all troops and civilians from Gaza despite widespread domestic opprobrium, especially among Gaza's Jewish residents. Israel continues to permit free trade and transportation between Gaza and Israel. In addition, it leaves behind a district of greenhouses vital to the Gazan economy.

---

[338] *Legal Consequences of the Construction of a Wall in the Occupied Palestinian Territory*, Advisory Opinion, 2004 I.C.J. 131 (July 9) [hereinafter the ICJ *Advisory Opinion*].

Thousands of Gaza Palestinians immediately fill the vacant territory and vandalize the greenhouses. They destroy the local synagogues. As Palestinian security forces stand by, Palestinian militant factions post their flags on the ruins.

Israel simultaneously evacuates four Israeli settlements in the northern West Bank to give West Bank Palestinians more territorial continuity. A related accommodation improves the West Bank transportation infrastructure to reduce travel delays caused by the Barrier.

2006 (January): Hamas wins Palestinian election. Hamas defeats the Fatah party in the Palestinian Legislative Council election to gain control of the PA. Fatah refuses to recognize the result. Middle East observers view the political transformation as a victory of Islamic fundamentalism over secular nationalism.

2006 (July- October): Israel-Hezbollah Lebanon War. Hezbollah fires rockets into Israel and ambushes an Israeli border patrol, killing three soldiers and kidnapping two. Five more Israeli troops are killed in a rescue attempt. Israel retaliates with air strikes and a ground invasion of southern Lebanon. Additional volleys of Hezbollah rockets lead to expanded combat. The UN brokers an end to the war. The UN expands UNIFIL's mission in southern Lebanon to keep the zone free of non-state fighters and weapons. But Hezbollah continues to stockpile missiles, anti-tank artillery, and other weapons in the UN-controlled zone.

2007: Hamas Rule in Gaza. Hamas and Fatah fight a brief war in Gaza. By shooting and lynching Fatah members, Hamas expels Fatah and seizes control of the enclave. Hamas imposes authoritarian rule based on Sharia law, strictly controlling all functions of government and the media. Its educational curriculum teaches militant Islam.

Fatah restructures the PA in a manner that excludes Hamas and retains Fatah's control of the West Bank. The Palestinian legislature ceases to function. While Hamas continues to seek Israel's destruction exclusively through war and terrorism, the PA emphasizes "resistance" through political pressure. PA security forces cooperate with the IDF to restrain Hamas sympathizers in the West Bank. Israel maintains communications with the PA. Meanwhile, Israel closes its border with Gaza and seals off the enclave to prevent the smuggling of weapons to Hamas. The land, air, and sea blockade (the "Blockade") stifles the already-weakened Gaza economy. Hamas digs tunnels into Egypt to smuggle weapons and consumer goods.

Two years later, Egypt imposes its own blockade of Gaza. The multi-year effort includes the construction of a steel wall, the demolition of over 1,000 Hamas smuggling tunnels, the digging and flooding of trenches to deter future tunnel construction, and the eviction of thousands of civilians along the Egyptian side to create a "buffer zone."

2008 (September) The Olmert Plan. In a private meeting between Israeli Prime Minister Ehud Olmert and Palestinian President and PA Chairperson Mahmound Abbas, the former verbally proposes a two-state solution slightly more generous than the Taba Summit proposal of 2001 (see Map 25: The Olmert Peace Plan, 2008).

MAP 25
THE OLMERT PEACE PLAN (2008)

Israeli proposal at Annapolis, 2008 - Israel-Palestine Border:
6.5% of the Palestinian territories will be Annexed to Israel,
including 85% of the Israeli population in the West Bank

	Israel	Palestine	Total
Israeli built area	33.83 sq. km	21.6 sq. km	55.43 sq. km
	0.0%	0.4%	1%
Palestinian built area	6.62 sq. km	375.21 sq. km	381.83 sq. km
	0.1%	6.4%	6.5%
Israeli locality up to 2,000 inhabitants	31	67	98
	32%	68%	100%
Israeli locality up to 10,000 inhabitants	15	8	23
	65%	35%	100%
Israeli locality over 20,000 inhabitants	3	0	3
	100%	0%	100%
Cultivated land by Israelis		38.4 sq. km	
		0.6%	

Mediterranean sea

Tel Aviv

Jaffa

Palestine West Bank

Israel

Legend

1967 Lines

Barrier

The Municipal boundaries of Jerusalem

Palestinian Locality

Jewish Locality

Up to 2,000 inhabitants

Up to 10,000 inhabitants

Over 20,000 inhabitants

Cultivated land by Israelis

Dead sea

N

Designed by SAYA © Shaul Arieli

0 5 10 20 30 40 km

*This map does not show the areas offered by Israel to the Palestinians in exchange ** Data does not include Jerusalem
Separation of West Bank population centers according to borders between Israel and Palestine proposed by Israel in 2008**

Note: To see this map in its original color version (with a zoom-in feature for more detailed viewing), download the PDF in the Appendix.

The Olmert Plan proposes:

145

1. Borders: The Palestinians acquire 93.7% of the West Bank. Israel annexes the remaining 6.3% and surrenders to the State of Palestine an equivalent area from pre-1967 Israel. A safe passage between Gaza and the West Bank makes Palestine contiguous.
2. Settlements: Settlers in the major settlement blocs remain; all other settlers relocate to pre-1967 Israel.
3. Jerusalem: Sovereignty over the neighborhoods of East Jerusalem is divided as proposed in the Clinton Parameters. The Haram/Temple Mount compound, along with other pieces of the Old City, would be managed by a committee composed of five nations: Israel, Palestine, Jordan, Saudi Arabia, and the US.
4. Security: as proposed at the Taba Summit.
5. Refugees: Israel acknowledges the suffering of the Palestinian refugees but does not accept responsibility for their plight. Israel lets 5,000 refugees relocate to Israel over a five-year period. Israel compensates other refugees, though the amount of compensation is undetermined.

The Olmert Plan, like the Taba Summit, nearly bridges the remaining differences between the parties.[339] President Abbas leaves the meeting,

---

[339] DOWTY, *supra* at 226.

makes a written record of the Plan, and consults with the Jordanians and Egyptians, but does not give Olmert a response to the Plan.[340]

The PA launches a diplomatic initiative to seek statehood through UN recognition instead of the Oslo-structured bilateral exchanges. Prime Minister Olmert leaves office, and the peace concessions he floated are repudiated by his successor.

2008 (December): The Gaza War/Operation Cast Lead. A fragile truce between Israel and Hamas is interrupted, sometimes by Hamas rockets and mortars aimed at civilian populations in southern Israel, and at other times by IDF "targeted assassinations" of Hamas leaders. When one Israeli air strike hits a group of militants, thousands of Hamas rockets rain down on Israeli civilian areas. Israel expands its air campaign. It also invades with infantry to explode Hamas tunnels used for weapons-smuggling. After three weeks, another truce takes hold.

2009: Israeli Settlement Freeze. Israel observes a ten-month moratorium on the construction of new housing in the West Bank as a "confidence-building measure" to induce the Palestinians to resume the permanent status negotiations.[341] The PA counters that only a complete halt to settlement construction would demonstrate a good faith

---

[340] For details on the Olmert Plan negotiation, see Avi Isacharoff, *Revealed: Olmert's 2008 Peace Offer to Palestinians*, JERUSALEM POST (May 24, 2013), available at http://www.jpost.com/Diplomacy-and-Politics/Details-of-Olmerts-peace-offer-to-Palestinians-exposed-314261.

[341] *Israel to End Settlement Moratorium*, September 12, 2010, AL JAZEERA, available at http://www.aljazeera.com/news/middleeast/2010/09/2010912201832209651.html.

willingness to negotiate peace.[342] Nevertheless, towards the end of the ten-month period the Palestinians agree to re-start the discussion. However, they soon request an indefinite extension of the moratorium as a condition of further talks. Israel rejects the idea, and the meeting disbands.

2012 (November): The Gaza War/Operation Pillar of Defense. In a protest against the Gaza Blockade and the West Bank Barrier, Hamas fires 100 rockets in a 24-hour period at Israel's civilian population centers. The group also attacks an IDF patrol jeep in Israel. Israel counters the assault with a series of air strikes on Hamas targets in Gaza. Hamas fires over 1,000 rockets into Israel. Some of the salvos are long-range rockets that can reach as far as Tel Aviv and Jerusalem. After eight days of combat, Egypt mediates a cease-fire.

2012: Recognition of Palestine. The UN General Assembly passes a resolution upgrading the status of "Palestine" from "observer mission" to non-member "observer state."[343]

2013: The US Sponsors Peace Talks. The U.S. persuades Israel and the PA to negotiate the core issues in dispute: borders, land swaps, and mutual recognition. In March of 2013 the parties begin observing a set of confidence-building measures, including an Israeli freeze on new settlement construction, a phased Israeli release of Palestinian prisoners, and a Palestinian pledge not to circumvent the negotiations by seeking recognition from the UN. A year later, after intensive

---

[342] DOWTY, *supra* at 211.

[343] G.A. Res. 67/19, *Status of Palestine in the United Nations*, U.N. Doc. A/RES/67/19, 67th Session (Nov. 29, 2012), available at: https://undocs.org/en/A/RES/67/19.

negotiations, an argument over the timing of the confidence-building requirements causes the talks to break down.

2014 (April): Kerry Peace Talks. US Secretary of State John Kerry coaxes the Israeli and Palestinian leaderships to re-start peace negotiations. The talks quickly end with each side blaming the other for the breakdown. **2014 (April): Hamas/Fatah Unity Government.** Ending seven years of alienation, Hamas and Fatah forge a unity government. But six months later, the arrangement collapses, with Hamas accusing Fatah of withholding salaries from Hamas's Gaza employees and Fatah accusing Hamas of plotting to overthrow the PA. Subsequent attempts at unity also fail.

2014 (June): The Gaza War/Protective Edge. Palestinian terrorists kill three Israeli teenagers in the West Bank. Israeli terrorists retaliate by killing a Palestinian teen. Hamas intensifies its Gaza-based rocket and mortar fire from a sporadic rate to a sudden barrage of thousands. The militant group fires rockets powerful enough to reach most major cities in Israel (see Map 26: Hamas Rocket Ranges, 2014).

MAP 26
HAMAS ROCKET RANGES (2014)

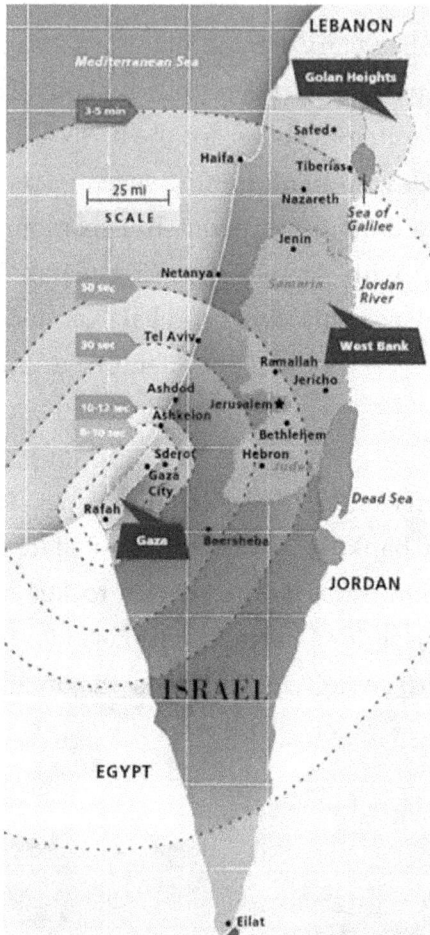

HAMAS ROCKET RANGES

The Gaza-based terrorist group Hamas has rockets that can reach most major cities in Israel.

Hamas' Rockets
Range (in miles)

- Heavy Mortar — 8 mi
- Qassam Rocket — 11 mi
- Grad Rocket — 30 mi
- M-75 / FAJR-5 / Syrian 220mm — 45 mi
- M-302 Long-Range Rocket — 100 mi

Source: American-Israel Political Action Committee (AIPAC). This map is copyrighted by AIPAC and reprinted with AIPAC's prior approval. It is for educational and illustrative purposes and does not imply AIPAC's policy positions on the peace process and final status issues.

Note: To see this map in its original color version (with a zoom-in feature for more detailed viewing), download the PDF in the Appendix.

150

Although the salvos aim for the Israeli population centers, most miss their mark, due in part to a lack of guidance systems and in part to Israel's Iron Dome missile defense system. Israel intercepts Hamas frogmen trying to infiltrate into Israel by sea.

An Israeli counteroffensive called Operation Protective Edge mobilizes to stop the rocket fire and knock out a network of tunnels used by Hamas to conceal its fighters and infiltrate into Israel for military operations. IDF bombing missions in Gaza blow up missile launchers, weapon-storage sites, and related military infrastructure, but also hit thousands of homes, which Israel claims are used for military purposes. Israel follows up with a ground invasion of Gaza's eastern fringe to explode the tunnels.

Arab nations generally withhold military and political support for Hamas's operations. Egypt brokers a series of truces until one ultimately ends the 51-day conflict.

Addressing the Hamas murders in the West Bank, Israel tightens its West Bank access restrictions (see Map 27: West Bank Access Restrictions, 2014).

MAP 27
WEST BANK ACCESS RESTRICTIONS (2014)

(Red line = Barrier constructed)
(Pink line = Barrier under construction)
(Gray line = Barrier planned route)
(Red, green and blue-circled "X" marks = checkpoints)

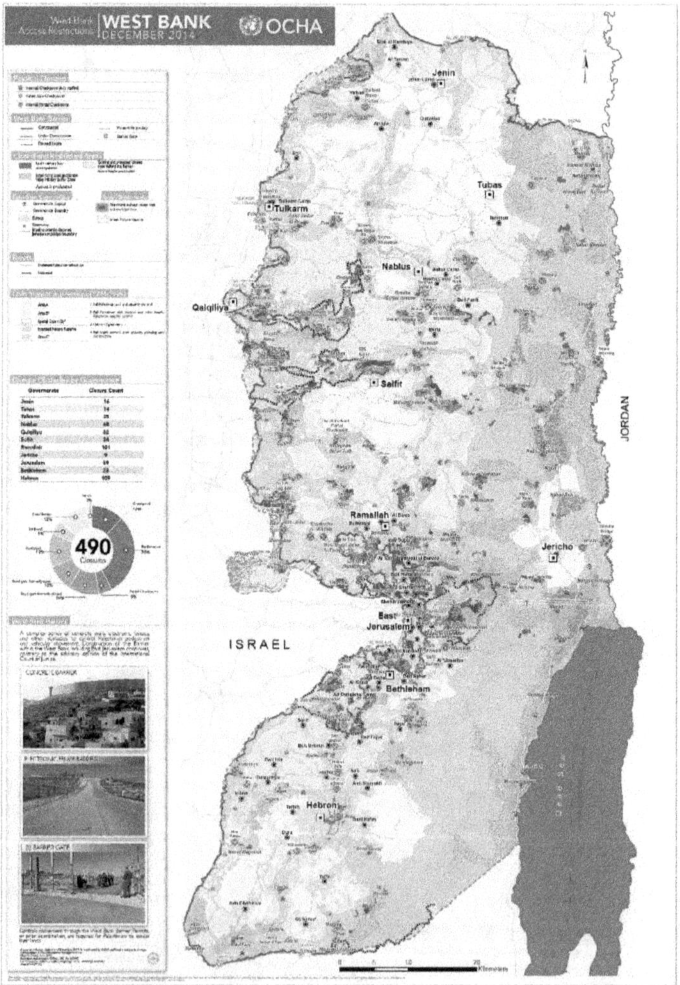

Source: UN Office for the Coordination of Humanitarian Affairs in the Occupied
Palestinian Territories

Note: To see this map in its original color version (with a zoom-in feature for
more detailed viewing), download the PDF in the Appendix.

Special restrictions are maintained in the West Bank town of Hebron, where fewer than 1,000 Jews live among a population of 250,000 Arabs who generally support Hamas (see Map 28: Restrictions on Movement in Hebron, 2011). The Blockade of Gaza remains in force (see Map 29: The Gaza Strip, 2014).

MAP 28
RESTRICTIONS ON MOVEMENT
IN HEBRON (2011)

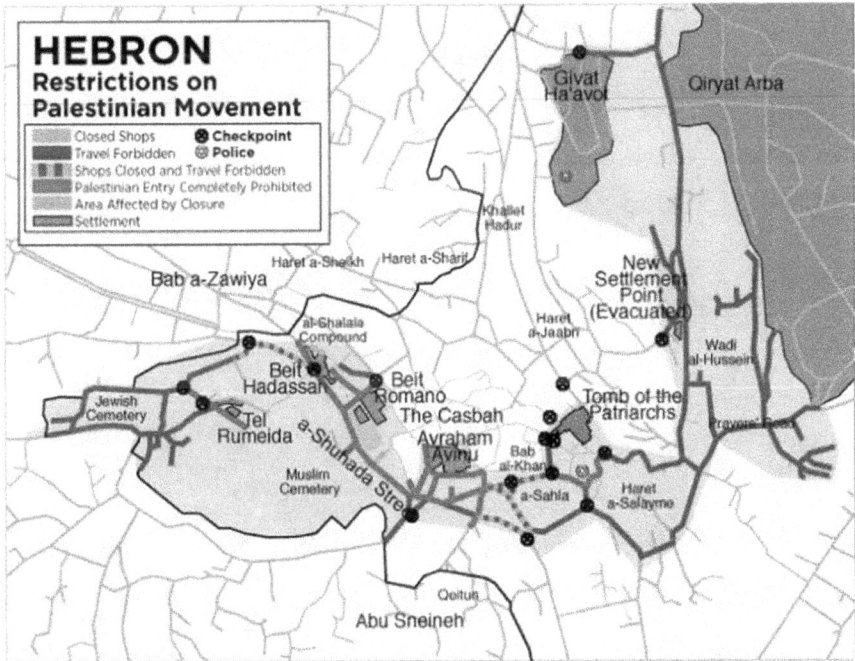

HEBRON
Restrictions on Palestinian Movement

Closed Shops · Checkpoint
Travel Forbidden · Police
Shops Closed and Travel Forbidden
Palestinian Entry Completely Prohibited
Area Affected by Closure
Settlement

Source: B'Tselem

Note: To see this map in its original color version (with a zoom-in feature for more detailed viewing), download the PDF in the Appendix.

MAP 29
GAZA STRIP (2014)

(Red line = "no go" zone, 300 meters)
(Pink line = "risk zone" within range of Israeli fire, 1,000 meters)

Source: UN OCHA, Office of the Occupied Palestinian Territories

Note: To see this map in its original color version (with a zoom-in feature for more detailed viewing), download the PDF in the Appendix.

2015 (January): The PA Accedes to the International Criminal Court. The PA ratifies and accedes to the Rome Statute, making "Palestine" a member state of the ICC, and later assents to the Rome Statute amendments on the crime of aggression.[344] The ICC opens an inquiry into Palestinian allegations of war crimes committed in the Gaza War of 2014.

2015-2016: The Knife Intifada. During the Jewish high holidays of 2015, false rumors of an Israeli scheme to seize control of the Al Aqsa Mosque in Jerusalem incite Palestinians to commit random knife attacks, as well as shootings, car rammings, and rock-throwing assaults, on Israelis. A disproportionate number of victims are Orthodox Jews, who are easily identified by their traditional attire. PA leaders praise the lone wolf attacks.[345] PA President Mahmoud Abbas announces that the Palestinians are no longer bound by the Oslo Accords. Hamas publicly urges more attacks.

---

[344] UN NEWS CENTRE, *International Criminal Court welcomes Palestine as State Party to the Rome Statute*, April 1, 2015, available at: http://www.un.org/apps/news/story.asp?NewsID=50477; United Nations, ICC, *State of Palestine becomes the thirtieth State to ratify the Kampala amendments on the crime of aggression*, June 29, 2016, available at https://www.icc-cpi.int/Pages/item.aspx?name=pr1225.

[345] *The Knives of Jerusalem*, WALL STREET JOURNAL, October 16, 2015, available at: http://www.wsj.com/articles/the-knives-of-jerusalem-1444950148; *The Paranoid, Supremacist Roots of the Stabbing Intifada*, THE ATLANTIC, October 16, 2015, available at http://www.theatlantic.com/international/archive/2015/10/the-roots-of-the-palestinian-uprising-against-israel/410944/.

Israel strengthens security measures and stops many of the attacks by shooting the assailants. Far more Palestinians than Israelis die in the violent exchanges.

2016 (September): The PA Reconfirms Commitment to Oslo Accords. In an address to the UN General Assembly, PA President Mahmoud Abbas reiterates the Palestinian desire for peace and pledges to comply with the Oslo Accords. He blames the conflict on the Israeli occupation and related hardships imposed on Palestinians.

2016 (December): UN Security Council Declares Settlements Illegal. The dense entanglement of Arab and Israeli communities in West Bank Area C leads to widespread anxiety that the Israeli towns and villages not only violate occupation law but pose an intolerable obstacle to peace (see Map 30: West Bank Communities, 2014). Similar concerns are directed at the Jewish residents of East Jerusalem (see Map 31: East Jerusalem, 2014). Many fear the Israeli presence in these portions of the Territories will soon grow too large to remove for purposes of creating a viable Palestinian state.

MAP 30
WEST BANK COMMUNITIES (2014)

(Blue dots = Palestinian settlements)
(Pink areas = Israeli settlements)

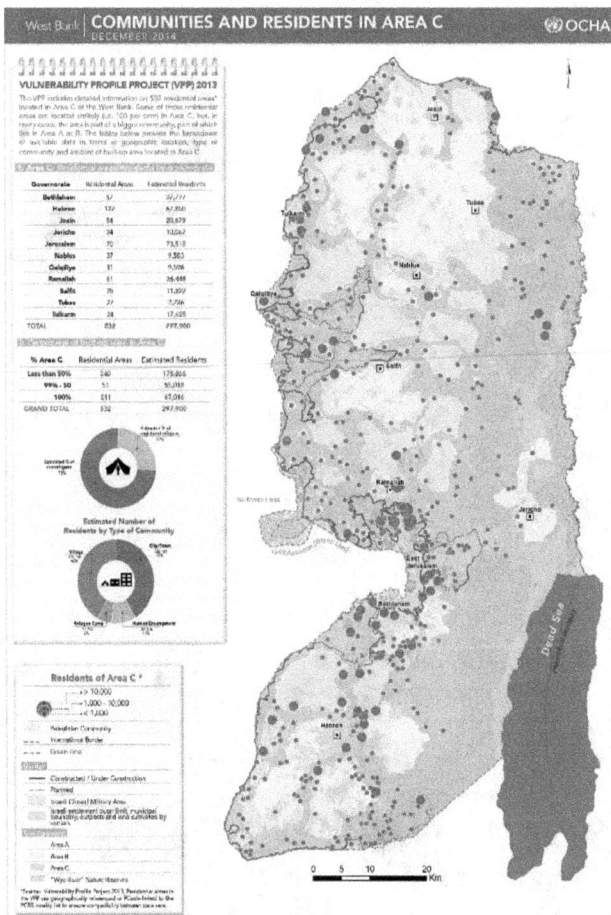

Source: UN OCHA, Office of the Occupied Palestinian Territories

Note: To see this map in its original color version (with a zoom-in feature for more detailed viewing), download the PDF in the Appendix.

MAP 31
EAST JERUSALEM (2014)

(Yellow = Palestinian communities)
(Purple = Jewish communities)
(Green dotted line = Green Line)
(Red line = the Barrier)
(Red, green and blue-circled "X" marks = checkpoints)

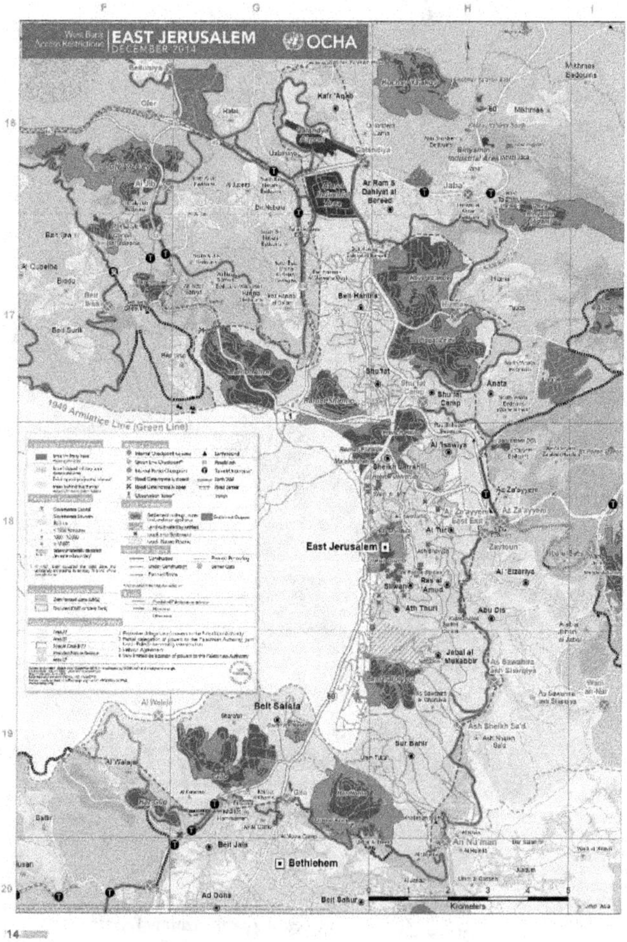

Source: UN OCHA Office of the Occupied Palestinian Territories

Note: To see this map in its original color version (with a zoom-in feature for more detailed viewing), download the PDF in the Appendix.

158

To forestall the demographic tipping point, the UN Security Council adopts Resolution 2334.[346] The Resolution declares that Israel's settlement construction in East Jerusalem and the West Bank are in "flagrant violation" of international law and "a major obstacle" to achieving a two-state solution.[347] To cure the violation, the decree states that Israel must immediately and completely cease all settlement activities in the occupied Palestinian territory, including East Jerusalem. The document also urges the rivals to negotiate all final status issues. Although the US traditionally votes against such UN resolutions, this time it abstains.

2017 (June) New settlement. Israel breaks ground on the first government-approved new settlement in the Territories in 25 years.[348] The settlement, called Amichai, is located north of Ramallah in the West Bank and replaces the nearby village of Amona, which has been declared illegal by an Israeli court. Amona was built on privately-owned Palestinian land without meeting the requirements of military justification and compensation to the property owner. Meanwhile, Israel continues to add housing units to existing West Bank settlements. Palestinians cite the construction initiatives as further evidence that Israel is sabotaging the peace process.

---

[346] *UNSC 2334*, UN/RES/2334, December 23, 2016.

[347] *Id.*

[348] *Israel begins work on first settlement in 25 years as Jared Kushner flies in*, THE GUARDIAN (June 20, 2017), https://www.theguardian.com/world/2017/jun/20/israel-new-settlement-benjamin-netanyahu-jared-kushner-amichai-amona.

2017 (December) US recognizes Jerusalem as Israel's capital. The US administration of President Donald Trump recognizes Jerusalem as Israel's capital and in the following year relocates its embassy there from Tel Aviv. The decision implements a 1995 act of Congress that was delayed by the presidential waiver of prior administrations. An overwhelming majority of UN members vote for a General Assembly resolution declaring the US decision null and void and demanding that the superpower rescind its decision. The PA declares the US disqualified as a neutral mediator of the Israeli-Palestinian dispute.

As of 2020, Jerusalem is recognized as Israel's capital by the US, Guatemala, Honduras, Serbia, Kosovo, Malawi, and Nauru. West Jerusalem is recognized as Israel's capital by Russia, Australia, Argentina and the Czech Republic. However, as of 2020 Jerusalem is recognized as the Palestinian capital by Iran, Pakistan, and Venezuela, and East Jerusalem is recognized as Palestine's capital by Russia and Saudi Arabia.

2019 US announces West Bank settlements are not illegal. After removing the label "occupied territories" from the discussion of the West Bank in the State Department's annual human rights report, the Trump administration declares that Israel's settlements in the West Bank are not inconsistent with international law. The announcement revives a legal position of the Ronald Reagan administration in the 1980's, defies a legal position of the Jimmy Carter administration in the 1970's, and ignores the views of all post-Reagan administrations, which sidestepped the legal issue but called the settlements "illegitimate" or "an obstacle to peace." The Palestinians are outraged by the apparent dismissal of their perceived national rights to the West Bank.

2020 US proposes Israeli-Palestinian peace plan. In 2019, the US releases a proposal of large-scale economic aid to the Palestinians conditioned on Palestinian acceptance of a companion proposal to solve the political dimensions of the Israeli-Palestinian dispute. The political offer is unveiled in 2020. It is formally titled "Peace to Prosperity" and informally billed as "the Deal of the Century." The Peace to Prosperity proposal would, most importantly, give Palestinians: (a) territory comparable in size to the pre-1967 West Bank and Gaza; (b) a sovereign state; (c) a sector of East Jerusalem to serve as the state's capital; (d) continued freedom of worship at the Haram al Sharif in East Jerusalem; (e) relocation of the Palestinian refugees to the Palestinian state; and (f) $50 billion in investment over ten years. The plan is not reconciled with the Oslo Accords, which requires Israel and the Palestinians to negotiate "permanent status issues" such as borders, settlements and Jerusalem through mutual negotiation.

The Palestinians reject the Peace to Prosperity proposal. Their main complaint is that the plan was developed without their input. As a substantive matter, they note the deal would: (a) convert Israel's West Bank settlements – plus the Jordan Valley – into sovereign Israeli territory; (b) leave the vast majority of Jerusalem in Israeli hands; (c) preclude the right of Palestinians to return to Israel; and (d) require Palestine to be demilitarized.

Later that year, the US shelves the Peace to Prosperity Plan and brokers an agreement between Israel and two Arab states: the United Arab Emirates and Bahrain. The agreement, called the Abraham Accords, establishes terms of "normalization" (trade and cultural exchanges) between the former adversaries. Soon after, other Muslim states, including Sudan, Morocco, and Kosovo, join the pact. The Palestinians decry the Accords as a betrayal of their national cause.

2021 President Biden restores prior US foreign policy. The election of U.S. President Joe Biden begins a restoration of pre-Trump policies towards the Israeli-Palestinian conflict. Although the new administration signals an intention to keep the U.S. Embassy in Jerusalem, it ignores the "Peace to Prosperity" plan, reiterates the need for a two-state solution to the conflict, pledges fairer treatment to the Palestinians, and opposes Israeli settlements in the West Bank.

CHAPTER 4:
LEGAL CLAIMS IN THE
ISRAELI-PALESTINIAN DISPUTE

The preceding chapter reviewed the legal history of the Israeli-Palestinian conflict. With this background we see how the conflict culminated in the current legal controversies. Those are the permanent status issues enumerated in the Oslo Accords.

The sections of this chapter explore the main Oslo-assigned final status issues in the Israeli-Palestinian dispute. Each section begins with an "Author's Prologue," an orientation to the given issue. After each Author's Prologue comes the "Palestinian Arguments" and then the "Israeli Arguments." These are the opinions of the parties, as opposed to those of the author. The two camps are represented by the narratives on their government websites, writings of thought leaders who appear to be their most prominent legal advocates, and other respected authorities. Prefacing each party's pleadings is a summary of its position.

4.1: Is Palestine a state in the Territories?

Author's Prologue

In the Oslo Accords, one of the five permanent status issues that Israelis and Palestinians agreed to negotiate was the determination of borders.[349] Israel's borders have never been fully defined, but they could be, depending on the outcome of the Oslo negotiation. For Palestinians, a set of recognized borders would not only define the contours of their state but also signify their independence from Israeli control.

Before the parties negotiate mutual borders, they must contend with the possibility that the Palestinians already have borders by virtue of establishing a state. Is Palestine a state? This chapter examines the question.

At what point does a community associated with a given territory legally qualify as a state? Is statehood a "declaratory" condition, meaning a set of objective facts? Or is the status "constitutive," meaning, it depends on recognition by other/existing states? Scholars have debated this question for centuries without complete resolution.

The most respected definition of a "state" has been articulated by James Crawford in his landmark treatise, "The Creation of States in International Law."[350] Crawford primarily endorses the declaratory

---

[349] *Oslo I*, Art. V.3.

[350] JAMES CRAWFORD, *THE CREATION OF STATES IN INTERNATIONAL LAW* (2006) [hereinafter CRAWFORD]. Judge Crawford is a judge on the ICJ. Previously he served as Dean of the Sydney Law School, where he was also Challis Professor of International Law. Prior to that position, he was Whewell Professor of International Law at the University of Cambridge and worked as Director of the Lauterpacht Centre for International Law, also at Cambridge. As the first Australian member of the United Nations International Law Commission (ILC) he was responsible for the ILC's work on the ICJ and the ILC's Articles on State Responsibility. He appeared in over 40 cases before the ICJ. His award-winning landmark study, *THE CREATION OF STATES IN INTERNATIONAL LAW*, is considered a bible of international law.

criteria but acknowledges the important role of constitutive factors.[351] For example, where a political body has not convincingly met the declaratory test, he believes constitutive evidence may resolve the uncertainty. Likewise, he says that a case of virtually-unanimous recognition may be practically conclusive.[352] He adds that recognition itself has a declaratory effect.[353] That is, when a group of states acknowledge the given assembly as a state, they help prove the objective fact that the claimant is a state.

The following summarizes Crawford's interpretation of the declaratory test of statehood. The would-be state must meet the four criteria of statehood established in Article I of the 1933 Montevideo Convention on the Rights and Duties of States. Specifically, the polity must demonstrate: (a) a permanent population; (b) a defined territory; (c) government; and (d) capacity to enter into relations with other countries. The related "principle of effectiveness" adds that the candidate must maintain the four qualities in an effective manner, not just symbolically."[354] At a minimum, this means the entity should effectively exercise the full scope of governmental powers exclusively over some territory, regardless of size, and some population, regardless of size.[355] An additional principle of "independence" requires that the given government should exercise the above powers – in both the

---

[351] *Id.* at 3-95.

[352] *Id.* at 27.

[353] *Id.* at pp. 23-24.

[354] *Id. at* 45-46.

[355] *Id.* 46-55.

formal and actual sense – to the exclusion of any other state.[356] Exceptions to these guidelines should sometimes be observed.[357]

"Sovereignty," according to Crawford, is the "totality of powers a state may exercise independently under international law." [358] It is not a criterion for statehood but a consequence of that status.[359]

With this guidance in mind, does Palestine qualify as a State? To answer the question requires an understanding of how Palestine's existence became an object of legal debate.

The Kingdom of Israel was established in the late 11th Century B.C.E.[360] Its rule stretched from present-day southern Israel to southern Lebanon and from the Mediterranean Sea to Jordan.[361] A dynastic feud split the Kingdom into two Israelite states: Israel in the north and Judea in the south.[362] The Babylonians, and eventually the Romans, conquered Judea. Resistance to Roman rule culminated in two disastrously futile rebellions. When the fighting ended in 135 C.E. the Romans invented the place name *Syria Palaestina* to erase the area's Jewish identity.[363]

---

[356] *Id.* at 62-89.

[357] See *Id.*

[358] *Id.* at pp. 32-33.

[359] *Id.* at p. 89.

[360] TESSLER, *supra* at 8.

[361] *Id.* at 9-10.

[362] *Id.* at 10.

[363] MATTHIJS DE BLOIS AND ANDREW TUCKER, *ISRAEL ON TRIAL* 272 (2018) [hereinafter DE BLOIS AND TUCKER].

After the Roman era, the province disguised as *Syria Palaestina* succumbed to a series of additional foreign invasions, including the Arab conquest, which transformed the Middle East in the 7th Century. As of the 13th Century, due to changes in political boundaries, there was no longer a province or any other place on a map labeled "Syria Palaestina."[364] The Turkish Ottoman Empire ruled a vast swath of the globe that included the Eastern Mediterranean region from 1517 to 1917. During that 400-year span, we still do not find a "Syria Palaestina."[365] There was only the province of Syria, and later, the province of Beirut, with Jerusalem, Jaffa, and points south forming an independent sub district.[366]

Christians continued to recount their history with references to "Palestine," though the term offered no more definition than its synonyms, "Promised Land" and "Holy Land."[367] Jews described the same amorphous geography as "the Land of Israel."[368] Through the 1920s and perhaps the 1930s, Arabs knew the place as "southern Syria."[369] To all concerned, the multi-named venue lacked any independent legal status.[370]

After World War I the defeated German and Ottoman empires surrendered their colonies, including the Eastern Mediterranean region,

---

[364] *See* TESSLER, *supra* at 162.

[365] MORRIS, *BIRTH REVISITED, supra* at 36, n. 2.

[366] *Id.*

[367] *Id.*

[368] *Id.*

[369] *Id.* at p. 42.

[370] CRAWFORD, *supra* at pp. 421-22.

to the Principal Allied Powers: Great Britain, France, Russia, Italy, Portugal, and Japan. The transfer of ownership left the Ottomans stateless.

The new sovereigns of the transferred colonies decided to re-map the possessions into "mandatory districts" pursuant to the authority of the League of Nations and usher different "peoples" to statehood in the designated areas, each under the supervision of a designated temporary administrator, called a "mandatory." In the Middle East, the nation builders enacted the treaty-like mandates in a way that birthed four Arab states[371] and one Jewish state.

The world powers planned for the Jewish state by delineating an area on the eastern Mediterranean they called "Palestine." The San Remo Resolution and the British Mandate for Palestine (BMP) recognized "the historical connection of the Jewish people with Palestine and... the grounds for reconstituting their national home in that country."[372] The BMP disavowed any intent to "prejudice the civil and religious rights of existing non-Jewish communities in Palestine."[373] Another important clause in the BMP promoted Jewish immigration to the area.[374] In view of the outpouring of Jews from Europe to Mandatory Palestine, the BMP's intent was to let Jewish Palestinians become a majority in the district and then establish their state under Jewish majority rule.[375] To

---

[371] The four were Lebanon, Syria, Iraq, and Transjordan (later Jordan).

[372] BMP, pmbl.; DE BLOIS AND TUCKER, *supra*, at 272.

[373] BMP, pmbl.

[374] BMP, art. 6.

[375] *See* CHARLES SMITH, *PALESTINE AND THE ARAB-ISRAELI CONFLICT* 77 (2017) [hereinafter SMITH].

supervise the sovereign emancipation, the League appointed Great Britain as the district's mandatory.

Arabs rejected the mandate system as an imperial encroachment.[376] In response to the Middle East mandates, a group of effendis (members of the Arab upper-class) in 1920 declared their own king of the area, which they had known for centuries as "Greater Syria."[377] Greater Syria encompassed some or all of present-day Syria, Lebanon, Israel (with all of Jerusalem), Gaza, the West Bank, and Jordan.[378] The new king, however, was promptly overthrown by the French military.

Having failed to establish a single giant Arab state, the Arab leaders opted to pursue independence separately in their respective localities.[379] In Mandatory Palestine, the new political agenda catalyzed the Arab Palestinian national movement.[380]

Early 20th Century depictions of Palestine in the maps of Great Britain and other western nations resembled the ancient Kingdom of Israel.[381] The original district of Mandatory Palestine therefore contained present-day Israel (with all of Jerusalem), Gaza, the West Bank, and

---

[376] See TESSLER supra at 155-56; DOWTY, supra at 79-80; RASHID KHALIDI, PALESTINIAN IDENTITY 148 (1997) [hereinafter KHALIDI PALESTINIAN IDENTITY].

[377] SHA'I BEN-TEKOA, PHANTOM NATION 17-22 (2013) [hereinafter "BEN-TAKOA"]; TESSLER, supra at 159.

[378] See Id.

[379] MORRIS 1948, supra at pp 19-21; TESSLER, supra at 165; KHALIDI PALESTINIAN IDENTITY supra at 149-50.

[380] MORRIS 1948, supra at 21.

[381] BEN-TEKOA at 6-7 and 13.

Jordan.[382] Soon after the League approved the BMP in 1922, Great Britain exercised its discretion to reallocate the eastern 77% of the district. The British sought to quell the violence between Arab and Jewish Palestinians by creating an additional Arab state.[383] That eastern expanse of Palestine became the Transjordan the following year, when the BMP took effect.

After the removal of eastern Mandatory Palestine from the intended Jewish state, the western remainder of the district became known simply as "Mandatory Palestine." Unfortunately, the territorial compromise failed to ease inter-ethnic tensions. In 1947, the UN adopted its Partition Plan, which proposed to split the downsized Mandatory Palestine into a Jewish state and another Arab state. But the Plan never materialized.[384] Instead, Arab Palestinian militias waged war against the Jewish Palestinians to capture the entire district by force.[385] Unable to stop the war, the British withdrew from the district on May 14, 1948.

The 1947 UN deliberators had struggled to chart an appropriate territorial division of the truncated Mandatory Palestine. Jews emphasized that they had populated the entire area over a thousand and six hundred years before the arrival of the first Arabs in the 7th Century. Arabs countered that their population in Mandatory Palestine was vastly larger than the Jewish presence. However, neither argument found support in the League Covenant. Nothing in the Covenant

---

[382] See Id. *See also* CRAWFORD at 570, n. 28.

[383] TESSLER, *supra*, at 164.

[384] CRAWFORD, *supra* at 431-32.

[385] TESSLER, *supra* at 261-63.

required the League's members to draw any particular mandatory district boundaries, give preferences to the ethnicities that lived there first, or prioritize those groups by size.

May 14, 1948 was the date when the Jewish Palestinians issued their Proclamation of Independence. The decree did not define the borders of their self-declared state. But by the end of the 1947-1948 Arab-Israeli war, the new State of Israel controlled three quarters of Mandatory Palestine, including West Jerusalem.

After the war, Israel received UN membership as a State. And many world powers recognized its statehood as well, including the U.S. and the Soviet Union.[386] The international acceptance extended to present-day Israel, but not any part of Jerusalem. This is because the Partition Plan had proposed to reserve the city as a multinational zone of unspecified governance.[387] The rest of Mandatory Palestine fell to three of the five Arab regimes that had joined in the War. Egypt occupied Gaza, Jordan declared sovereignty over East Jerusalem and the West Bank, and Syria snatched a small piece of the eastern Galilee.

The Arab world refused to recognize the State of Israel.[388] From a base in Egyptian-controlled Gaza, Arab Palestinians formed a government they called "the Arab Government of all Palestine."[389] The new assembly did not, however, gain influence, largely due to the strictures of

---

[386] *Id.* at 269.

[387] *Id.* at 274.

[388] *Id.* at pp. 273-74.

[389] *Id.* at 275.

Egyptian military rule.[390] Jordan's annexation of the West Bank was more successful.[391] The Hashemite King empowered a new parliament that included Palestinian representatives of the West Bank [392] The maneuver attempted to apply a gloss of legitimacy to his control over that slab of western Palestine. But not even the Arab League recognized the Jordanian annexation.

During the mandatory period, the word "Palestinian" was used mostly to describe the Jewish Palestinians. However, when the PLO issued its PLO Charter of 1964, it referred to area Arabs as "Palestinians" and asserted a claim of sovereignty over "Palestine."[393] In the PLO manifesto, the Palestinians declared ownership of Israel but disclaimed any rights to the portions of former Mandatory Palestine that had been acquired by Egypt, Jordan, and Syria (i.e. the Territories)[394] to avoid conflicts with their fellow Arabs.

In the 1967 Six-Day War, Israel captured the Territories and held them under martial law. It then reunified Jerusalem under its municipal law, thereby asserting sovereignty over the city. The world community refused to recognize the gesture.

---

[390] *Id.*

[391] *Id.* at 276.

[392] *Id.*

[393] *See PLO Charter of 1964*, arts. 2 and 3, in *Palestine Liberation Organization, The Original Palestine National Charter (1964)*, JEWISH VIRTUAL LIBRARY, https://www.jewishvirtuallibrary. org/the-original-palestine-national-charter-1964.

[394] *See Id.*, art. 24.

Two events simplified the rivalry over title to western Palestine. In 1979, upon signing the Egypt-Israel Peace Treaty, Egypt disclaimed any right to Gaza. In the 1994 Jordan-Israel Peace Treaty, Jordan relinquished its claim to East Jerusalem and the West Bank. Both treaties were signed without prejudice to the territorial rights of Israel or the Palestinians.

Post-1967, the Palestinians replaced Egypt and Jordan as claimants to former Mandatory Palestine. Unlike the PLO Charter of 1964, the PLO Charter of 1968 claimed the right to both Israel and the Territories.[395] The widely-recognized 1988 Palestinian Declaration of Independence portrayed a blueprint of "Palestine" that matched the Arab share of the aborted 1947 UN Partition Plan.[396] The implementation of that 1988 plan would have secured the Territories for Palestinians and removed some but not all of Israel. A map of Palestine that would have entirely replaced Israel appeared in the 1987 Covenant of Hamas, the Islamic militant group of Palestinians that rivaled the PLO.[397] Meanwhile, the UN General Assembly adopted a series of resolutions that increasingly supported the Palestinian quest for statehood.

In the Oslo Accords of the 1990's, Israel and the PLO did not decide whether or where Palestine was a state. They agreed to settle their differences over borders, Jerusalem, settlements, security, refugees, and other matters through negotiation based on the principles of UN Resolutions 242 and 338.[398] The parties have not reached agreement on those "permanent status" issues. Nevertheless, the Palestinians have

---

[395] See PLO Charter of 1968, arts. 1 and 2.

[396] See Palestinian Declaration of Independence of 1988, para. 6.

[397] See Hamas Covenant of 1987, pmbl., paras. 2 and 8; art. 6.

[398] See TESSLER, supra at 757.

found acceptance in numerous international treaties, many of which were designed for state membership.

One more international development is worth mentioning to put the Israeli-Palestinian sovereignty debate in perspective. On September 13, 2007, the UN General Assembly adopted a resolution titled "Declaration of Rights of Indigenous Peoples."[399] Palestinians and Israelis have both described themselves as indigenous to Israel and the Territories.[400] However, the Declaration did not support either party's claim of sovereignty. The document was merely a non-binding political statement, and it addressed only cultural rights, not sovereignty rights. At any rate, it could not be applied retroactively to resolve pre-2007 claims.

Given this legal history, is Palestine a state?

---

[399] United Nations Human Rights, Office of the High Commissioner, *Declaration on the Rights of Indigenous Peoples*, (September 13, 2007), https://www.ohchr.org/en/issues /ipeoples/pages/declaration.aspx.

[400] *See* Palestine Liberation Organization - Negotiations Affairs Department, *Negotiations Primer*, p. 21 ("Israel's settlement enterprise [confiscates] Palestinian lands ... while confining the indigenous Palestinian population in enclaves and severing East Jerusalem from the West Bank.") (May, 2008), http://www.sadaka.ie/Articles/OtherReports/OTHER-PLO_Negotiations_Primer.pdf. *See also* Israeli Ministry of Foreign Affairs, *Historic Jewish Presence in Israel*, Facebook.com, ("Israel joins the world today in marking International Day of Indigenous Peoples. On this day, we are proud to recall the ancient Jewish connection to the Land of Israel, unbroken for three thousand years and still going strong.") (Aug. 9, 2017), https://www.facebook.com/IsraelMFA/photos/a.459511111316/10154935950161317/?type=3 &source=57 .

A summary of the opposing views on the issue appeared in a proceeding brought by the Palestinians before the International Criminal Court (the "ICC Proceeding").[401] The ICC Proceeding may ultimately determine whether Israel has committed war crimes in the Territories. In the first stage of the Proceeding, the Court considered whether it had received the requisite criminal jurisdiction from Palestine as an ICC member "State."

The ICC prosecutor filed a legal "request" with the Court asking it to treat Palestine as a State.[402] Israel was not an ICC member or a participant in the ICC Proceeding. However, Israel's attorney general issued a rebuttal to the Prosecutor's Request in the form of a

---

[401] *The Prosecutor of the International Criminal Court, Fatou Bensouda, opens a preliminary examination of the situation in Palestine*, Office of the Prosecutor, ICC-OTP-20150116-PR1083 (Jan. 16, 2015), https://www.icc-cpi.int//Pages/item.aspx?name=pr1083.

[402] *Prosecution request pursuant to article 19(3) for a ruling on the Court's territorial jurisdiction in Palestine, Situation in the State of Palestine*, Office of the Prosecutor, ICC, ICC-01/18-12 (Dec. 20, 2019) [hereinafter the *Prosecutor's Request*], https://www.icc-cpi.int/Pages/record.aspx?docNo=ICC-01/18-12. Although the prosecutor is not necessarily a Palestinian sympathizer, her analysis of Palestinian statehood tracks the publicly stated Palestinian position on the subject. An Israeli news outlet and an Israeli NGO claims she coordinated closely with Palestinian organizations to prepare her prosecution. *See ICC reportedly spurned Israelis, met Palestinian group before probe decision*, THE TIMES OF ISRAEL (Dec. 23, 2019), https://www.timesofisrael.com/icc-reportedly-spurned-israelis-met-palestinian-group-before-probe-decision/; Brig.-Gen. (res.) Yossi Kuperwasser, Dan Diker, *Legal Assault: How the ICC Has Been Weaponized Against the U.S. and Israel*, Jerusalem Center for Public Affairs (May 5, 2020), https://jcpa.org/legal-assault-how-the-icc-has-been-weaponized-against-the-u-s-and-israel/. At any rate, her statement offers a reliable summary of Palestinian thinking on the issue.

Memorandum of Law.[403] Numerous parties then participated in the ICC proceeding through friend-of-the-court ("amicus") briefs. One amicus party that seemed to provide a complete and accurate summary of the Israeli perspective was a group led by an NGO called the *Lawfare Project* [404] which "provides pro bono legal services to protect the civil and rights of the Jewish people worldwide." In response to the briefs, the prosecutor published a formal "response." [405] The relevant portions of these legal statements are recounted in this part of the study.

On February 5, 2021 the Court ruled that Palestine was a state–with territory consisting of Gaza, East Jerusalem, and the West Bank–for the limited purposes of the ICC's jurisdiction.[406] The judges sidestepped the question of whether Palestine was a state as defined by general international law.[407] Nevertheless, the above-cited materials offer the

---

[403] *Memorandum of Israel's Attorney General* (Dec. 20, 2019) [hereinafter the *Attorney General's Memo*], https://mfa.gov.il/MFA/PressRoom/2019/Documents/ICCs%20 lack%20of%20jurisdiction%20over%20socalled%20%E2%80%9Csituation%20in%20Palestine% E2%80%9D%20-%20AG.pdf.

[404] *Observations on the Prosecutor's Request on behalf of the Non-Governmental Organisations: The Lawfare Project, the Institute for NGO Research, Palestinian Media Watch, and the Jerusalem Center for Public Affairs, Amicus Curiae, Situation in the State of Palestine*, ICC, ICC-01/18 (March 16, 2020) [hereinafter *Lawfare Project*], https://www.icc-cpi.int/CourtRecords/CR2020_01023. PDF.

[405] *Prosecution Response to the Observations of Amici Curiae, Legal Representatives of Victims, and States, Situation in the State of Palestine*, Office of the Prosecutor, ICC, ICC-01/18-131 (April 30, 2020) [hereinafter *Prosecutor's Response*], https://www.icc-cpi.int/Pages/record.aspx?docNo=ICC-01/18-131.

[406] The *Pre-Trial Chamber I, Situation in the State of Palestine*, ICC, ICC-01/18, paras. 89-131 (Feb. 5, 2021), https://www.icc-cpi.int/Pages/record.aspx?docNo=ICC-01/18-143.

[407] *Id.* at paras. 93, 103, 108, 113, and 130.

most current expositions of the two opposing views on the statehood issue.

A. The Palestinian Arguments

Summary of Arguments

An entity may be deemed a State under the primary assessment of sovereignty – the Montevideo test – if it has a population, a defined territory, effective and independent government, and international relations. Palestine has a population of millions. Its territory is readily defined to include Gaza, East Jerusalem, and the West Bank. Palestine's international relations are manifested through the numerous treaties it has signed and the many international institutions it has joined.

Regarding the element of effective and independent government, a strict construction of Montevideo is not necessary. Scholars have advised that flexibility in the statehood analysis may be warranted by special circumstances. Palestine presents a special case. It has earned a widely recognized right of self-determination. Many of the recognizing parties have asserted that Palestinian self-determination should be expressed in the form of statehood. Equally important, Palestinian efforts to establish effective and independent government have been frustrated by the construction of Israeli settlements. The UN, the ICJ, and other authorities have confirmed that Israel's settlement building has dimmed hopes for a two-state solution to the Israeli-Palestinian conflict. These realities should influence the analysis of Palestinian sovereignty.

Aside from the Montevideo test, certain other factors compel a finding of a Palestinian state. At least 138 states already recognize Palestine as a state. That is strong constitutive evidence of statehood. Israel has disengaged from Gaza. And because Israel is an occupying power, it is legally barred from acquiring title to the occupied lands.

The Oslo Accords do not prevent the Palestinians from possessing their own state. A provision of Oslo II confirmed that neither party to the Accords waived any of its preexisting rights. Thus, the Palestinians did not waive their right of self-determination.

i. Palestine meets three of the four Montevideo criteria of statehood

As explained above, the prevailing Montevideo (declarative) test of sovereignty examines whether the candidate for statehood has a population, a defined territory, effective and independent governance, and international relations. Palestine certainly has a population.[408] About three million people live in the West Bank, with nearly two million more in Gaza and another half a million in East Jerusalem.[409]

Palestine also has a defined territory.[410] Numerous pronouncements by the U.N., the ICJ, and international institutions have referred to "Palestine," the area east of "the Green Line," and/or "the occupied Palestinian territory" as the land of the Palestinians.[411] The precise area at issue is the Territories, which consist of Gaza, East Jerusalem, and the West Bank.

The capacity of Palestine to conduct international relations is demonstrated by its internationally recognized rights and responsibilities.[412] Palestine has signed numerous international treaties, including the four Geneva Conventions, their 1997 Additional Protocols, and other human rights and humanitarian law conventions.[413] Furthermore, Palestine has joined a bevy of international

---

[408] *The Prosecutor's Request, supra,* para. 145.

[409] *Id.,* para. 88.

[410] *Id.,* para. 145.

[411] *Id.,* paras. 193-215.

[412] *Id.,* para. 145.

[413] *Id.,* para. 127.

organizations.[414] The state belongs to UNESCO, the UN Economic and Social Commission for Western Asia, the Group of Asia-Pacific States, the League of Arab States, the Movement of Non-Aligned Countries, the Organization of Islamic Cooperation, the Group of 77 and China, the Union for the Mediterranean, and Interpol.[415] Moreover, Palestine has achieved observer status in the U.N. General Assembly and membership in five other U.N. agencies.[416]

Palestine's international activities include the filing of complaints against Israel before three international bodies: the International Convention on the Elimination of All Forms of Racial Discrimination, the Committee on the Elimination of Racial Discrimination, and the ICJ.[417]

ii. The remaining Montevideo criterion need not be applied strictly

The remaining criterion of the Montevideo test – the element of effective and independent governance – need not be applied strictly.[418] Leading scholars have opined that Montevideo may be read flexibly where circumstances warrant.[419] One must closely examine alternative factors to accurately assess the special context of decolonization. [420] In this case,

---

[414] *Id.*, para. 128.

[415] *Id.*

[416] *Id.*

[417] *Id.*, para. 129.

[418] *Id.*, para. 137.

[419] *Id.*, para. 141.

[420] *Id.*, para. 141.

the complete fulfillment of the Montevideo criteria is no longer considered the exclusive measure of statehood.[421]

A special analysis is appropriate in this case for two reasons: 1) the Palestinians have earned a widely recognized right of self-determination, and 2) Israel's illegal settlements have wrongly blocked that right from ripening into statehood.[422]

Self-determination is a fundamental human right, which commands *jus cogens* (inalienable) status and applies *erga omnes* (towards all).[423] Accordingly, all states are bound to accept it, regardless of political preference.[424] Indeed, the right of self-determination is a foundational guarantee of the U.N. Charter.[425] It has been viewed by some as a customary norm.[426] State parties to the International Covenant on Civil and Political Rights and International Covenant on Economic, Social and Cultural Rights are obligated to promote self-determination.[427] Under the International Law Commission's 2001 Articles on State Responsibility for Internationally Wrongful Acts, states must refrain from supporting any serious breach of the right.[428]

---

[421] *Id.*, n. 470.

[422] *Id.*, para. 138.

[423] *Id.*, para. 147

[424] *Id.*

[425] *Id.*, para. 148 (citing U.N. Charter art. 1(2).

[426] *Id.*

[427] *Id.*, para. 149.

[428] *Id.* (citing *Draft Articles on the Responsibility of States for Internationally Wrongful Acts, Report of the ILC on the Work of its Fifty-third Session,* UN GAOR, 56th Sess, Supp No 10, p 43, U.N. Doc A/56/10 (2001).

The international community has endorsed the Palestinian right of self-determination.[429] More to the point, the consensus favors the establishment of a Palestinian state.[430] Although self-determination may be expressed in non-sovereign ways, many authorities agree the Palestinians deserve their own state.[431] In 1974, the General Assembly adopted a resolution recognizing the Palestinian right to an independent state.[432] The U.N. Human Rights Council also confirmed that the Palestinians should have a state.[433] A Palestinian state would fulfill the dream of a two-state solution to the Israeli-Palestinian conflict, which the international community has widely endorsed.[434]

The esteemed jurist James Crawford analyzed the issue of whether Palestine is a state. He said:

> There may come a point where international law may be justified in regarding as done that which ought to have been done, if the reason it has not been done is the serious default of one party and if the consequence of its not being done is serious prejudice to another. The principle that a State cannot rely on its own wrongful

---

[429] *Id.*, para. 150.

[430] *Id.*

[431] *Id.*

[432] *Id.* (citing G.A. Res. 3326 (XXIX), U.N. Doc. A/RES/3326(XXIX) (Nov. 22, 1974), available at: https://documents-dds-ny.un.org/doc/RESOLUTION/GEN/NR0/738/38/IMG/NR073838.pdf?OpenElement).

[433] *Id.* (citing *Human Rights Council Resolution 37/34* (March 23, 2018), available at https://undocs.org/A/HRC/RES/37/34).

[434] *Prosecutor's Response*, para. 47.

conduct to avoid the consequences of its international obligations is capable of novel applications; and circumstances can be imagined where the international community would be entitled to treat a new State as existing on a given territory, notwithstanding the facts.[435]

Although Crawford did not believe the above proposition applied to Palestine,[436] a case could be made that Israel has committed a serious default and that its wrongdoing has prejudiced the Palestinians. In 2012, when the UN accepted Palestine as a non-member observer State, the world body praised the impressive progress the State had made in building its governing institutions.[437] Six year later, however, the United Nations Development Program reported a loss of momentum in the progress toward statehood due to the continuing rift between the PA, which governs the West Bank, and Hamas, which controls Gaza.[438]

Similarly, the UN's Special Rapporteur on human rights in Palestine lamented the contradiction of trying to build a sovereign economy under conditions of belligerent occupation.[439] Describing the Territories, the Special Rapporteur said:

---

[435] *Prosecutor's Request, supra,* para. 142 (citing CRAWFORD, *supra* at 447-48).

[436] *Id.,* para. 143.

[437] *Id.,* para. 145 (citing *UN Resolution 67/19,* Doc. GA/RES/67/19 (Nov. 29, 2012)

[438] *Id.* (citing the *United Nations Assistance Development Framework State of Palestine 2018-2022,* p. 3, https://www.undp.org/content/dam/papp/docs/Publications/UNDP-papp-research-undaf_2018-2022.pdf.)

[439] *Id.* (citing *Report of the Special Rapporteur on the situation of human rights in the Palestinian territories occupied since 1967,* UN General Assembly, seventy-first session, A/71/554 (Oct. 19, 2016), https://digitallibrary.un.org/record/845877/files/A_71_554-AR.pdf).

Its territorial components – the West Bank... East Jerusalem, and Gaza – are separated physically from one another ... The West Bank... has been divided by Israel into an archipelago of small islands ... Within these areas... the local political authority is likewise splintered [between] the Palestinian Authority... in the West Bank... and a separate political authority [in Gaza]... and Israel has illegally annexed East Jerusalem. Furthermore, Israel has imposed a comprehensive land, sea and air blockade on Gaza since 2007. Within the West Bank, Israel exercises full civil and security authority over "Area C", which makes up over 60 percent of this part of the territory and completely surrounds and divides the archipelago of Palestinian cities and towns ... All of [Palestine's] borders, with one exception, are controlled by Israel. No other society in the world faces such an array of cumulative challenges that includes belligerent occupation, territorial discontinuity, political and administrative divergence, geographic confinement and economic disconnectedness.[440]

At root, Palestinian progress toward statehood is suffocated by Israel's campaign of settlement construction in the Territories and the related Barrier in East Jerusalem and the West Bank.[441] The settlements disrupt Palestine's territorial continuity, endanger its territorial integrity, and otherwise prevent Palestinians from fulfilling their right of self-

---

[440] *Id.*

[441] *See* Id., para. 157.

determination.[442] The detrimental trend is both profound and irreversible.[443]

In response, the U.N. Security Council, General Assembly, and other intergovernmental bodies have consistently declared the settlements illegal and urged states not to assist the wrongful activity.[444] The ICJ Barrier Opinion underscored the obligation not to recognize or assist the development of the settlements.[445]

Halting Israel's settlement project is ubiquitously considered essential for the Palestinians to achieve statehood.[446] The ICJ Barrier Opinion ruled that the settlements severely impede the Palestinians from fulfilling their right of self-determination.[447] Reemphasizing the ICJ view, the UN Security Council announced that the cessation of all Israeli settlement activity was crucial to the goal of forging a two-state solution between the two rival peoples.[448] Specifically, the 2016 UN resolution stated:

> Continuing Israeli settlement activities are dangerously imperiling the viability of the two-State solution based

---

[442] *Id.*

[443] *Id.*, para. 159 (citing *UNSC RES 446*, Doc. S/RES/446 (March 22, 1979), https://digitallibrary.un.org/record/1696/files/S_RES_446%281979%29-EN.pdf).

[444] *Id.*, paras. 151-56.

[445] *Id.*, para. 152 (citing the *ICJ Barrier Opinion*, para. 159).

[446] *Id.*, para. 157.

[447] *Id.*, para. 158 (citing the *ICJ Barrier Opinion*, paras. 120 and 122).

[448] *Id.*, para. 161 (citing *UNSC Res. 2334*, U.N. Doc. S/RES/2334 (Dec. 23, 2016), available at https://undocs.org/S/RES/2334(2016)). *See also* para. 167 (citing *Human Rights Council Resolution 37/36* (March 23, 2018), https://undocs.org/A/HRC/RES/37/36).

on the 1967 lines [and] the cessation of all Israeli settlement activities is essential for salvaging the two-State solution.[449]

Other UN bodies have echoed the point.[450] So has the European Council[451] and the African Union.[452]

Israel has ignored the international condemnation of its settlements in the Territories.[453] If anything, Israel has signaled a determination to annex the Territories.[454] Yet Israel's abdication of its occupation duties does not deprive Palestinians of their sovereign rights. The occupation strengthens Palestinian rights. After the dissolution of the Ottoman Empire, there was no successor to its sovereignty in the Territories. There were only occupying powers. Israel has greatly prolonged the period of legal limbo, even though occupations are intended to be temporary. To resolve the sovereignty issue, it therefore makes sense to follow a current theory of occupation law, which is to recognize that sovereignty is vested in the occupied population.[455]

---

[449] *Id.*

[450] *Id.*, paras. 164 to 170.

[451] *Id.*, para. 171 (citing the *European Council Conclusions on the Middle East Peace Process* (Jan. 18, 2016), para. 7, available at https://www.consilium.europa.eu/en/press/press-releases/2016/01/18/fac-conclusions-mepp/.

[452] *Id.*, para. 173 (citing the *African Union's 30th Assembly Declaration* (Jan. 28-29, 2018), preamble, available at https://au.int/sites/default/files/decisions/33908-assembly_decisions_665_-_689_e.pdf).

[453] *Id.*, para. 177.

[454] *Id.*

[455] *Prosecutor's Response*, para. 42.

Any review of the Palestinians' eligibility for statehood under the scrutiny of Montevideo should therefore take two factors into account: 1) Palestinians have a right of self-determination that deserves to be expressed in the form of statehood; and, 2) this worthy cause is obstructed by Israel's illegal settlement project.[456] It is the settlements that prevent Palestinians from exercising effective and independent self-governance, as Montevideo normally requires.[457]

At any rate, the PA's lack of effective control over all the Territories should pose no barrier towards a conclusion that there exists, in fact, a Palestinian state.[458] UN resolutions have consistently considered Gaza, East Jerusalem, and the West Bank to all be part of the single territorial unit known as "the Occupied Palestinian Territory."[459] The Oslo Accords likewise treat the Territories as a single territory.[460] Therefore, all the Territories lie within the PA's sovereign reach.

iii. **Statehood for the Palestinians is compelled by other factors**

The Montevideo-based argument for Palestinian statehood is buttressed by a strong constitutive factor: at least 138 states already recognize Palestine as a state.[461] This growing mass of recognition prompted

---

[456] *Prosecutor's Request, supra*, para. 178.

[457] *Id.*

[458] *See Prosecutor's Response, supra*, para. 96.

[459] *Id.*

[460] *Id.*

[461] *Prosecutor's Request, supra*, para. 179.

Professor Crawford to remark in 2014 that Palestine "seems to be eking its way toward statehood." [462]

The UN General Assembly formalized the international recognition in 2012 when it passed a resolution upgrading the status of Palestine from "Observer Mission" to "Non-member Observer State."

The fact that Israel has disengaged from Gaza should also be considered.[463] That area of Palestine is thus uniquely conducive to statehood.

In any event, it is well-settled that a state such as Israel may not acquire territory by force, and therefore, an occupation cannot transfer title to the occupying power.[464] This principle bars Israel from annexing the Territories.

The Oslo Accords do not preclude the Palestinians from exercising their peremptory right of self-determination to establish a state.[465] On the contrary, the Accords established the rudiments of a Palestinian state.[466]

Those legal seeds were expected to blossom into Palestinian sovereignty based on the completion of the final status negotiation.[467] Meanwhile,

---

[462] *Id.*, para. 143 (citing JAMES CRAWFORD, *CHANCE, ORDER, CHANGE: THE COURSE OF INTERNATIONAL LAW, GENERAL COURSE ON PUBLIC INTERNATIONAL LAW* 199-200 (2014).

[463] *Id.*

[464] *Id.* (citing Resolution 242).

[465] *Id.*, para. 186.

[466] *Prosecutor's Response, supra*, paras. 63-66.

[467] *Id.*, para. 67.

Oslo II clearly documented the intent of the signatories to implement the Accords without waiving any preexisting rights.[468] Self-determination is one such preexisting Palestinian right.

B. The Israeli Arguments

Summary of Arguments

There has never been a state called "Palestine." After World War I, the League authorized the creation of Mandatory Palestine and allocated it for the self-determination of the Jewish people. The BMP held sovereignty over the district in abeyance until the Jews could rule it as a state. That binding international law covered all present-day Israel and the Territories. It remains in force to this day. Israel has forborne from applying its sovereign rights to the entirety of the Territories. Instead, it has strived to negotiate the borders of those lands, along with related existential matters, to make peace with its Arab neighbors.

Although the Palestinians claim to have a state, they lack the elements of statehood required by the applicable Montevideo standard. The Palestinians try to offset their lack of Montevideo qualifications with a self-styled theory of statehood that combines a right of self-determination with complaints of Israeli wrongdoing. However, no law or precedent supports such an amalgamation.

The constitutive evidence of an extant Palestine also falls short. Although many states recognize Palestine, several major states do not. Some of the governments that supposedly recognize the purported state continue to describe it as a mere aspiration. So do the Palestinian leaders themselves.

---

[468] *Prosecutor's Request, supra,* para. 187 (citing *Oslo II,* art. XXX1(6)).

189

i. Sovereignty over the Territories remains in abeyance

There has never been a State of Palestine.[469] After World War I, when the Ottoman Empire surrendered its colonies to the Allied Powers, the new owners lawfully allocated those lands through the auspices of the League to different peoples.[470] In the process, they created a mandatory district they called "Palestine." The 1920 San Remo Resolution and the 1922 BMP reserved Mandatory Palestine for the self-determination and statehood of the Jewish people.[471]

The San Remo treaty and the treaty-equivalent BMP were instruments of binding international law that recognized the 3,000-year connection of the Jewish people with their ancestral homeland.[472] The legal decrees, after Great Britain reallocated eastern Mandatory Palestine to create Jordan, covered all of Mandatory Palestine, including present-day Israel and the Territories.[473] BMP Article 5 stated that "no Palestine [sic] territory shall be ceded or leased to, or in any way placed under the control of, the government of any foreign power."[474]

In Mandatory Palestine, like the mandatory districts that produced the states of Lebanon, Syria, and Iraq, sovereignty over the area remained

---

[469] *The Attorney General's Memo*, paras. 27 and 32.

[470] *Id.*, paras. 27-28.

[471] *Id.*, para. 27.

[472] *Id.*

[473] *See Id.* (citing BMP arts. 5 and 25).

[474] *Id.* (citing BMP art. 5).

in abeyance until the targeted population could rule it as a state.[475] The concept of suspended sovereignty flowed from the League of Nations Covenant, wherein the world powers agreed to treat the development of the local populations as a "sacred trust." [476] Sovereignty remained in abeyance in Mandatory Palestine throughout the period of administration by Great Britain.[477] Under the BMP plan, continued Jewish immigration to the mandatory district would enable the Jews to build the institutions of government, declare independence, and exercise sovereignty by majority rule.[478] When the League transitioned its authority to the UN, the UN Charter contained a special provision that preserved the Zionist path to statehood.[479]

The State of Israel declared independence on May 16, 1948 but could not govern its entire mandatory bequest due to an Arab invasion, which conquered the Territories.[480] Despite the illegal Arab aggression,

---

[475] Id. (citing *Territorial Sovereignty and Scope of the Dispute (Eritrea v. Yemen)*, R.I.A.A. Vol XXII 209, para. 445 (Perm. Ct. Arb. 1996).

[476] See Id. *Also see League of Nations Covenant*, art. 22.

[477] Id. (citing Malcolm N. Shaw, *The League of Nations Mandate System and the Palestine Mandate: What Did and Does it Say About International Law and What Did and Does it Say About Palestine?*, 49 ISR. L. REV. 287, 295 (2016); *International Status of South-West Africa, Advisory Opinion*, 1950 I.C.J. 128, at 150 (July 11, 1950) (Separate Opinion of Judge McNair); JAMES CRAWFORD, BROWNLIE'S PRINCIPLES OF PUBLIC INTERNATIONAL LAW 235 (9th ed., 2019)).

[478] See Id. (citing BMP, art. 6).

[479] Id., para. 28 (citing *UN Charter art. 80(1)*).

[480] Id., para. 29.

sovereignty in the Territories remained in abeyance, available as ever for inclusion in the Jewish state.[481]

Israel gained possession of the Territories in a defensive military campaign during the 1967 war.[482] Confusion over the issue of whether Israel had "occupied" the Territories did not diminish the state's sovereign right to the land.[483] On the contrary, the Israeli government validly exercised that right by extending its sovereignty to East Jerusalem, thereby reunifying the city that had been severed by the Arab invasion.[484] Israel refrained from extending its sovereignty to the rest of the Territories. Instead, it left the status of those lands in abeyance for the sake of negotiating peace with its Arab neighbors.[485]

No one has a stronger legal right to the Territories than Israel.

ii. The Palestinians fail to meet the Montevideo standard of statehood

The Palestinians meet none of the four Montevideo requirements of sovereignty. The imagined "Palestine" lacks a defined territory because

---

[481] *See Id.* (noting that even the Arab League refused to recognize Jordan's purported annexation of East Jerusalem and the West Bank.)

[482] *Id.*, para. 30.

[483] *Id.*

[484] *Id.*

[485] *Id.*, paras. 30-31.

it has no borders. "Borders" is one of the final status issues the Palestinians have agreed to negotiate pursuant to the Oslo Accords.[486]

The claimed Palestinian state also lacks the required permanent population. Not until the Palestinian borders are fixed can anyone count the number of Palestinians within that circumference.[487] Moreover, because the final status negotiation may require Israel to evacuate hundreds of thousands of Jewish residents from East Jerusalem and/or the West Bank, the Territory's population cannot be considered permanent.[488]

Under Montevideo, the would-be sovereign must also maintain the full range of governmental powers exclusively over the territory it claims.[489] The PA never attained such status in the Territories.[490] It is merely an administrative entity created by the Oslo Accords.[491] Its only purpose is to perform certain limited tasks provisionally delegated by Israel under the agreement.[492] Those powers hardly amount to the degree of control

---

[486] *Id.*, para. 49.

[487] *Lawfare Project, supra*, para. 10.

[488] *Id.*, para. 10, n. 18.

[489] *Id.*, para. 33.

[490] *Id.*

[491] *Id.*, 34.

[492] *Id.*

that a genuine government wields.[493] The Palestinians' own negotiation team has admitted as much.[494]

A close look at Oslo II reveals that the PA's powers are strictly limited. Oslo II assigns the critical governmental role of external security over the Territories to Israel.[495] The same goes for control over airspace and the crucial function of tax collection.[496] Operation of radio frequencies, the telecommunications network, the monetary system, and water and sewer management are subject to Israel's cooperation or consent.[497] The few powers vested in the PA govern only Palestinians – not Israelis – and extend only to certain small enclaves in the Territories.[498] The PA exercises no control whatsoever over Gaza (where its rival, Hamas, exercises de facto control), Jerusalem (governed by Israel), or 60 percent of the West Bank (under Israeli administration).[499]

When Palestinians claim the Territories are "occupied," they implicitly acknowledge a lack of sufficient control to assert sovereignty over those lands. An occupation, by definition, means the land at issue has fallen

---

[493] *Id.*, 35.

[494] *Id.* (citing Internal Memorandum from the Negotiations Support Unit to Dr. Saeb Erekat, *Implications of Change in de facto Control in Gaza* (June 19, 2007). In the Internal Memorandum, the Palestinian negotiation team secretly advised the Palestinian leadership that Palestine was not a state due to the lack of required legal elements such as effective, independent control. Available at http://www.ajtransparency.com/en/projects/ thepalestinepapers/20121822587187346.html).

[495] *Id.*

[496] *Id.*

[497] *Id.*

[498] *Id.*, paras. 35-36.

[499] *See Id.*, para. 37.

under a foreigner's effective control. This point has also been conceded by the Palestinian negotiating team.[500]

Finally, the PA lacks the Montevideo-required capacity to engage in foreign relations because the Oslo Accords prohibit it from such activity.[501]

A long history of UN resolutions has confirmed the Oslo-enshrined principle that the only lawful way Palestinians may attain statehood is through bilateral negotiation with Israel.[502]

Notwithstanding their dearth of qualifications for sovereignty under Montevideo, and despite their Oslo duty to negotiate their sovereignty demands with Israel, the Palestinians attempt to snatch the mantle of statehood by unilateral decree. Their self-styled logic lacks merit.

Palestinians claim their lack of traditional qualifications is offset by other factors but cite no law or relevant precedent to support that novel

---

[500] Id., para. 38 (citing Memorandum from the Negotiations Support Unit to Palestinian Leadership, Legal approaches to be advanced at the ICC in order to protect overall Palestinian strategy and realize rights and interests (25 Mar. 2009), in "The Palestine Papers," wherein it was stated that "a state of occupation arguably negates the effective control required for the emergence of a state"). http://www. ajtransparency.com/en/projects/thepalestinepapers/201218205613718519.html.

[501] *Lawfare Project, supra*, para. 18. *See also* Oslo II, art. IX(5).

[502] *Attorney General's Memo, supra*, para. 36 (citing, by way of example, *G.A. Res. 73/19*, U.N. Doc. A/RES/73/19, preambular para. 25 and operative paras. 16 and 19 (Jan. 23, 2019); *G.A. Res. 73/256*, U.N. Doc. A/RES/73/256, preambular para. 2 (Dec. 5, 2018); *S.C. Res. 2334*, U.N. Doc. S/RES/2334, para 8 (Dec. 23, 2016); *G.A. Res. 67/19*, U.N. Doc. A/RES/67/19, note 35, at para. 5).

claim.[503] Next, they say their state exists primarily due to their right of self-determination. However, a right of self-determination is not evidence of an existing state or a license to create one.[504] The right entitles people to nothing more than a voice in their political, economic, cultural, and social conditions.[505] It may validly be manifested in the form of conditional autonomy without statehood.[506]

The Palestinians try to inflate their legal argument with complaints about Israel's settlements. However, the settlements comply fully with the Oslo Accords and other applicable laws.[507] The UN resolutions to the contrary were mere political statements without legal effect.[508] In particular, they were the political contrivances of a dominant UN voting bloc consisting of 56 Islamic states, other developing world states, and Soviet republics dedicated to a Cold War agenda that was fanatically hostile to Israel.[509] Israelis know the antagonistic alliance as the "automatic majority."

---

[503] *Id.*, para. 41.

[504] *Id.*, para. 40.

[505] *Id.*

[506] *See Id.*

[507] *See Id.*, para. 39.

[508] *Id.*, para. 28, n. 61.

[509] *Lawfare Project, supra*, paras. 35-44.

The ICJ Barrier Opinion was likewise purely advisory (non-binding).[510] The Opinion was also biased.[511] Specifically, it: (a) resulted from a petition by the UN's anti-Israel voting block; (b) ignored the fact that Israel lawfully built the Barrier to defend against relentless Palestinian suicide bombings; and (c) misrepresented the disputed Territories as "Palestinian land."[512] In any event, no law or precedent contemplates that the building of settlements by one party in a given territory can help justify the creation of a state by another party in that land.[513]

The allegation that Israel impedes Palestinian statehood is particularly surprising.[514] Apart from recognizing the Palestinian right of self-determination, Israel has also: 1) facilitated partial Palestinian self-governance though the Oslo Accords; 2) agreed to negotiate fuller Palestinian self-rule; 3) withdrawn from Gaza – a large Palestinian enclave; and 4) repeatedly proposed detailed plans for a two-state solution.[515] The Palestinians squandered these opportunities for statehood by ignoring or rejecting Israel's peace offers and otherwise refusing to negotiate.[516]

---

[510] *See* discussion titled *"2004: The ICJ Barrier Opinion," supra* at p. 103.

[511] Israeli Ministry of Foreign Affairs, *Saving Lives: Israel's Anti-Terrorist Fence*, pp. 22-23 (Jan. 1, 2004), http://www.israel.org/MFA/MFA-Archive/2003/Pages/Saving%20Lives-%20Israel-s%20anti-terrorist%20fence%20-%20Answ.aspx#:~:text=The%20purpose%20of%20the%20fence%20is%20to%20keep%20the%20terrorists,the%20chances%20of%20achieving%20peace.

[512] *Id.*

[513] *See Attorney General's Memo, supra*, para. 28, n. 61.

[514] *Id.*

[515] *See Id.*, para. 41.

[516] *Id.*, paras. 31, n. 69 and 41.

iii. **The constitutive evidence of Palestinian statehood is unavailing**

Unfortunately, it makes no difference that many governments recognize Palestine as a state.[517] Their support falls well short of unanimity and therefore cannot compensate for the missing Montevideo merits.[518] Several leading states reject the notion of an existing Palestine. The list includes Australia, Austria, Belgium, Canada, Cameroon, Denmark, France, Germany, Japan, Mexico, the Netherlands, New Zealand, Norway, Panama, Singapore, South Korea, Switzerland, the United Kingdom, and the United States.[519]

Over two-thirds of the governments that announced their recognition of Palestine's statehood did so in 1988, when the Palestinians declared independence. However, long after that date many of those same parties described Palestinian statehood as a future event, or something not yet realized.[520]

Palestinian leaders themselves speak of statehood in the future tense.[521] For example, in a pleading on the record of the 2004 ICJ Advisory Opinion, they represented that the Territories were "destined" for a

---

[517] *Id.*, para. 42.

[518] *Id.* (citing CRAWFORD, *supra* at 93, wherein the author explained that "[a]n entity is not a State because it is recognized; it is recognized because it is a State").

[519] *Id.*, para. 43, n. 107.

[520] *Id.*, para. 43 (citing as examples speeches by the Russian, Chinese, and Indian heads of state).

[521] *Id.* (citing as examples remarks by Yasser Arafat in 1998 and Mahmoud Abbas in 2000).

Palestinian state.[522] In October of 2017, Palestinian President Mahmoud Abbas publicly stated that "[i]n due time there will be a Palestinian State but this will not happen soon. We are building the Palestinian State one step at a time, and this takes time."[523] In recent years various Palestinian leaders have expressed similar remarks.[524]

Signing a treaty does not transform an entity into a State.[525] The political nature of international organizations sometimes permits non-States to join treaties meant only for States.[526] When the Palestinians have signed treaties, other signatories have cautioned that the Palestinian accessions did not make Palestine a State.[527]

The UN designation of Palestine as a Non-voting Member Observer State and related UN resolutions did not make Palestine a State.[528] The UN Charter does not give the UN authority to create States or recognize entities as States.

---

[522] *Id.*, n. 105 (citing *Written Statement submitted by Palestine*, para. 375 (29 Jan. 2004) in the *ICJ Barrier Opinion* proceeding).

[523] *Id.*, para. 45 (citing *President Mahmoud Abbas's interview to the Egyptian Channel CBC* (Oct. 3, 2017), https://www.youtube.com/watch?v=huJVJK5FUf0).

[524] *Id.*

[525] *Id.*, para. 44 (citing *Report of the International Law Commission, Sixty-Third Session* (April 26 - June 3 and July 4 – Aug. 12, 2011), U.N. Doc. A/66/10/Add.1, pp. 95-96 (2011).

[526] *Id.*, para. 25, n. 48.

[527] *Id.* (citing *Statement by Canada, Germany, the Netherlands and the United Kingdom of Great Britain and Northern Ireland in explanation of their position concerning the use of the term 'State of Palestine'*, Bureau of the Assembly of States Parties, 7th meeting, Annex II (Nov. 15 2016)).

[528] *See Id.*, paras. 31 and 40.

As noted above, the Oslo Accords require the Palestinians to resolve their sovereign ambitions through bilateral negotiations with Israel.[529] The Accords prohibit the Palestinians from trying to "change the status" of the Territories by other means, such as treaty accessions.[530]

4.2: Does Israel have a sovereign claim to the Territories?

Author's Prologue

After Israel captured the Territories in the 1967 war, the question arose whether Israel could lawfully annex those lands. Resolution 242 stated that the acquisition of territory by war was inadmissible. Yet if Israel had withdrawn from the Territories, no sovereignty would have reverted to Egypt or Jordan because those Arab states never held valid title to the lands. They had violated the acquisition-by-war prohibition by acting as owners of Gaza, Jerusalem and the West Bank after the 1947-1948 War.

Resolution 242 addressed the war over the Territories between Israel and its neighboring Arab states. But after the Resolution was passed, the dispute produced a new claimant to the Territories: the Palestinians.

The Arab defeat in 1967 motivated the Palestinians to expand their territorial ambitions. Having lost confidence in the Arab states to spearhead the liberation/destruction of Israel, the Palestinians took the

---

[529] *Id.*, para. 30.

[530] *Id.* (citing *Oslo II*, art. XXXI(7)).

lead in that campaign.[531] At the same time, they amended the PLO Charter to clarify that their ownership claim included not only recognized-Israel (also called "Israel proper") but also the Territories.[532] The PLO erected a quasi-state in Jordan along the east bank of the Jordan River.[533] From there the militant group launched guerrilla attacks on Israelis. Meanwhile PLO spokesmen lobbied the international community for endorsement of a Palestinian state.

The next two decades of Palestinian military action failed to gain territory. The Palestinians then narrowed their territorial claim. In their 1988 Declaration of Independence they said they owned a "State of Palestine" apparently limited to the Territories. Nations worldwide recognized the reconceived state. However, Israel never relinquished its BMP-based claim to the Territories.

A dispute over territorial sovereignty may not be susceptible to a binary determination that one party is completely right and the other wrong. Most often the question is which party holds the relatively stronger legal entitlement.[534] Even if Palestine is not yet a state, the Palestinians may deserve the Territories more than Israel.

---

[531] EDWARD SAID, THE QUESTION OF PALESTINE 158-59 (1992) [hereinafter SAID]. Professor Said (pronounced sah-EED) was a professor of literature at Columbia University and one-time member of the Palestinian legislature in exile. He became a world-renowned proponent of Palestinian rights.

[532] Article 2 of the 1968 Charter said, "Palestine [exists] with the boundaries it had during the British Mandate . . . " The boundaries of the British Mandate, once the British severed eastern Palestine to create Transjordan, included present-day Israel and the Territories.

[533] SAID, *supra* at 159.

[534] SHAW, *supra* at 354-55.

To explore this possibility, we must examine Israel's claim to the land.

A. The Palestinian Arguments

Summary of Arguments

Israel has no legal claim to the Territories. The Territories belong to the Palestinians by virtue of their right of self-determination and despite Israel's attempts to frustrate that right.

Israel's status in the Territories is that of an occupying power. Occupation law instructs that an occupation is a temporary affair, not an opportunity for the occupying power to enlarge its borders. Regrettably, ever since the 1967 war, Israel has abused its occupying powers to expand its recognized terrain. It has done so through a pattern of illegal *de jure* and *de facto* annexation. The international community should preserve the distinction between Israel and the Territories while working actively to constrain Israel's expansion.

---

i. Israel lacks any legal claim to the Territories

Israel has no right to any portion of the Territories.[535]

Even if Palestine is not already a state, it should be. The Palestinians are legally entitled to express their self-determination throughout the

---

[535] Saeb Erekat, *Palestine Liberation Organization legal brief in support of recognition of the State of Palestine*, PALESTINE NEWS NETWORK, in Australians for Palestine (Feb. 25, 2013) [hereinafter *"Erekat Recognition"*), http://australiansforpalestine.com/76584. Mr. Erekat heads the Palestinian negotiation team.

Territories via a sovereign State with borders on the Green Line.[536] Palestinians may lack effective control over that entire domain, as is normally expected under the Montevideo standard of sovereignty. But this deficiency is due to Israel's illegal occupation activities.[537] And Israeli denial of Palestinian rights only strengthens the case for Palestinian statehood.[538]

Palestinians must rule the entirety of the Territories, not only to fulfill their political destiny but to satisfy their fundamental human rights to freedom, dignity, and equality.[539] This vision of sovereignty is nothing less than what is required by international law.[540] It flows from numerous UN resolutions that have upheld the Palestinian cause and resisted Israel's countervailing measures.[541] Any peace plan that would legitimize Israel's theft of the Territories would not produce peace.[542]

For Palestine to be a truly independent and viable state, its control over the Territories would require a land corridor linking Gaza, East Jerusalem, and the West Bank, thereby making the country a single territorial unit.[543] The link would permit the unfettered movement of

---

[536] *Id.*

[537] *Id.*

[538] *Id.*

[539] Palestine Liberation Organization - Negotiations Affairs Department, *Palestinian Vision of Peace and Official Palestinian Positions on Final Status Issues* (Feb. 3, 2020) [hereinafter PLO-NAD *Final Status*], https://www.nad.ps/en/media-room/media-briefs/palestinian-vision-peace-and-official-palestinian-positions-final-status.

[540] *Id.*

[541] *Id.*

[542] *Id.*

[543] *Id.*

persons, goods, and resources (e.g. gas, water, electricity) among the three areas.[544] Sovereign viability would also entail exclusive rights to the state's airspace and the full gamut of maritime rights along the Gaza coast.[545] The state's capital would be East Jerusalem, the political, economic and spiritual heart of the Palestinian people.[546]

Palestinians may agree to minor deviations from the Green Line, if found to be in their interest, for the sake of peace.[547]

ii. Israel is an occupying power, which illegally annexes the occupied lands

When Israel conquered the Territories in the 1967 War, it commenced a military occupation of those lands.[548] An occupation is legally framed as a temporary arrangement, a status quo to be preserved until a peace treaty is signed. It is not an opportunity for the occupying power to attain ownership of the occupied ground.[549] Such a wrongful taking, called an annexation, occurs where one State seizes another State's territory by force.[550] Article 2(4) of the UN Charter expressly prohibits

---

[544] *Id.*

[545] *Id.*

[546] *Id.*

[547] *Id.*

[548] *See* Erekat *Recognition, supra.*

[549] *Id.*

[550] Negotiation Affairs Department - Palestine Liberation Organization, *From Temporary Occupation to Permanent Annexation: Israel's Acquisition of Palestinian Territory by Force*, 3 (Oct.

the "threat or use of force against the territorial integrity or political independence of any state."[551] The UN applied the anti-annexation dictum to the Israeli-Palestinian conflict. Resolution 242 emphasized "the inadmissibility of the acquisition of territory by war."[552]

Israel has already learned the futility of annexation. After the 1967 war, when the nation annexed East Jerusalem, the move was not recognized anywhere, not even by the US. The UN nullified the land grab.[553] The same legal roadblock confronts any further Israeli annexation of the Territories.[554]

Despite the law that Israel may not exploit its power as an occupant to annex the Territories, Israel continues to do just that.[555] Since 1967, Israel has steadily striven to redraw its borders to include all Territories from

---

15, 2019) [hereinafter "PLO-NAD *Annexation*"] (citing R. Hoffmann, *Annexation*, in Max Planck Encyclopedia of Public International Law (2013), https://www.nad.ps/en/publication-resources/factsheets/temporary-occupation-permanent-annexation-israel%E2%80%99s-acquisition.

[551] *Id.* (citing UN Charter, art. 2(4)).

[552] Erekat, *supra* (citing the preamble of UN Resolution 242). *See also* Iain Scobbie, *The Israeli-Palestinian Conflict in International Law: Territorial Issues*, SSRN ELECTRONIC JOURNAL, pp. 85-86 (Jan. 2010) [hereinafter Scobbie], https://www.researchgate.net/publication/228151495_The_Israel-Palestine_Conflict_in_International_Law_Territorial_Issues. Professor Scobbie is the Chair of International Law at the Manchester Law School, University of Manchester. He is also a member of the Scientific Advisory Board of the European Journal of International Law.

[553] Erekat *Recognition*, *supra* (citing UNSC Resolution 252, Doc. S/RES/252 (May 21, 1968), https://undocs.org/en/S/RES/252(1968)).

[554] Scobbie, *supra* at 88.

[555] PLO-NAD *Annexation*, *supra* 1-2.

the Jordan Valley to Jerusalem.[556] The taking of East Jerusalem was a *de jure* annexation because it was formally announced.[557] By contrast, Israel's incremental confiscation of the geography, infrastructure, and demography of the West Bank is a *de facto* annexation.[558] The West Bank illegality was condemned in the ICJ Barrier Opinion. Therein, the Court determined that the Barrier and its accompanying regime created "a 'fait accompli' on the ground that could well become permanent, in which case... it would be tantamount to a *de facto* annexation."[559]

The global community must distinguish between Israel and Israeli-occupied territory.[560] Nations should reject any action that may assist the annexation of the Territories.[561]

---

[556] *Id.*

[557] *Id.*, 3.

[558] *Id.*

[559] *Id.*, 5 (citing the ICJ Barrier Opinion at para. 21).

[560] *Id.*, 8.

[561] *Id.*

B. The Israeli Arguments

Summary of Arguments

Based on ICJ rulings and UN resolutions in past international territorial disputes, sovereign ownership of the Territories vests in Israel. The decisional factors in the territorial analysis are treaty law, the doctrine of *"uti possidetis juris"* (explained below), and effective control. Israel prevails on all three counts.

Rulings on territorial disputes give little credence to ill-supported claims of self-determination, such as the one advanced by the Palestinians. The Palestinian claim of self-determination was not even internationally recognized until 1970 – 50 years after the Territories had already been lawfully reserved for the self-determination of the Jewish people.

i. Israel holds a binding sovereign right to the Territories

The ICJ has consistently resolved international territorial disputes by applying three factors in the following order of priority: (1) treaty law; (2) the doctrine of *"uti possidetis juris;"* and (3) effective control.[562]

Where a disputed territory is allocated by treaty, the treaty decides who owns the land.[563] As explained above, the 1920 San Remo treaty and the 1922 treaty-equivalent BMP held Mandatory Palestine, including the Territories, in trust for the Jewish people to form the state that became

---

[562] Brian Taylor Sumner, *Territorial Disputes at the International Court of Justice*, 53.6 DUKE LAW JOURNAL 1779, 1780, 1804-1808 (2004) [hereinafter Sumner].
[563] *Id.* at 1782-1804.

Israel.[564] As also noted, the UN Charter continued the legal entitlement through the transition of authority from the League to the UN. Accordingly, Israel holds a treaty-based right to the Territories.

In the absence of a treaty, the factor that decides international land disputes is the doctrine of *uti possidetis juris* ("as you possess it by law").[565] *Uti possidetis juris* ensures that when a politically distinct territory such as a mandatory district graduates to an independent state, the administrative boundaries at the time of independence become the state's international borders.[566] Under this doctrine, Israel inherited the borders of the BMP (present-day Israel and the Territories) on May 16, 1948, when the Jewish state declared independence.[567] The same doctrine ensured borders for Lebanon, Syria and Iraq that matched their preexisting mandatory boundaries.[568] The rule of *uti possidetis juris* was later used to set borders for the States that emerged from the decolonization of Latin America and Africa, the dissolution of the Soviet Union, and the break-up of Yugoslavia.[569]

The third highest factor in the ICJ's decisional hierarchy is "effective control."[570] As explained above, Israel has effective control over most of

---

[564] *Id.*

[565] *Id.* at 1790-91.

[566] *Id.* at 1779, n. 5; SHAW, *supra* at 211.

[567] Abraham Bell & Eugene Kontorovich, *Palestine, Uti Posseditis Juris, and the Borders of Israel,* 58 Ariz. L. Rev. 633, 681-84 (2016) [hereinafter Bell & Kontorovich].

[568] *Id.* at 648-57.

[569] See Alain Pellet, *The Opinions of the Badinter Arbitration Committee, a Second Breath for the Self-Determination of Peoples,* 3 Eur. J. Int'l L. 178, 180 and 184-85. (1992) [hereinafter Pellet].

[570] Sumner, *supra* at 1787-88.

the Territories, including East Jerusalem and West Bank Area C, which covers 60% of the West Bank.

In sum, the factors of treaty rights, *uti possidetis juris*, and effective control give Israel a dispositive sovereign claim to the Territories.

When Israel took possession of the Territories from Egypt, Jordan and Syria in the 1967 War, it did not start an occupation.[571] It ended the occupations of those three Arab regimes. Israel's presence in the Territories was not an occupation because a state cannot be said to occupy land that has already been legally reserved for its sovereignty.[572] Israel removed itself further from the status of an occupying power to the extent that it surrendered effective control over the Palestinian populated portions of the Territories.[573] In the Oslo Accords, Israel gave the Territory-based Palestinians full administrative control over the major Palestinian population centers (Area A) and shared control over certain outlying areas (Area B). Palestinians cannot claim to be occupied in areas where they exercise such full or joint functional control. Even if one views Israel as an occupying power, that status would be lawful until the disputed land is allocated through a peace treaty.[574] The mere

---

[571] *Disputed Territories: Forgotten Facts about the West Bank and the Gaza Strip*, Israel Ministry of Foreign Affairs (Feb. 2003) [hereinafter "MFA Forgotten Facts"], https://mfa.gov.il/MFA/MFA-Archive/2003/Pages/DISPUTED%20TERRITORIES-%20Forgotten%20Facts%20About%20the%20We.aspx.

[572] *See* Eugene Kontorovich, *Why President Trump is keeping the promise made at San Remo in 1920*, Jerusalem Post (Jan. 1, 2020).

[573] The "Effective Control" test of occupation law is discussed more fully at Chapter 4.5 (May Israel Keep Settlements in the Territories), Author's Prologue.

[574] *See* DE BLOIS AND TUCKER, *supra* at 155-57.

fact that a territory is occupied does not give the occupied people a sovereign right to the land. [575]

ii. Israel's right to the Territories supersedes the conflicting Palestinian claim

Territorial claims based on self-determination, such as the one averred by the Palestinians, carry little weight in international land disputes.[576] The ICJ has ruled that a territorial claim grounded on an ethnic group's longevity in the land "cannot prevail over an established treaty title."[577] Self-determination also yields to the doctrine of *uti possidetis juris*.[578] As stated by the international "Arbitration Committee" that supervised the break-up of Yugoslavia, "the right to self-determination must not involve changes to existing frontiers at the time of independence (*uti possidetis juris*)."[579]

UN practice accords with the above-described pronouncements. In 2014, the Russian Federation annexed the Crimean Peninsula of

---

[575] *Id.*; The Attorney General's Memo, para. 30.

[576] *See* Sumner, *supra* at 1785-86 and 1789-90.

[577] ICJ, Case Concerning Land and Maritime Boundary between Cameroon and Nigeria, Judgment, ICJ Reports 2002, paras. 65-70, available at:
http://www.worldcourts.com/icj/eng/decisions/2002.10.10_boundary.htm.

[578] Sumner, *supra* at 1779. *See, e.g.* Frontier Dispute (Burk. Faso/Mali), Judgment, 1986 I.C.J. 554, 556, paras. 20-26 (Dec. 22), [hereinafter Burk. Faso/Mali], available at: https://www.icj-cij.org/en/case/69 (holding that where the principle of *uti possidetis juris* "conflicts outright with [the principle of] self-determination . . . the maintenance of the territorial status quo [is] the wisest course . . . .").

[579] Pellet, *supra* at 184.

Ukraine. The UN voted to uphold Ukraine's treaty right to Crimea, even though most Crimeans were ethnic Russians who had dwelled there for generations and voted by referendum to join Russia.[580] Again in the cases of South Ossetia and Abkhazia, two autonomous regions of the Republic of Georgia where indigenous ethnic groups asserted rights of self-determination to declare independence, the UN objected out of respect for the territorial integrity of Georgia.[581]

The Palestinian right of self-determination was not even globally recognized until 1970, when the UN adopted Resolution 2672C. That was 50 years after Israel and the Territories had already been dedicated by the BMP for the self-determination of the Jewish people.[582] The supremacy of first-in-time rights to territories is a "principle of special importance" that conditions rights of self-determination.[583] Accordingly, Israel's claim to the Territories supersedes the conflicting Palestinian claim.[584]

---

[580] G.A. Res. 68/262, U.N. Doc. A/RES/68/262 (March 27, 2014), available at: http://www.un.org/press/en/2014/ga11493.doc.htm.

[581] *Georgia: Abkhazia and South Ossetia*, Encyclopedia Princetoniensis, the Princeton Encyclopedia of Self-Determination, https://pesd.princeton.edu/node/706 (last viewed September 21, 2016; *See also* S.C. Res. 1808, U.N. Doc. S/RES/1808 (April 15, 2008) (affirming "the commitment of all Member States to the sovereignty, independence and territorial integrity of Georgia within its internationally recognized borders . . . ."), http://www.un.org/press/en/2008/sc9299.doc.htm.

[582] STONE, *supra* at 21-22.

[583] Cristescu, *supra* at para. 279. *See* Declaration on Colonial Countries, *supra* and Declaration on Principles, *supra* at subheading, "The principle of equal rights and self-determination of peoples."

[584] *See* STONE, *supra* at 19-20. *See also* BARNIDGE, *supra* at 84, 87, and 96.

Although a bevy of UN resolutions has uniformly supported Palestinian rights and lambasted Israel's exercise of sovereignty, those non-binding barbs have no legal effect. Since the late 1960's, the aforementioned "automatic majority" of UN members, composed of Muslim regimes and assorted anti-American governments, has politically harassed Israel with hateful resolutions.[585]

4.3: Should the two-state border be the Green Line?

Author's Prologue

The League's mandatory system aimed to rehabilitate the colonies of the collapsed Ottoman Empire by reorganizing them into mandatory districts and preparing them to become independent states. At least, that was the official plan.[586] The Allied Powers actually managed the mandatory areas more like their own colonies.[587] In the Middle East, the three mandatory districts consisted of Syria (which originally included present-day Lebanon), Mesopotamia (now known as Iraq), and Palestine (which originally included present-day Gaza, Israel, the West Bank, and Jordan). The mandatory borders were established by treaty in the wake of the 1920 San Remo Resolution.[588]

Arabs abhorred the mandate system. From their perspective, there was no justification to re-zoning the Middle East into the three League-

---

[585] DEBLOIS AND TAYLOR, *supra* at 62-79.

[586] DAVID LESCH, *THE ARAB-ISRAELI CONFLICT* 70 (2008) [hereinafter LESCH].

[587] *Id.*

[588] *See* DE BLOIS AND TUCKER, *supra* at 66-68.

designed countries. Arabs vented their anger violently in all three mandatory areas.

To quell the unrest in Palestine, the League decided to divide the proto-state into two parts: one Arab and one Jewish. Thus, in September of 1922, two months after the League approved the BMP, Great Britain reallocated the eastern 77% of the mandatory district to create the Arab emirate that became Jordan. The residual 23% of Palestine – western Palestine – remained earmarked for the planned Jewish state. As a result, the Jordan River became the border between the Arab and Jewish realms,[589] and Mandatory Palestine was reduced to western Palestine.

The League's two-state solution for Palestine was denounced by Arabs as another intolerable offense. They insisted both eastern and western Palestine belonged to Arabs, given the long history of majority Arab life in both halves of the territory. The Jews also cried foul. To them, the creation of an Arab state in Palestine unfairly truncated the Jewish National Home established in San Remo.[590] Attacks and reprisals among Arabs, Jews, and the British mandatory administrators ricocheted throughout the mandatory period.

In 1947, a controversial UN General Assembly vote created a non-binding proposal to the UN Security Council and Great Britain. The proposal, called the UN Partition Plan, recommended a second two-state solution by dividing the already reduced Mandatory Palestine. Essentially, the Plan designated 4,500 square miles (45% of Mandatory Palestine), containing 804,000 Arabs and 10,000 Jews, for an Arab state,

---

[589] See TESSLER, supra at 159-165.

[590] Id. at 162-165.

while earmarking 5,500 square miles (55% of Mandatory Palestine), containing 538,000 Jews and 397,000 Arabs, for a Jewish state.[591]

The Zionists reluctantly accepted the Partition Plan. The Arabs rejected it. In their view, they deserved all western Palestine based on their majority population and centuries-long history in the land. Immediately after the UN vote, armed Arab bands launched the 1947-1948 war by killing and looting Jewish civilians throughout the mandatory district.[592] The war drove Great Britain to abandon its mandatory role and evacuate its personnel from the mandatory district. Amidst the blood-soaked fight for survival, the Zionists declared independence for a state they called Israel without specifying its borders. In response, five surrounding Arab armies immediately invaded Israel to destroy it.[593] The Partition proposal was therefore never approved by the Security Council or the British.

The Zionists not only repelled the Arab invasion but captured about 80% of western Palestine, 21% more than what they would have received from the Partition Plan.[594] The rest of western Palestine fell to Egypt (which seized control of Gaza), Jordan (which captured East Jerusalem and the West Bank), and Syria (which grabbed a corner of western Palestine's northeast).[595]

---

[591] *See* SACHAR, *supra* at 292.

[592] GILBERT, *supra* at 154.

[593] *Id.* at 191-2. The five attacking nations were Egypt, Lebanon, Syria, Jordan, and Iraq.

[594] LESCH, *supra* at 145.

[595] *Id.*

The 1947-1948 war did not conclude with a peace treaty. Instead, the parties signed armistice (cease-fire) agreements and thus remained legally at war.[596] The armistice lines traced the military fronts on the cease-fire date. Those routes differed dramatically from the suggested UN Partition Plan borders. Because the armistice negotiators used a green pen to map the demarcation lines, they called the finished drawing the Green Line. The Green Line separated Israel from its surrounding Arab-held terrain as follows: Lebanon to the north, Syria to the northeast, East Jerusalem, the West Bank, and Jordan to the east, and Gaza and Egypt to the southwest.[597]

In the 1967 War, Israel captured all western Palestine (including Gaza, East Jerusalem, and the West Bank), the Golan Heights, and Egypt's Sinai Desert. Israel thereby seized territory in nearly all directions across the Green Line.

In November of 1967, the UN Security Council hoped to resolve the Arab-Israeli conflict by adopting the landmark Resolution 242. Among other things, the nonbinding Resolution instructed: (1) Israel to withdraw its armed forces from "territories" occupied in the war; and (2) Israel and the five Arab combatant states to negotiate "secure and recognized boundaries."[598] After the 1973 war, UN Resolution 338 repeated the call to negotiate the issues framed in Resolution 242.

Egypt and Jordan eventually signed peace treaties with Israel. In those agreements, Egypt abandoned its claim to Gaza and Jordan recanted its

---

[596] SMITH, *supra* at 218.

[597] *See* MAP 13 (Armistice Lines, 1949).

[598] Resolution 242, paras. 1-4.

claim to the West Bank. The resulting international borders between Israel and the two Arab states therefore tracked the contours of Mandatory Palestine, as opposed to the Green Line.[599] On Israel's western and southern sides, Israel and Egypt established the BMP boundary as their international border everywhere their territories touched. Likewise, on Israel's eastern side, Israel and Jordan made the BMP boundary their international border everywhere their lands touched. The treaties were signed without prejudice to the Israeli-Palestinian conflict, meaning the Israelis and Palestinians remained free to negotiate an international border where their respective lands met.[600] The Palestinians did not accept the BMP boundaries. That would have effectively ceded the Territories to Israel. Instead, they demanded that the Green Line be their border with Israel.

One of the final status controversies slated for negotiation by the Oslo Accords was the issue of borders.[601] More specifically, the Accords envisioned that the border negotiation (like all final status talks) would "lead to the implementation of Security Council Resolutions 242 and 338."[602]

---

[599] See *Egypt-Israel Peace Treaty*, art. II (stating, "The permanent boundary between Egypt and Israel [is] the recognized international boundary between Egypt and the former mandated territory of Palestine . . . without prejudice to the issue of the status of the Gaza Strip.") *See also Jordan-Israel Peace Treaty*, art. 3 (stating, "The international boundary between Israel and Jordan is delimited with reference to the boundary definition under the Mandate . . . without prejudice to the status of any territories that came under Israeli military government control in 1967.")

[600] See *Id*.

[601] Oslo I, art. V.3.

[602] *Id*., art. 1.

If the final status negotiation results in two mutually-recognized sovereign states – Israel and Palestine – should their border be the Green Line?

A. The Palestinian Arguments

Summary of Arguments

A maxim of international law, which appears in the preamble of Resolution 242, states that territory may not be acquired by war. For this reason, Israel may not annex the Territories it occupied in 1967. It must withdraw to the Green Line, which separates Israel from the Territories.

An Israeli withdrawal to the Green Line is additionally compelled by the operative terms of Resolution 242. The UN pronouncement instructed Israel to withdraw its armed forces from "territories" occupied in the 1967 war. As interpreted by most UN Security Council members, the clause meant Israel should remove its forces from all the territories it captured in the war. The Oslo Accords refocused Resolution 242 by instructing Israel to conduct a phased withdrawal of troops from the Territories. Completing that mission would require the IDF to retreat to the Green Line.

An Israeli withdrawal to the Green Line would also harmonize the peace process with the 1988 Palestinian Declaration of Independence. The Declaration made a huge territorial concession by claiming statehood only in the portion of western Palestine that did not lie within recognized Israel. In Oslo, the Palestinians reinforced this concessionary approach by recognizing Israel's right to exist on its side of the Green Line.

Formalizing the Green Line is therefore central to reaching a two-state solution. Israel has persistently refused to establish the Green Line as an international border. Instead, it has increasingly wrested control over the Territories, which belong in a future Palestinian state. The subterfuge has worsened Palestinian life and frustrated the peace process.

---

i. Israel may not acquire territory by war

Resolution 242 emphasized a classic principle of international law: "the inadmissibility of the acquisition of territory by war."[603] Israel acquired the Territories in the 1967 war. Accordingly, Israel cannot lawfully assert sovereignty over any of those wartime gains.[604] Because the dividing line between Israel and the Territories is the Green Line, that should be the Israeli-Palestinian border and the line to which Israel withdraws. [605]

One of the Territories Israel conquered in 1967 was East Jerusalem. Although Israel subsequently annexed that half of the city, the UN rightly condemned the move. The UN decision demonstrated that the international community recognized the Green Line as the international border between Israel and the State of Palestine.[606] If Israel would accept that reality, the border issue would be settled.

---

[603] Resolution 242, pmbl.; Palestine Liberation Organization, *Borders*, Negotiation Affairs Department, State of Palestine, https://www.nad.ps/en/our-position/borders [hereinafter PLO *Borders*]; Iain Scobbie, *The Israeli–Palestinian Conflict in International Law: Territorial Issues*, SSRN ELECTRONIC JOURNAL 85-91 (Jan. 2010) [hereinafter Scobbie], available at: https://www.researchgate.net/publication/228151495_The_Israel-Palestine_Conflict_in_International_Law_Territorial_Issues.

[604] PLO *Borders*, *supra*.

[605] *Id.*

[606] *Id.*

ii. Resolution 242 requires Israel to withdraw to the Green Line

The Green Line should be the Israeli-Palestinian border for the additional reason that Resolution 242 required Israel to withdraw its armed forces from "territories" it captured in the 1967 war.[607] The word "territories" referred to all the lands occupied by Israel in the war and thus indicated Israel should retreat to the Green Line.[608] In fact, ten of the fifteen Security Council members supported that interpretation of the text.[609]

In 2016, the UN Security Council adopted Resolution 2334, which again identified the Green Line as the presumptive border for Israel and the State of Palestine.[610] Specifically, the UN vowed it would "not recognize any changes to the 4 June 1967 lines, including with regard to Jerusalem, other than those agreed by the parties through negotiations."[611]

---

[607] *See The Green Line is a Red Line: The 1967 Border and the Two State*, NAD, (June 27, 2011), https://www.nad.ps/en/publication-resources/factsheets/green-line-red-line-1967-border-and-two-state.

[608] Iain Scobbie, *The Israeli–Palestinian Conflict in International Law: Territorial Issues*, SSRN ELECTRONIC JOURNAL, pp. 74-81 (Jan. 2010) [hereinafter Scobbie], available at: https://www.researchgate.net/publication/228151495_The_Israel-Palestine_Conflict_in_International_Law_Territorial_Issues.

[609] *Id.* at 81.

[610] S.C. Res. 2334, U.N. Doc. S/RES/2334 (Dec. 23, 2016), https://www.un.org/webcast/pdfs/SRES2334-2016.pdf.

[611] *Id.* at para. 3.

iii. A Green Line border would suit the Palestinians' Declaration of Independence

The geographic ambit of recognized Palestine impliedly consists of at least the Territories, given that a 1988 Palestinian communique attached to the Declaration of Independence cited to Resolution 242, and that Resolution called for Israel to withdraw from the Territories.[612] In the process, the Declaration evidenced a major territorial concession.[613] Instead of seeking the replacement of Israel with an Arab Palestinian state, as envisioned by the 1964 PLO Charter, the widely-endorsed 1988 position implicitly accepted Israel's existence by proposing to create a Palestinian state on just a fraction of the disputed land.[614] The 1988 approach demonstrated the Palestinians' commitment to a two-state solution.[615]

The above-described territorial concession was reinforced, upon signing of Oslo I, by the PLO's recognition of Israel's right to exist west of the Green Line.[616] This action furthered the logic of making the Green Line the appropriate border between Israel and the State of Palestine.[617]

Based on the above, the State of Palestine should be deemed to include the Territories with its capital in East Jerusalem and no occupying

---

[612] QUIGLEY CASE FOR PALESTINE, supra at 212.

[613] RASHID KHALIDI, supra at 193-95.

[614] PLO Borders, supra.

[615] KHALIDI PALESTINIAN IDENTITY, supra at 195.

[616] Scobbie, supra at 62.

[617] Id.

forces.[618] That delimitation of territorial rights is central to reaching a two-state solution.[619]

iv. Israel's refusal to recognize the Green Line obstructs the peace process

The border issue remains unsettled because Israel never fully complied with its Oslo withdrawal obligation.[620] In fact, the Israeli-controlled Area C still consumes as much as 60% of the West Bank. In the first stage of the withdrawal, Israel was required to pull its troops from 80 percent of the Gaza Strip and all of the Jericho area within two months, but the process actually took seven months.[621] No matter how scrupulously the lawyers negotiated the scope and timing of the IDF redeployments, Israel repeatedly found excuses for delay.[622] When the IDF did redeploy, it did so in unilateral moves without seeking the Palestinians' prior consent.[623]

During the Second Intifada of 2000 to 2005, the IDF undercut Oslo II even more egregiously by re-occupying the West Bank Area A and B urban centers from which it had withdrawn.[624] Exacerbating the offense,

---

[618] PLO *Borders, supra.*

[619] Id.

[620] PLO, *20 Years After Oslo*, Negotiation Affairs Department, State of Palestine, p. 6, http://www.nad.ps/en/publication-resources/publication/oslo-process-20-years. To clamp down the West Bank, Israel installed hundreds of checkpoints throughout the West Bank.

[621] DOWTY, *supra* at 157.

[622] *Id.*

[623] *Id.*

[624] SACHAR, *supra* at 1038, 1050, and 1054-55.

the troops acted as though Oslo I and II had never been signed.[625] Even after the UN Security Council ordered Israel to cure its Oslo breaches, Israel ignored the command.[626] The ensuing IDF raids and arrests in Palestinian communities ruined the peace process.

Israel also tries to change facts on the ground by maintaining the Barrier and filling the Territories with Israeli settlements.[627] The Barrier, by swallowing as much as 9.4% of the West Bank, evidences an attempt to annex that occupied land.[628] Owing to the Barrier, as many as 650,000 settlers already live illegally in the West Bank, and another 225,000 illegally occupy East Jerusalem.[629]

Because the path of the Barrier deviates from the Green Line it accomplishes a de facto annexation of land that belongs to a Palestinian state.[630] The incursion deprives Palestinians of their agricultural plots, constricts their water supply, limits their freedom of movement, and distances them from their schools, hospitals, and job sites.[631] Studies of the ongoing Barrier construction project that when the structure is

---

[625] *Id.* at 1054.

[626] *See* S.C. Res. 1435, U.N. Doc. S/RES/1435 (Sept. 24, 2002), https://undocs.org/en/S/RES/1435(2002)

[627] PLO *Borders.*

[628] *Id.*

[629] *Id.*

[630] *The Barrier to Peace*, PLO Negotiation Affairs Department, in *THE QUESTION OF PALESTINE*, United Nations (July 2013), https://www.un.org/unispal/document/auto-insert-199543/.

[631] *Id.*

completed, as many as 249,000 Palestinians will be trapped between the Barrier and the Green Line.[632]

In sum, Israel's continuing resistance to territorial compromise has frustrated the two-state solution.[633]

B. The Israeli Arguments

Summary of Arguments

Israel acquired the Territories by law, not by war. The Territories were part of the territory granted by the San Remo Resolution and the BMP to the Jewish people for purposes of reconstituting their state in their ancestral homeland.

Resolution 242 did not require Israel to withdraw to the Green Line. The document did not even mention the Green Line. It required Israel to withdraw its armed forces from undefined "territories," not "the territories." The UN Security Council deliberately omitted the word "the" from the final text.

The Oslo Accords did not require Israel to withdraw to the Green Line as a border. They merely framed a process to negotiate borders.

Resolution 242 and the Oslo Accords recognize Israel's right to secure borders. For Israel, the Green Line would not be a secure border. It would leave the nation's major population centers vulnerable to close-range Palestinian attack.

---

[632] *Id.*

[633] *Diplomatic Quartet releases report on advancing two-state solution to Israel-Palestine conflict,* UN NEWS CENTRE (July 1, 2016) [hereinafter *Quartet Report*], http://www.un.org/apps/news/story.asp?NewsID=54379#.WLIiHeQzXbJ. The "Quartet" that produced this report was the same alliance of four leading international bodies – the UN, EU, US, and Russia – that authored the Israeli-Palestinian Roadmap for Peace in 2002.

i. Israel earned the Territories by law, not by war

Resolution 242 rightly stated that territory may not be acquired by war. This rule of non-annexation prohibits an occupying power from assuming title to the occupied land without first resolving the legal status of the property through a peace treaty.[634] However, the rule does not prohibit a state from taking possession of territory to which it is already entitled by treaty.

As explained above, the Territories were part of Mandatory Palestine. As also noted, two instruments of binding international law – the San Remo Resolution and the BMP – assigned Mandatory Palestine to the Jewish people to reconstitute their state in their ancestral homeland. Israel was initially blocked by an illegal multi-state Arab invasion from exercising sovereignty over the Territories. But when Israel subsequently captured the Territories in its 1967 military campaign of self-defense,[635] it validly took control of its own land.

It has also been shown that even if Israel is viewed as an occupying power, it retains the same sovereign right to the Territories and the same

---

[634] *See* DINSTEIN, *WAR, AGGRESSION AND SELF-DEFENCE* 181 (5th Ed. 2011). Professor Dinstein is Professor Emeritus at Tel Aviv University, where he served as President and Dean of Law. He also taught at the U.S. Naval War College and the Max Planck Institute for Comparative Public Law and International Law. His treatise, "War, Aggression and Self-Defence," has been described an indispensable guide to the law of war and self-defense.

[635] *See* Schwebel, *supra* at 345-46; STONE, *supra* at 46. See also Miriam Sapiro, *Iraq: the shifting sands of preemptive self-defense*, 97.3 Am. J. INT'L L. 599-607, 600-601 (2003); DINSTEIN, *WAR, supra* at 206-07.

right to negotiate their ultimate disposition pursuant to a peace agreement such as the Oslo Accords.

ii. Resolution 242 does not require Israel to withdraw to the Green Line

Resolution 242 was non-binding.[636] Moreover, the UN statement did not require Israel to withdraw to the Green Line. It deliberately omitted any reference to the Green Line to avoid pre-judging the outcome of the requirement to negotiate "secure and recognized boundaries."[637] Likewise, Resolution 242 asked Israel to withdraw its armed forces from "territories" occupied in the 1967 war, not "the territories" captured in the war. Proposals to add the article "the" were rejected.[638] Indeed, the requirement to negotiate "secure and recognized boundaries" would have been meaningless, had Israel been obligated to return all the territories taken in the war.[639] The Security Council left out the word

---

[636] Ruth Lapidoth, Security Council Resolution 242 at Twenty Five, 26 Isr. L. Rev. 298-99 (1992), https://www.cambridge.org/core/journals/israel-law-review/article/security-council-resolution-242-at-twenty-five/7B4BB36D54E0001900707E9785F8FD9C.

[637] Arthur J. Goldberg, *United Nations Security Council Resolution 242 and the Prospects for Peace in the Middle East*, 12 Colum. J. Transnat'l L. 187, 189-91 (1973), http://heinonline.org/HOL/LandingPage?handle=hein.journals/cjtl12&div=16&id=&page. Arthur Goldberg was a justice on the US Supreme Court, the US ambassador to the UN, and a principal negotiator of Resolution 242.

[638] *Id.* at 307.

[639] *Id.* at 309-10 and 312-13.

"the" so the opposing parties could negotiate borders other than the Green Line, in deference to Israel's security needs.[640]

Although the Arab states stressed that Resolution 242 should include the word "the," Egypt and Jordan accepted the language that was ultimately approved.[641] After the October 1973 war, Syria also endorsed the Resolution despite the missing "the."[642]

Israel has arguably fulfilled its Resolution 242 withdrawal obligation because it has pulled its troops from over 90% of the land it captured from Egypt, Syria and Jordan in the 1967 war.[643] Specifically, IDF units left the Sinai Peninsula, Gaza, Areas A and B of the West Bank, and small parts of the Golan Heights.[644]

Resolution 2334 of 2014 was also non-binding.[645] In any event, it made no difference that the Resolution prodded Israel to withdraw to the

---

[640] Eugene Rostow, *The Future of Palestine*, Institute for National Strategic Studies, National Defense University, McNair Paper 24, 6-8 (1993) [hereinafter Rostow], available at http://permanent.access.gpo.gov/websites/nduedu/www.ndu.edu/inss/mcnair/mcnair24/mcnair 24.pdf. Dean Rostow was Dean of Yale Law School, and during the 1960's, Under Secretary of State for Political Affairs under President Lyndon B. Johnson. While serving in the Johnson administration he was one of the drafters of UN Resolution 242, the seminal UN pronouncement that outlined terms of Arab-Israeli peace in the wake of the 1967 Six-Day War. *See also* Kontorovich Resolution 242, *supra* at 130.

[641] TESSLER, *supra* at 419. Syria followed suit after the 1973 war.

[642] *See* DOWTY, *supra* at 124.

[643] Rostow, *supra* at 10.

[644] Kontorovich *Resolution 242*, *supra* at 130.

[645] Ruth Lapidoth, *Some Reflections on Security Council Resolution 2334 (2016) that Condemned Israel*, 59 Justice 5 (Spring-Summer 2017).

Green Line. That legal marker had already disappeared in 1994, when the underlying Jordan-Israel Armistice Agreement was replaced by the Jordan-Israel Peace Treaty and the two countries therein established an international border along the BMP line.[646]

Beyond Resolution 242, Palestinians give no legal reason no make the Green Line a border. They could not have inherited any Green Line-delineated border from Egypt, Syria, or Jordan. Those Arab regimes were mere occupying powers in the Territories with no right to keep them.[647] In fact, during the 19-year period when the Arab regimes occupied the Territories they did not make that region a Palestinian state. They had no territorial rights to transfer to a third party such as the Palestinians.[648]

iii. **The Green Line would not be a secure boundary as planned by Resolution 242**

As noted above, Resolution 242 and the Oslo Accords guaranteed Israel's right to secure borders. Moreover, the armistice agreements of 1949 expressly stipulated that the Green Line would not be a border at all.[649] The Green Line marked nothing more than the place where the

---

[646] *Id.*

[647] Lawfare, *supra*, para. 31.

[648] *Id.*

[649] *The Egypt-Israeli Armistice Agreement* stated at Article V.2.: "The Armistice Demarcation Line is not to be construed in any sense as a political or territorial boundary, and is delineated without prejudice to rights, claims and positions of either Party to the Armistice as regards ultimate settlement of the Palestine question." *Cf Jordan-Israel Armistice Agreement*, Art. VI.9.; *Syria-Israel Armistice Agreement*, Art. V(a).

fighting happened to stop in 1949. At the time, the adversaries intended to change that temporary cease-fire boundary when transitioning from the armistice agreements to peace treaties.[650] Since then, the military capabilities of Israelis and Palestinians have evolved dramatically. The arbitrary, temporary, and obsolete Green Line of 1949 says nothing about where the Israeli-Palestinian border may be securely drawn today.

The Green Line would not be secure today because it would not meet Israel's minimal security needs.[651] If anything, leaving Israel's major population centers so vulnerable to close-range Palestinian attack would virtually invite another war.[652] Israel's largest city is Jerusalem. If an international border of Palestine were to follow the Green Line, West Jerusalem would fall within point-blank range of a Palestinian-ruled East Jerusalem. Another segment of the Green Line is just nine miles from Israel's Mediterranean coast, an area that includes Israel's second-largest city, Tel Aviv.[653] The Green Line would place Palestine within four miles of Ben Gurion Airport, Israel's airline gateway to the world.[654] More generally, a Palestine positioned along the Green Line

---

[650] Rostow, *supra* at 7-8.

[651] Lt.-Gen. (ret.) Moshe Yaalon, *Introduction: Restoring a Security-First Peace Policy*, in ISRAEL'S CRITICAL Jerusalem Center for Public Affairs (JCPA), *Israel's Critical Requirements For Defensible Borders: The Foundation for a Secure Peace*, p. 8 (2014) [hereinafter Yaalon], http://jcpa.org/requirements-for-defensible-borders/.

[652] *Id.*

[653] Israel Ministry of Foreign Affairs, About Israel, *Range of Fire from Judea & Samaria (West Bank)*, (2018), https://mfa.gov.il/MFA/AboutIsrael/Maps/Pages/Range-of-Fire-from-West-Bank.aspx.

[654] *Id.*

could fire rockets and/or mortal shells on all of Israel's major communities and strategic locations.[655]

Some contend that if Israel would evacuate the Territories, Palestinians would lose their motivation to attack Israelis.[656] But the opposite is true. In a scenario of complete evacuation, the Palestinian terror groups would likely escalate their attacks, just as they did after Israel's troop redeployments from the West Bank and its removal of all troops and civilians from Gaza.[657] Another risk is that the desired State of Palestine may be led by a Hamas-style regime.[658] If such a government were to control all of East Jerusalem and the West Bank, the military consequences for Israel would be devastating.[659]

4.4: Which party should govern Jerusalem?

Author's Prologue

Great Britain named Jerusalem the capital of Mandatory Palestine.[660] At the inception of the BMP in 1922, the population of Mandatory Palestine was overwhelmingly Arab. But even before the turn of the century,

---

[655] *Id.*

[656] *See* Eric R. Mandel, *What Would Happen if Israel Withdrew from the West Bank and Ended the 'Siege' of Gaza*, THE JERUSALEM POST (Jan. 26, 2016), http://www.jpost.com/Opinion/What-would-happen-if-Israel-withdrew-from-the-West-Bank-and-ended-the-siege-of-Gaza-442855.

[657] *Id.*

[658] *Id.*

[659] *Id.*

[660] DOWTY, *supra* at 234.

Jerusalem had been majority Jewish.[661] Jerusalem also features a special history. It has been conquered by numerous ethnic groups since antiquity. What makes Jerusalem even more exceptional is its spiritual significance. Its ancient vistas include sites holy to all three of the world's major monotheistic religions: Judaism, Christianity and Islam.

By 1947, the violent competition between Arabs and Jews for control of Mandatory Palestine drove Great Britain to announce that it would abandon its role as the governing mandatory. The UN General Assembly scrambled to contain the crisis. Its solution, the UN Partition Plan, was a proposal to the UN Security Council and Great Britain. The Partition Plan proposed to divide most of Palestine into Arab and Jewish states. As for Jerusalem, the Plan resolved to split the city into three boroughs: one for the Arab Palestinians; one for the Jewish Palestinians; and one for international use consisting of the Old City, which housed the "Holy Places" sacred to the three Abrahamic faiths. An additional provision arranged to expand Jerusalem's municipal boundaries to include more Arab neighborhoods and thereby equalize the two alienated populations.[662] The city would be a demilitarized *corpus separatum* (separate land) subject to international control.[663]

Unfortunately, the UN found no nations willing to contribute the policemen needed to secure the proposed international presence.[664] The security issue then became moot. Immediately after the Partition vote,

---

[661] LARRY COLLINS & DOMINIQUE LAPIERRE, *O JERUSALEM* 22 (1972) [hereinafter COLLINS LAPIERRE].

[662] *Id.* at 148.

[663] *Id.* at 148-49.

[664] *Id.* at 149.

Arab Palestinians launched the 1947-1948 war, rendering the Plan impossible to implement. For that reason, neither the UN Security Council nor Great Britain bothered to approve the Plan.

The war ended with a cease-fire. At that point, Israeli troops controlled much of Mandatory Palestine, including most of Jerusalem. The Egyptian army occupied Gaza. And Jordanian forces occupied the West Bank, as well as a cluster of neighborhoods on the east side of Jerusalem. Armistice agreements marked the cease-fire lines between Israel and the four surrounding enemy states.

In 1949, Israel proclaimed Jerusalem its capital and began to install its governmental institutions in the city.[665] The Knesset formalized the city's official designation the following year.[666] However, the fledgling state could not govern all of Jerusalem due to the partial seizure of the city by Jordan. Jordan sealed off the corner of the city it occupied, called it East Jerusalem, and annexed it to its own territory in 1950.

No state outside Israel recognized Jerusalem as Israeli territory. Only Pakistan recognized East Jerusalem as part of Jordan.[667] Many nations continued to believe Jerusalem should be internationalized, despite the collapse of the Partition Plan. But in 1952, the scheme of special governance was abandoned.[668]

---

[665] *Id.* at 564.

[666] LESCH, *supra* at 187, n. 5.

[667] By comparison, Jordan's claim of sovereignty over the West Bank was recognized only by Pakistan and Great Britain.

[668] DE BLOIS & TAYLOR, *supra* at 217-18.

Included in the Jordanian-annexed portion of Jerusalem was the Old City. Until the late 19th Century, Jerusalem consisted of nothing more than the Old City.[669] But municipal expansion in the Mandatory years reduced the Old City to just one percent of Jerusalem's acreage.[670] From 1949 to 1967, when Jordan asserted ownership of East Jerusalem, the eastern and western sides of the city were separated by a segment of the armistice line, otherwise known as "The Green Line." [671] The Green Line in Jerusalem consisted of a barbed-wire fence, fortified by concrete barriers and land mines. No one could cross it in either direction.

In the 1967 war, Israel conquered the Territories, including East Jerusalem. Also seized were Egypt's Sinai Desert and Syria's Golan Heights. Israel expressed a general willingness to arrange land-for-peace deals.[672] In response, Israel's Arab enemies issued their Khartoum Resolution of "three noes:" no peace; no recognition; and no negotiation.[673]

East Jerusalem was the one parcel Israel refused to trade.[674] The government removed the municipality's Green Line fortifications and reunified the east and west sides, restoring the city to its pre-1948 status. Without using the word "sovereignty" the Knesset passed legislation

---

[669] DOWTY, *supra* at 234.

[670] *Id.*

[671] Other segments of the Green Line separated Israel from Egypt, Lebanon and Syria. The Line bore no relation to the contours of the UN Partition Plan.

[672] GORDIS, *supra* at 402; *See also* SACHAR, *supra* at 673-77, and GILBERT, *supra* at 398 and 402.

[673] SACHAR, *supra* at 675-77;

[674] SACHAR , *supra* at 668 and 673.

extending its "law, jurisdiction and administration" citywide.[675] Jerusalem's municipal boundaries were expanded to incorporate certain strategically important points, including Mount Scopus, the Mount of Olives, and adjacent Arab villages.[676] With government assistance, Israelis took up residence in East Jerusalem, some refilling neighborhoods from which they had been expelled by Jordanian forces 19 years before.

The world community viewed Israel's presence in all the 1967-conquered lands as an occupation. Observing that the rights of occupation included no right of sovereignty, the UN condemned Israel's apparent annexation of East Jerusalem.[677]

Even as East Jerusalem came under Israeli governance, the Arab residents of that city sector remained citizens of Jordan. For them, the adjustment to foreign rule was bewildering.[678] Israel invested heavily in the reunification initiative, upgrading the east side infrastructure, creating local employment opportunities, and permitting freedom of movement, education, and religion citywide.[679]

---

[675] DINSTEIN, *THE INTERNATIONAL LAW OF BELLIGERENT OCCUPATION (2009)* 18 (citing Law and Administration Ordinance (Amendment No. 11) Law, June 27, 1967. Municipal Corporation Ordinance (Amendment No. 6) Law, 1967.)

[676] *See* TESSLER, *supra* at 404

[677] *Id.* at 18-19. *See* General Assembly Resolution 2253, GA/RES/2253 (July 4, 1967) (calling on Israel to rescind all measures taken to alter the status of Jerusalem).

[678] *See* GORDIS, *supra* at 285; GILBERT, *supra* at 397.

[679] SACHAR, *supra* at 667-73.

Israel offered the Jerusalemite Jordanians Israeli citizenship. Nearly all of them declined. As a fallback, Israel let them remain as "permanent residents." Permanent residents could hold Israeli identity cards, vote in municipal (but not national) elections, work in Israel, and receive Israeli government benefits such as social security and health insurance.

A UN Security Council consensus to ease tensions between Israel and its enemies culminated in Resolution 242 of November 1967. The Resolution did not mention Jerusalem or revive the *corpus separatum* theme. Instead, the new UN approach urged the warring states to settle their border dispute and other differences through negotiation.

Of all the lands earmarked for negotiation, the Old City presented a unique challenge. Israel ended the Jordanian practice of excluding Jews from visiting the Holy Places. The new policy, expressed in the Protection of Holy Places Law of 1967, opened that historic basin to freedom of access for people of all faiths.[680]

An especially delicate controversy was how to manage a certain Holy Place sacred to all three monotheistic faiths. The structure was known to Jews and Christians as the Temple Mount, the site where Jews built their First Temple in the 10th Century B.C.E. and the Second Temple in the 5th Century B.C.E. According to the Bible, the Temple Mount was the setting where Abraham nearly sacrificed his son Isaac to prove his devotion to God. It is the holiest site in Judaism and a revered site in Christianity. To ascend the Temple Mount, one walks from ground

---

[680] Israel Ministry of Foreign Affairs, *Protection of Holy Places Law, June 27, 1967* (last viewed February 28, 2017), available at http://www.mfa.gov.il/mfa/foreignpolic y/mfadocuments/yearbook1/pages/14%20protection%20of%20holy%20places%20law.aspx.

level, at the Temple's still-surviving "Western Wall," to an upper level, where the building once featured the chambers of the ancient Jewish priests.

The Temple's upper level is known to Muslims as the Haram al-Sharif (Noble Sanctuary). The Haram consists principally of the Al-Aqsa Mosque and the Dome of the Rock. According to the Koran, Mohammed dreamed that he flew in a miraculous night journey from Mecca to the Al-Aqsa Mosque. The Haram is the third holiest site in Islam after the Masjid al-Haram (the Sacred Mosque) of Mecca and the al-Masjid an-Nabawi (Mosque of the Prophet) in Medina. The original incarnations of the two Haram structures date back to 692 C.E. The current versions were completed in the 11th Century.

During Jordan's tenure in East Jerusalem, the Temple Mount/Haram was managed by a special religious ministry called the Waqf (pronounced "wakf" or "wakif") Islamic Trust. It was a role the Waqf had performed since the 18th Century. The Waqf permitted only Muslims to access the site, so only Muslims could pray there. After the 1967 war, Muslims demanded that Israel preserve the Muslim-only prayer policy. Israel agreed.[681] The Israeli leadership hoped the concession would dispel any suspicion that they had captured the site for religious reasons.[682]

---

[681] See TESSLER, *supra* at 679.

[682] Yossi Klein Halevi, *The Astonishing Israeli Concession of 1967*, THE ATLANTIC, June 7, 2017, https://www.theatlantic.com/international/archive/2017/06/israel-paratroopers-temple-mount-1967/529365/.

Based on Israel's peace gesture, the Israelis and Jordanians observed an informal arrangement for preserving Muslim tradition at the Temple Mount/Haram. The deal became known as "the status quo agreement."

The status quo agreement was later referenced in the 1994 Israel-Jordan Peace Treaty,[683] though the particulars of the plan remained murky.[684]

In practice, the Waqf became responsible for administering prayer at the Temple Mount/Haram, while Israel handled matters of security and access to the site.[685] Israeli police patrolled within and around the Temple Mount/Haram but did not enter the Muslim Holy Places.[686] Another of Israel's responsibilities was to regulate non-Muslim access to the site. Small numbers of Christians, Jews, and other non-Muslims were admitted during limited hours of the day. The few entrants were prohibited from bringing religious objects to the site or praying there. Waqf monitors could eject any Christian or Jew from the site for moving lips in prayer.[687]

From time to time, Israeli police restricted access to the Temple Mount/Haram, typically with temporary exclusions of Muslim men

---

[683] *Israel-Jordan Peace Treaty*, art. 9 (stating that the participants promise to "provide freedom of access to places of religious and historical significance," impliedly including the Temple Mount/Haram).

[684] International Crisis Group, *The Status of the Status Quo on Jerusalem's Holy Esplanade* (June 30, 2015) [hereinafter Crisis Group], https://d2071andvip0wj.cloudfront.net/159-the-status-of-the-status-quo-at-jerusalem-s-holy-esplanade.pdf.

[685] *Id.* at 5.

[686] *Id.*

[687] *Id.* at 10.

under age 30 or 40 when individuals of that age sparked riots at the site.[688] The police originally coordinated such restrictions with the Waqf. However, the customary coordination broke down during the Second Intifada, when the Temple Mount/Haram became a frequent flashpoint of violence.[689]

Tensions over the status quo policy continue today. Jewish worshipers complain the policy abridges their freedom of religion at the holiest site in Judaism. Palestinians accuse Israel of scheming to abolish the status quo by seizing full control of the site.

In 1980, the Knesset amended its Basic Law with language reaffirming the 1950 declaration of Jerusalem as the nation's capital. Israel has since referred to the city as its "undivided eternal capital." The Basic Law amendment enraged the international community. In their view, the amendment exacerbated the illegal 1967 annexation of East Jerusalem. A backlash of UN resolutions declared Israel's control of East Jerusalem invalid. The international statements repeatedly urged Israel to stop all construction and Israeli migration to the eastern zone.

In 1988, the Jerusalem controversy grew more complex. Jordan renounced its claim to East Jerusalem and the West Bank. Pursuant to the decision, Jordan revoked the citizenship of the Jordanians living in both enclaves, leaving them stateless. But the affected Arabs had already developed national aspirations as "Palestinians." They formalized that political framework in 1988 by issuing a declaration of

---

[688] *See Id.* at 8-9.

[689] *Id.* at 9.

independence to create the State of Palestine. The pronouncement named all of Jerusalem as their nation's capital.

In 1993, the Oslo Accords listed "Jerusalem" as an issue to be resolved at the permanent status stage of the peace process.[690] Oslo II let the Palestinians of Jerusalem vote in PA elections.[691] For all other purposes, the Accords tacitly left the city under Israeli control.[692]

During the Second Intifada of 2000-2005 Israel constructed the Barrier to defend against a wave of Palestinian suicide bombings and other terrorist attacks. A stretch of that separation line ran through East Jerusalem. The wall/fence structure separated many Jerusalemite Palestinians from the rest of their community.

On December 6, 2017 the US recognized Jerusalem as Israel's capital, and on May 14, 2018 it relocated the US embassy to that city. The UN General Assembly met in emergency session to register its objection. The resulting pronouncement said the US decision had no legal effect, that it must be rescinded due to past UN statements, and that all states should refrain from installing diplomatic missions in Jerusalem.[693]

As of 2017, the core city of Jerusalem (as opposed to the entire metropolitan area) contained a population of 901,300, including 546,100

---

[690] Oslo I, art. V.3.

[691] Oslo II, art II.3 and annex II, art. VI.

[692] See Oslo II, art. XVII.4.a. (Giving Israel authority over all parts of the Territories not under PA control)

[693] UN General Assembly Resolution ES-10/19, G.A Res. ES-10/19, A/RES/ES-10/19 (Dec. 21, 2017), https://www.securitycouncilreport.org/un-documents/document/areses-1019.php.

Jews (60.5%), 341,500 Arabs (37.8%), and 13,700 "others" (1.5%).[694] However, East Jerusalem was majority Palestinian, with roughly 300,000 Palestinians (60%) and 200,000 Jews (40%).[695]

Israel continues to govern Jerusalem as a unified whole. For example, the municipality is served by a single electric grid, light rail network, and postal system. Arabs and Israelis live, work, and travel throughout the city. And nowhere in the ecosystem is the Green Line detectable.

Israel's governance of East Jerusalem remains a central controversy in the Israeli-Palestinian dispute. Is the arrangement lawful?

---

[694] Israel Central Bureau of Statistics, *Localities, Population, and Density per SQ. KM.*, 2017 (September 4, 2018), https://www.cbs.gov.il/he/publications/DocLib /2018/2.%20ShnatonPopulation/st02_25.pdf.

[695] Isabel Kershner, *New Proposal to Divide Jerusalem Unites People against It*, N.Y. TIMES (March 6, 2016), available at: http://www.nytimes.com/2016/03/07/world/middleeast/new-proposal-to-divide-jerusalem-unites-people-against-it.html?_r=0.

A. The Palestinian Arguments

Summary of Arguments

Any resolution of the Israeli-Palestinian conflict must recognize the significance of Jerusalem to Muslims. Jerusalem houses the third-holiest site in Islam – the Haram-al Sharif – and figures prominently in Muslim history.

Israel's attempt to annex East Jerusalem and make Jerusalem its capital defied international law. The UN Partition Plan made Jerusalem a *corpus separatum* under international control. In any event, an occupying power such as Israel may not annex the occupied land.

After capturing East Jerusalem in 1967, Israel multiplied its occupation law violations by merging the east and west sides of the city, colonizing the eastern neighborhoods, and repressing their Palestinian inhabitants.

Israel exploited its control over East Jerusalem's Old City by restricting Muslim access to the Holy Places. That action violated Israel's status quo agreement with Jordan.

The Holy Places are best left under Arab control. Arabs respect all three monotheistic religions because Arabs are followers of all three faiths.

Israel's Judaization of East Jerusalem undercuts the spirit of the Oslo Accords by preventing Palestine from exercising sovereignty over East Jerusalem as its capital.

---

i. Jerusalem is uniquely important to Palestinians

The importance of Jerusalem to the Muslim people was well-described in a 1995 article published in the Palestine-Israel Journal.[696] The article noted the following.

Jerusalem is the spiritual apex of the Palestinian homeland.

Arabs have lived in Jerusalem for 13 centuries. Until the Prophet Muhammad's migration to Medina in 622 AD, he and his followers prayed in the direction of Jerusalem. According to the Koran, Muhammad dreamed that the archangel Gabriel appeared to him and transported him on a winged horse from Mecca to "the furthest place of prayer." The event was known as the "Night Journey" (the "Mi'raj"). Islamic theologians later identified the "furthest place" as Jerusalem. While in Jerusalem, it is said that Muhammad led Abraham, Moses and Jesus in prayer and then ascended to heaven.

Soon after the 637 AD Arab conquest of Palestine, the region's Arab ruler, Umayyad Caliph Abd al-Malik, ordered the construction of the Dome of the Rock on the site of the Jewish Temples. The placement of the shrine signaled that Islam had completed the spiritual journey begun by Judaism and Christianity. Inside the Muslim monument, worshipers gazed on the "Foundation Stone," which marked the spot where Muhammad had risen to heaven. Ever since, the structure's golden dome has iconized Jerusalem's skyline.

---

[696] Ziad Abu-Amr, *The Significance of Jerusalem: a Muslim Perspective*, PALESTINE-ISRAEL JOURNAL, Vol 2, No. 2, 1995, http://www.pij.org/details.php?id=646.

In 661 AD, the Umayyad Caliph Mu'awiyah regarded Jerusalem with such reverence that he proclaimed himself caliph (the religious and political leader of the Islamic empire) in that city, even though his political capital was Damascus. Subsequent Muslim caliphs, including those of the Abbasids, Mamelukes, and Ottomans, accorded Jerusalem the same respect.

In 715, AD the Umayyads complemented the Dome of the Rock by building the nearby Al Aqsa Mosque (the Further Mosque). Together, the Dome of the Rock and the Al Aqsa Mosque became known as the Haram al-Sharif. The Haram established Jerusalem as the third holiest city in Islam after Mecca and Medina. Islamic law has taught Muslims to protect the Haram from encroachment by non-believers.

Through the centuries, Jerusalem became a magnet for Muslim pilgrimage, study, and prayer. Muslim scholars came from distant lands to study at the Al-Aqsa Mosque.

Muslim caliphs practiced religious tolerance towards Christians and Jews – "the people of the book" – because Islam revered the prophets of all three religions. Muslim rule was continuous from 637 to 1917 with only a brief interruption of about a century due to the Crusader invasion of 1099. In 1187 the Muslim Sultan Saladin liberated Jerusalem on the same date as the Prophet's Night Journey. His victory was a crowning achievement in Islamic history.

In 1988, the Palestinian Declaration of Independence named Jerusalem as the capital of the new Arab state. Palestinians validly exercised their sovereign right to name their capital city. Consistent with that sovereign act, the Arab League Peace Plan of 2002 proposed to preserve East

Jerusalem as the state's capital. Since then, most of the world community, including the US, has endorsed the idea.

Palestine celebrates Jerusalem every year on Al-Quds (Jerusalem) Day. That annual event is held on the last Friday of the Muslim holy month of Ramadan as an international day of struggle to defeat Israel and liberate Jerusalem.

From 1948 to 1967, there were no Jews in East Jerusalem. After Israel captured East Jerusalem in the 1967 war, it offered citizenship to the city's Palestinians. Nearly all of them refused. They would not submit to a foreign power. To the contrary, they engaged in armed struggle to defend their national rights.

Israel's occupation of Jerusalem was an offense and humiliation equal to the crime of the Crusaders. By conquering West Jerusalem in 1948, capturing East Jerusalem in 1967, and then annexing the eastern side in 1980, Israel robbed local Muslims of their position as custodians of the hallowed city. Fortunately, Jordan's King Hussein made a commitment, when he assumed control of East Jerusalem in 1948, to protect the Haram. Jordan's Waqf Islamic Trust has guarded and nurtured the holy place ever since. For now, East Jerusalem remains majority-Arab, but a relentless inflow of Jewish settlers has eroded the area's Arab character.

The reason Muslims worldwide, including many Palestinians, denounced the Oslo Accords is because the pact made Jerusalem a matter of negotiation. To bargain away any part of Jerusalem would betray Islam.

Judaism survived for thousands of years without Jews controlling Jerusalem. Israel has no reason to alter that condition today. By contrast, the Haram has been an exclusive and continuous place of Muslim worship for 13 centuries. That tradition of active worship should remain undisturbed.

ii. **Israel illegally attempted to annex East Jerusalem**

Israel's administration of East Jerusalem is doubly illegal under occupation law.[697] This subsection addresses the first category of violations: those that illegally asserted ownership of the city and misrepresented it as Israel's capital. [698] The next subsection discusses the second category: acts that persecute the city's occupied population. [699]

Soon after Israel declared independence in 1948, the UN began adopting a series of resolutions reiterating the importance of making Jerusalem a *corpus separatum*, as contemplated by the UN Partition Plan. One General Assembly resolution stated that:

> [I]n view of its association with three world religions, the Jerusalem area... should be accorded special and separate treatment from the rest of Palestine and should be placed under effective United Nations control ... [700]

---

[697] Amy Goodman, *Noam Chomsky Blasts United States for Supporting Israel, Blocking Palestinian State*, DEMOCRACY NOW (October 22, 2014), available at: http://www.democracynow.org/2014/10/22/in_un_speech_noam_chomsky_blasts.

[698] *Id.*

[699] *Id.*

[700] G.A Res. 194(III), para. 8, U.N. Doc. A/RES/194(III) (Dec. 11, 1948), https://undocs.org/en/A/RES/194(III).

Israel ignored the UN guidance. In 1949, the nation named Jerusalem its capital. Nevertheless, Jerusalem stands outside Israel's sovereignty. A state may not acquire territory by force, as Israel did in the 1947-1948 war.[701] Israel's only recognized borders are the ones defined by the UN Partition Plan, under which Jerusalem remains a *corpus separatum*.[702]

After the 1967 war, when Israel occupied the Territories, it applied its civil law to East Jerusalem, thereby treating the entire city as Israeli land. It meanwhile expanded the city's boundaries extensively. The enlargement reached 105 kilometers (65 miles) to the north, east and south of Jerusalem proper.[703] By artificially increasing the city's size, Israel tried to maximize the territory it could declare nonnegotiable.[704] The new borders were drawn to include the maximum amount of Palestinian land while excluding the maximum number of Palestinians.[705] In 1980, the Knesset ossified the purported status of Jerusalem as Israel's capital by incorporating the designation in the country's Basic Law.

As noted above, a state may not acquire territory by force. The UN accordingly censured Israel's acquisitive activities in East Jerusalem after the 1967 war. The UN Security Council stated in 1968 that all

---

[701] Palestine Liberation Organization - Negotiations Affairs Department, *Occupied East Jerusalem – Legal Status, State of Palestine* (January 9, 2016) [hereinafter PLO-NAD *Occupied East Jerusalem*](citing UN Charter Article 2, paragraph 4), https://www.nad.ps/en/publication-resources/factsheets/occupied-east-jerusalem-%E2%80%93-legal-status.

[702] *Id.*

[703] SMITH, *supra at 439.*

[704] *Id.*

[705] PLO-NAD *Occupied East Jerusalem, supra.*

actions taken by Israel to change the legal status of Jerusalem were "invalid."[706] In response to Israel's 1980 amendment to its Basic Law, the Council emphasized that the action had "no legal validity" and constituted "a flagrant violation" of occupation law.[707]

Later that year, the Security Council denounced the 1980 legislation "in the strongest terms" and urged all states having diplomatic relations with Israel to withdraw their missions from Jerusalem.[708] The affected nations complied by moving their foreign embassies from Jerusalem to Tel Aviv.

Neither of the above post-occupation legislative steps accomplished a valid annexation.[709] The 1967 decree merely reflected an acknowledgement that East Jerusalem was occupied territory, not a sovereign part of Israel.[710] Similarly, the 1980 amendment stated that "Jerusalem, complete and united, is the capital of Israel," but nothing in that phrase mentioned annexation or sovereignty.[711] An earlier version of the bill had proposed to declare that "the integrity and unity of greater Jerusalem... in its boundaries after the Six-Day War shall not be

---

[706] *Id.* (citing S.C. Res. 252, U.N. Doc. S/RES/252 (May 21, 1968), https://undocs.org/en/S/RES/252(1968).

[707] *Id.* (citing S.C. Res. 476, U.N. Doc. S/RES/476 (June 30, 1980)), https://undocs.org/en/S/RES/476 (1980).

[708] S.C. Res. 478, U.N. Doc. S/RES/478 (Aug. 20, 1980), available at: https://undocs.org/en/S/RES/478(1980).

[709] Ian S. Lustick, *Has Israel Annexed East Jerusalem?* 5 *Middle East Policy* 34-45, 35 (1997), https://www.polisci.upenn.edu/sites/default/files/Lustick_Has_Israel_Annexed_Jerusalem_1997.pdf.

[710] *Id.* at 36-37.

[711] *Id.* at 40.

violated."[712] Such border-defining language would have effected an annexation. But, significantly, the wording was rejected.[713] As a result, East Jerusalem legally remains available as ever for Palestinian rule.[714]

The dubious nature of Israeli sovereignty in East Jerusalem is echoed in Israel's classification of the local residents. Israel labeled the local Palestinians "permanent residents." In a genuine annexation, that population would become Israeli citizens.[715] Similarly, the government did not apply its educational curriculum to local Palestinian schools or impose its commercial regulations on local Palestinian businessmen and professionals.[716]

Four reasons for Israel's ambiguous acquisition strategy are inferable. First, Israel must have known an actual annexation of East Jerusalem would violate occupation law.[717] Second, the government likely sought to avoid a legal confrontation with the world community.[718] Third, annexing East Jerusalem without claiming ownership of any more territory may have angered internal constituencies seeking annexation for all of western Palestine.[719] Finally, the policy avoided the need to offer Israeli citizenship to the Palestinians of East Jerusalem.[720]

---

[712] *Id.*

[713] *Id.*

[714] *Id.* at 45.

[715] *Id.* at 38.

[716] *Id.*

[717] *Id.* at 36.

[718] *Id.*

[719] *Id.*

[720] *Id.*

East Jerusalem is part of sovereign Palestine.[721] In 1988, when Palestinians declared independence in the Territories, including Jerusalem, the global community recognized the new state overwhelmingly. In 2017, the Organization of Islamic Conference specifically recognized East Jerusalem as Palestine's capital.[722] This was in reaction to the US pronouncement recognizing Jerusalem as the capital of Israel. The US recognition was an act that the UN Security Council would have repudiated, if not for the US veto.[723]

iii. Israel's reunification of East and West Jerusalem violated occupation law

An occupying power must serve the needs of the protected population.[724] Israel violated this occupation law duty as it absorbed East Jerusalem into Israel.

---

[721] State of Palestine, *Referral by the State of Palestine Pursuant to Articles13(a) and 14 of the Rome Statute*, submitted to the International Criminal Court (May 15, 2018), n.4 (explaining that, "The State of Palestine comprises the Palestinian Territory occupied in 1967 by Israel, as defined by the 1949 Armistice Line, and includes the West Bank, including East Jerusalem, and the Gaza Strip"), https://www.icc-cpi.int/itemsDocuments/2018-05-22_ref-palestine.pdf.

[722] *Islamic Cooperation declares East Jerusalem as Palestine's capital*, HURRIYET DAILY NEWS (Dec. 13, 2017), http://www.hurriyetdailynews.com/oic-agrees-to-recognize-east-jerusalem-as-palestinian-capital-124064

[723] Edith Lederer, *UN denounces US recognition of Jerusalem as Israeli capital*, ASSOCIATED PRESS NEWS (Dec. 22, 2017), https://apnews.com/article/united-nations-donald-trump-us-news-ap-top-news-international-news-1703c751741142abb9ddad8a90bc41bb.

[724] *Hague Regulations*, art. 43.

One occupation law rule disallows the transfer of an occupier's citizens into the occupied environment.[725] Yet Israel has systematically colonized the eastern sector of Jerusalem.[726] Public and private funding sources have moved Jewish families into the East Jerusalem, either by acquiring property never owned by Jews or reclaiming land bought by Jews before Israel's founding in 1948. The illegal settlements also surround East Jerusalem and isolate it from the Palestinian communities in the West Bank.[727] In June of 2016, the Jerusalem City Council approved the construction of an Israeli apartment building in Silwan, the largest Palestinian neighborhood in East Jerusalem.[728]

By boosting the Jewish population of East Jerusalem, Israel hopes to outnumber the local Palestinians and thereby prevent any re-division of the city along ethnic lines.[729] The contrived influx of Jews should not count for purposes of any self-determination analysis.[730] East Jerusalem should remain recognized as "Arab Jerusalem."[731]

---

[725] *Fourth Convention*, art. 49.

[726] Rashid Khalidi, *Introduction*, in *Commentary: Jerusalem at Boiling Point*, JOURNAL OF PALESTINE STUDIES, Vol. XLV, No. 2, p. 2 (Winter, 2016) [hereinafter *Boiling Point*], http://jps.ucpress.edu/content/45/2/1.5.

[727] Palestine Liberation Organization - Negotiations Affairs Department, *Jerusalem*, [hereinafter PLO-NAD *Jerusalem*], https://www.nad.ps/en/our-position/jerusalem.

[728] *Id.*

[729] Michael Eisner, *Jerusalem: An Analysis of Legal Claims and Political Realities*, 12 *Wis. Int'l LJ* 221, 238-240 (1993) [hereinafter Eisner]; *See also* PLO-NAD *Jerusalem, supra*.

[730] Eisner, *supra* at 242-43.

[731] *Id.* at 244.

Israel seeks to transform East Jerusalem not only by inflating the Jewish population but by expelling Palestinians.[732] Palestinians are mere permanent residents of Israel, prohibited from voting in national elections. [733] At any time, the government may strip a Palestinian of his or her permanent resident permit for law enforcement reasons or political activity deemed hostile to Israel.[734] "Revocation of residency" may also be invoked when a permanent resident leaves East Jerusalem to live elsewhere.[735] As many as 14,600 permits have been revoked between 1967 and today.[736] Under this policy Palestinians have lost families, homes and jobs.[737]

Israel contends permanent residency is a privilege that can be revoked.[738] But this thinking is inhumane. Many of the victimized Palestinians were born in Jerusalem, have lived there for many years, contributed to its economy, and never held legal status anywhere else.[739]

Another scheme to constrict East Jerusalem's Palestinian community operates through prejudicial housing policies. On paper, the policies appear neutral, but they promote the expansion of Jewish

---

[732] *Revocation of Residency in East Jerusalem*, B'TSELEM (Jan. 1, 2011, updated Aug. 18, 2013) [hereinafter B'Tselem *Residency*], http://www.btselem.org/jerusalem/revocation_of_residency.

[733] Daniel Seidemann, *East Jerusalem: The Myth of Benign Occupation Disintegrates* [hereinafter Seidemann], in Boiling Point, *supra*, pp. 4-5, available at https://www.palestine-studies.org/en/node/198543 .

[734] *Id.*

[735] B'Tselem *Residency*, *supra*.

[736] PLO-NAD *Jerusalem*, *supra*.

[737] B'Tselem *Residency*, *supra*.

[738] *Id.*

[739] *Id.*

neighborhoods at the expense of the Palestinian ones.[740] In addition, they permit the demolition of unauthorized housing, something that Palestinians are forced to undertake due to difficulties in obtaining building permits in East Jerusalem.[741]

Economically, Israel pressures East Jerusalem Palestinians by relegating them to a low standard of living. Seventy-nine percent of them earned incomes below Israel's poverty line in 2014, according to an Israeli study.[742] A major cause of Palestinian poverty in East Jerusalem is the Barrier.[743] When the structure tore through Palestinian East Jerusalem, it severed much of that eastern dominion from the rest of the West Bank, thus separating East Jerusalem businesses from many of their customers and forcing local consumers to buy higher-priced Israeli goods.[744] The Barrier also limits space for Palestinian growth while abetting the spread of Israeli settlements.[745]

Yet another technique used to repress East Jerusalem's Palestinian community is police harassment. The police frequently arrest local,

---

[740] Francesco Chiodelli, *The Jerusalem Master Plan: Planning into the Conflict*, 51 JERUSALEM QUARTERLY 5, 7-12 (2012), https://www.palestine-studies.org/en/node/78505.

[741] *Id.* at 12-13. *See also* PLO-NAD, *Jerusalem, supra* (noting that about 40% of homes in the Palestinian neighborhoods of Jerusalem are built without permits).

[742] *Standard of Living and Welfare*, Chapter VI, The Jerusalem Institute for Israel Studies, Statistical Yearbook, 2016 Edition, available at:
https://jerusaleminstitute.org.il/en/?cmd=statistic.550#.V23FVOT2YhU.

[743] *Israel's Separation Wall Causes Poverty in East Jerusalem*, THE PALESTINE CHRONICLE, June 22, 2016, available at: http://www.palestinechronicle.com/israels-separation-wall-causes-poverty-increase-east-jerusalem/.

[744] *Id.*; PLO-NAD *Jerusalem, supra*.

[745] PLO-NAD *Jerusalem, supra*.

working-age Palestinians. In a single week in 2016, Israeli forces arrested 11 Palestinians, including four children and three women, in occupied Jerusalem.[746] An arrest record can ruin a person's chances for employment.[747]

In response to Israel's occupation law crimes, the UN General Assembly and Security Council have passed numerous condemnatory resolutions. One representative announcement emphasized that:

> All legislative and administrative measures and actions taken by Israel, including expropriation of land and properties thereon, which tend to change the legal status of Jerusalem are invalid and cannot change that status;... [and Israel should] rescind all such measures already taken and... desist forthwith from taking any further action which tends to change the status of Jerusalem ...[748]

Israel has consistently ignored the UN's legal alarm bells.

iv. Israel illegally curtails Muslim access to the Holy Places

The status quo agreement was memorialized in Article 9 of the Israel-Jordan Peace Treaty. That provision required Israel, among other

---

[746] *Palestinian Center for Human Rights Report on Israeli Human Rights Violations in the oPt* (16 – 22 June 2016), INTERNATIONAL MIDDLE EAST MEDIA CENTER (June 23, 2016), available at http://imemc.org/article/pchr-report-on-israeli-human-rights-violations-in-the-opt-16-22-june-2016/.

[747] *Id.*

[748] S.C. Res. 252, U.N. Doc. S/RES/252 (May 21, 1968), available at: https://undocs.org/en/S/RES/252(1968).

things, to let Muslims pray at the Temple Mount/Haram. Accompanying that ground rule, Israel agreed to prohibit non-Muslims from praying at the site.

Israel violates the status quo policy by asserting excessive control over the Holy Place. In recent years, an increasing number of Jews have visited the site.[749] These "Temple activists" often try to pray at the site, and some succeed.[750] Some of them have even built models of an imagined Third Temple that would replace the Al Aqsa Mosque.[751]

In the face of these provocations, Palestinians have little recourse because the status quo is an understanding between Israel and a third party: the Jordanian Waqf.[752] Palestinians cannot rely on such an alliance to represent their rights.[753]

Visits to the Temple Mount/Haram by Christians or Jews frequently result in violent confrontations.[754] Israeli police inappropriately respond to the skirmishes by curtailing Muslim access to the site.

In July of 2017, after a shooting incident at the Temple Mount/Haram, Israel installed metal detectors at the Lions Gate entrance to the site.

---

[749] Crisis Group, *supra*, p. 14.

[750] *Id.*

[751] *Id.*

[752] *Id.*, p. ii.

[753] *Id.*

[754] *Why Jordan is installing cameras at Al-Aqsa Mosque*, AL-MONITOR, March 31, 2016, available at: http://www.al-monitor.com/pulse/originals/2016/03/jordan-cameras-al-aqsa-mosque-palestine.html.

Israel violated the status quo by failing to coordinate the action with the Waqf. Moreover, the metal detectors changed the status of the site in violation of Israel's duty to preserve the status quo.[755] Most disturbing of all, the Israeli action reflected a pretense of sovereignty over East Jerusalem in defiance of Israel's responsibility as an occupying power not to annex occupied land.[756] These encroachments instigated such an uproar from Palestinian protestors that Israel was forced to remove the security devices.[757]

v. The Holy Places should remain under Arab control

Jordan's detractors criticize the country for having prevented Jews from accessing the Holy Places of the Old City, when it ruled East Jerusalem from 1949 to 1967. However, that claim is unfair.[758] In 1949, Jordan joined Egypt, Lebanon and Syria in a UN-backed declaration pledging to guarantee access to the Holy Places for visitors of all faiths.[759] Israel refused to sign the declaration and also ignored UN resolutions to

---

[755] Osama Al-Sharif, *Netanyahu's failed game of brinkmanship*, ARAB NEWS (July 25, 2017), http://www.arabnews.com/node/1134711.

[756] *Id.*

[757] *Id.*

[758] *Israel's 1967 Annexation of Arab Jerusalem: Walid Khalidi's Address to the UN General Assembly Special Emergency Session, 14 July 1967*, in 42.1 Institute for Palestine Studies 71 (2012/2013), https://www.palestine-studies.org/en/node/162553. Professor Khalidi is General Secretary and co-founder of the Institute for Palestine Studies, an independent research center focusing on Palestinian rights and the Arab-Israeli conflict. He has taught at Oxford University, the Harvard Center for International Affairs, and Princeton University.

[759] *Id.*

repatriate and compensate Palestinian refugees.[760] Those were the real reasons why Jews were denied access to the holy sites.[761]

Arabs are uniquely suited to be guardians of the Holy Places.[762] There are Arab Muslims, Arab Christians and Arab Jews. Arab Muslims have historically respected the other two major monotheistic religions.[763] Jews lack such a track record of tolerance for the other two faiths.[764]

Israel's contempt for Islam is demonstrated by its scheme to Judaize Jerusalem and thereby erase its Islamic and Palestinian identity.[765] Israeli excavation tunnels beneath the Temple Mount/Haram have endangered local lives and properties.[766] The government has imposed Jewish vacation schedules on both the Israeli and Palestinian schools of Jerusalem.[767] And Street names in the Old City have been changed to Hebrew.[768]

vi. Israel undercuts the Oslo vision for Jerusalem

There can be no Palestinian state, and therefore no sustainable settlement of the conflict, unless the state includes East Jerusalem as its

---

[760] *Id.*

[761] *Id.*

[762] *Id.*

[763] *Id.*

[764] *Id.*

[765] *Mufti slams Israeli 'Judaization' policies in Old City of Jerusalem*, MA'AN NEWS AGENCY (Dec. 28, 2016), https://www.jstor.org/stable/2537436?seq=1.

[766] *Id.*

[767] *Id.*

[768] *Id.*

capital.[769] East Jerusalem is central to the political, economic, and spiritual life of the future state.[770] If Palestinians find it in their interest, they may accept Jerusalem as the capital of two nations.[771]

Article V of Oslo I listed Jerusalem as an issue to be resolved in the permanent status negotiations.[772] Thus, Article V preserved the potential for Israel to withdraw from East Jerusalem and make way for a Palestinian capital. The Article in no way allocated Jerusalem to Israel. By expanding its presence in East Jerusalem, pressuring local Palestinians to leave, and continuing to declare Jerusalem its "undivided eternal capital," Israel has undercut Article V by trying to predetermine the outcome of the final status talks.[773] The international community must act urgently before Israel completely forecloses hope for a viable Palestinian capital in East Jerusalem.[774]

The United States could compel Israel to accept the Palestinians' legitimate rights in Jerusalem. Unfortunately, US policy on Jerusalem has undermined that goal. In 1995, the US Congress passed a law to recognize Jerusalem as the undivided capital of Israel and move the US

---

[769] PLO-NAD *Final Status, supra.*

[770] *Id.*

[771] *Id.*

[772] Oslo I, art. V.

[773] *See Displacement and the 'Jerusalem Question': An Overview of the Negotiation over East Jerusalem and Developments on the Ground, Background Report,* Norwegian Refugee Council (April, 2015), p. 29, https://www.nrc.no/globalassets/pdf/reports/displacement-and-the-jerusalem-question.pdf.

[774] *Id.*

embassy from Tel Aviv to Jerusalem.[775] For over 20 years, a succession of US presidents declined to implement the law. They wisely recognized that Jerusalem should not be anyone's capital until the city's status is resolved through the Oslo-arranged final status talks. In support of the executive branch position, the US Supreme Court ruled that the US Constitution gives the president exclusive power to recognize foreign sovereigns such as Israel.[776] Regrettably, the US broke from the executive tradition in 2017 by recognizing Jerusalem as the capital of Israel and relocating its embassy to Jerusalem the following year.

The American reversal on Jerusalem breached the Vienna Convention on Diplomatic Relations (VCDR).[777] In particular, the US embassy in Jerusalem does not represent the US in the "receiving state" (i.e. Israel) as required by the VCDR because the facility is not located in the sovereign territory of that state.[778]

---

[775] *Jerusalem Embassy Act of 1995*, Pub.L. 104-45, November 8, 1995, 109 Stat. 398.

[776] *Zivotofsky v. Kerry*, 135 S. Ct. 2076 (2015), https://www.oyez.org/cases/2014/13-628.

[777] State of Palestine, *Application Instituting Proceedings in the International Court of Justice, State of Palestine v. United States of America* (Sept. 28, 2018), https://www.icj-cij.org/en/case/176.

[778] *Id.* at paras. 36-50. *See also* Victor Kattan, *It's Time to Take Palestine v. United States of America Seriously*, Comment, OPINIO JURIS (Oct. 18, 2018) (arguing that because Israel lacks sovereignty over Jerusalem, the US cannot lawfully conduct diplomatic relations with Israel in that city), http://opiniojuris.org/2018/10/16/its-time-to-take-palestine-v-united-states-of-america-seriously/.

B. The Israeli Arguments

Summary of Arguments

Jerusalem is the political head and spiritual heart of Israel. The city has been central to Jewish life for over 3,000 years.

Jerusalem validly became part of sovereign Israel in 1948, when Israel declared independence pursuant to the San Remo Resolution and the BMP. In 1949, Israel exercised its sovereign discretion to name Jerusalem its capital.

When Israel captured East Jerusalem in the 1967 war, it finally possessed the portion of its capital that Jordan had illegally invaded and occupied for 19 years. Israel then implemented its sovereign authority to reunify the eastern and western sides of the city. Although various UN resolutions tried to characterize Israel's control of East Jerusalem as an occupation, those non-binding political statements failed to diminish Israel's binding legal right to the land.

Israel has protected the Holy Places for all three of the monotheistic religions. Its agreement to maintain the status quo at the Haram/Temple Mount pays special deference to Islam.

East Jerusalem is best left in Israel's hands to preserve the Holy Places for all faiths.

Nothing in the Oslo Accords prevents Israelis from living in East Jerusalem and developing those neighborhoods pending the final status talks. The US merely stated the obvious by recognizing Jerusalem as Israel's capital.

i. Jerusalem is uniquely important to Israel

The importance of Jerusalem to the Jewish people was well-described in a 1995 article published in the Palestine-Israel Journal.[779] The following summarizes the article.

Of all the ethnic groups with a history in Jerusalem, the Jews have planted the longest and deepest roots. It was the "historical connexion of the Jewish people with Palestine" that supplied the San Remo Resolution and the BMP with "the grounds for reconstituting their national home in that country."[780]

The first Israelites lived in the vicinity of Jerusalem in the 13th Century B.C.E. That was about 1,900 years before the region was invaded by Arabs. Jerusalem became the political, spiritual, and cultural capital of the Kingdom of Israel on or about 1006 B.C.E. No other group has ever established a state in that portion of the Levant or made Jerusalem its capital. Since ancient times, Jews have lived in Jerusalem almost continuously, and their compatriots in the Jewish Diaspora have persistently returned to that home base, despite persecution and expulsion by foreign invaders. The majority population of Jerusalem was Jewish in antiquity, again in medieval times, yet again in the 19th Century, and ever since.

The Bible situates Jerusalem as the fulcrum of Judaism. In fact, the holy book references the city 669 times by the name "Jerusalem" and another

---

[779] Raphael Jospe, *The Significance of Jerusalem: A Jewish Perspective*, PALESTINE-ISRAEL JOURNAL, Vol. 2, No. 2 (1995), http://www.pij.org/details.php?id=647.

[780] *San Remo Resolution*, pmbl.; BMP, pmbl.

150 times by the name "Zion" (the root word of Zionism). The city is not named at all in the Koran.

According to the Bible, Jerusalem is where Abraham nearly sacrificed his son Isaac to prove his faith. At the site of that seminal event, the Jews built the First and Second Jewish Temples. Hence the Temple Mount is the holiest place in Judaism. The co-located Haram al-Sharif is the third holiest site in Islam after Mecca and Medina.

The only remaining structural remnant of the Second Temple is the Western Wall (also known as the "Wailing Wall"). Jews worldwide make pilgrimages to the Wall to pray, conduct Jewish ceremonies, and insert paper messages to God in the gaps between the hewn blocks of Jerusalem stone. The ancient monument symbolizes the survival of the Jewish people.

Jews worldwide build synagogues facing Jerusalem and pray facing the city. Muslim worshipers face Mecca. The climax of the Jewish prayer service is a period of silence in which Jews pray for, among other things, the coming of the messiah to Jerusalem. In the Jewish wedding ceremony, the groom crushes a glass under foot to remember Jerusalem and then recites the Israelite King David's psalm, "If I forget thee, O Jerusalem, let my right hand lose its cunning..." Jews observe the 9th day of the Hebrew month of Av as a day of fasting and mourning for the loss of the First and Second Temples in Jerusalem. On two major Jewish holidays, Yom Kippur (the "Day of Atonement") and Passover, worshipers recite the hopeful words, "Next year in Jerusalem."

The Israeli national anthem is an ode to Jerusalem. All of Israel's major governmental institutions are located there. Archeological digs in the city have broadened the nation's understanding of its ancient past. On

Jerusalem Day, Israel celebrates the reunification of the city after the 1967 war.

ii. Israel validly assumed sovereignty over Jerusalem

The legally binding San Remo Resolution and the binding BMP dedicated Mandatory Palestine, including all of Jerusalem and the rest of the Territories, for the Jewish National Home.[781] In 1948, that Jewish state-in-waiting ripened into the sovereign State of Israel. Because the Arab-initiated 1947-1948 war prevented Israel from taking sovereign possession of the Territories, the sovereign right to those quarters remained in abeyance.[782]

Israel then exercised its sovereign right in 1949 to declare Jerusalem its capital – just as every other state freely chooses its capital – and erected its primary governmental institutions in that city.[783] Up until that point, no people other than the Jews had ever made Jerusalem their capital.[784]

Israel was finally able to gain possession of the eastern flank of Jerusalem in the 1967 war. The act was an exercise of sovereign

---

[781] Dore Gold, *Defending Israel's Legal Rights to Jerusalem*, p. 101, JCPA (June 1, 2011) [hereinafter Gold], http://jcpa.org/article/israels-rights-to-jerusalem/. Ambassador Gold is President of the Jerusalem Center for Public Affairs. He served as advisor to two Israeli Prime Ministers, Israel's ambassador to the UN, and Director General of Israel's Ministry of Foreign Affairs.

[782] *Attorney General's Memo, supra* at para. 29.

[783] *See* Israel Ministry of Foreign Affairs, *What is the status of Jerusalem?* [hereinafter MFA Status of Jerusalem], https://mfa.gov.il/MFA/ForeignPolicy/FAQ/Pages/Israel-%20the%20Conflict%20and%20Peace-%20Answers%20to%20Frequen.aspx#jerusalem.

[784] *Id.*

prerogative and self-defense, not an "occupation."[785] By the same token, when the Jewish state subsequently reunified its capital city and extended its civil law to the city's entire acreage, there was no need to declare an "annexation" because the legal action merely implemented a pre-existing sovereign right. The 1980 legislation that codified the status of Jerusalem in Israel's basic law solidified the city's prominence as the nation's eternal, undivided capital.

The US and Guatemala recognize Jerusalem as Israel's capital and maintain embassies in the city.[786] Honduras, the Republic of Nauru, and the Republic of Vanuatu also recognize Jerusalem as Israel's capital, though they have not moved their embassies to the city.[787] Russia, Australia and the Czech Republic recognize West Jerusalem as Israel's capital but have not moved their embassies there.[788]

Jerusalem never became a *corpus separatum* as proposed by the UN Partition Plan because neither the Security Council nor Great Britain ever authorized the Plan. The UN abandoned the Plan when it declined to defend Jerusalem from capture in the 1947-1948 war. Then the world body dropped the subject from its Arab-Israeli deliberations.[789] The

---

[785] *See The Attorney General's Memo, supra* at paras. 29 and 30.

[786] *Nauru, Honduras recognize Jerusalem as Israel's capital*, JERUSALEM POST (Aug. 30, 2019), https://www.jpost.com/breaking-news/israel-republic-of-nauru-recognizes-jerusalem-as-israels-capital-600071.

[787] *Id.*

[788] *Id.*

[789] STONE, *supra* at 117.

Arabs denounced the Plan and then effectively aborted it by launching the 1947-1948 war.[790]

Jordan never acquired rights to East Jerusalem because it captured those neighborhoods in an illegal offensive war.[791] It follows that Jordan had no sovereignty to transfer to another party like the Palestinians.[792]

The Palestinians have never publicly explained how their supposed State of Palestine acquired a sovereign right to East Jerusalem.[793] They cannot logically claim sovereignty over Jerusalem and still call the city a *corpus separatum* where no state is sovereign.[794] While they have installed governmental institutions in Ramallah and Gaza they have never done so in Jerusalem. Countries that recognize Palestine maintain their embassies in Ramallah.[795]

---

[790] Michel Gurfinkiel, *The Mirage of an International Jerusalem*, MOSAIC (July 8, 2019) [hereinafter Gurfinkiel], https://mosaicmagazine.com/essay/israel-zionism/2019/07/the-mirage-of-an-international-jerusalem/.

[791] STONE, *supra* at 116-120.

[792] *See Id.*

[793] Avi Bell, *Is 'East Jerusalem' Palestinian Territory?*, THE TIMES OF ISRAEL, The Blogs (Dec. 18, 2016), https://blogs.timesofisrael.com/is-east-jerusalem-palestinian-territory/.

[794] *Id.*

[795] Noga Tarnopolsky, *U.S. declaration of Jerusalem as Israel's capital has sparked worldwide anger. But there's been plenty of precedent*, L.A. TIMES (Jan. 2, 2018), http://www.latimes.com/world/middleeast/la-fg-israel-jerusalem-status-20180102-htmlstory.html.

iii. **The reunification of Jerusalem was unaffected by subsequent UN resolutions**

The reunification of Jerusalem was a domestic act not subject to foreign challenge.

UN attempts to impose occupation law obligations on Israel in East Jerusalem were mere non-binding resolutions, which were subordinate to the binding San Remo Resolution and BMP.[796] The non-binding statements opposing Jewish habitation in East Jerusalem were specifically preempted by BMP Article 6. That provision required "close settlement [i.e. dense population] by Jews on the land."[797] The UN assertions were also nullified by BMP Article 15, which instructed that "no discrimination of any kind shall be made between the inhabitants of Palestine based on the ground of race, religion, or language."[798] Later non-binding resolutions attempting to reserve East Jerusalem for a new State of Palestine were overridden by force of BMP Article 5: "[N]o Palestine [sic] territory shall be ceded or leased to, or in any way placed under the control of, the government of any foreign power" (i.e. foreign to the state that became Israel).[799]

Far from creating an IHL violation, Israel's reunification of Jerusalem corrected the past IHL violations of Jordan. Jordan had illegally invaded East Jerusalem in the 1947-1948 war. It destroyed the local Jewish

---

[796] *See* Gold, *supra*, p. 102.

[797] BMP, art. 6.

[798] BMP, art. 15.

[799] BMP, art. 5.

community, killed many of its inhabitants, expelled 2,000 more,[800] and dynamited its historic synagogues. Then it unlawfully annexed the area.

Israel's permanent residency law is not a scheme to banish Jerusalemite Palestinians, as their sympathizers contend. Permanent residency is a privilege, not a right. When residents abuse the privilege, especially when they threaten Israel's national security, their permits are validly revoked. Between 1967 and 2017, as the number of Palestinian residents of East Jerusalem grew from 70,000 to 300,000, fewer than 15,000 permits were revoked.[801] From 1967 to 2015, 24,000 of the permanent residents became citizens.[802] Moreover, the rate of conversion from permanent residency to citizenship has risen, indicating a welcome trend of demographic integration.[803]

Almost half the Palestinians of East Jerusalem enjoy a lower-middle class or higher standard of living.[804] Their material lives are much better than those of Palestinians in the West Bank and Gaza.[805] Even more heartening for the city's future, a 2011 opinion poll revealed that more Jerusalemite Palestinians would rather be citizens of Israel than citizens

---

[800] Gurfinkiel, *supra.*

[801] *See* Maha Hilal, *Revoking citizenship: Israel's new repressive tool,* AL-JAZEERA, (Aug. 14, 2017), http://www.aljazeera.com/indepth/opinion/2017/08/revoking-citizenship-israel-repressive-tool-170813160204870.html.

[802] Maayan Lubell, *Breaking taboo, Jerusalem Palestinians seek Israeli citizenship,* REUTERS (Aug. 3, 2015), http://www.reuters.com/article/us-israel-palestinians-jerusalem-insight/breaking-taboo-jerusalem-palestinians-seek-israeli-citizenship-idUSKCN0Q81HP20150803.

[803] *See Id.*

[804] David Pollock, *What Do the Arabs of East Jerusalem Really Want?* Vol. 11, No.14 JCPA (Sept 7, 2011), http://jcpa.org/article/what-do-the-arabs-of-east-jerusalem-really-want/.

[805] *Id.*

of a new Palestinian state.[806] The poll also found that 40 percent of these Palestinians would probably or definitely rather live in Israel than in a State of Palestine.[807] These respondents preferred Israel because of its higher living standards and basic freedoms.[808]

In 2015, Israel approved a multi-billion dollar "economic peace" initiative to improve living conditions for the country's Arabs.[809] The effort dispelled accusations that Israel oppressed its Arab population.

Both of the dominant populations of East Jerusalem – Palestinians and ultra-Orthodox Jews – experience high poverty rates for similar reasons. The first reason involves education. The Palestinians take pride in managing their own schools with their own curriculum, but the academic standards are low.[810] The ultra-Orthodox Jews likewise run their own schools, where the curriculum is religious, not secular.[811] Employment choices also correlate to poverty. Palestinians discourage women from working. Haredi wives work while their unemployed

---

[806] *Id.*

[807] *Id.*

[808] *Id.*

[809] *State okays $4 billion upgrade plan for Arab communities*, TIMES OF ISRAEL, December 30, 2015, available at: https://www.timesofisrael.com/government-okays-nis-15b-upgrade-plan-for-arab-communities/.

[810] *Israel's Education Ministry to Pay East Jerusalem Schools to 'Israelize' Curriculum*, HAARETZ, January 29, 2016, available at: http://www.haaretz.com/israel-news/.premium-1.700219.

[811] 10,000 Students Attending Unregulated Haredi Schools in Jerusalem, HAARETZ, September 14, 2015, available at: http://www.haaretz.com/israel-news/.premium-1.675855.

husbands study Torah. The third commonality: both Palestinians and ultra-Orthodox Jews have large families.[812]

iv. Israel exceeds its obligation to protect the Holy Places

After the 1967 war, Israel allowed free access and worship for people of all faiths visiting the Holy Places of the Old City.[813] The government could have reserved the Haram/Temple Mount compound exclusively for Jewish and Christian worship. However, the authorities did the opposite. They let the Waqf Islamic Trust continue managing religious affairs at the site, even though the decision gave the Jordanian agency control over the holiest site in Judaism.[814]

Consistent with the Haram/Temple Mount status quo policy, Israel prohibits Christians and Jews from praying there. The policy persists even though most Israeli Jews oppose the no-prayer restriction.[815] Some complain the ban violates international standards that ensure freedom of religion. Only one ultra-orthodox contingent, representing roughly 10% of Israelis, supports the 'no-prayer' rule.[816] They believe entering

---

[812] *Lydia Saad, Attitudes towards Family Size among Palestinians and Israelis,* Gallop News Service (March 17, 2006), http://news.gallup.com/poll/21940/attitudes-toward-family-size-among-palestinians-israelis.aspx.

[813] SACHAR, *supra* at 1037.

[814] Nadav Shragai, *The 'Al-Aksa is in Danger' Libel,* pp. 14-17, JCPA (2012) [hereinafter Shragai], available at http://jcpa.org/text/downloads/the-al-aksa-is-in-danger-libel-the-history-of-a-lie.pdf.

[815] Crisis Group, *supra,* pp. 13-15.

[816] *Id.,* pp. 14-15.

the site is religiously prohibited until the end of days, a time when they believe the Third Temple will descend from heaven.[817]

Israel's extreme deference to Islam at the Haram/Temple Mount is ignored by Palestinians. They violate the status quo policy by exploiting the Holy Place to stage anti-Israel riots. Since the 1930's, Palestinian clergymen have repeatedly circulated rumors that Jews are about to commandeer or otherwise desecrate the Al-Aqsa Mosque, goading Palestinian followers to respond with anti-Semitic violence.[818] A gang of young East Jerusalem males known as the Shabab A-Aqsa (Al Aqsa Youth) use the Mosque as a cover for their attacks on Israeli police and Jewish worshipers.[819] They stock the Holy Place with make-shift weapons such as rocks, cinder blocks, iron rods, building materials, and fireworks fashioned for lethality.[820] Then, at designated times, they unleash the ammunition in surprise attacks on their perceived enemies. The "Al Aqsa is in danger" libel was the catalyst for the 2015-2016 wave of terrorism called the "Knife Intifada," in which Palestinian youths murdered Jews nationwide.[821]

Just as the Al Aqsa libel incites Palestinian violence, Palestinian violence revives the libel. In July of 2017, a group of Arab Israelis smuggled machine guns into the Temple Mount/Haram and used them to kill two

---

[817] *Id.*

[818] Shragai, *supra*, pp. 19-31, 60-78.

[819] Crisis Group, *supra*, pp. 2, 6-7 and 17.

[820] Shragai, *supra*, p. 76.

[821] Jeffrey Goldberg, *The Paranoid, Supremacist Roots of the Stabbing Intifada*, THE ATLANTIC, (October 16, 2015), https://www.theatlantic.com/international/archive/2015/10/the-roots-of-the-palestinian-uprising-against-israel/410944/.

Israeli police officers. Israel then exercised its status quo security authority to prevent further shootings by installing metal detectors at the Lions Gate entrance to the site.[822] The PA's ruling Fatah party reacted with outrage, as if the safety measure were an assertion of Israeli sovereignty over the Al Aqsa Mosque. The leaders encouraged more violence by calling for a "day of rage," an incitement that caused Palestinian riots and more terrorist murders.[823] The threat of another Intifada forced Israel to remove the security devices.

For the status quo policy at the Temple Mount/Haram to survive, Israel must retain the right to control access and maintain security at the site. One sensible form of access control is to limit admission by age when Palestinian youths wreak havoc at the site.[824] A common security tool to deter gun smuggling is a metal detector. Such technology is not an emblem of sovereignty.

v. The Holy Places should remain under Israeli control

The only reliable way to protect the Holy Places for all believers is to keep the sites under Israeli control.[825] Israel's 1948 Proclamation of Independence promised to "safeguard the Holy Places of all

---

[822] *Watch: Jerusalem Attackers Smuggle Weapons into Holy Site Before Deadly Ambush*, NEWSWEEK (July 20, 2017), http://www.newsweek.com/watch-jerusalem-attackers-smuggle-weapons-holy-site-deadly-ambush-639806.

[823] *The Latest: UN chief urges no provocative action, restraint*, SAN FRANCISCO CHRONICLE (July 26, 2017), http://www.sfchronicle.com/news/crime/article/The-Latest-Israel-tells-Turkey-its-criticism-is-11437132.php.

[824] Shragai, *supra, p. 76.*

[825] Gold, *supra* at 113.

religions."[826] In 1967, Israel legislated the policy with its Protection of the Holy Places Law. It has upheld the law ever since.

By contrast, the Jordanians in Jerusalem who became Palestinians have treated the Jewish holy sites with contempt. In the 1947-1948 war, when the Jordanians invaded East Jerusalem, they killed local Jews and expelled the rest of the local Jewish population.[827] The attackers destroyed 58 historic synagogues.[828] In the ancient Mount of Olives cemetery, where Jewish prophets and other legendary religious leaders were buried, they smashed thousands of tombstones and used much of the stonework as building material or paving stones for latrines.[829] Graves were demolished to make room for a highway.[830] And the Western Wall was reduced to a slum.[831] During its 19-year occupation of East Jerusalem, Jordan barred Jews from entering that side of the city or even visiting its Jewish Holy Places.

Jordan's policy of religious exclusion at the Haram/Temple Mount paid homage to the original purpose of the Haram. The 7th Century shrine was built atop the Jewish temples as a message to Jews and Christians that their faiths had been replaced by Islam.[832] To emphasize the point,

---

[826] Proclamation of Independence, para. 12.

[827] Jerusalem: 1948-1967: Jordanian occupation of Eastern Jerusalem, The Six-Day War, Committee for Accuracy in Middle East Reporting in America (2007), http://www.sixdaywar.org/content/jordanianocuupationjerusalem.asp.

[828] *Id.*

[829] *Id.*

[830] *Id.*

[831] *Id.*

[832] BERNARD LEWIS, *THE CRISIS OF ISLAM* 43-44 (2004) [hereinafter LEWIS].

an inscription on the Dome of the Rock faulted Christians for their belief in Jesus Christ.[833]

Rather than protect the Jewish inhabitants of East Jerusalem in accordance with occupation law, Jordan victimized that population. The religious discrimination specifically violated Article VIII (2) of the Israel-Jordan Armistice Agreement, which had promised "free access to the Holy Places" and "use of the cemetery on the Mount of Olives."[834]

After Jordan relinquished its claim to the Territories in 1988, the Palestinians continued to desecrate the sacred sites of non-Muslims. In 2000, Palestinian rioters ransacked and torched Joseph's Tomb, a site in the West Bank town of Nablus that is holy to Christians and Jews. They burned the Tomb again in 2015.[835] In January of 2016 at the Cave of the Patriarchs, a site in the West Bank town of Hebron that is holy to both Muslims and Jews, a stabbing incident left one Israeli dead and a sniper attack wounded a teenage female Israeli soldier.[836] Palestinian militants in 2002 burst into the Church of the Nativity in Bethlehem and held the clergy hostage for 39 days.[837]

---

[833] *Id.*

[834] Israel-Jordan Armistice Agreement, Art. VIII(2).

[835] *Joseph's Tomb site set ablaze amid wave of Israeli-Palestinian violence*, CNN.com, Friday, October 16, 2015, available at: http://www.cnn.com/2015/10/16/middleeast/israel-palestinian-tensions/.

[836] *IDF Soldier Wounded in Suspected Sniper Attack near Hebron*, January 3, 2016, available at: http://www.jpost.com/Arab-Israeli-Conflict/Initial-report-Israeli-woman-wounded-in-suspected-shooting-attack-near-Hebron-439232.

[837] Gold, *supra* at 111.

vi. **Israel complies with the Oslo vision for Jerusalem**

The Oslo Accords slated the issue of Jerusalem for the final status negotiation. When Israel agreed to that provision, its intent was to negotiate religious rights among Jerusalem's Holy Places, not to re-divide the city.[838] The Accords did not even mention East Jerusalem.[839] Rather, the agreement left that portion of the city under Israel's unfettered control.[840]

The negotiation over Jerusalem should not be viewed as an existential struggle for Palestinians. Throughout the centuries of Muslim dominance in Jerusalem, Muslims did not consider Jerusalem politically significant.[841] During the age of Muslim rule, the Temple Mount/Haram never inspired Muslims to call Jerusalem a holy city.[842] Jerusalem did not become politically or spiritually important to Muslims until the 20th Century, when the Mufti revised Islamic doctrine to compete with Jewish claims to the city.[843] Until then, no Arab rulers other than Jordan's kings visited Jerusalem. And after 1948, when Jordan captured East Jerusalem, the Kingdom kept its capital in Amman.[844] The PLO

---

[838] Gold, *supra*, p. 103.

[839] SMITH, *supra* at 439.

[840] Allegra Pacheco, *Flouting Convention: The Oslo Agreements*, in THE NEW INTIFADA, RESISTING ISRAEL'S APARTHEID 186, 189 (2001).

[841] *See* LEWIS, *supra* at 50. *See also* Shragai, *supra* at 31-33.

[842] Morton A. Klein and Daniel Mandel, *Op-Ed: End the Propaganda Myth that Jerusalem is Holy to Muslims*, ZOA in the News, Zionist Organization of America, ZOA.org (May 25, 2017), http://zoa.org/2017/05/10364082-end-the-propaganda-myth-that-jerusalem-is-holy-to-muslims/.

[843] *Id.*

[844] *Id.*

Charters of 1964 and 1968 did not even mention Jerusalem, let alone name it as a desired capital.

4.5: May Israel keep settlements in the Territories?

Author's Prologue

After the 1967 Six-Day War Israel prepared to negotiate land-for-peace treaties with its Arab neighbors. But the Arab states issued their Khartoum Resolution with its Three No's: no peace; no recognition; no negotiation. Arabs continued to regard Israel as an illegal entity that had expelled Arabs from Palestine and stolen their land, injustices that Arabs believed should be remedied by force.

To guard against future attacks, Israel fortified the Territories with IDF bases and cordoned off military zones. Meanwhile, Israeli civilians began relocating to the captured lands. Some returned to the same neighborhoods from which Jews had been expelled in the 1947-1948 war.[845] The military positioning and civilian relocation left Palestinians demoralized. After fighting to remove Israel from its 1948-limited subset of western Palestine, the defeated Arabs watched helplessly as the enemy implanted military bases and communities throughout western Palestine. Even more discouraging for Palestinians, Israel reunified East and West Jerusalem by applying its domestic law to both sides of the city.

---

[845] *See, e.g.* SACHAR, *supra* at 674 (describing the return of Jews to the West Bank town of Kfar Etzion, where their parents had been killed in the 1948 War).

In subsequent decades, the Israeli population of the Territories grew to the hundreds of thousands. Some of the growth came from Israeli relocation, some from childbirth within the relocated community, and the rest from immigration. Israel not only permitted this demographic evolution but encouraged it through housing subsidies and tax abatements.

In the Oslo Accords of the 1990's, the adversaries agreed to split the Territories temporarily into sectors, with each party controlling its assigned area pending completion of the final status negotiation. They relegated the issue of "settlements" to the final status talks.

In 2005, Israel voluntarily withdrew all troops and nearly 9,000 civilians from Gaza. The decision rendered the settlement issue moot for purposes of that enclave. But in East Jerusalem and the West Bank, Israeli homes, businesses, roads, and other infrastructure continued to proliferate.

The larger settlements are authorized under Israeli property law. They are congregated mainly in East Jerusalem and three West Bank Area C domains: the "major settlement blocs" on the west side, where the West Bank abuts Jerusalem; the towns in the Jordan Valley on the east side, which borders Jordan; and the high-elevation communities dotting the "Mountain Strip" in between.

In addition, about 110 Israeli "outposts" are scattered throughout Israeli-controlled Area C of the West Bank.[846] An outpost is typically a small cluster of mobile homes and flimsy structures thrown together without Israeli authority. Normally, any construction in West Bank Area C would require the issuance of a building permit by Israel's Civil Administration, the division of the IDF responsible for civilian planning and development. Israeli citizens began building the unapproved encampments in 1996, when the Civil Administration throttled down its permitting process. Since then, Israel has enforced its property law unevenly, removing some of the outposts but leaving others intact.

Defining the geographic dimensions of an Israeli settlement is a subjective exercise. At a minimum, most agree that a settlement includes "built-up areas," which contain settler housing or other buildings. Casting a wider net, a settlement may be said to include the farms, fields, or orchards that surround a built-up area. This broader concept of settlement is defined by its municipal boundaries. Alternatively, one may count the roads that connect the municipalities, as well as the land between them, to identify an even larger sphere of control that could be called a settlement.

As of 2010, an estimated 0.99 percent of East Jerusalem and West Bank settlements consisted of built-up areas, 9.28 percent fell within municipal boundaries, and 42.8 percent remained under Israeli

---

[846] *Statistics on Settlements and Settler Population* (Jan. 16, 2019), B'TSELEM [hereinafter B'Tselem *Statistics* on *Settlements*], https://www.btselem.org/settlements/statistics. B'Tselem is a human rights nongovernmental organization ("NGO") that advocates for Palestinian rights in the Territories and specializes in the study of settlements in those areas.

control.[847] All these lands fell within the 60 percent of the West Bank provisionally allocated to Israel under the Oslo Accords. Since then, the settlements have grown significantly in population but not in geographic extent.

Population estimates for Israel and the vicinity are fiercely debated.[848] Generally speaking, about 400,000 Israelis live in the West Bank and 200,000 in East Jerusalem.[849] By comparison, nearly three million Palestinians live in the West Bank and over 300,000 in East Jerusalem.[850] Over 90% of West Bank Palestinians dwell in Area A under PA rule. Another 180,000 to 300,000 live in the Israeli-controlled West Bank Area C.[851]

As Israelis build housing and infrastructure in East Jerusalem and West Bank Area C, the developments increasingly defy Palestinian aspirations for statehood on the same ground. Palestinians respond with occupation law challenges before Israel's courts and world bodies. In addition, they wage acts of terrorism against Israelis in both the Territories and Israel proper. Certain Israeli settlers engage in anti-

---

[847] *By Hook and By Crook, Israeli Settlement Policy in the West Bank*, B'TSELEM (July, 2010), p. 11, https://www.btselem.org/download/201007_by_hook_and_by_crook_eng.pdf.

[848] Yotam Berger & Jack Khoury, *How Many Palestinians Live in Gaza and the West Bank? It's Complicated*, HAARETZ (March 28, 2018), https://www.haaretz.com/israel-news/how-many-palestinians-live-in-gaza-and-the-west-bank-it-s-complicated-1.5956630.

[849] *Id.*

[850] *Id.*

[851] *Planning Policy in the West Bank, Area C* (Feb. 6, 2019), B'TSELEM, https://www.btselem.org/topic/area_c.

Palestinian violence, mostly through vandalism of structures and arson attacks on cropland.

Israel claimed it built the Barrier to defend its citizens from attack. But the construction immediately drew Palestinian accusations of de facto annexation. To Palestinians, the winding path of walls and fences also effects a widespread scheme of harassment that frustrates their travel, commerce, and social life.

Israel's Civil Administration rarely grants permits for Palestinian construction of homes or other buildings in West Bank Area C.[852] The reason, according to Israel, is because few Palestinians apply for the permits. Palestinians say the application process is usually futile because Israel opposes the expansion of Palestinian communities in Area C. Based on this premise, Palestinians often build in Area C without approval.[853] A Civil Administration "stop order" to halt the unapproved project can spawn protracted litigation before Israel's courts. If a court declares the construction illegal, it may order the demolition of the unauthorized structure.[854]

If Israel is subject to occupation law, which is embodied in The Hague Regulations and the Fourth Convention, it owes significant obligations to Palestinians in the Territories. The adversaries' debate whether

---

[852] Tovah Lazaroff, *Report: Cabinet Approved Permits for 700 Palestinian Homes in Area C,* JERUSALEM POST (July 30, 2019), https://www.jpost.com/Middle-East/Report-Cabinet-approved-permits-for-700-Palestinian-homes-in-Area-C-597187.

[853] *See Id.*

[854] *See* Id.

occupation law applies to the conflict, when any occupation may have begun, and whether it has since ended.

The ICRC advises that in an armed conflict, an occupation begins when an invading power acquires "effective control" over the subject territory and ends when such control is surrendered or lost. [855] According to this "Effective Control Test," a power achieves effective control when it meets the following conditions:

1. The armed forces of a State are physically present in a foreign territory without the consent of the effective local government in place at the time of the invasion;
2. The effective local government in place at the time of the invasion has been, or can be rendered, substantially or completely, incapable of exerting its powers by virtue of the foreign forces' unconsented presence; and

---

[855] *Report, International humanitarian law and the challenges of contemporary armed conflicts,* 32nd International Conference of the Red Cross and Red Crescent, Geneva, Switzerland, 8-10 December, 2015, ICRC, pp. 11-12 (October 31, 2015), [hereinafter ICRC *2015 Report*], https://www.icrc.org/en/document/international-humanitarian-law-and-challenges-contemporary-armed-conflicts. The Effective Control Test was derived from three legal sources: Hague Regulation, art. 42; Fourth Convention, art. 6; and *United States v. List (Hostages Case),* U.N. War Crimes Commission, Law Reports of Trials of War Criminals, Vol. 6-10, at 55-56 (William S. Hein 1997) (1948). *See also* Elizabeth Samson, *Is Gaza Occupied?: Redefining the Status of Gaza under International* Law, 25 Am. U. Int'l L. Rev. 915, 925-26 (2010) [hereinafter Samson].

3. The foreign forces are in a position to exercise authority instead of the local government over the concerned territory (or parts thereof).[856]

Article 42 of the Hague Regulations adds that when an occupation has begun, it extends "only to the territory where such authority has been established and can be exercised."[857]

Hague Article 43 summarizes the duties of the occupying power. The law states:

> The authority of the legitimate power having, in fact, passed into the hands of the occupant, the latter shall take all the measures in his power to restore and ensure, as far as possible, public order and safety, while respecting, unless absolutely prevented, the laws in force in the country.[858]

Under this standard, the military commander of the occupation must balance three interests: its own interests of military necessity as authorized by Fourth Convention Article 64; the goals of the ousted sovereign government; and the needs the local population.[859] Military necessity includes the needs of IHL, security, orderly government, and the effective administration of justice.[860]

---

[856] *Id.*

[857] Hague Regulations, art. 42.

[858] Hague Regulations, art. 43.

[859] *See* BENVENISTI, *supra* at 69-72.

[860] DINSTEIN, *OCCUPATION, supra* at 110-11.

Against this legal backdrop, the question becomes: Under what legal conditions, if any, may Israel build settlements in East Jerusalem or the West Bank?

A. The Palestinian Arguments

Summary of Arguments

The Israeli settlements in East Jerusalem and West Bank Area C violate the no-change-in-status provision of the Oslo Accords. Israel has dramatically changed the status of the Territories with its urbanizing developments.

Israel's settlements are subject to occupation law. Although Israel contests this legal determination, it is the majority interpretation of the Fourth Convention. Occupation law remained the controlling law even after the signing of the Oslo Accords. The consequence is that Israel must obey a panoply of responsibilities incumbent on an occupying power.

Nearly all nations and international law authorities agree that Israel's settlements contravene the occupation law provision embodied in Fourth Convention Article 49(6), which states that an occupying power may not deport or transfer its citizens to the occupied territory. Israel transfers its citizens to the Territories by incentivizing the relocations.

Other occupation laws breached by Israel concern its use of the occupied land. The violations involve Israel's treatment of absentee land, state land, and land seizures. In the aggregate, these offenses cause special harm to Palestinians living in West Bank Area C. Yet another violation of occupation law occurs when Israel demolishes Palestinian property.

Some of the demolitions are wrongly rationalized as enforcements of Israel's construction permit laws. Others are inflicted in response to perceived acts of terrorism. The latter sanction may render a suspect's entire family homeless, thereby imposing a prohibited collective punishment. Israel's governance of the West Bank illegally discriminates against Palestinians. The double-standard handicaps the protected persons in both their civil interactions and criminal trials.

Although an occupying power is entitled to the normal use of local resources, Israel exploits the resources of the Territories for the benefit of the settlements. Settlers divert scarce water supplies for their own use. Similarly, they dominate the local mineral extraction industry. Israel's settlements pose an obstacle to peace by encumbering the land Palestinians desire for their own state. The more Israel expands the settlements, the more they stoke anti-Israel militancy.

i.   The settlements violate the Oslo Accords

Under Oslo II, Article XXXI(7), the contracting parties must not "initiate or take any step that will change the status of the [Territories] pending the outcome of the permanent status negotiations."[861] Israel undercut this no-change-of-status clause by continuing to add settlements and settlers in the Territories, leaving less land to partition in the Oslo final status negotiation.[862]

---

[861] Oslo II, art. XXXI(7).

[862] *See* State of Palestine, Palestine Liberation Organization-Negotiations Affairs Department, *The Oslo Interim Agreement* (Jan. 21, 2018), https://www.nad.ps/en/publication-resources/faqs/oslo-interim-agreement.

The settlements are designed to limit Palestinian development.[863] In particular, they block Palestinians from building the kind of large-scale infrastructure projects needed to improve Palestinian life.[864] The settlement project also separates the West Bank from East Jerusalem and creates a disconnected archipelago of Palestinian population centers.[865] As a result, the settlements frustrate the potential for a contiguous, independent Palestinian state.[866]

Israel built the Barrier primarily to confiscate Palestinian land.[867] The Barrier accomplishes three goals. It annexes over nine percent of the West Bank, separates the Palestinians of East Jerusalem from their compatriots in the West Bank, and enables Israel to seize scarce water and other resources.[868] The impact on the daily life of Palestinians is harsh. It distances Palestinian family members from each other and separates Palestinians from their farmland.[869]

Over time, the settlement problem has grown worse. In the 20-year period after the signing of Oslo I, the number of Israeli settlers

---

[863]State of Palestine, Palestine Liberation Organization, Negotiations Affairs Department, *Palestine, the Drive Toward Justice, Freedom, and Peace, Frequently Asked Questions, Israel's Illegal Colonial Settlements* [hereinafter PLO-NAD *Settlements*], p. 12, https://www.nad.ps/sites/default/files/01012019_1.pdf.

[864] *Id.*

[865] *Id.*

[866] *Id.*

[867] *Id.* at p. 20.

[868] *Id.*

[869] *Id.*

doubled.[870] It was hard enough for Israel to relocate 9,000 settlers from Gaza during the disengagement of 2005. Removing 600,000 more from the rest of the Territories may prove infeasible.[871] Israel willfully deposited these "facts on the ground," thus belying any sincere desire to complete the Oslo peace process.[872]

ii. The settlements are subject to occupation law

Israel's settlements violate multiple provisions of occupation law. At the outset, one must understand why the settlements are subject to occupation law. Article 2, paragraph 1 of the Fourth Convention applies the Convention to "all cases of declared war or... any other armed conflict which may arise between two or more of the High Contracting Parties [i.e. the Fourth Convention signatory states] ..."[873] Paragraph 2 adds: "The Convention shall also apply to all cases of partial or total occupation of the territory of a High Contracting Party, even if the said occupation meets with no armed resistance."[874] Article 2, paragraph 1 addresses cases of declared war and occupations.[875] This means the

---

[870] *Diplomatic Quartet releases report on advancing two-state solution to Israel-Palestine conflict,* UN News Centre (July 1, 2016) [hereinafter Quartet *Report*], p. 4, http://www.un.org/apps/news/story.asp?NewsID=54379#.WLIiHeQzXbJ. The "Quartet" that produced this report was the same alliance of four leading international bodies – the UN, EU, US, and Russia – that authored the Israeli-Palestinian Roadmap for Peace in 2002.

[871] Richard Klass, *Facts on the Ground: Israel and the Palestinians,* HUFFINGTON POST (March 26, 2015), http://www.huffingtonpost.com/richard-klass/facts-on-the-ground-israe_b_6949126.html.

[872] *See Id.*

[873] Fourth Convention, art. 2(1).

[874] *Id.*, art. 2(2).

[875] ICJ Barrier Opinion, paras. 94-101.

entire Fourth Convention, including its occupation law provisions, applies whenever an armed conflict leads to a capture of territory. It does not matter whether the territory happens to belong to a High Contracting Party.

Israel contends its 1967 military expansion was not governed by occupation law. First, Israel states that Fourth Convention Article 2 limits the applicability of occupation law to the territories of a High Contracting Party. It then argues Egypt and Jordan failed to meet the above condition because neither state ever held recognized sovereign title to its respectively controlled portion of the Territories.

Israel's interpretation of the Fourth Convention was rejected by the ICJ in its Barrier Opinion.[876] In that ruling, the Court explained that the entire Fourth Convention applies wherever there is an armed conflict between two parties.[877] The Court then confirmed that if an armed conflict produces a capture of territory, the Fourth Convention's occupation law provisions apply.[878] Where the language of Article 2 addressed the matter of occupations, the Court said, the purpose was not to limit the applicability of occupation law to the territory of a High Contracting party but merely to clarify that the occupation provisions would take effect even if the occupation meets with no armed resistance.[879]

---

[876] ICJ Barrier Opinion, paras. 93-101.

[877] *Id.*, para. 95.

[878] *Id.*

[879] *Id.*

For these reasons, the Court rightly declined to second-guess the legitimacy of the governments that ruled the Territories before the 1967 war.[880]

The ICJ's analysis aligns with Fourth Convention Article 4, which defines "protected persons" for purposes of an occupation.[881] Article 4 stated that:

> Persons protected by the Convention are those who, at a given moment and in any manner whatsoever, find themselves, in case of a conflict or occupation, in the hands of a Party to the conflict or Occupying Power of which they are not nationals.[882]

The 1967 war was undeniably a "conflict." And the Palestinians of the Territories found themselves in the hands of a party to the conflict – Israel – of which they were not nationals. Therefore, the Palestinians were persons protected by the Convention.

The ICJ's logic tracked the longstanding position of the ICRC[883] and the consensus of international law scholars. They say the Article 2 term

---

[880] *See Id.*, para. 101.

[881] Fourth Convention, art. 4.

[882] *Id.*

[883] *Declaration, Conference of High Contracting Parties to the Fourth Geneva Convention*, Government of Switzerland, para. 3 (Dec. 5, 2001), available at https://unispal.un.org/DPA/DPR/unispal.nsf/0/8FC4F064B9BE5BAD85256C1400722951. *See also* Peter Maurer, *Challenges to International Humanitarian Law: Israel's Occupation Policy*,

"state or High Contracting Party" should be read flexibly to include both sovereign states and de facto states.[884] The purpose of the Fourth Convention is to protect the civilian population, regardless of the sovereign status of the ousted government.[885]

The UN Security Council also agreed that Israel's control of the Territories after the 1967 war subjected it to occupation law.[886] The same view was reiterated in numerous resolutions of the Security Council and General Assembly.

The Oslo Accords did not relieve Israel of its IHL obligations as an occupying power. Israel must continue to protect the Palestinian population of the Territories in accordance with occupation law because Israel continues to maintain authority in the Territories for external

---

94 Int'l Rev. Red Cross 888, 1504-05 (Winter 2012) [hereinafter Maurer] (stating that, "Israel has exercised 'actual authority' over the West Bank and the Gaza Strip for almost half a century, making its presence in these areas one of the longest sustained military occupations in modern history." [footnote omitted]),

https://www.icrc.org/eng/resources/documents/article/review-2012/irrc-888-maurer.htm.

Ambassador Maurer is President of the ICRC. Formerly, he was Switzerland's ambassador to the United Nations and secretary of state for foreign affairs.

[884] *See, e.g.* Orna Ben-Naftali *et. al., Illegal Occupation: Framing the Occupied Palestinian Territory*, 23 BERKELEY J. INT'L LAW. 551, 567 (2005) [hereinafter Naftali].

[885] BENVENISTI, *supra* at 207.

[886] S.C. Res. 446, U.N. Doc. S/RES/446 (March 22, 1979), available at https://undocs.org/en/S/RES/446(1979).

security, border control, the Israeli settlements, and matters of joint cooperation with the PA.[887]

Under the Effective Control Test, Israel has begun an occupation in the Territories. The following applies the Effective Control Test in each of the relevant geographic zones. In the process, we will incorporate additional guidance from the ICRC. In 2015, the agency theorized that "the end of an occupation" should be identified using a standard known as the "functional approach."[888]

The functional approach is used in certain specific and exceptional cases, where foreign forces withdraw from the occupied territory but retain "key elements of authority or other important governmental functions usually performed by an occupying power."[889] In those scenarios, the occupier may still have effective control, at least to the extent of its continuing competencies.[890] In particular, a belligerent military stationed outside a foreign territory would be regarded as still having effective control if it can still "reassert its full authority inside the territory within a reasonably short period of time."[891] The functional

---

[887] *AHuman Rights Assessment of the Declaration of Principles on Interim Self-Government Arrangements for Palestinians*, Al Haq (West Bank), p. 9 (1993), https://www.alhaq.org/publications/8121.html . Al Haq is a Palestinian non-governmental organization based in the West Bank that defends human rights in the Territories. The NGO reports on violations of law and advocates in national and international fora to hold violators accountable.

[888] ICRC 2015 Report, p. 12

[889] *Id.*

[890] *Id.*

[891] *Id.*

approach is useful in an age when states use high-tech means to project power.[892]

A functional approach to the Israeli occupation reveals that Israel has met the Effective Control Test in each of the Territories and remains an occupying power in those lands.

The first of the Territories to be analyzed is Gaza. Since 2007, Israel has closed most of Gaza's crossings into Israel.[893] Few people and goods are permitted to pass through the remaining openings.[894] At Gaza's Rafah Crossing, which leads to Egypt, movement is also heavily regulated due to a security agreement between Egypt and Israel.[895]

Applying the functional approach of the Effective Control Test to Gaza, Israel has not shed its status as an occupying power for three reasons.[896] First, because Israel has accepted that Gaza, East Jerusalem and the West Bank comprise "a single territorial unit,"[897] a withdrawal from only the Gazan slice of that unit must be considered a mere partial pull-out.[898] Second, Israel has not relinquished core ingredients of effective control over Gaza. It still regulates Gaza's land, sea and air perimeters, as noted above.[899] Finally, Israel represents that it may conduct IDF operations in

---

[892] *Id.*

[893] *Id.*, pp. 14-17.

[894] *Id.*

[895] *Id.*

[896] DINSTEIN *OCCUPATION, supra* at 274-79.

[897] Oslo II, art. XI(1).

[898] DINSTEIN *OCCUPATION, supra* at 277.

[899] *Id.* at 278.

Gaza whenever necessary for national security.[900] As a result, the only elements of Gazan control for which Israel may disclaim responsibility are those assigned to the Palestinians under the Oslo Accords.[901]

In East Jerusalem, the functional analysis is more straightforward. Israel seized control of East Jerusalem in the 1967 war. It then merged the eastern and western halves of the city and applied its domestic law citywide. When Israel and the PLO negotiated the Oslo Accords, they agreed to prohibit the PA from operating in East Jerusalem.[902] Israel therefore controls East Jerusalem exclusively. City planners have exploited this control to increase the Jewish population, reduce the Palestinian presence, and isolate East Jerusalem from the West Bank.[903]

Israel also exercises effective control over the West Bank. In West Bank Areas A and B the Oslo Accords divide the functions of government into three categories.[904] Municipal affairs (e.g. taxation, internal security,

---

[900] *Id.* at 279.

[901] *Id.* at 279-80.

[902] Oslo II, art. XVII(1).

[903] *East Jerusalem*, B'TSELEM (April 3, 2017), http://www.btselem.org/jerusalem. B'Tselem is The Israeli Information Center for Human Rights in the Occupied Territories, an Israeli human rights organization dedicated to protecting the rights of Palestinians in the Territories. Funded by foundations in Europe and North America, as well as private individuals, the NGO distributes educational materials to policymakers, as well as the Israeli public, documenting Israeli violations of international law in the Territories. Its goal is to create a human rights culture in Israel.

[904] Omar Dajani, *No Security Without Law: Prospects for Implementing a Rights-Based Approach in Palestinian– Israeli Security Negotiations*, pp. 65-69, in INTERNATIONAL LAW AND THE ISRAELI-PALESTINIAN CONFLICT: A RIGHTS-BASED APPROACH TO MIDDLE EAST PEACE 192 (Susan Akram, Michael Dumper, Michael Lynk, and Iain Scobbie eds., 2011).

housing, health, education) are run by the PA.[905] Civic responsibilities implicating the Israeli government (e.g. infrastructure issues such as electric and water supply) require coordination between the PA and Israel.[906] In Area B, Israel retains the additional power of external security.[907] Israel's involvement in the coordinated functions and external security gives it effective control over both areas.[908] In West Bank Area C, representing 60% of the West Bank, Israeli control includes all security responsibilities, land allocation, zoning, housing, other construction, infrastructure development, and most civic matters.[909] The PA handles only education and medical services for the Area's approximately 200,000 Palestinian residents.[910]

iii. The settlements violate the occupation law ban on population transfers

Having established that all the Territories are subject to occupation law, we may examine Israel's occupation law violations. Chief among the offenses is the violation of Article 49(6) of the Fourth Convention.[911] Article 49(6) states that an occupying power may not "deport or transfer parts of its civilian population into the territory it occupies."[912] The Israeli settlements flout this prohibition. Indeed, the settlements have

---

[905] *Id.*

[906] *Id.*

[907] *Id.*

[908] *Id.*

[909] *Area C*, B'TSELEM (May 18, 2014), https://www.btselem.org/topic/area_c.

[910] *Id.*

[911] Fourth Convention, art. 49(6).

[912] *Id.*

been declared illegal by UN Security Council Resolutions 446,[913] 465,[914] 452,[915] and 2334.[916] Condemning Israel in the strongest terms, the Council's most recent anti-settlement vote reaffirmed that:

> the establishment by Israel of settlements in the Palestinian territory occupied since 1967, including East Jerusalem, has no legal validity and constitutes a flagrant violation under international law ...[917]

Similar condemnations of the Israeli settlements have been issued by the UN General Assembly.[918] Joining the anti-settlement chorus are the ICRC,[919] the ICJ,[920] the UN Human Rights Council,[921] Human Rights

---

[913] S.C. Res. 446, U.N. Doc. S/RES/446 (March 22, 1979) (the US abstained), https://unispal.un.org/DPA/DPR/unispal.nsf/0/BA123CDED3EA84A5852560E50077C2DC.

[914] S.C. Res. 465, U.N. Doc. S/RES/465 (March 1, 1980) (the US mistakenly voted in favor and then clarified that it meant to abstain), https://undocs.org/en/S/RES/465(1980).

[915] S.C. Res. 452, U.N. Doc. S/RES/452 (July 20, 1979) (the US abstained), http://avalon.law.yale.edu/20th_century/un452.asp.

[916] S.C. Res. 2334, U.N. Doc. S/RES/2334 (Dec. 23, 2016) (the US abstained) [hereinafter Resolution 2334], http://www.un.org/webcast/pdfs/SRES2334-2016.pdf.

[917] Resolution 2334, *supra*, paras. 1-4.

[918] *See, e.g.* G.A. Res. 3005(XXVII), U.N. Doc. A/RES/3005(XXVII) (Dec.15, 1972); G.A. Res. 65/105, U.N. Doc. A/RES/65/105. (Dec. 10, 2010).

[919] Maurer, *supra*, pp. 1503-1510 and 1507.

[920] *Legal Consequences of the Construction of a Wall in the Occupied Palestinian Territory, Advisory Opinion*, 2004 I.C.J. 131 (July 9, 2004) [hereinafter ICJ *Barrier Opinion*], para. 120.

[921] *Report of the Special Committee to Investigate Israeli Practices Affecting the Human Rights of the Palestinian People and Other Arabs of the Occupied Territories*, submitted to the U.N. General Assembly, Seventieth Session, Agenda Item 55, U.N. Doc. A/70/406 (Oct. 5, 2015), available at: http://www.un.org/ga/search/view_doc.asp?symbol=A/70/406.

Watch,[922] and Amnesty International.[923]

The US could have vetoed any of the four above-referenced UN Security Council resolutions but chose instead to abstain. In 1978, the administration of US President Carter did more than abstain. It expressly determined that the Israeli settlements were illegal. [924]

ICRC President Peter Maurer has advised that the phrase "deport or transfer" includes any type of transfer – mandatory or voluntary – that is performed with government support and imposes certain effects on the occupied territory. Applying Article 49(6) to the Israeli occupation, President Maurer said:

> [t]his provision aims to prevent the Occupying Power from modifying the social, demographic, and economic pattern of the occupied territory, against the interests of the population living there. The Israeli government's decisive and systematic support over the years to the establishment of settlements, including by taking away land, has effectively achieved just that: a profound

---

[922] *Occupation, Inc.: How Settlement Businesses Contribute to Israel's Violations of Palestinian Rights*, Human Rights Watch (January 19, 2016) [hereinafter HRW Report of 2016], https://www.hrw.org/news/2016/01/19/occupation-inc-how-settlement-businesses-contribute-israels-violations-palestinian.

[923] Amnesty International, *Israel must halt construction of West Bank settlements* (Dec. 3, 2012), https://www.amnesty.org/en/latest/news/2012/12/israel-must-halt-construction-west-bank-settlements/.

[924] *Letter of the State Department Legal Advisor, Mr. Herbert J. Hansell, Concerning the Legality of Israeli Settlements in the Occupied Territories of April 21, 1978*, https://www.hlrn.org/img/documents/USSDLegalAdvisorHansell_ltr.pdf.

alteration of the economic and social landscape of the West Bank ...[925]

Since 1967 the Israeli government has transferred parts of its civilian population to the Territories by underwriting the migrations.[926] The subsidies, which defray up to 50-70% of the settlement costs, are expressly designed to promote the relocation movement.[927]

As of May, 2015, the above polices of population transfer incentivized nearly 500,000 Israelis to occupy 247 settlements throughout East Jerusalem and the West Bank, including the unauthorized outposts.[928] The influx not only transformed the demographic complexion of the Territories but restructured the area economically by granting privileges to settler businesses while restricting Palestinian firms.[929]

Israel accelerated its settlement program after US President Donald Trump took office in January of 2017. Counting on a more permissive

---

[925] Maurer, *supra* at 1507.

[926] Amnesty International, 1. Background: The Israeli Occupation, in Destination: Occupation, Digital Tourism and Israel's Illegal Settlements in the Occupied Palestinian Territories, p. 22 (2019), https://www.amnesty.org/en/latest/campaigns/2019/01/chapter-1-background/.

[927] *U.S. Criticizes Israel Plan to Subsidize West Bank Settlement Construction*, HAARETZ, January 31, 2012, http://www.haaretz.com/israel-news/u-s-criticizes-israel-plan-to-subsidize-west-bank-settlement-construction-1.410271.

[928] B'TSELEM *Statistics on Settlements, supra.*

[929] HRW Report of 2016, p. 4.

US approach to settlements, the Knesset approved thousands of new housing units in West Bank Area C.[930]

iv. Settlement policies breach occupation law limits on property acquisition

The European empires of the 19th and 20th Centuries employed legal rationales to whitewash oppressive policies of property acquisition for colonial settlement.[931] Israel used similar strategies to colonize Palestine.[932] The following describes each of these tactics in turn.

Absentee land:

During the 1947-1948 war, numerous Arab Palestinians were driven from their homes in the territory that became recognized Israel. Israel kept the refugees from returning to the real estate they left behind. The government classified the outcasts as "absentees," declared their plots "abandoned," and reclassified them as state land.[933]

---

[930] Nickolay Mladenov, Special Coordinator for the Middle East Peace Process, *Briefing to the Security Council on the Situation in the Middle East*, UN Department of Political Affairs (Feb. 16, 2017), https://dppa.un.org/en/security-council-briefing-situation-middle-east-special-coordinator-nickolay-mladenov-6.

[931] George Bisharat, *Land, Law, and Legitimacy in Israel and the Occupied Territories*, 43 Am. U. L. REV. 468-71 (1993) [hereinafter Bisharat *Land Law*], available at: https://digitalcommons.wcl.american.edu/aulr/vol43/iss2/3/. Professor Bisharat is a Senior Fellow of the Institute for Palestinian Studies. He also serves as professor of law at Hastings College of the Law in San Francisco, where he teaches criminal procedure and practice, law and anthropology, Islamic law, and law in Middle East societies.

[932] *Id.* at 471.

[933] *Id.* at 512-14.

By 1954, over a third of Israel's Jewish population lived on absentee property, and nearly a third (350,000) of new Jewish immigrants made their homes in communities abandoned by Arabs.[934] In effect, the absentee property law transferred Arab property to Jews.[935] Later Israeli governments attempted to mitigate the hardship of the property takings by furnishing replacement plots and cash compensation, but the efforts were largely ineffective.[936] In only 209 cases did the government return properties to their original Arab owners.[937]

State Land:

Article 43 of the Hague Regulations implies that occupiers must preserve the status quo of land use in an occupied territory, or at least ensure that any land use changes serve the interest of the occupied population.[938] The provision states that the occupant must:

> take all the measures in his power to restore, and ensure, as far as possible, public order and safety, while respecting, unless absolutely prevented, the laws in force in the country.[939]

---

[934] *Id.* at 438-39.

[935] *Id.* at 386.

[936] *Id.* at 387-89.

[937] *Id.* at 514.

[938] Marya Farah, *Planning in Area C: Discrimination in Law and Practice*, Vol. 21 Palestine-Israel Journal para. 3 and n. 24 (2016), http://www.pij.org/details.php?id=1685.

[939] Hague Regulations, art. 43.

After 1967, Israel upset the status quo by acquiring Palestinian property throughout the Territories[940] and thereby displacing Palestinians from their land.[941] One way Israel accomplished this goal was by reclassifying Palestinian land as state land.

As of 1967, 13% of the West Bank was registered as state land, one-third was privately owned by Arabs, and the rest remained in dispute.[942] Several years later, an Israeli land survey team analyzed the legally questionable West Bank lands. They classified all non-private tracts as "state land."[943] During the investigation, Palestinian land owners tried to defend their titles but often lacked deeds, sales contracts, tax receipts or other evidence to challenge the official determinations.[944] By 2001, Israel had enlarged the state land category to 40% of the West Bank.[945] The government initiative dramatically altered the status quo in the Territories in breach of Hague Article 43.

The way Israel altered the status quo in the Territories caused an additional violation of occupation law. Specifically, Israel exceeded its

---

[940] *Israel's Obligations as An Occupying Power Under International Law, its Violations and Implications for EU Policy*, The European Coordination of Committees and Associations for Palestine, Part II.g. (Jan. 29, 2014) [hereinafter *European Coordination*], available at: http://www.eccpalestine.org/israels-obligations-as-an-occupying-power-under-international-law-its-violations-and-implications-for-eu-policy/#sdfootnote19sym.

[941] *See, e.g.* Orna Ben-Naftali *et. al.*, *Illegal Occupation: Framing the Occupied Palestinian Territory*, 23 BERKELEY J. INT'L LAW. 551, 582-83 (2005) [hereinafter Naftali].

[942] Stacy Howlett, *Palestinian Private Property Rights in Israel and the Occupied Territories*, 34 Vand. J. Transnat'l L. 117, 140-42 (2001) [hereinafter Howlett].

[943] *Id.* at 142-45.

[944] *Id.*

[945] *See Id.* at 145.

Hague Article 55 power as a "usufructuary" (one with a temporary right to make normal use of another's property) to make "normal use" of occupied land. The establishment of settlements exceeded the limit of normal use; it changed the land's essential character.[946] The IDF's Civil Administration has dedicated much of the occupied acreage to housing, business development, roads and other infrastructure.[947] Some parcels have been closed to Palestinians as military "buffer zones," while others have been earmarked for nature reserves and recreational parks.[948]

Private Land:

Hague Article 46(2) states that "private property cannot be confiscated."[949] However, Israel has confiscated Palestinian land by seizure under the pretext of military needs.[950] The confiscated land is then used for urbanization and buffer zones surrounding the urban developments.[951]

In areas of the Territories seized by Israel, Palestinian land development is generally precluded.[952] Palestinians may not enter the 400-meter

---

[946] DAVID KRETZMER, *THE OCCUPATION OF JUSTICE* 93 (2002) [hereinafter KRETZMER *OCCUPATION*]. A right of usufruct permits a non-owner of public buildings, real estate, forests, agricultural estates, or other natural resources to make normal use of the property. VON GLAHN, *supra* at 176-77.

[947] European Coordination, *supra.*

[948] *Id.*

[949] Hague Resolutions, art. 46.

[950] European Coordination, *supra.*

[951] *Id.*

[952] *Id.*

buffer zone surrounding each West Bank settlement.[953] Israeli roads serve the dual function of linking the settlements to each other and isolating the Palestinian towns.[954] Israel's fortifications in the Jordan Valley block cross-border passage between the West Bank and Jordan.[955] Meanwhile, about 100 military checkpoints surround the Palestinian pockets.[956] And countless roadblocks seal off Palestinian roads with concrete blocks or mounds of stone-filled earth.[957]

The Impact in West Bank Area C:

Israel's land acquisition policies severely harm the 180,000 Palestinians – 6.6 percent of the West Bank Palestinian population – who live in West Bank Area C.[958] Less than one percent of Area C is available for Palestinian land development due to the Civil Administration's zoning restrictions.[959] This impediment has contributed to a decades-long decline in the rate of Palestinian construction in the West Bank.[960] Development constraints in Area C also inflate land prices in Areas A and B.[961]

---

[953] JIMMY CARTER, *PALESTINE: PEACE NOT APARTHEID* 151-54 (2006).

[954] *Id.*

[955] *Id.*

[956] *Id.*

[957] *Id.*

[958] *West Bank and Gaza: Area C and the Future of the Palestinian Economy*, World Bank Report No. AUS2922, p. 17 (Oct. 2, 2013) [hereinafter World Bank Report of 2013], available at https://openknowledge.worldbank.org/bitstream/handle/10986/16686/AUS29220REPLAC0 EVISION0January02014.pdf?sequence=1.

[959] *Id.*, pp. 17 and 28.

[960] *Id.*, pp. 30-31.

[961] *Id.*, pp. 28-32.

Palestinian villagers who live in Area B but own farmland or pastures in Area C are also victimized by Israel's Area C land policies.[962] In these situations, Israel treats the farms and pastures as if they exist exclusively for Israel's benefit.[963] Palestinian requests to develop their Area C land are rarely granted.[964] Instead, Israel builds "bypass roads" (purportedly to bypass the danger of Palestinian communities) that create physical boundaries between Palestinians and their Area C agricultural resources.[965] Then Israeli settlers encroach on the parcels and exploit them for their own use.[966] The local Jews establish settlements or illegal settlement outposts, as noted above.[967] They cultivate their own crops, graze their own sheep, and monopolize local water resources.[968] This systematic consumption of Palestinian land by Israeli settlers tightens their grip on the West Bank, even as their government claims the province remains available for a Palestinian state.[969] All told, the land theft devastates the Palestinian economy, violates their rights, and undermines their way of life.[970]

---

[962] *Expel and Exploit: The Israeli Practice of Taking Over Rural Palestinian Land*, B'TSELEM (Dec. 2016), pp. 10-11.
http://www.btselem.org/download/201612_expel_and_exploit_eng.pdf.

[963] *Id.*

[964] *Id.*

[965] *Id.*, pp. 11-12.

[966] *Id.*, pp. 13-24.

[967] *Id.*

[968] *Id.*

[969] *Id.*

[970] *Id.*, pp. 24-30.

v. Settlement policies breach occupation law limits on property demolition

Under Fourth Convention Article 53, "Any destruction by the occupying power of real or personal property belonging to [protected persons] is prohibited, except where such destruction is rendered absolutely necessary by military operations."[971] The standard of absolute necessity calls for a situation of extreme military urgency.[972] Israel's settlement policy violates this rule of occupation law in two respects.

First, the Civil Administration allows construction in West Bank Area C only pursuant to the agency's grant of construction permits. Such permits are rarely granted to Palestinians, and when they are approved they are confined to a zoned district amounting to one percent of Area C.[973] Between 2000 and 2012, the Administration approved only 210 out of 3,565 building permit requests by Palestinians.[974] As a result, Palestinians must often build homes without them.

The lack of construction documents gives Israel a pretext to demolish the resulting structures, even where there is no absolute military necessity. In 2014, Israeli authorities demolished 590 Palestinian structures in West Bank Area C and East Jerusalem, displacing 1,177

---

[971] Fourth Convention, art. 53.

[972] GERHARD VON GLAHN, *THE OCCUPATION OF ENEMY TERRITORY* 227 (1957) [hereinafter VON GLAHN]. Professor Von Glahn was among the most respected scholars on international law in general, and occupation law in particular, in the post -World War II era.

[973] HRW Report of 2016, p. 37.

[974] *Id.*

residents, according to OCHA statistics.[975] In 2015, the demolitions erased another 601 Palestinian structures in those districts, evicting another 1,215 people.[976] In 2016, the pace of demolition quickened to 165 per month.[977] The structures included houses, Bedouin tents, livestock pens, outhouses and schools.[978] In some cases, the structures were built with European Union funds earmarked to assist victims of prior demolitions.[979] These Palestinians lost their homes and livelihoods more than once.[980]

Another Israeli demolition policy destroys Palestinian homes belonging to terrorist suspects. If an Israeli military commander suspects that an individual has participated in a terrorist act, the person's house may be demolished[981] or sealed to keep the home unoccupied.

---

[975] OCHA, *United Nations Resident and Humanitarian Coordinator Calls for an Immediate Halt to Demolitions and Forced Displacement in the West Bank* (Jan. 23, 2015), available at https://www.ochaopt.org/content/united-nations-resident-and-humanitarian-coordinator-calls-immediate-halt-demolitions-and.

[976] HRW Report of 2016, p. 31.

[977] *With demolitions, Israel tightens squeeze on West Bank Palestinians*, REUTERS (April 7, 2016), available at: http://www.reuters.com/article/us-israel-palestinians-demolitions-idUSKCN0X41TA.

[978] *Id.*

[979] *Id.*

[980] *See Israeli Forces Compel Nablus Villager to Destroy Structures*, PALESTINIAN NEWS AND INFORMATION AGENCY (Aug. 8, 2016), http://english.wafa.ps/page.aspx?id=6rN2dta38898145110a6rN2dt.

[981] *Claiming lack of building permits, Israel continues to demolish Palestinian homes*, AL MONITOR (June 1, 2016), available at http://www.al-monitor.com/pulse/originals/2016/05/israel-demolishes-palestinian-buildings-lack-permits.html.

The stated military justification for these security demolitions is to deter terrorist attacks. But the destructive measures violate two occupation laws: the prohibition against property destruction; and the ban on collective punishment.[982] A "collective punishment," considered a war crime of customary international law, is any criminal sanction or other penalty imposed without a basis of "individual criminal responsibility."[983] The rule is meant to stop a belligerent party from punishing an entire group of persons for a given offense, regardless of which individual actually committed the act, typically when the real motive for the punishment is oppression, as opposed to legitimate law enforcement.[984]

As noted above, Fourth Convention Article 53 prohibits an occupying power from destroying property unless it considers the act "absolutely necessary for military operations." Israel cannot validly consider a security demolition of a terrorist suspect's home absolutely necessary for military operations because once the suspect has been identified, captured, or killed, there is no military need to destroy the person's home.[985] The demolition is more properly classified as a punitive measure, which lacks any military justification at all.[986]

---

[982] KRETZMER *OCCUPATION*, *supra* at 145-163.

[983] ICRC, *Customary IHL, Rule 103. Collective Punishments*, https://ihl-databases.icrc .org/customary-ihl/eng/docs/v1_rul_rule103.

[984] Shane Darcy, *Prosecuting the War Crime of Collective Punishment, Is it Time to Amend the Rome Statute?* 8 Journal of International Criminal Justice 29, 29-30 (2010), https://academic.oup.com/jicj/article/8/1/29/821405.

[985] Farrell, *supra.* at 926.

[986] *Israel's Punitive House Demolition Policy: Collective Punishment in Violation of International Law*, AL HAQ, p. 49 (2003) [hereinafter Al Haq *Demolition*], http://www.alhaq .org/publications/publications-index/item/israel-s-punitive-house-demolition-policy.

Security demolitions amount to collective punishment when they harm residents of the homes other than the terror suspects. Specifically, in situations where the suspect lives with his or her family, and the family members lack awareness of the alleged terror plot, the fate of sudden homelessness would devastate the lives of innocent parties.[987]

Israel claims the purpose of a security demolition is deterrence. But in the context of such a destructive act, deterrence and punishment are inseparable, and the harm to the family members is direct, not merely incidental.[988] The deterrence argument fails for the additional reason that deterrence never worked.[989] Palestinians have continued to mount attacks despite the demolition policy.[990] Even if security demolitions produce some deterrent effect, they depart from the principle of individual responsibility on which the rule against collective punishment is based.[991]

vi. **Settlement policies breach occupation limits on the use of natural resources**

---

[987] *Id.* at 53; DINSTEIN OCCUPATION, *supra* at 155-59 (2009).

[988] Brian Farrell, *Israeli Demolition of Palestinian Houses as a Punitive Measure: Application of International Law to Regulation 119, 28.3* Brook. J. Int'l L., 871, 928 (2002) [hereinafter Farrell], http://brooklynworks.brooklaw.edu/cgi/viewcontent.cgi?article=1351&context=bjil.

[989] Al Haq *Demolition, supra* at 49.

[990] *Id.*

[991] KRETZMER OCCUPATION, *supra* at 151.

As an occupying power, Israel is merely a usufructuary of the Territories, not their owner.[992] This classification implies a duty to use the natural resources of the occupied countryside only for the temporary needs of the military. The amount of usage should be no more than it was in pre-occupation days.[993] Despite this guidance, Israel has excessively exploited the natural resources of water and minerals in the Territories.

Israelis divert the environment's scarce water resources for their own use, even though the practice cannot be justified as a military necessity.[994] Immediately after the 1967 war, Israel's military seized control of all water resources in the Territories and issued an order forcing any community desiring to construct a new water facility such as a water well to obtain a permit from the commander.[995] The commander granted very few permits to Palestinians.[996]

On paper, Israel and the PA currently control West Bank water resources jointly under Oslo II.[997] But in practice, Israel has the upper hand, owing to its superior access to information on water supplies, as well as to the water itself.[998] In fact, Israel's per-capita water

---

[992] *See* Hague Regulations, Article 55.

[993] VON GLAHN, *supra* at 177.

[994] European Coordination, Part 2.h.

[995] Stephen Gasteyer et. al., 5.2 *Water Grabbing in Colonial Perspective: Land and Water in Israel/Palestine*, WATER ALTERNATIVES 450, 461 (2012) [hereinafter Gasteyer], available at: http://www.water-alternatives.org/index.php/volume5/v5issue2/179-a5-2-15/file.

[996] *Id.*

[997] *Id.* at 462.

[998] *Id.*

consumption is four to five times higher than the Palestinian per-capita consumption.[999] Anyone may view the discrimination by comparing the lush green landscapes of Israeli settlements with the brown, semi-arid West Bank lands inhabited by Palestinians. The lopsided Oslo-governed water management system produces frequent water shortages for Palestinian households, industries, and farms.[1000] Ultimately, the systematic denial of the vital resource endangers public health and hinders economic development in West Bank Palestinian communities.[1001]

Israel's domination of water in the West Bank is a common colonial strategy called "water grabbing." [1002] In this case, the wrongdoing may leave the ecology permanently altered.[1003]

A similar violation of occupation law is found in the mining industry. An occupant may not use local mineral resources at a greater rate than the population did in pre-occupation days.[1004] But because Israel maintains exclusive control of the Dead Sea, they dominate the local mineral extraction industry. They similarly control most area mining operations. All these Israeli businesses are conducted without military justification and therefore violate occupation law.[1005]

---

[999] *Id.* at 461.

[1000] *Id.* at 464.

[1001] *Id.* at 462-3.

[1002] *Id.* at 464-65.

[1003] *Id.*

[1004] VON GLAHN, *supra* at 177.

[1005] European Coordination, Part 2.h.

Since 1994, Israel has issued no new quarrying permits to Palestinian businesses in Area C.[1006] As of 2012 only nine Palestinian quarries operated legally in Area C.[1007] If the Civil Administration discovers a Palestinian quarry in operation without a permit, the agency may confiscate the business equipment and penalize the owner with a heavy fine.[1008]

In 2013, the UN responded to Israel's abuse of the local water and mineral resources. The General Assembly adopted Resolution 235, which recognized the "permanent sovereignty of the Palestinian people" over the natural resources of the Territories and called on Israel to stop exploiting them.[1009] Israel ignored the plea.

vii. Settlement policies illegally discriminate against Palestinians

Israel's settlement policies violate Palestinian human rights by creating a legal double-standard based on nationality.[1010] The discrimination is institutionalized and colors every aspect of West Bank life.[1011]

[1006] HRW Report of 2016, pp. 31 and 42.

[1007] *Id.*, p. 42.

[1008] *Id.*, pp. 42–43 and 51–52.

[1009] G.A. Res. 68/235, U.N. Doc. A/RES/68/235 (Dec. 20, 2013).

[1010] Hiba Husseini, *Legal Duality in the Occupied West Bank*, PALESTINE-ISRAEL JOURNAL, Vol. 21, No. 3 (2016), at subtitle "Duality of Operation of Law in the West Bank: Israeli Law for Settlers and Palestinian and Israeli Military Orders for Palestinian Inhabitants" [hereinafter Husseini], http://www.pij.org/details.php?id=1683.

[1011] *Id.*

For example, all governmental services for settlers – from health care to education to agricultural activities – are controlled exclusively by Israeli law.[1012] In matters of criminal law, there are two systems: one with plenary due process for settlers and another with reduced standards for Palestinians.[1013] Settlers enjoy freedom of movement, including a system of Israeli-only roads, while Palestinians struggle against a labyrinth of military checkpoints, roadblocks and the Barrier.[1014]

The dual legal regime treats the Palestinian people as a *bete noire* to be strictly monitored and restrained.

viii. **The settlements pose an obstacle to peace**

Virtually the entire world community, including past US State Department spokespersons, have described Israel's settlements as "an obstacle to peace."[1015] They agree that the illegal homes, businesses, and infrastructure stymie efforts to create a Palestinian state. Israel's settlement project threatens the two-state solution through its population growth and geographic layout.

The more Israelis populate the Territories, the harder it is for Palestinians to bring the land under self-rule. Removing all East Jerusalem and West Bank Area C settlers would require a major

---

[1012] *Id.*

[1013] *Id.*

[1014] *Id.*

[1015] Oren Liebermann, *What you need to know about the Israeli settlements*, CNN (Feb. 3, 2017) [hereinafter CNN *Need to Know*], http://www.cnn.com/2017/02/01/middleeast/settlements-explainer/index.html.

undertaking, something beyond Israel's political will.[1016] Indeed, as the settler crowd grows, so do the number of Knesset votes against evacuation.[1017]

The geographic threat to peace is apparent from the settlement locations. For example, if a certain strip of West Bank settlements continues to elongate its east-west arc it may eventually cut the would-be Palestinian state in half.[1018] The lack of a contiguous Palestinian state would kill the concept of a two-state solution.[1019] Already, there is a settlement, *Ma'ale Efraim*, which stands closer to Jordan than the Green Line.[1020]

The Palestinian cities of the West Bank are separated from each other by Israeli settlements and/or military-patrolled zones. East Jerusalem, the city where Palestinians want to establish their capital, is almost completely severed from the West Bank. The disconnected cantons trap Palestinians indefinitely under Israeli control.[1021]

[1016] Robert Wright, *Who is Responsible for the Israeli-Palestinian Impasse?*, THE ATLANTIC (March 21, 2012), https://www.theatlantic.com/international/archive/2012/03/who-is-responsible-for-the-israeli-palestinian-impasse/254890/.

[1017] *Id.*

[1018] *Id.*

[1019] *Id.*

[1020] *Id.*

[1021] EDWARD SAID, *THE QUESTION OF PALESTINE* 192 (1992) [hereinafter SAID]. Professor Said (pronounced sah-EED) was a professor of literature at Columbia University and one-time member of the Palestinian legislature in exile. He became a world-renowned proponent of Palestinian rights.

Israel has deliberately placed civilian settlements in the Territories since the 1967 war to make the disputed environment permanently Israeli.[1022] A post-war development scheme planted Kibbutz farming collectives along the western shore of the Jordan River, which separated Israel from Jordan.[1023] Additional settlements soon appeared throughout the West Bank.[1024] One was interposed in the West Bank town of Hebron, a major Arab community.[1025] Settlements also emerged throughout East Jerusalem.[1026] Israel's strategy all along was to preclude Palestinian statehood.

Looking ahead, Israel may effectively absorb the Territories without any formal determination of sovereignty. As stated in ICJ Barrier Opinion:

> the construction of the wall and its associated régime create a "fait accompli" on the ground that could well become permanent, in which case, and notwithstanding the formal characterization of the wall by Israel, it would be tantamount to a de facto annexation.[1027]

Palestinians cannot be expected to negotiate the return of their land with an adversary that increasingly confiscates that land. This is why, since 2009 Palestinians have demanded a freeze on Israeli settlement construction before agreeing to continue the final status talks.[1028]

[1022] SACHAR, *supra* at 681-82.

[1023] *Id.*

[1024] *Id.* at 865.

[1025] *Id.* at 681-82.

[1026] *Id.*

[1027] ICJ Barrier Opinion, para. 121.

[1028] *See* CNN Need to Know, *supra.*

A former US secretary of state observed that frustration over Israel's settlement expansion drives Palestinians to violence.[1029] Under the circumstances, violence is inevitable. Verbal condemnations have proven inadequate to halt the illegal building spree.[1030] Even when the Ramallah government warns that settlement growth will explode the peace process, Israel pays no attention.[1031] Thus, the only effective way to stop the seizure of Palestinian land is with violence.[1032] Palestinians must disrupt the settlers, wreck their plans, and impose a new reality on the ground.[1033]

[1029] Michael Wilner, *Kerry Links Wave of Terrorism in Israel to Settlement Activity*, JERUSALEM POST (Oct. 14, 2014), http://www.jpost.com/Israel-News/Politics-And-Diplomacy/Kerry-to-visit-Israel-amid-crisis-423892.

[1030] Dr. Fayez Abu Shamaleh, *Who will stop the Israeli settlements?* MIDDLE EAST MONITOR (Sept. 8, 2017), https://www.middleeastmonitor.com/20170908-who-will-stop-the-israeli-settlements/.

[1031] *Id.*

[1032] *Id.*

[1033] *Id.*

B. The Israeli Arguments

Summary of Arguments

The Olso Accords imposed no limits on settlements. They designated the settlement dispute as one of the final status issues to resolve in the final status negotiation. Until then, neither party may prejudge the outcome of that negotiation by pressuring the other side to stop building settlements. Israel may cultivate communities in East Jerusalem and West Bank Area C just as freely as Palestinians build in Areas A and B.

Occupation law does not apply to the Territories. A state such as Israel cannot be said to occupy land that is already within its sovereign reach. Moreover, Israel did not capture the Territories from any party that held them legitimately in the first place. Even if occupation law did apply to Israel at some point, the law became moot when Israel transferred control to the Palestinians under the Oslo Accords. Nevertheless, Israel complies with the humanitarian provisions of occupation law voluntarily.

The occupation law embodied in Fourth Convention Article 49(6) is superseded by the BMP. The BMP expressly requires the "close settlement" of Jews in Mandatory Palestine, including the Territories. Moreover, Article 49(6) does not fit the facts of Israel's situation. The Article states that an occupying power may not "deport or transfer" its population to the occupied territory. Israel does not deport or transfer Israelis to the Territories. Israelis relocate to the Territories voluntarily.

The occupation laws that guide property use have all been met in the Territories. Israel's compliance with these property rules extends to absentee land, state land, and land seizure.

Israel validly demolishes homes in the Territories under one of two narrow circumstances: where the structures were built without Civil Administration approval; or where necessary to deter terrorism.

Consistent with the Oslo Accords and IHL, two bodies of law govern the Territories: Israeli law for Israeli citizens; and martial law for non-citizens. The arrangement does not amount to illegal discrimination. Any application of Israeli law to Palestinian-controlled Areas A or B would be scorned as an illegal annexation.

Israel's management of water in the Territories exceeds the minimum requirements of the Oslo Accords and occupation law. As a result, Palestinian access to water has greatly improved.

Israel's mineral extraction business in the Territories likewise benefits Palestinians and otherwise meets the relevant occupation law standard.

Neither Israeli nor Palestinian settlements pose an obstacle to peace. Local Arabs started killing their Jewish neighbors long before there were any settlements. The main obstacle to peace is Palestinian extremism.

i. Both Israeli and Palestinian settlements are permitted under the Oslo Accords

The Oslo Accords gave each contracting party temporary control over certain portions of the Territories. This right of control does not limit either party's right to build settlements in its respective area.[1034] If anything, Oslo requires Israel to ensure the security of its settlements.[1035] The Accords also acknowledge that neither party, by entering into the

---

[1034] Israel Ministry of Foreign Affairs, *Israeli Settlements and International Law* (Nov. 30, 2015) [hereinafter MFA *Settlements*], https://www.mfa.gov.il/mfa/foreignpolicy/peace/guide/pages/israeli%20settlements%20and%20international%20law.aspx.

[1035] Oslo II Art XII(1).

agreements, has "waived any of its existing rights."[1036] Under this legal condition, neither party has waived its right to build settlements.

Oslo I reserves the settlement issue (among others) for resolution in the permanent status negotiation.[1037] Until then, neither party may prejudice the other party's final status rights by ordering the other party to halt settlement construction. Israelis may cultivate communities in East Jerusalem and West Bank Area C just as Palestinians may pursue such developments in Areas A and B.

During the Oslo negotiation, the parties considered a clause that would freeze the construction of settlements but ultimately discarded the idea.[1038] The PLO's own lead negotiator later admitted that Oslo did not limit settlement building.[1039] Accordingly, the PLO accepted Israeli settlement growth during the Oslo interim period.[1040]

The Oslo II "no-change-of-status" clause prohibited unilateral acts of sovereignty, not unilateral settlement construction. That is, the clause precluded Israel from annexing the Territories and blocked the

---

[1036] Oslo II, art. 31(6).

[1037] Oslo I, art. V.3.

[1038] *See* WATSON, *supra* at 134. *See also* Israel Ministry of Foreign Affairs, *The Peace Process and the Settlements* (Oct. 5, 2016) [hereinafter MFA *Peace Process*], https://www.mfa.gov.il/ MFA/ForeignPolicy/Pages/The-Peace-Process-and-the-Settlements-5-October-2016.aspx.

[1039] SMITH, *supra* at 442.

[1040] *Id.* at 486.

Palestinians from establishing a state.[1041] An analogous provision of occupation law stops the occupying power from changing the political status of the occupied territory.[1042]

ii. The Israeli settlements are not subject to occupation law

Occupation law does not apply to the Territories. By the time Israel captured the Territories, it had already earned legal, historic, and indigenous claims to those lands, based on the Balfour Declaration, the San Remo Resolution, and the BMP.[1043] A state cannot be said to occupy land that is already within its sovereign entitlement.[1044] Plainly, occupation law never contemplated circumstances where land is lawfully dedicated to one party, illegally conquered by others, and then acquired by the intended beneficiary. Thus, the situation should be considered *sui generis* (anomalous), which means it falls outside occupation law.[1045]

[1041] MFA Settlements, *supra*; RUTH LAPIDOTH, AUTONOMY: *FLEXIBLE SOLUTIONS TO ETHNIC CONFLICTS* 165 (1997) [hereinafter LAPIDOTH *AUTONOMY*]. Professor Lapidoth is a member of the International Editorial and Advisory Board of the Israel Council on Foreign Relations, Senior Researcher at the Jerusalem Institute for Israel Studies, and Professor Emeritus of International Law at the Hebrew University of Jerusalem. She served as a member of the Israeli delegation to the United Nations and also participated in the negotiations that led to the Egyptian-Israeli Peace Treaty of 1979.

[1042] *See* BENVENISTI, *supra* at 6.

[1043] Alan Baker, *The Legality of the Settlements: Flaws in the Carter-Era Hansell Memorandum*, JERUSALEM CENTER FOR PUBLIC AFFAIRS Vol. 19, No. 20 (Nov. 21, 2019) [hereinafter Baker *Legality of Settlements*], http://jcpa.org/article/the-legality-of-israels-settlements/.

[1044] STONE, *supra*, p. 10.

[1045] Baker *Legality of Settlements*, *supra*; Sharon, *supra* at 20.

Even if the Territories had not been legally reserved for the Jewish state, those properties would still not be subject to occupation law because they never met the definition of an occupation. Article 2, paragraph 1 of the Fourth Convention states that occupation law applies to "all cases of declared war or... any other armed conflict which may arise between two or more of the High Contracting Parties ..."[1046] Paragraph 2 adds: "The Convention shall also apply to all cases of partial or total occupation of the territory of a High Contracting Party, even if the said occupation meets with no armed resistance."[1047]

Article 2, paragraph 1 addresses only cases of declared war and other armed conflicts, not occupations. Paragraph 2 addresses occupations. This paragraph plainly limits the applicability of the Fourth Convention to occupations involving the territory of "a High Contracting Party," meaning a sovereign state signatory to the Convention. The Territories were not under the sovereign possession of Egypt or Jordan before they were captured by Israel in 1967. Egypt and Jordan were mere occupying powers in those lands. Accordingly, the Israeli capture did not activate occupation law.

This reading of Article 2 is consistent with the Hague Regulation. Hague Regulation Article 43 requires each occupying power to preserve the laws of "the legitimate power." Before Israel assumed control over the Territories, they lacked a legitimate power.

[1046] Fourth Convention, art. 2(1).

[1047] Fourth Convention, art. 2(2).

Focusing on the legitimacy of the ousted power to determine the applicability of occupation law makes sense because the foundational purpose of the law is to protect the inalienability of sovereignty.[1048] Where there is no sovereignty to alienate, occupation law has no use. International lawyers would only invert justice by enforcing occupation law to protect states such as Egypt or Jordan, which seized land offensively.[1049]

Israel's interpretation of the Fourth Convention is also consistent with state practice. As of 2018, the Trump Administration discontinued the US government practice of referring to the Territories as the "Occupied Territories."[1050] The UN never attributed the term "occupying power" to Egypt or Jordan when their military forces held the Territories. Likewise, the agency did not assign occupier status to the military administrations of Turkey in Northern Cyprus, Indonesia in East Timor,

---

[1048] STONE, *supra* at 119; Avinoam Sharon, *Why is Israel's Presence in the Territories Still Called "Occupation"?*, pp. 5-8 LEGACY HERITAGE FUND, JCPA (2009) [hereinafter Sharon], http://jcpa.org/wp-content/uploads/2011/11/Occupation-Sharon.pdf.

[1049] Sharon, *supra* p. 9 (citing Meir Shamgar, *Legal Concepts and Problems of the Israeli Military Government – The Initial Stage*, in Meir Shamgar, ed., *Military Government in the Territories Administered by Israel 1967-1980* (1982), p. 37.) Justice Shamgar was President of Israel's Supreme Court from 1983 to 1995. Before his tenure on the Court, he served as chief military prosecutor and then attorney general. He set the legal guidelines of Israel's military government in Gaza and the West Bank after the 1967 war. He also permitted Palestinians subject to Israel's military courts appeal their cases to Israel's Supreme Court.

[1050] Carol Morello, *State Department strikes reproductive rights, 'Occupied Territories' from human rights report*, WASHINGTON POST (April 20, 2018), https://www.washingtonpost.com/world/national-security/state-department-strikes-reproductive-rights-occupied-territories-from-annual-report/2018/04/20/46ef0874-44a6-11e8-ad8f-27a8c409298b_story.html.

Morocco in Western Sahara, Vietnam in Cambodia, Armenia in Azerbaijan, Russia in parts of Georgia, or Russia in the Crimean Peninsula.[1051] In territorial disputes the UN normally uses the term "disputed" land, not the pejorative "occupied" land.[1052] In that sense, Israel and the United States are the only states since the advent of occupation law to observe that law at all.[1053]

Even if Israel's 1967 capture of the Territories did trigger occupation law, the law was rendered moot by the Oslo Accords, The Hague Regulations, and the Effective Control Test.

Leading scholars have recognized that the Oslo Accords ended any alleged occupation in Gaza and West Bank Area A because, in those environs, the PA assumed full governmental authority.[1054] It is hard to believe West Bank Area B remains occupied because in that precinct, Israel has largely withdrawn its control and the PA exercises substantial authority.[1055]

The Territories' only other apportionments are East Jerusalem and West Bank Area C. Those confines are governed by the Oslo Accords.

[1051] *See* Eugene Kontorovich, *At the UN, Only Israel is an Occupying Power*, KOHELET POLICY FORUM (Sept. 19, 2016), http://en.kohelet.org.il/publication/u-n-israel-occupying-power.

[1052] Sharon, *supra* at 19 and 21.

[1053] BENVENISTI, *supra* at 203.

[1054] Sharon Weill, *The judicial arm of the occupation: the Israeli military courts in the occupied territories*, 89.866 INTERNATIONAL REVIEW OF THE RED CROSS 395, 402 (June, 2007), https://www.icrc.org/eng/assets/files/other/irrc_866_weill.pdf. For example, Professor Watson finds West Bank Area A is no longer occupied territory. WATSON, *supra* at 176.

[1055] WATSON, *supra* at 176.

Considering the comprehensive scope of the Oslo permanent status negotiation, the arrangement reveals an intent to resolve the entire Israeli-Palestinian dispute through the framework of the Accords, as opposed to any branch of IHL.[1056] Therefore the Accords should be deemed the *lex specialis* (the law governing a particular subject matter) that has replaced the edicts of occupation law.[1057]

Palestinian proponents who raise occupation law grievances against Israel forget a crucial stage of the Oslo negotiation. Palestinian lawyers proposed a clause for the Accords that would have made the pact subject to Fourth Convention occupation law. But they were overruled by Yasser Arafat and his negotiating team, who disregarded the Fourth Convention in their haste to finalize Oslo I.[1058] Thus, the Palestinians conceded that the Accords suspended the Fourth Convention and established a *lex specialis*.[1059]

Any occupation of the Territories was also dissolved by Article 42 of the Hague Regulations. Article 42 states that an occupation exists only in "the territory where such authority has been established and can be exercised." In the Oslo Accords, Israel significantly reduced the scope

---

[1056] *See* Alan Baker, *The Settlements Issue: Distorting the Geneva Convention and the Oslo Accords,* JCPA (Jan. 5, 2011), http://jcpa.org/article/the-settlements-issue-distorting-the-geneva-convention-and-the-oslo-accords/.

[1057] *Id.*

[1058] Allegra Pacheco, *Flouting Convention: The Oslo Agreements,* in THE NEW INTIFADA, RESISTING ISRAEL'S APARTHEID 186-88 (2001) [hereinafter Pacheco]; NOURA ERAKAT, JUSTICE FOR SOME: LAW AND THE QUESTION OF PALESTINE 163-64 (2019) [hereinafter ERAKAT].

[1059] ERAKAT, *supra* at 163-64.

of territory where its authority had been established and exercised. Specifically, it disengaged from its authority in Gaza, delegated authority to the PA in West Bank Area A, where over 90% of West Bank Palestinians live, and delegated to the PA all authority in West Bank Area B except for external security matters and certain coordination functions.

Any occupation was further extinguished by dint of the Effective Control Test.[1060] Under this Test, if the occupier loses any of the three requisite elements of effective control, the occupation ends.[1061] The following explores the Effective Control Test in detail.

It is not appropriate to modify the Effective Control Test with the ICRC's relatively recent "functional approach" because the approach improperly detaches the Effective Control Test from the governing IHL treaties. When drafting The Hague Regulations and Fourth Convention, the authors believed an occupation could not exist without a physical troop presence in the foreign land.[1062] The ICJ has expressly recognized the need to find a physical troop presence in an area before declaring it

---

[1060] ICRC 2015 Report, *supra* at 12.

[1061] *Id.*

[1062] Tristan Ferraro, *Determining the beginning and end of an occupation under international humanitarian law*, 94.885 INTERNATIONAL REVIEW OF THE RED CROSS 133, 144 (2012) [hereinafter Ferraro].

subject to occupation law.[1063] Moreover, the importance of the physical presence factor is widely reflected in legal scholarship.[1064]

Even taking the functional approach into account, one should not find that Israel maintains Effective Control over any of the Territories.[1065] If one examines Gaza – none of the three elements of effective control appear in that prefecture. Israel ended its physical presence in 2005 when it evacuated all its troops and civilians. The eviction of an occupant is proof that the occupation no longer exists.[1066] Moreover, Hamas is substantially capable of exercising power in Gaza. Hamas dictates all of Gaza's governmental affairs, including the police force, schools, hospitals, religious rites, sanitation, and local media. Indeed, Hamas's totalitarian grip is so tight that Gaza has no elections. Israel was never able to wield authority in lieu of that iron-fisted regime.

[1063] Margaret E. McGuinness, *Case Concerning Armed Activities on the Territory of the Congo: The ICJ Finds Uganda Acted Unlawfully and Orders Reparations*, International Law, INTERNATIONAL LAW, Vol. 10, Issue 1 (Jan. 9, 2006), https://www.asil.org/insights/volume/10/issue/1/case-concerning-armed-activities-territory-congo-icj-finds-uganda-acted#:~:text=On%20December%2019%2C%202005%2C%20the,Republic%20of%20the%20Congo%20v.&text=The%20Court%20ordered%20Uganda%20to%20pay%20reparations%20to%20the%20DRC.

[1064] Ferraro, *supra* at 146. But see *Id.* at 158 (supporting the functional approach in circumstances where a state withdraws unilaterally from an occupied territory and retains "key elements of authority" without the local government's consent).

[1065] Hanne Cuyckens, *Is Israel Still an Occupying Power in Gaza?*" 63 NETH INT LAW REV 275, 285-86 (2016) [hereinafter Cuyckens].

[1066] VON GLAHN, *supra*, at 29.

The Oslo agreement to treat the Territories as "a single territorial unit" did not alter the meaning of Hague Article 42. [1067] Article 42 states that an occupation extends "only to the territory where such authority has been established and can be exercised."[1068] Consequently, no occupation can be found in Gaza, even if it exists elsewhere in the Territories.[1069]

Israel's supervision of Gaza's airspace, territorial waters, and boundaries are products of Palestinian consent under the Oslo Accords.[1070] As for Gaza's entry points, consent to Israel's control was established in agreements signed with the PA after the disengagement.[1071] These instruments of consent prove Gaza fails the no-consent criteria of the Effective Control Test. Even without the consents, effective control cannot reside in Israel merely because it controls another country's borders. Otherwise, states-within-states such as Lesotho, San Marino, and the Vatican would be considered permanently occupied.[1072] In any event, Hamas cannot claim ownership

---

[1067] Cuyckens, *supra*, at 287.

[1068] *Id.* (citing Hague Article 42).

[1069] *Id.*

[1070] *See* Oslo II, art. XII(1) (permitting Israel to "carry the responsibility for defense against external threats, including the responsibility for protecting the Egyptian and Jordanian borders, and for defense against external threats from the sea and from the air . . . .").

[1071] Israel Ministry of Foreign Affairs, *Agreed Documents on Movement and Access from and to Gaza* (Nov. 15, 2005), available at http://www.mfa.gov.il/mfa/foreignpolicy/peace/mfadocuments/pages/agreed%20documents%20on%20movement%20and%20access%20from%20and%20to%20gaza%2015-nov-2005.aspx.

[1072] Justus Reid Weiner, *Israel and the Gaza Strip: Why Economic Sanctions Are Not Collective Punishment*, p. 22, JCPA (2016) [hereinafter Weiner], http://jcpa.org/gaza-economic-sanctions/.

of any coastline or airspace that could be occupied because such rights adhere only to sovereign states.[1073]

Under the functional approach, effective control exists in the absence of a physical troop presence only where the belligerent military stationed outside the foreign territory is able to "reassert its full authority inside the territory within a reasonably short period of time."[1074] Israel lacks that ability.[1075] The Gaza War of 2008-2009 proved Israel could not reassert its authority in Gaza at all.[1076] The Gaza Wars of 2012 and 2014 reemphasized the point. Clearly, the only way Israel could regain effective control over Gaza would be through an even longer and costlier war.[1077] It is precisely because Israel lacks effective control over terrorist-led Gaza that it must resort to defensive measures like the Gaza Blockade.

This line of reasoning is supported by state practice. Egypt enforces the Gaza Blockade jointly with Israel but is not accused of occupying Gaza. Similarly, during the Persian Gulf War of 1990-1991, when the US

[1073] See Convention on the Territorial Sea and the Contiguous Zone, art. 1(1), Apr. 29, 1958, http://legal.un.org/ilc/texts/instruments/english/conventions/8_1_1958_territorial_sea.pdf; Convention on International Civil Aviation, art. 1, Dec. 7, 1944, http://www.icao.int/publications/Documents/7300_orig.pdf.

[1074] ICRC 2015 Report, p. 12.

[1075] Cuyckens, supra at 285-86.

[1076] BENVENISTI, supra at 210-11.

[1077] See Yuval Shany, The Law Applicable to Non-Occupied Gaza: A Comment on Bassiouni v. Prime Minister of Israel, HEBREW UNIVERSITY INTERNATIONAL LAW RESEARCH PAPER No. 13-09, 7 (2009) [hereinafter Shany], http://ssrn.com/abstract=1350307.

enforced a naval blockade and a "no-fly-zone" in Iraq, the measure was not called an occupation.

It is unnecessary to measure effective control in East Jerusalem. Israel governs the entire city by sovereign right based on the San Remo Resolution and the BMP. A state cannot be said to occupy its own land.

Meanwhile, West Bank Areas A and B lack all three elements of effective control. The IDF lacks an actual physical presence in Area A and conducts external security operations in Area B with Palestinian consent.[1078] The IDF cannot substitute its authority for that of the PA, and the PA continues to execute its own directives.

Even under the ICRC's functional approach to the Effective Control Test, Israel lacks effective control over West Bank Areas A and B because the only way the IDF could fully assert its authority in those spaces would be through a long and costly war.[1079] Israel needs the Barrier precisely because it lacks sufficient control to stop the terrorism originating from Areas A and B.

West Bank Area C lacks the no-consent element of the Effective Control Test because Israel administers that expanse with Palestinian consent under Oslo.[1080]

[1078] See Oslo II, art. XII(1).

[1079] See Shany, *supra* at 7.

[1080] See Oslo II, art. XII(1).

iii. Israel's settlements are not subject to the ban on population transfers

Even assuming occupation law governs the Territories, the occupation law provision embodied by Fourth Convention Article 49(6), which governs civilian population transfers, does not apply because it is superseded by the BMP. The BMP requires Jewish settlement growth throughout Mandatory Palestine, including the Territories.[1081] Specifically, BMP Article 6 calls for "close settlement by Jews on the land."[1082]

Even if Article 49(6) could apply to the Territories, it would not prohibit Israel's settlements. The Article states that an occupying power may not "deport or transfer" parts of its own civilian population into the occupied territory. Israel does not deport or transfer anyone to the Territories. The individuals relocate voluntarily.[1083]

Israel's plain-meaning interpretation of Article 49(6) is confirmed by the ICRC's original 1958 commentary on the provision. The ICRC determined that Article 49(6):

> ... is intended to prevent a practice adopted during the Second World War by certain Powers, which transferred portions of their own population to occupied territory for political and racial reasons or in order, as they claimed, to colonize those territories. Such transfers

---

[1081] Rostow, *supra* at 9-11.

[1082] MFA *Settlements*, *supra* (citing BMP, art. 6).

[1083] MFA *Settlements*, *supra*; STONE, *supra* at 177-78.

worsened the economic situation of the native population and endangered their separate existence as a race.[1084]

The above-described practices of World War II were government-mandated mass-expulsions of over 40 million people, including 15 million Germans, five million Soviet citizens, and millions more from Poland, Czechoslovakia, Ukraine, and Hungary.[1085] Israel's citizens are not subject to any mandate of expulsion.

The Israeli migrants are certainly not subject to expulsions imposed "for political or racial reasons" or to "colonize" the Territories. In the first decade after the 1967 war, Israelis moved to certain spots in the Territories to revive former Jewish communities and help defend Israel from further Arab attacks.[1086] A subsequent wave of migration to the Territories was spiritually motivated.[1087] The third and largest flow of settlers was attracted to the area for "quality of life" reasons.[1088]

[1084] *Geneva Convention relative to the Protection of Civilian Persons in Time of War*, COMMENTARY ON THE GENEVA CONVENTIONS OF 12 AUGUST 1949, Jean Pictet (ed.), ICRC (1958), p. 283. https://www.loc.gov/rr/frd/Military_Law/pdf/GC_1949-IV.pdf.

[1085] Alan Baker, *The Settlements Issue: Distorting the Geneva Convention and the Oslo Accords*, JERUSALEM CENTER FOR PUBLIC AFFAIRS, Vol. 10, No. 20 (Jan. 5, 2011), https://jcpa.org/article/the-settlements-issue-distorting-the-geneva-convention-and-the-oslo-accords/.

[1086] DOWTY, *supra* at 230-31.

[1087] *Id.*

[1088] *Id.*

Moreover, the settlers have not "worsened the economic situation" of Palestinians in the Territories.[1089] Israel's merger of the Palestinian and Israeli economies brought Palestinians significant economic growth.[1090] Israel also built seven universities in Gaza and the West Bank. The Territories previously had none.[1091] In any event, Israel has not "endangered" the Arabs' "separate existence as a race."[1092]

Decades after the ICRC described the words "deport or transfer" to mean a government-mandated mass-expulsion committed for offensive reasons to harm a native population, the advisory agency unaccountably reinterpreted "deport or transfer" to mean any government action modifying the social, demographic, and economic pattern of the territory. Then the agency unfairly applied the new definition only to Israel.[1093] The unwarranted reinterpretation of Article 49(6) betrayed the intent of the law.

The ICRC is required to dispense its IHL advice according to standards of "impartiality," "neutrality," and "independence."[1094] However, when

---

[1089] STONE, *supra* at 177-181.

[1090] TESSLER, *supra* at 524-26 (noting that between 1968 and 1978, the Palestinian standard of living greatly improved).

[1091] GORDIS *supra* at 353.

[1092] STONE, *supra* at 177-181.

[1093] Eugene Kontorovich, *Unsettled: a Global Study of Settlements in Occupied Territories*, 9 J. LEGAL ANALYSIS, 285, 286 (Jan. 1, 2017).

[1094] Statutes of the International Committee of the Red Cross (as amended October 3, 2013), Art. 4.1 (a), https://www.icrc.org/eng/resources/documents/misc/icrc-statutes-080503.htm.

it comes to the issue of occupation law in the Territories, the agency's advice is politicized.[1095]

Not all nations have succumbed to the ICRC bias. In 2019, the US clarified its mixed record of official opinion on the settlements by stating they were not inconsistent with international law.[1096]

Just as Arabs are permitted to live in Israel, Jews should be free to live in the Territories.[1097] It would be an ironic perversion of IHL to make any portion of the Jewish homeland *Judenrein* (the Nazi expression meaning "Jew-free").[1098]

iv. Israel's settlements comply with the limits on property acquisition

Although occupation law does not apply to the Territories, Israel voluntarily complies with the humanitarian provisions of the law. The following explains how Israel's voluntary efforts meet the occupation law standards governing the use of occupied property.

Absentee Land:

[1095] Alan Baker, *Hijacking the Laws of Occupation*, Institute for Contemporary Affairs, No. 613 (Sept. 2017), http://jcpa.org/article/hijacking-laws-occupation/.

[1096] *See Secretary Michael R. Pompeo Remarks to the Press*, Remarks, US Department of State (Nov. 18, 2019), https://www.un.org/unispal/document/us-secretary-of-state-pompeos-remarks-to-the-press-on-us-policy-towards-israeli-settlements/.

[1097] DINSTEIN *OCCUPATION*, *supra* at 242.

[1098] STONE, *supra* at 123.

The land left behind by Arab Palestinian refugees in 1947-1948 was classified as "abandoned" and converted to state land. After armed conflicts, states often adopt abandonment laws.[1099] When Arab nations drove out their Jewish populations in the 1940's and '50's, the Arab governments immediately acquired the properties left behind.[1100] In fact, many Jews who moved into housing abandoned by Arab Palestinians were refugees from Arab lands where their own property had been seized.[1101] The UN has observed that some abandonment laws are fair and others unfair.[1102] But to date, there is no judicial mechanism to resolve property abandonment disputes in post-conflict settings.[1103]

State Land:

The Ottoman Empire classified most of pre-mandatory Palestine as "state land."[1104] There was no "Palestinian land" in the sense of national rights or private property. Great Britain preserved the state land designation, and so did Israel. Due to sparse land records, the status of other properties in the Territories was unknown.[1105] Israel's land survey

---

[1099] Scott Leckie, *Legal and Protection Policy Research Series, Housing, Land and Property Rights in Post-Conflict Societies: Proposals for a New United Nations Institutional and Policy Framework*, Department of International Protection, PPLA 2005/01, UNHCR, para. 13 (March 2005) [hereinafter Leckie], http://www.unhcr.org/afr/425683e02a5.pdf.

[1100] SACHAR, *supra* at 438.

[1101] *Id.*

[1102] Leckie, *supra*, para. 13.

[1103] *Id.*, para. 14.

[1104] Bisharat, *supra* at 492-93.

[1105] Canadian Anti-Semitism Education Foundation, *The Levy Commission Report on the Legal Status of Building in Judea and Samaria*, p. 61 (June 21, 2012) [hereinafter *Levy Report*], English translation available at https://www.israelslegalrights.org/the-levy-report.

team endeavored to fill in the blanks. Where a question of property ownership could not be resolved, the experts added the parcel to the inventory of state land, as permitted by occupation law.[1106] Israel's West Bank settlements were built on state land.

As noted above, Hague Regulation Article 55 permits an occupying power to manage occupied territory as a usufructuary by making normal use of the land. In the Territories, Israel observes this norm by making normal use of state lands.[1107] Simply put, the government permits the normal development of settlements in the lands.[1108] At the same time, it requires the residents to remain renters and prevents them from acquiring ownership interests in the properties pending resolution of the sovereignty dispute.[1109]

As also observed, Hague Article 43 requires an occupying power to ensure public order and respect the laws in force in the occupied territory. The Article does not regulate land use, as some Palestinians believe. It certainly does not require property management decisions to maintain any pre-occupation "status quo." Among scholars, the rigid status quo concept has encountered significant challenge.[1110] The better interpretation of the law gives an occupier flexibility to make land use changes to defend military positions, improve the occupied ecosystem, or serve the larger interests of IHL.[1111]

[1106] *See* VON GLAHN, *supra* at 179-80.

[1107] Baker *Legality of Settlements, supra.*

[1108] *Id.*

[1109] *Id.*

[1110] *Contemporary challenges to IHL – Occupation: overview,* ICRC, (June 11, 2012).

[1111] BENVENISTI, *supra* at 90-92.

Private Land:

Hague Article 46 states that in an occupied zone, "[p]rivate property cannot be confiscated."[1112]

In other words, the occupier may not transfer ownership of the parcel without a demonstration of military necessity and payment to the owner of just compensation.[1113] However, occupied private real property may be "expropriated," that is, taken temporarily for military necessity after paying just compensation.[1114]

Israel has upheld the above standard, as shown in the landmark 1979 case known as *"Elon Moreh."*[1115] In *Elon Moreh*, Israel's Supreme Court struck down an IDF expropriation order for failure to demonstrate a genuine military need.

The lands Israel seized after the 1967 war were objects of military necessity. Specifically, Israel's Ministry of Defense designated the sites for settlements to help monitor the country's vulnerable frontiers.[1116] That is why most Israeli West Bankers reside along the Green Line, the last battle line of 1948. Other Israelis dwell in Mountain Strip communities with high-elevation views of hostile populations. Still

---

[1112] Hague Regulations, art. 46.

[1113] *See* VON GLAHN, *supra* at 185-86; DINSTEIN *OCCUPATION, supra* at 224-27 and 242-45.

[1114] *Id.*

[1115] Dweikat et. al. v. Government of Israel et. al., High Court of Justice (H.C.J.) 390/79, decided Oct. 22, 1979, http://www.hamoked.org/Document.aspx?dID=1670.

[1116] *See* BENVENISTI, *supra* at 233.

others live in the Jordan Valley, the corridor along the strategically sensitive Jordanian border. These positions help defend Israel from Arab terrorist attacks and terrorist smuggling operations.

The Impact in West Bank Area C:

Palestinians cannot validly complain of Israeli land use in West Bank Area C. The Oslo Accords provisionally granted Israel plenary zoning authority in Area C, just as it gave Palestinians full zoning rights in Areas A and B.

The Oslo land assignments work to the Palestinians' advantage. The six percent of West Bank Palestinians who settled in Israeli-controlled Area C are permitted to stay. By contrast, Israel must prohibit its citizens from entering Palestinian-controlled West Bank Area A for fear of abduction and/or murder.[1117] Thus, Palestinians are free to live in all three West Bank jurisdictions, whereas Israelis are confined to two.

v. Israeli settlement policies validly permit property demolitions

Palestinians frequently build homes in West Bank Area C without building permits.[1118] They hope these "facts on the ground" will shift de

---

[1117] Amos Harel, *IDF Mulls Lifting Ban on Israelis Entering Palestinian-controlled West Bank*, HAARETZ (July 19, 2010), https://www.haaretz.com/idf-mulls-lifting-ban-on-israelis-entering-palestinian-controlled-west-bank-1.302689.

[1118] *PA plans to bypass Israel by issuing construction permits, rebuilding demolished homes*, AL-MONITOR (Feb. 26, 2020), https://www.al-monitor.com/originals/2020/02/construction-permit-israel-area-c-demolition-oslo-accords.html.

facto control over Area C from Israel to themselves. However, the unlicensed home-building evades the Civil Administration's land registration process, which derives from Israel's Oslo-granted authority over Area C. Therefore, the illegal dwellings are properly demolished.

In response to certain acts of terrorism, Israel demolishes the terrorist's home. The purpose of such security demolitions is to render the home unavailable for military purposes (e.g. as a bomb-making lab, rocket-launching site, or munitions warehouse) and deter would-be terrorists from carrying out attacks.[1119]

The deterrence strategy works because Palestinians are reluctant to engage in hostilities that may render their families homeless.[1120] Likewise, relatives of terrorists sometimes decide to stop the offenses rather than lose their homes.[1121] The demolitions are conducted under the supervision of Israel's courts and disallowed where there is no apparent deterrent value.[1122]

[1119] *See* Emanuel Gross, *Democracy's Struggle Against Terrorism: The Powers of Military Commanders to Decide Upon the Demolition of Houses, the Imposition of Curfews, Blockades, Encirclements and the Declaration of an Area as a Closed Military Area*, 30.2 GA. J.INT'L & COMP. L. 165, 186-191 (2002) [hereinafter Gross], https://digitalcommons.law.uga.edu/gjicl/vol30/iss2/2/.

[1120] *Id.*

[1121] *Id.*

[1122] *See, e.g. Supreme Court Cancels Demolition of Terrorist's Home*, YNETNEWS.COM (Dec. 1, 2015, available at http://www.ynetnews.com/articles/0,7340,L-4733372,00.html.

Less drastic measures to deter terrorism have not worked. For example, suicide bombers are not deterred by the threat of prosecution because they do not expect to survive their attacks.[1123]

Security demolitions are justified by the public order and safety mandate of Hague Regulation Article 43.[1124] They are also supported by Fourth Convention Article 53, which permits property destruction where the occupant considers it "absolutely necessary [for] military operations." Especially in cases where someone learns a family member is about to commit an attack and neglects to stop it, demolition is necessary.[1125]

A security demolition is not a collective punishment. The ICRC has recognized that a home used for a military purpose is a valid military target.[1126] Moreover, judicial oversight ensures the demolitions are not carried out indiscriminately. Each proceeding considers a variety of factors, including the severity of the terrorist act, any evidence of involvement by the family, and the degree of hardship that would result from the demolition.[1127]

vi. Israeli settlement policies comply with the limits on use of natural resources

---

[1123] Gross, *supra* at 201.

[1124] Gross, *supra* at 193.

[1125] *Id.* at 194-95.

[1126] *See Practice Relating to Rule 10. Civilian Objects' Loss of Protection from Attack,* Customary IHL, ICRC, https://ihl-databases.icrc.org/customary-ihl/eng/docs/v2_rul_rule10.

[1127] Gross, *supra* at 199-200.

Hague Regulation Article 55 requires an occupying power to administer the area's natural resources as a usufruct. Israel is not an occupying power but still meets this standard. In the process, it has dramatically improved the supply of water to Palestinians.

In 1967, few Palestinians in the Territories were connected to a water system. By 2012, thanks to Israeli intervention, 96 percent of Palestinians were connected, and another two percent were scheduled to come on line.[1128] The progress gave Palestinians better water access than their brethren in the surrounding Arab states.[1129]

Oslo II defers the issue of water rights to the final status negotiation.[1130] During the Oslo interim period, the parties share the resource under the auspices of a Joint Water Committee.[1131] The Committee was considered necessary to control the dual risks of water scarcity and salination of area aquifers by unlicensed and unregulated water use. Israel has fully cooperated in the Committee's proceedings. In fact, it has exceeded the minimum delivery quota of water to Palestinians.[1132] The Joint Water Committee agreed that during the Oslo interim period, Israel would

---

[1128] Haim Gvirtzman, *The Israeli-Palestinian Water Conflict: An Israeli Perspective*, The Begin-Sadat Center for Strategic Studies Bar-Ilan University, No. 94 MIDEAST SECURITY AND POLICY STUDIES 9 (2012) [hereinafter Gvirtzman] available at: http://besacenter.org/wp-content/uploads/2012/01/MSPS94.pdf.

[1129] *Id.*

[1130] Oslo II, appendix 1, art. 40.1.

[1131] *Id.*, appendix 1, art. 40.

[1132] *Id.*, p. 8.

increase the supply of water to Palestinians by 20 percent, yet during that time Israel actually increased the supply by 50 percent.[1133]

There is no material difference in per-capita water consumption between Israelis and Palestinians.[1134] The disparity quoted by Palestinians is based on reports from the Palestinian Central Bureau of Statistics, which inflates Palestinian population figures by hundreds of thousands.[1135] For example, some Palestinians counted as "residents" of the Territories actually immigrated to Israel proper through Israel's family unification program, while others relocated to Israel through intermarriage and still others moved abroad.[1136]

The reason why Israeli lawns are green and Palestinian yards are brown is due to differences in water management. Israel stretches its water supply through programs of recycling, desalination, and conservation.[1137] Palestinians neglect the simplest steps of water management.[1138] Despite numerous Joint Committee approvals for new wells and offers of international aid, the PA has failed to pursue even basic projects to increase its water supply or maintain existing pipes,

---

[1133] Water Authority, State of Israel, *The Issue of Water between Israel and the Palestinians* (March, 2009) [hereinafter Water Authority], p. 7, https://www.gov.il/BlobFolder/reports/water_israel_palestinians/he/Israel_and_the_Palestinian s.pdf.

[1134] Gvirtzman, *supra*, pp. 12-13.

[1135] *Id.*

[1136] *Id.*

[1137] *Id.*, pp. 27-28.

[1138] *Id.*, p. 28-29.

which are now prone to massive leaking.[1139] Instead, Palestinians steal water from Israeli pipelines in violation of the Oslo Accords.[1140]

Israel also meets Hague Article 55 in its mining operations. Oslo II authorizes Israeli mining companies to operate in West Bank Area C pending the final status negotiation.[1141] But even if Israel is viewed as an occupying power, it may mine the quarries of the West Bank. As a usufruct, an occupying power may use resources in the occupied territory to the same degree as in pre-war days.[1142] In a prolonged occupation, the occupier may also make normal technological improvements in the productivity of the resource-extracting enterprise.[1143]

Based on the above, Israeli mining companies operate quarries and mines in Israel's Oslo-assigned Area C, while permitting Palestinians to conduct such operations in Areas A, B, and C.[1144] The Israeli-controlled quarries and mines benefit the economies of both populations in the Territories and are not excessively productive.[1145] The reason Palestinians may not mine the quarries abandoned by Israeli companies in West Bank Areas A and B is because the Oslo agreement made them

---

[1139] *Id.*, p. 21-29.

[1140] *Id.*, pp. 9-11; Water Authority, p. 9-11 and 21.

[1141] *See* Oslo II, Annex III, Art. 31.2.

[1142] Hague Article 55; DINSTEIN *OCCUPATION, supra* at 215-16.

[1143] DINSTEIN *OCCUPATION, supra* at 215-16.

[1144] *See* Yesh Din – Volunteers for Human Rights v. The Commander of the IDF Forces in the West Bank, HCJ 2164/09, December 26, 2011, paras. 3-6, available at https://casebook.icrc .org/case-study/israel-high-court-justice-quarrying-occupied-territory.

[1145] *Id.*, paras. 8-13.

inoperative during the interim period.[1146] Meanwhile, Israel voluntarily refrained from opening new quarries in West Bank Area C.[1147]

vii. Israeli settlement policies do not discriminate against Palestinians

The legal system that oversees the Territories does not discriminate against Palestinians.

Oslo II allocates civil jurisdiction in the Territories to both Israeli and Palestinian courts.[1148] Pursuant to this system of concurrent jurisdiction, Israeli civil courts exercise jurisdiction over Israeli citizens in both Israel proper and the Territories.[1149] This "personal jurisdiction" doctrine gives all Israelis equal rights.[1150] The doctrine cannot allow Israel to apply its civil law to the Territories as a geographic unit and thereby encompass Palestinians. Any such extension of Israeli law to those disputed confines would likely be denounced as an annexation of territory in violation of Oslo's no-change-in-status clause[1151] and occupation law.[1152]

[1146] Oslo II, Annex III, Art. 31.3.a.

[1147] David Kretzmer, *The law of belligerent occupation in the Supreme Court of Israel*, 94 Int'l Rev. of the Red Cross 207, 222 (Spring 2012), https://papers.ssrn.com/sol3/papers.cfm?abstract_id=2657530.

[1148] Oslo II, Annex IV, art. III.

[1149] BENVENISTI, *supra*, at 227-29.

[1150] Michael M. Karayanni, *the Quest for Creative Jurisdiction: The Evolution of Personal Jurisdiction Doctrine of Israeli Courts toward the Palestinian Territories*, 29 MICH. J. INT'L L., 665, 677 (2008), available at http://repository.law.umich.edu/cgi/viewcontent.cgi?article=1154&context=mjil.

[1151] *See Id. See also* Oslo II, art. XXXI (7).

[1152] *See* VON GLAHN, *supra* at 94.

Civil matters involving Palestinians in West Bank Areas A and B are properly adjudicated in Palestinian courts under Palestinian law.[1153] West Bank Area C Palestinians may seek civil relief under either legal system.

Overlaying the above-described civil law structure is a military administration necessitated by the armed conflict.[1154] Hague Article 43 requires an occupying power to enforce such martial law for the sake of public order and safety. Thus, when Palestinians commit acts of terrorism they are naturally tried in military courts.[1155] An Israeli criminal court would lack jurisdiction over such non-citizens.

Israel affords Palestinian terrorist defendants a right not compelled by the Fourth Amendment and never observed anywhere else in the world. The defendants may appeal cases to Israel's Supreme Court as the legal supervisor of the IDF.[1156] The procedural innovation has successfully protected Palestinian due process rights.[1157]

Israel maintains defensive roads, roadblocks, checkpoints, and other movement restrictions in the West Bank pursuant to its "responsibility for overall security of Israelis" under Oslo II.[1158] Having agreed to that Oslo provision, Palestinians cannot credibly bemoan its consequences.

[1153] See BENVENISTI, *supra* at 231 and 239.

[1154] See *Id.* at 212-213.

[1155] See *Id.* at 239.

[1156] *Id.* at 217-18.

[1157] *Id.* at 220 and 232.

[1158] Oslo II, art. VIII.

viii. Israel's settlements are not obstacles to peace

Israel's settlements are not obstacles to peace. In fact, there is no correlation between settlement construction and peace talks. Long before 1967, when Israel began building settlements in the Territories, Arab Palestinian terrorists relentlessly attacked Israeli civilians. From December 1992 to 1999, while both parties built settlements in the Territories, they successfully negotiated the Oslo Accords.[1159] In 2005, when Israel withdrew all its settlements from Gaza, Palestinians eschewed peace talks and instead exploited the vacated land as a launching pad for rocket and missile attacks on Israeli civilian populations.[1160] Then in 2009 and 2013, when Israel froze all new settlement projects, the concessions failed to induce any flexibility on the other side of the negotiating table.[1161] Palestinian terrorism continued unabated.

Palestinians complain that Israel's settlements effect a de facto annexation of the Territories as measured by land use and population growth. Only a small percentage of the West Bank contains Israeli settlements.[1162] The built-up portion of the settlements covers only one percent of the West Bank and just 1.9% of the ground spanning both the West Bank and East Jerusalem.[1163] Within that 1.9% ambit stands the

---

[1159] See SACHAR, *supra* at 1003.

[1160] MFA *Peace Talks*, *supra*.

[1161] MFA *Peace Talks*, *supra*.

[1162] MFA *Peace Talks*, *supra*.

[1163] Col. (res.) Shaul Arieli, *Why Settlements Have Not Killed the Two-State Solution*, BRITAIN ISRAEL COMMUNICATIONS & RESEARCH CENTRE 3, (Jan. 2013), https://www.bicom.org.uk/analysis/11038/.

major settlement blocs, which house eighty percent of Territory-based Israelis.[1164] Keeping those blocs intact would require nothing more than a border assigning six percent of the West Bank to Israel.[1165] That six percent sliver could be offset by a land-swap allocating an equal expanse of Israeli land to the proposed Palestinian state.[1166] As for the unauthorized outposts, they contain fewer than 2,000 residents each and collectively consume less than 0.4% of the West Bank.[1167] Thus, the encampments could be readily removed. The Ehud Olmert peace proposal of 2008 proposed just such a plan. Regrettably, the Palestinians snubbed the offer without proposing an alternative.

More generally, Palestinians blame the entire Israeli-Palestinian conflict on the so-called "occupation." That supposed encroachment started during the 1967 war. Yet area Arabs have been terrorizing their Jewish neighbors since long before then.[1168] The militants organized attacks on Jewish villages in 1886, 1888, 1890, 1892, 1893, 1896, 1899, 1908, and 1909.[1169] Following those hostilities were the Nebi Musa riots of 1920,[1170] which killed a group of orthodox Jewish civilians, and another mass-murder of Jews in 1929. Numerous acts of terrorism marred the next

---

[1164] *Id.*

[1165] *Id.*

[1166] *Id.*

[1167] *Factsheet: Myths and Facts about the growth of Israel's West Bank settlements*, AIJAC (May 4, 2015), http://www.aijac.org.au/news/article/factsheet-myths-and-facts-about-the-growth-of-is.

[1168] MFA *Peace Talks, supra.*

[1169] DOWTY, *supra* at 65.

[1170] *See* Mario Loyola, *For Peace in Palestine, Start From Scratch*, NATIONAL REVIEW (Jan. 4, 2017) [hereinafter Loyola], http://www.nationalreview.com/article/443501/israeli-palestinian-peace-requires-total-overhaul.

three decades of Arab-Jewish life. The violence reached even greater extremes with the founding of the PLO in 1964.

The greatest obstacle to Israeli-Palestinian peace is Palestinian radicalism.[1171] Opinion polls in the Territories have consistently found that regardless of how many Israeli settlers leave the Territories, most Palestinians believe they deserve all of former Mandatory Palestine and Israel should not exist.[1172] Time and again, Palestinian terrorism has discouraged both sides from making peace.[1173] In fact, Yassir Arafat orchestrated anti-Israeli violence as an instrument of diplomacy and never even spoke of making compromises for peace.[1174]

Anti-Semitic violence is the cause, not the effect, of the Israeli-Palestinian conflict.[1175] Many Palestinians simply oppose equal co-existence with Jews.[1176] Similar storms of Islamic bigotry have wreaked havoc worldwide.[1177]

A point often overlooked is that Israeli settlements nurture seeds of reconciliation with peace-loving Palestinians. In the West Bank, Israelis

---

[1171] MFA *Peace Talks, supra.*

[1172] Daniel Polisar, *Do Palestinians Want a Two-State Solution?* MOSAIC (April 3, 2017), https://mosaicmagazine.com/essay/2017/04/do-palestinians-want-a-two-state-solution/.

[1173] ROSS *MISSING PEACE, supra,* at 761-62.

[1174] *Id.* at 766.

[1175] *Id.*

[1176] Jeffrey Goldberg, *The Paranoid, Supremacist Roots of the Stabbing Intifada,* THE ATLANTIC (Oct. 16, 2015), https://www.theatlantic.com/international/archive/2015/10/the-roots-of-the-palestinian-uprising-against-israel/410944/.

[1177] Loyola, *supra.*

and Palestinians increasingly form business partnerships that improve local conditions.[1178] Palestinians and Israelis also work side-by-side in West Bank companies. Hardline Palestinians violently oppose such collaborations as treasonous "normalization."[1179] But the interethnic associations advance hopes for peace.[1180]

4.6: Do Palestinians have a right of return to Israel?

Author's Prologue

During the 1947-1948 war, frantic population movements in and around Mandatory Palestine transformed the region's demographics. Refugee figures from the period are disputed,[1181] but approximately 600,000 to 760,000 Arab Palestinians were expelled or fled from the territory that became recognized as Israel.[1182] About a third of the Arab migrants rushed to Gaza (then occupied by Egypt), another third ran to the

---

[1178] Richard Behar, *Peace through Profits? Inside the Secret Tech Ventures That Are Reshaping The Israeli-Arab-Palestinian World*, FORBES (Aug. 12, 2013), https://www.forbes.com/sites/richardbehar/2013/07/24/peace-through-profits-a-private-sector-detente-is-drawing-israelis-palestinians-closer/#135c08893614.

[1179] *See* Cary Nelson, *Anti-Normalization*, in DREAMS DEFERRED, *supra* 32-36.

[1180] *Id.*

[1181] The circumstances of the human dispersals are unclear due to the chaotic nature of the War and lack of records. BENNY MORRIS, *THE BIRTH OF THE PALESTINIAN REFUGEE PROBLEM REVISITED* 593 and 599 (2004) [hereinafter MORRIS *BIRTH REVISITED*].

[1182] BENNY MORRIS, *THE BIRTH OF THE PALESTINIAN REFUGEE PROBLEM*, 1947-1949 1 (1987). Other estimates of the figure range from 500,000 to over 940,000. TESSLER, *supra* at 279.

present-day West Bank (annexed by Jordan), and the rest went mainly to Lebanon, Syria and Jordan.[1183]

Jewish Palestinians were expelled or fled from their homes in Mandatory Palestine.[1184] About 1,600 Jews left the Jewish Quarter of the Old City in Jerusalem and roughly 10,000 more emptied various other locales in the mandatory district.[1185] The uprooted residents flocked to the Jewish strongholds in the district.[1186]

During and after the War, 700,000 or more Jews were expelled or fled from Muslim lands across the Middle East and North Africa, including states not involved in the military clash.[1187]

[1183] *Palestinian Refugees*, ANTI-DEFAMATION LEAGUE, https://www.adl.org/resources/glossary-terms/palestinian-refugees. For a more detailed breakdown of the Arab Palestinian exodus, see TESSLER, *supra* at 279-280.

[1184] Gilead Ini, *Backgrounder: Palestinian Arab and Jewish Refugees*, CAMERA (May 12, 2009) [hereinafter CAMERA *Backgrounder on Refugees*], https://www.camera.org/article/backgrounder-palestinian-arab-and-jewish-refugees/. CAMERA stands for "Committee for Accuracy in Middle East Reporting in America." CAMERA describes itself as "a media-monitoring, research and membership organization devoted to promoting accurate and balanced coverage of Israel and the Middle East." *Mission*, CAMERA, https://www.camera.org/about/mission/.

[1185] *See id.* Another source estimates 2,500 Jews left the Jewish Quarter. GILBERT, *supra at 156*.

[1186] CAMERA *Backgrounder on Refugees*, *supra*.

[1187] GORDIS, *supra* at 185. Another estimate of the Jewish refugee population was 820,000. *Fact Sheet, Jewish Refugees from Arab Countries*, JEWISH VIRTUAL LIBRARY, https://www.jewishvirtuallibrary.org/jewish-refugees-from-arab-countries. According to Israel's Ministry of Foreign Affairs, the figure exceeded 850,000. *Jewish Refugees Expelled from Arab*

Given the geography of the warfare, where neighbors fought neighbors, each belligerent used its towns and villages as military bases while striving to capture and destroy the opposing municipalities.[1188] The Jewish Palestinians implemented this strategy more successfully than their rivals.[1189] In the end, the War displaced far more Arab Palestinians than Jewish Palestinians and destroyed far more Arab homes than Jewish homes.[1190] The dual displacement across the entire Middle East and North Africa was about equal. All the involved nations confiscated the properties abandoned in their jurisdictions.

The War ended with armistice (cease-fire fire) agreements, not peace treaties. The Arab coalition remained implacably opposed to Israel's existence.[1191] Armed bands from Gaza, Syria and Jordan sporadically

---

Lands and from Iran, ISRAELI MINISTRY OF FOREIGN AFFAIRS (Nov. 30, 2017), https://mfa.gov.il/MFA/ForeignPolicy/Issues/Pages/Jewish-refugees-expelled-from-Arab-lands-and-from-Iran-29-November-2016.aspx. The involved Muslim states were Egypt, Lebanon, Syria, Turkey, Iraq, Morocco, Algeria, Libya, Tunisia, Yemen, and Iran. *Id.*

[1188] Benny Morris, *"The Birth of the Palestinian Refugee Problem, 1947-49,"* in *1948 Refugees, Proceedings of an international workshop*, Hebrew University of Jerusalem Faculty of Law, *14-15 December, 2016*, 51(1) ISRAEL LAW REVIEW 47,48 (2018) [hereinafter Morris *Refugee Workshop*].

[1189] *Id.*

[1190] *See* Mahmoud Yazbak, *"The Nakba and the Palestinian Silence,"* in *1948 Refugees, Proceedings of an international workshop*, Hebrew University of Jerusalem Faculty of Law, *14-15 December, 2016*, 51(1) ISRAEL LAW REVIEW 51 (2018) [hereinafter Yazbak *Refugee Workshop*], https://www.cambridge.org/core/journals/israel-law-review/article/1948-refugees/1E997E364691F4379C6F77EC05BC84AD/core-reader.

[1191] GILBERT, *supra* at 255.

attacked Israeli communities despite the armistice terms, and Israel launched retaliatory raids.

After the War, Lebanon, Syria and Jordan refused to resettle their populations of Arab refugees. According to these states, Israel was an illegal colonial enterprise that had usurped Arab land and unjustly expelled its inhabitants. The Arabs reiterated their determination to extinguish the "Zionist entity" and let the Arab refugees return to their pre-war homes.

Israel would not repatriate the Arab refugees. The fledgling nation sealed its armistice borders based on the claim that opening its doors to the enemy population would imperil its national security.[1192] The closure served the military purpose of defending against guerilla infiltrations and the political purpose of preventing the reintroduction of a large, hostile Arab minority.[1193] In the process, the barrier blocked both Arab militants and other Arabs who simply wished to go home.

The impasse over the dislocated Arabs generally left them stateless and homeless with no rescue plan.[1194] Decades later, many Arabs looked back on the event as the "Nakba" (catastrophe).

The UN responded to the humanitarian crisis by building refugee camps in the three Arab refugee host states, as well as Gaza, East Jerusalem, and the West Bank. Just as the UN established the United

---

[1192] TESSLER, *supra* at 280.

[1193] MORRIS *BIRTH REVISITED*, *supra* at 341, 505, and 598.

[1194] Jordan's policy differed from that of Lebanon and Syria; it granted citizenship to most of its Palestinian entrants.

Nations High Commissioner for Refugees (UNHCR) to care for the refugees of World War II, the world body also created the United Nations Relief and Works Agency (UNRWA) to serve the Arab Palestinian refugees of the 1947-1948 war.[1195] UNRWA's mission was meant to be temporary, but the organization survives to this day, with the fate of its wards unresolved.

Not all Arab Palestinians left the portion of Mandatory Palestine that became Israel. Those who stayed – approximately 160,000 – became citizens of the new Jewish state and elected two Arab representatives to Israel's first Knesset (parliament).[1196] On the other hand, many of those Arabs could not remain in their pre-war villages because they had been demolished.[1197]

Israel resettled the Jewish Palestinian refugees from East Jerusalem and the West Bank, as well as the hundreds of thousands of Jews who had arrived from the Muslim world. Many of the internally displaced persons could not go home because their homes had been destroyed. The UN did not assist Israel's refugee integration efforts.

Under pressure from the US in 1949, Israel offered to admit 65,000 to 70,000 Arab refugees as part of a comprehensive peace plan.[1198] The Arabs rejected the offer.[1199] They did not want to legitimize Israel by engaging the state in peace talks. In any event, their goal was to restore

---

[1195] *See* G.A. Res. 302, U.N. Doc. A/RES/302 (Dec. 8, 1949).

[1196] *See* MORRIS *BIRTH REVISITED*, *supra* at 61, n. 6; GILBERT, *supra* at 250.

[1197] KIMMERLING, *supra* at 127.

[1198] MORRIS *BIRTH REVISITED*, *supra* at 600.

[1199] *Id.*

the entire Arab Palestinian refugee population, not just a token few. Even after the UN sweetened the deal by promising Egypt, Lebanon, Syria and Jordan vast resources to revitalize their moribund economies, the Arab states kept their thumbs down.[1200]

The 1967 war further complicated the refugee situation. During the fighting, some 150,000 Palestinians fled the West Bank to Jordan's East Bank and Syria.[1201] As many as 80,000 of them had already suffered the hardship of relocation during the 1947-1948 war.[1202] The 1967 conflict did not involve expulsions.[1203] However, those who left the area were generally not permitted to return.[1204]

Instead of demolishing Arab villages, as it had done in the 1947-1948 war, Israel, in 1967, generally left Arab villages intact, rebuilt some Arab homes that had been destroyed,[1205] and helped the inhabitants establish their first-ever set of self-governing institutions, pending the outcome of expected peace talks.[1206] In addition, over 50,000 Palestinian refugees were readmitted to the Territories as an exception to Israel's no-return policy.[1207]

[1200] Nitza Nachmias, *UNRWA Betrays its Mission*, 19:4 MIDDLE EAST QUARTERLY 27, 28 (2012), http://www.meforum.org/3354/unrwa-mission.

[1201] SACHAR, *supra* at 669.

[1202] *Id.*

[1203] *Id.*

[1204] *Id.*

[1205] GILBERT, *supra* at 396-97.

[1206] SACHAR, *supra* at 677-78.

[1207] *See Id.* at 670.

After the war, the Arab League issued its Khartoum ("Three No's") Resolution: no recognition, no negotiation, and no peace. Egypt, Syria and Jordan continued to torment Israel with terrorist attacks. Israel resumed its retaliatory strikes and sealed its new boundaries (which now encompassed the Territories), blocking entry by militants and refugees alike.

The Oslo Accords of the 1990's slated the issue of "refugees" for resolution in the final status negotiation. However, the vague wording of the documents did not assign blame for the problem or suggest how it should be solved.

Arabs and Israelis endlessly debate two issues: who was to blame for the outpouring of Arab and Jewish refugees during their two 20th Century wars; and how should the victims be "rehabilitated" (compensated)?

The rehabilitation issue boils down to a basic question: should the refugees be "resettled" in their states of asylum, "repatriated" to their pre-war homes," or awarded monetary compensation?

Palestinians argue for repatriation of their people under a "right of return." They believe the right could be satisfied through a physical relocation to the former Mandatory Palestine or monetary compensation. Jews relocated to East Jerusalem and the West Bank after Israel captured those lands in the 1967 war. Jewish repatriation to their Muslim countries of origin is considered infeasible due to the instability of those nations and their continuing hostility to Jews. Therefore, the affected Jewish expatriates would probably have to accept monetary compensation.

Why so many Arabs and Jews migrated en masse during and after the 1947-1948 war is one of history's most heated controversies. This study provides only a summary of the dispute. Yet the issue is important to determine whether either exodus was caused by a legal violation. If a violation occurred, the next question is whether the victims may return to their pre-war homes or collect alternate compensation. These are the issues reserved for the Oslo final status negotiation. As discussed, the Jewish émigrés from the Muslim world cannot realistically return to their pre-war homes. A right of return could be implemented only for Palestinians.

Do Palestinians have a right of return?

A. The Palestinian Arguments

Summary of Arguments

Zionist ideology mandated the expulsion of Arab Palestinians from their homeland so the Jewish people could establish a state in Palestine. The Zionists engineered the ethnic cleansing via the 1947-1948 war. In that conflict, Jewish armed forces employed a combination of military attacks, massacres, and psychological terror to force about 700,000 Arabs from their homes. The brutal mass-removal was just the kind of conduct recognized as a war crime in the Nuremberg and Tokyo Tribunals.

The expelled Palestinians have a right of return to the territory now called Israel. Because Israel's violation of Palestinian refugee rights has been "of a continuing character", this return is required under modern-day treaties and customary law – even though these legal tools were not available in 1948.

In addition, UN Resolution 194(III) of 1948 established that all Palestinian refugees who wished to return to Israel and live at peace with their neighbors were immediately permitted to do so. A long chain of UN resolutions passed after Resolution 194(III) have reiterated the Palestinian right of return. The pronouncements have recognized that such repatriation is instrumental to the Palestinian right of self-determination.

When Israelis and Palestinians enter the final stage of the Oslo Accords, they will be expected to reach a "just settlement" of the refugee issue, as memorialized in UN Resolution 242. A just settlement would permit the abused innocents to decide whether they will live in Israel, the Territories, or somewhere else. The resolution of the conflict will also compensate Palestinian refugees for the confiscation of their property and other losses.

UNRWA, the UN relief agency that provides essential humanitarian services to Palestinian refugees, serves the world's largest refugee population. The aggrieved population amounted to nearly 6 million as of 2018 and continues to grow.

> The numbers tell a story of grave injustice. Israel attempts to minimize its responsibility for the crisis by assuming the count of Palestinian refugees should be determined under the narrow definition of "refugee" found in the Refugee Convention.
>
> However, Palestinian refugees are exempt from the Convention. Israel also argues that its duty to Palestinian refugees should be offset by an amount owed to Jewish refugees from all Arab lands. But this is erroneous. Any wrongdoing committed by a non-Palestinian state should be remedied by that state, not the Palestinians.

i. The Zionists illegally expelled the Arab Palestinian population

The term "Nakba" (catastrophe) refers to Israel's ethnic cleansing of Arabs from at least 418 cities and villages in Mandatory Palestine during and after the 1947-1948 war.[1208] The Nakba stripped Arab Palestinians of their human rights and national rights.[1209] And the crimes of expulsion and displacement continue to this day.[1210]

[1208] State of Palestine, Palestine Liberation Organization - Negotiations Affairs Department, *Factsheet, 70 Years of al-Nakba, in Focus, The Illegality of Moving the US Embassy to Jerusalem*, , https://www.nad.ps/sites/default/files/05092018.pdf.

[1209] *Id.*

[1210] *Id.*

The motivation for the Nakba was directly attributable to Zionism.[1211] Zionists expelled the Arab Palestinian population to facilitate the immigration of hundreds of thousands of Jews.[1212]

For decades after the Nakba, Israel propagated the lie that the Arab Palestinian exit was caused by their own leaders.[1213] The invented story was that Arab *mukhtars* (local political leaders) ordered their villagers to evacuate and thereby clear a path for the Arab army invasion of Israel.[1214] However, in the late 1980's Israel's "New Historians" corrected the record.[1215] They exposed the fact that before the 1947-1948 war, top Zionist leaders discussed how they might "transfer" the Arab population to make way for their planned Jewish state.[1216] What the academics failed to disclose was that the Zionists did not merely consider the possibility of expelling Arabs; they chose expulsion as an ideological imperative and then implemented the master plan through their wartime strategy.[1217] It was the only way they could seize possession of a land that was already owned by others.[1218]

[1211] Walid Khalidi, *Plan Dalet: Master Plan for the Conquest of Palestine*, 18:1 J. PALEST. STUD. 4 (1988) [hereinafter Walid Khalidi], http://pbble.com/doc/Khalidi-Plan-Dalet.pdf. Professor Khalidi is a Palestinian historian, founder of the Institute for Palestine Studies, and a Palestinian delegate to the Middle East peace negotiations held at the Madrid Conference. His scholarship has been instrumental in shaping Palestinian positions on the Arab-Israeli conflict.

[1212] *Id.* at 5-6.

[1213] *Id.* at 4-5.

[1214] *Id.*

[1215] *Id.*

[1216] *Id.*

[1217] *Id.* at 5-6.

[1218] *Id.* at 8-10. For a detailed study of the connection between Zionism and the expulsion of Arab Palestinians, see ILAN PAPPE, *THE ETHNIC CLEANSING OF PALESTINE* (2007).

The Zionist expulsion plot was hatched during internal discussions in the early 1930s and then articulated in the Peel Commission Report of 1937.[1219] The Report recommended an exchange of land and population between Arabs and Jews, even though the Arab population was overwhelmingly larger and Arabs owned all but a fraction of the land. A variation of the discriminatory theme emerged in the 1947 UN Partition Plan, when Zionists took the position that 55 percent of Mandatory Palestine was the "irreducible minimum" they could accept to form their desired state.[1220] The Partition Plan would have contrived a radical redistribution of territory in favor of the Zionists.[1221]

The IDF's own intelligence estimate from 1948 reveals that 70 percent of the Arab Palestinian displacement was caused by: (1) "direct, hostile Jewish operations against Arab settlements;" (2) "the effect of our hostile operations on nearby [Arab] settlements;" and (3) "operations of the [Jewish extremist militias Irgun and Lehi]."[1222] Some of those hostile operations impacted areas that had been designated for an Arab state by the 1947 UN Partition Plan.[1223]

"Plan Dalet," otherwise known as "Plan D," formed the heart of the premeditated military initiative that carried out the expulsion

---

[1219] *Id.* at 10-11.

[1220] *Id.* at 12-14.

[1221] *Id.* at 14.

[1222] VICTOR KATTAN, *FROM COEXISTENCE TO CONQUEST* 194-95 (2009) (hereinafter KATTAN *CONQUEST*) (citing a document in the private papers of Aharon Cohen, Director of Mapam, the labor party of early Israel).

[1223] *Id.*

scheme.[1224] The Plan orchestrated an all-out offensive to conquer and occupy the whole of western Palestine.[1225] In pertinent part, the text instructed Jewish military commanders that:

> ... in the event of resistance, the armed force must be wiped out and the population must be expelled outside the borders of the new state.[1226]

Supplementing the expulsions was a campaign of fear-mongering.[1227] The *Haganah* (the Zionists' regular army) used loudspeaker vans and Arab-language radio broadcasts to spread disinformation throughout Arab towns and villages.[1228] Some broadcasts threatened the Arabs with mass slaughter if they remained in their homes and promised safe passage if they would promptly leave.[1229] Other phony news alerts warned of fast-spreading deadly diseases. These tricks effectively drained hundreds of Arab communities.

One of the most potent catalysts of Arab Palestinian flight during the 1947-1948 war was the massacre at Deir Yassin.[1230] The term "Deir Yassin" has come to symbolize the Zionist policy of terror that stripped Mandatory Palestine of its Arab majority.[1231] In that village outside Jerusalem, two Jewish militant extremist groups – Irgun and Lehi –

[1224] Walid Khalidi, *supra* at 8.

[1225] *Id.* at 15-17.

[1226] *Id.*, Appendix B, p. 29.

[1227] *Id.* at 18-19; KHALIDI *IRON CAGE*, *supra* at 189.

[1228] TESSLER, *supra* at 294-300.

[1229] *Id.* at 294-300; MORRIS *BIRTH REVISITED*, *supra* at 591-92.

[1230] *See* KATTAN *CONQUEST*, *supra* at 191-92.

[1231] *See* TESSLER, *supra* at 291.

killed over 200 Arab men, women and children and blew up their homes.[1232] The bodies of entire families were found filled with bullets and shrapnel.[1233] Many of the civilians were cut down while escaping from their homes; others were pulled aside and shot.[1234] According to British authorities, the Haganah was aware of the operation.[1235] Zionist news reports of the massacre turned the Arab Palestinian departure into a frenzied rush for the exits.[1236] In subsequent months, Zionist forces perpetrated similar atrocities and hailed the results.[1237] This practice of excessive brutality is what drove many Arab Palestinians from their homes.[1238]

The exclusionist goal of Plan Dalet was also evidenced by the resulting pattern of Palestinian dispersion. As many as 80% of the Arab refugees left towns and villages in the geographic expanse now called Israel.[1239] All the refugees, not just those who were literally expelled, should be counted as expelled because they all migrated due to the war and expected to return.[1240] Even those Arab Palestinians who were internally displaced should be included in the refugee count because their transition to Israeli citizenship did not alter their refugee status.[1241]

[1232] *Id.*

[1233] *Id.* (citing BENNY MORRIS, *RIGHTEOUS VICTIMS: A HISTORY OF THE ZIONIST-ARAB CONFLICT*, 1881-1999 208 (1999)) [hereinafter MORRIS *RIGHTEOUS VICTIMS*].

[1234] *Id.* (citing MORRIS *RIGHTEOUS VICTIMS* at 208).

[1235] KATTAN CONQUEST, *supra* at 191.

[1236] *Id.* at 192.

[1237] *Id.* 191-94.

[1238] *Id.* at 199.

[1239] Yazbak Refugee Workshop, *supra* at 51.

[1240] *Id.* at 51-55 and 57.

[1241] *Id.*

After the 1947-1948 war, Israel's "emergency regulations" established security zones along the armistice lines to block Arab Palestinians from coming home.[1242] The zones deliberately foreclosed the possibility of any large-scale refugee return.[1243]

Israel's expulsionist activities triggered legal liability. After World War II, the military tribunals in Nuremberg and Tokyo confirmed that the practice of mass-expulsion breached customary international law.[1244] Thus, the subsequent Israeli expulsion of Arab Palestinians during the 1947-1948 war violated that law, even though the codified version of the war crime, which emerged in the Fourth Convention, had not yet entered into force.[1245]

ii. Palestinians have a right of return to Israel and rights to related reparations

Although a rule of international law -- called the intertemporal rule – generally prohibits judicial authorities from applying the laws of today to actions of the past, an exception is recognized for wrongdoing of "a continuing character."[1246] Where a violation is continuing, the applicable law is the law in force when the dispute is settled.[1247] Israel continued

---

[1242] SACHAR, *supra* at 385.

[1243] MORRIS *BIRTH REVISITED, supra* at 341-60.

[1244] KATTAN *CONQUEST, supra* at 203-04.

[1245] *Id.*

[1246] KATTAN, *supra* at 212-13 (citing the International Law Commission's Articles on *Responsibility of States for Internationally Wrongful Acts*, art. 14.)

[1247] *Id.* at 216.

the crime of expulsion in the 1947-1948 war by refusing to let the exiled individuals return to Israel.[1248] Accordingly, whether the Israeli-Palestinian conflict is resolved through negotiation or judicial decree, the parties should honor all refugee-related treaties adopted since 1948.[1249]

Such treaties include the Universal Declaration of Human Rights and the International Covenant on Civil and Political Rights.[1250] The Universal Declaration of Human Rights guarantees that "everyone has the right to leave any country, including his own, and return to his country."[1251] The International Covenant on Civil and Political Rights states that "No one shall be arbitrarily deprived of the right to enter his own country."[1252] Under these laws, Israel must accommodate the return of the Palestinian refugees and pay them post-war compensation ("reparations").[1253]

Even without reliance on post-1948 laws, Arab Palestinian refugees may be repatriated by virtue of UN action.[1254] As the 1947-1948 war concluded, the UN General Assembly adopted Resolution 194(III),

---

[1248] *Id.*

[1249] *Id.* at 216-17.

[1250] *Id.* at 217.

[1251] State of Palestine, Palestine Liberation Organization - Negotiation Affairs Department, "*Refugees," Our Position,* (citing Universal Declaration of Human Rights, art.13(2)), https://www.nad.ps/en/our-position/refugees.

[1252] *Id.* (citing International Covenant on Civil and Political Rights, art. 12(4)).

[1253] KATTAN, *supra* at 217.

[1254] *Id.* at 217-220.

which let Palestinian refugees return to Israel. Paragraph 11 resolved that:

> the refugees wishing to return to their homes and live at peace with their neighbors should be permitted to do so at the earliest practicable date, and that compensation should be paid for the property of those choosing not to return and for loss of or damage to property which, under principles of international law or in equity, should be made good by the Governments or authorities responsible ...[1255]

The intent of Paragraph 11 was to "facilitate the repatriation, resettlement and economic and social rehabilitation of the refugees and the payment of compensation ..."[1256]

Paragraph 11 created a right of return for Arab Palestinian refugees.[1257] As stated in 1948 by UN peace mediator Count Folke Bernadotte, the official whose report on the 1947-1948 war laid the foundation for Resolution 194(III), "no settlement can be just and complete if recognition is not accorded to the right of the Arab refugee to return to the home from which he has been dislodged ..."[1258]

[1255] Resolution 194 (III), para. 11.

[1256] *Id.*

[1257] KATTAN *CONQUEST, supra* at 217-20.

[1258] *Id.* at 218 (citing *Progress Report of the United Nations Mediator on Palestine submitted to the Secretary-General for Transmission to the Members of the United Nations*, UN Doc. A/648 (Sept. 16, 1948)).

Resolution 194(III) arranged the right of return in five components:[1259]

1) Refugees have a right to return "to their homes," and not just anywhere in Mandatory Palestine;[1260]

2) Right of return is a matter of each refugee's individual choice;[1261]

3) Timeframe for refugee relief as "the earliest practicable date," with no need to await the negotiation of a peace treaty;[1262]

4) Israel is obligated to readmit the refugees who wish to return;[1263] and

5) This measure applies to all refugees without discrimination.[1264]

Palestinian refugees should have the choice of exercising their right of return in one of the following ways: a return to Israel; resettlement in a future Palestinian state; integration into an existing host state; or

---

[1259] Gail J. Boling, *Palestinian Refugees and the Right of Return: An International Law Analysis*, BADIL RESOURCE CENTER FOR PALESTINIAN RESIDENCY AND REFUGEE RIGHTS, Information & Discussion Brief, Issue No. 8 (Jan. 2001). BADIL is "an independent, human rights non-profit organization committed to protect and promote the rights of Palestinian refugees and internally displaced persons." *About BADIL, Mission*, http://www.badil.org/en/about-us.html.

[1260] *Id.*

[1261] *Id.*

[1262] *Id.*

[1263] *Id.*

[1264] *Id.*

resettlement in other states.[1265] In addition, the remedy should involve rehabilitation services such as housing, education, medical services, and professional training.[1266]

The clause in Resolution 194(III) that mentions reparations under "principles of international law or in equity" was a reference to the international law of "state responsibility" and related standards for deciding when compensation is owed to injured claimants.[1267] Under the law of state responsibility, if a state commits an act that breaches an international obligation, it must:

1) discontinue the act and restore the status quo ante
2) apply remedies as shaped by its domestic law, including the payment of compensation if restoring the preexisting status is not possible; and
3) provide guarantees that the act will not recur.[1268]

Certain tribunals established after past wars have ordered states to pay compensation to injured parties, including the replacement of confiscated property ("restitution").[1269]

[1265] PLO-NAD *Final Status, supra.*

[1266] *Id.*

[1267] Donna E. Arzt, *The Right to Compensation: Basic Principles Under International Law, Compensation as Part of a Comprehensive Solution to the Palestinian Refugee Problem,* prepared for the International Development Research Center's Workshop on Compensation for Palestinian Refugees, PALESTINIAN REFUGEE RESEARCHNET (July 14-15, 1999) [hereinafter Arzt], available at http://prrn.mcgill.ca/research/papers/artz4.htm.

[1268] *Id.; See also* SHAW, *supra* at 582-83.

[1269] Arzt, *supra.*

In modern times, the international community has acknowledged the importance of reparations for refugees.[1270] For example, the 1995 Dayton Accord, which ended the war in Bosnia and Herzegovina, recognized the right of refugees from that war to recover their property.[1271] The principle was given universal currency in the UN's 2006 Principles on Housing and Property Restitution for Refugees and Displaced Persons.[1272] These precedents provide guidance to compute the funds owed to the Palestinians.

Applying the above blueprint to the Israeli-Palestinian dispute, Israel should pay reparations to the Palestinian refugees for their losses in the wars of 1947-1948 and 1967. The reparations should take three forms:

1) Israel must confess to its role in creating and perpetuating the Palestinian refugee crisis;[1273]
2) Israel must provide restitution by restoring the ownership of land and other property Palestinians lost in the wars.[1274] If restitution is impossible in a given case, Israel may grant

---

[1270] Rex Brynen *Compensation for Palestinian Refugees: Law, Politics and Praxis*, 51(1) ISRAEL LAW REVIEW, 29,34 (2018).

[1271] *Id.*

[1272] *Id.*

[1273] PLO-NAD *Final Status, supra. See also* Rex Brynen, Session 4, *Restitution and Compensation, Restitution and Compensation,* in *1948 Refugees, Proceedings of an international workshop*, HEBREW UNIVERSITY OF JERUSALEM FACULTY OF LAW, *14-15 December, 2016*, 51(1) Israel Law Review 47,78-79 (2018).

[1274] PLO-NAD *Final Status, supra.*

the individual vacant land in the country or monetary compensation.[1275]

3) Israel owes the refugees monetary compensation for other damages, such as the destruction of personal property, lost jobs, and pain and suffering.[1276]

Until now, Palestinian refugees residing in Arab states have been represented by the PLO. Assuming that the State of Palestine becomes fully recognized, some may question whether the representation of refugees in the diaspora should shift from the PLO to Palestine, with all Palestinians made citizens of Palestine.[1277] That is a political question to be decided by the Palestinian people. But under Resolution 194(III), the refugees will remain entitled as ever to the choice of returning to Israel.[1278] Therefore any refugee currently in Lebanon, Syria or Jordan who chooses to move to Israel should not be diverted to another destination such as the State of Palestine.[1279]

Israel believes any compensation owed to Arab Palestinian refugees should be offset by the amount owed to Jewish refugees, regardless of whether those injured parties originated from Mandatory Palestine or a surrounding Arab state.[1280] However, if a state, such as Iraq, evicted its

---

[1275] *Id.*

[1276] *Id.*

[1277] *Position Paper: PCHR Warns of Prejudice of Palestinian Refugees' Right of Return*, PALESTINIAN CENTER FOR HUMAN RIGHTS (Sept., 2011), http://pchrgaza.org/en/?p=5350.

[1278] *Id.*

[1279] *Id.*

[1280] *Id.*

Jewish residents during the 1947-1948 war, then only Iraq should pay damages.[1281]

iii. UN actions after Resolution 194(III) reinforced the Palestinian right of return

Israel's failure to implement Resolution 194(III) led the UN to reiterate the statement on a nearly annual basis.[1282] When the 1967 war produced the second wave of Palestinian refugees, the UN Security Council immediately responded with Resolution 237.[1283] The measure required Israel to "facilitate the return of those inhabitants who have fled the areas since the outbreak of hostilities."[1284] Israel ignored the obligation.

The following year, the UN chastised Israel, and strongly urged the latter to resolve the 1967 refugee crisis.[1285] Resolution 2452A said Israel should "take effective and immediate steps [to] return without delay... those inhabitants who have fled the area since the outbreak of hostilities." [1286] Unlike Resolution 194(III), Resolution 2452A did not ask the 1967 war refugees to "live at peace with their neighbors."[1287] The implication was that Israel should admit all the 1967 refugees, even if

---

[1281] *Id.*

[1282] Yoav Tadmor, *The Palestinian Refugees of 1948: The Right to Compensation and Return*, 8 TEMP. INT'L & COMP. *LJ* 403, 413-14 (1994) [hereinafter Tadmor].

[1283] S.C. Res. 237, U.N. Doc. S/RES/237 (June 14, 1967). https://undocs.org/en/S/RES/237 (1967).

[1284] *Id.*, para. 1.

[1285] G.A. Res. 2452A, U.N. Doc. A/RES/2452A (Dec. 19, 1968), available at https://undocs. org/en/A/RES/2452(XXIII) .

[1286] *Id.* at para. 1.

[1287] Tadmor, *supra* at 424-25.

some might pose a national security risk.[1288] Israel disregarded the UN directive.

In 1969, UN Resolution 2535B recognized that Palestinian refugees possessed more than a right of return.[1289] The statement observed that the refugee problem arose from the denial of their inalienable rights under the UN Charter and the Universal Declaration of Human Rights, and it affirmed "the inalienable rights of the people of Palestine."[1290] The reference to inalienable rights implied a right of self-determination.

Perhaps the most definitive articulation of the Palestinian right of return was embodied in General Assembly Resolution 3089D (XXVIII) of 1973.[1291] The Resolution stated that the right of return as recommended by Resolution 194(III) was "indispensable for the achievement of a just settlement of the refugee problem."[1292]

iv. The Oslo Accords support the Palestinian right of return

The fate of the Palestinian refugees is one of the issues reserved for the final status talks of the Oslo Accords. As stated in Oslo I, the Accords

---

[1288] *Id.*

[1289] G.A. Res. 2535B (XXIV), U.N. Doc. A/RES/2535B (XXIV)(Dec. 10, 1969), available at https://undocs.org/A/RES/2535(XXIV).

[1290] *Id.*, para. 1.

[1291] G.A. Res. 3089D (XXVIII), U.N. Doc. A/RES/3089D (XXVIII) (Dec. 7, 1973), https://undocs.org/A/RES/3089(XXVIII).

[1292] *Id.* at para. 3.

are based in part on the message of UN Resolution 242. And Resolution 242 speaks of "achieving a just settlement of the refugee problem."[1293]

A just settlement of the Palestinian refugee issue would permit the refugees to decide their own fate.[1294] Some refugees may decide to return to Israel. Others may venture to the portion of Mandatory Palestine that becomes the universally-recognized State of Palestine.[1295] Still others may prefer other destinations, including the US or Europe.[1296] Some may opt for payment in lieu of relocation.[1297] Any of these solutions would serve Israel's interest by settling the many legal claims emanating from Resolution 194.[1298]

v. The Palestinian refugees have become the world's largest refugee population

According to the Palestinian Central Bureau of Statistics, as of 2018 there were 5.9 million Palestinian refugees, the largest refugee population in the world.[1299] As the refugee population swells, so does the injustice of their situation.

[1293] Resolution 242, para 2(b).

[1294] Shibley Telhami, *Addressing the Palestinian Refugee Problem*, BROOKINGS INSTITUTE (May 8, 2007) [hereinafter Telhami], https://www.brookings.edu/testimonies/addressing-the-palestinian-refugee-problem/.

[1295] *Id.*

[1296] *Id.*

[1297] *Id.*

[1298] *Id.*

[1299] *World Refugee Day 2018 Report: Palestinians are the Largest Population of Refugees*, IMEMC NEWS (June 21, 2018), https://imemc.org/article/world-refugee-day-2018-report-palestinians-are-the-largest-population-of-refugees/.

After the 1947-1948 war, when observers realized there would be no immediate solution for the approximately 700,000 Palestinian refugees from the war, UNRWA began providing essential services to Palestinians in their refugee status until they could receive a "just and durable solution" to the problem.[1300] A just and durable solution would give the refugees a meaningful range of choices, including the choice of returning to Israel or the Territories.[1301] Some of the deserving individuals are "1948 refugees," others are "1967 refugees," and still others are "internally displaced" within Israel and the Territories.[1302] The following explains how UNRWA counted Palestinians as refugees, a population which now totals 5.4 million,[1303] and why it is so urgent to end their stateless plight.

UNRWA defines "Palestine refugees"[1304] as "persons whose normal place of residence was Palestine during the period 1 June, 1946 to 15 May, 1948 and who lost both home and means of livelihood as a result of the 1948 conflict."[1305] Descendants of Palestinian refugee males are also eligible for UNRWA services, provided they live in one of

---

[1300] *See* About UNRWA, p. 4, UNRWA (2015) [hereinafter About UNRWA], https://www.unrwa.org/sites/default/files/about_unrwa_2015.pdf.

[1301] State of Palestine, Palestine Liberation Organization - Negotiation Affairs Department, *"Refugees," Our Position,* https://www.nad.ps/en/our-position/refugees.

[1302] *Id.*

[1303] *Immense Support for the Renewal of the UNRWA Mandate at the UN General Assembly,* UNRWA (Dec. 16, 2019), https://www.unrwa.org/newsroom/press-releases/immense-support-renewal-unrwa-mandate-un-general-assembly.

[1304] UNRWA uses the term "Palestine," not "Palestinian," to preserve their national identity.

[1305] Palestine Refugees, UNRWA, https://www.unrwa.org/palestine-refugees.

UNRWA's five theaters of operation.[1306] The five areas are Lebanon, Syria, Jordan, Gaza, and the West Bank.

UNRWA serves the five above-named markets in 58 refugee camps. Nearly all of UNRWA's $747 million annual budget (as of 2018) comes from donor nations, not the UN.[1307] The largest donor is the European Union.[1308] Of the organization's 30,000 employees, most are Palestinian refugees.[1309] The arrangement offers clients a double benefit: relief services and employment income.

In the refugee camps, poverty levels are high and growing. The camps are overcrowded, dilapidated, unsanitary, and dangerous.

In Lebanon, the 260,000 to 280,000 UNRWA-registered Palestinian refugees are dependent on UNRWA for their living needs. They are denied citizenship and basic services by the government.[1310] Two-thirds of Lebanon's Palestinian population are rated poor or extremely poor.[1311] The Lebanese Army controls the entry and exit points of many UNRWA refugee camps, limiting Palestinian access to jobs and essential services, including health care.[1312] As many as 36 common professions

---

[1306] *Id.*

[1307] UNRWA, *Frequently Asked Questions* [hereinafter UNRWA Questions], https://www.unrwa.org/who-we-are/frequently-asked-questions.

[1308] *Id.*

[1309] UNRWA, *Working at UNRWA*, https://www.unrwa.org/careers/working-unrwa.

[1310] *The Situation of Palestinian Refugees in Lebanon*, p. 3, UNHCR (Feb. 2016), http://www.refworld.org/pdfid/56cc95484.pdf.

[1311] *Id.* at 6.

[1312] *Id.* at 5 and 17.

are officially off-limits to Palestinians.[1313] Lebanese law also disqualifies them from owning property[1314] and excludes them from its public schools.[1315]

The Syrian government denies its Palestinian refugees citizenship and basic services such as education and health care. Consequently, UNRWA is the primary provider of humanitarian assistance to the 438,000 refugees still living in the country.[1316] Their destitution and vulnerability have been compounded by Syria's civil war.

Jordan's census does not track the country's Palestinian residents. However, UNRWA statistics for Jordan show 2.1 million registered Palestinian refugees as of 2016.[1317] Jordan has granted citizenship to most refugees, including those who arrived from the West Bank but not from Gaza.[1318] The legal distinction is rooted in Jordanian history. The nation once ruled the West Bank but not the coastal redoubt.[1319]

Israelis deny the extent of the refugee crisis by rejecting UNRWA's broad definition of "refugee." Israel prefers the more restrictive

---

[1313] *Id.*

[1314] *Id.* at 7.

[1315] *Id.* at 9.

[1316] UNRWA *Questions, supra.*

[1317] UNRWA, *Where We Work* (last viewed Dec. 16, 2016), https://www.unrwa.org/where-we-work/jordan.

[1318] *Jordan's mixed plans for its Palestinian 'guests'*, MIDDLE EAST EYE (Feb. 25, 2016), http://www.middleeasteye.net/news/west-bank-vs-gaza-jordans-mixed-plans-its-palestinian-guests-1529473549.

[1319] *See Id.*

definition set forth in the Refugee Convention.[1320] However, the Refugee Convention does not apply to Palestinians. Article 1(D) of the Convention exempts from the scope of the law persons who are protected by relief agencies "other than the United Nations High Commissioner for Refugees" (the UNHCR).[1321] The Palestinian refugees were assigned to UNRWA, not UNHCR.

The longer Israel delays justice for the Palestinian refugees the more dire their situation becomes. For example, Palestinians fleeing Syria cannot receive relief services in other countries such as Egypt because those governments believe the displaced persons are UNRWA's responsibility, even though they no longer live in UNRWA's jurisdiction.[1322] Similarly, the status of Palestinians fleeing to Europe varies from one EU member state to the next.[1323]

[1320] See Refugee Convention: Protocol relating to the Status of Refugees, TREATY SERIES, vol. 606, p. 267, UN General Assembly, United Nations, 31 January 1967, available at http://www.refworld.org/docid/3ae6b3ae4.html.

[1321] Refugee Convention, art. 1(D).

[1322] Jinan Bastaki, The Legacy of the 1951 Refugee Convention and Palestinian Refugees: Multiple Displacements, Multiple Exclusions, 8 BERKELEY J. MIDDLE E. & ISLAMIC L. 1, 13-16 (2017), https://lawcat.berkeley.edu/record/1128121?ln=en.

[1323] Id. at 18-19.

B. The Israeli Arguments

Summary of Arguments

There was no Zionist plan to expel the Arabs of Mandatory Palestine, and there was no mass expulsion. The Zionists tried to resolve the conflict in Palestine diplomatically. It was the Arab Palestinians who waged war. The vast majority of Arab Palestinians who became refugees fled out of fear as their side lost ground in the war. By the time the Haganah/IDF commanders entered most Arab villages, there was no one left to expel. A minority of the refugees was expelled for lawful reasons of military necessity.

Israel has not committed any "continuing violation" that gives rise to a right of return. There is not even a concept of "continuing violation" in international law. Likewise, UN Resolution 194 (III) created no "right of return." It was a mere non-binding political proposal that the Arabs themselves rejected because they refused to accept the related condition of peaceful coexistence with Israel. Subsequent UN resolutions on the Palestinians' so-called right of return merely hurled more non-binding political attacks on Israel. The UN's primary refugee agency has always supported solutions for refugees that have promoted resettlement, not repatriation.

The Oslo Accords do not favor a Palestinian right of return. The agreements simply require the parties to negotiate the refugee issue at the final status stage of the peace process. Israel has no responsibility to rehabilitate Palestinian refugees; it was the Arab Palestinians and their Arab allies who caused the wars that created their refugee problem. To the extent the Oslo conversation produces refugee relief, it should compensate the Jews pushed out of Arab lands during the 1947-1948 war.

When assessing the number of Palestinian refugees, the parties should follow the legal definition of "refugee" set forth in the Refugee Convention. UNRWA's non-legal working definition of "refugee" was invented only to track those who needed services such as housing and education. The agency vastly exaggerates the number of Palestinians who may deserve legal relief.

i. The Zionists lawfully expelled a minority of Arab Palestinians

There was no Zionist plot to expel Palestine's Arabs.[1324] The Palestinian refugee problem was caused by the Arab Palestinians who started the 1947-1948 war.

During the violent Arab-Jewish clashes of the mandatory period, Zionist leaders rancorously debated diplomatic options to diffuse the conflict. [1325] The Jewish pre-state did not desire war, especially considering its lack of military preparedness.[1326] As the date of the British withdrawal neared, the Zionists repeatedly proposed offers of compromise with the Arabs.[1327]

Before the Jewish Palestinian leadership could form a position on the Arab question, events overtook them.[1328] The UN introduced the Partition Plan of 1947, which proposed to split the disputed territory with no population movement. The Jews reluctantly accepted the UN Plan. The Arabs did not. The Arabs instantly declared the Plan null and

---

[1324] MORRIS 1948, *supra* at 407-08; TESSLER, *supra* at 299; KIMMERLING, *supra* at 147-150; LESCH, *supra* at 137; DOWTY, *supra* at 99.

[1325] *See* Gershom Gorenberg, *The Mystery of 1948*, Slate.com (Nov. 7, 2011) [hereinafter Gorenberg], available at http://www.slate.com/articles/news_and_politics/foreigners/2011/11/israel_and_1948_did_israel_plan_to_expel_its_arabs_in_1948_or_not_.html.

[1326] DOWTY, *supra* at 44.

[1327] *Id.* at 79.

[1328] Gorenberg, *supra*.

void and began to seize the disputed land by force.[1329] For the first four months of the 17-month war, the Arab offensive made significant gains.[1330]

In April of 1948, as five of the surrounding Arab states joined the war while pledging to exterminate the Jewish Palestinians, the Jews realized their survival was at stake.[1331] Plan Dalet aimed to turn the tide of the war by taking control of certain strategic positions in the Mandatory district.[1332] The goal was to defend Jews, not to expel Arabs.[1333] Arab villages not located in the strategic sites or otherwise involved in the war were not disturbed.[1334]

Deir Yassin was a vital position outside Jerusalem where Arab militiamen established a base and besieged the local Jewish community.[1335] Haganah officers knew the Zionist splinter groups Irgun and Lehi were planning to capture the village but did not approve any extreme tactics.[1336] At first, the Zionist militias let hundreds of the Arab civilians escape unharmed.[1337] However, when some of the remaining inhabitants feigned surrender and then opened fire they triggered

---

[1329] *Id.*

[1330] TESSLER, *supra*, pp. 261-63; SACHAR, *supra*, pp. 299-301.

[1331] GILBERT, *supra* at 166-67; LESCH, *supra* at 143.

[1332] *See* GILBERT, *supra* at 166.

[1333] *Id.* at 166-67; TESSLER, *supra* at 295.

[1334] *See* GILBERT, *supra* at 163 and 166-67.

[1335] ERIC ROZENMAN, *JEWS MAKE THE BEST DEMONS* 227-28 (2019) [hereinafter ROZENMAN].

[1336] *See* TESSLER, *supra* at 293.

[1337] ROZENMAN, *supra* at 227-28.

ferocious house-to-house fighting.[1338] Arab women were killed because Arab men disguised themselves in dresses.[1339] News accounts varied on whether the resulting Arab death toll was as low as 107 or as high as 250.[1340] Arab reports exaggerated the conquerors' violence for propaganda purposes.[1341] But the strategy backfired. It only heightened the panic that turned Arabs into refugees.[1342] During the same week as the Deir Yassin incident, Arab attackers ambushed and killed 77 Jewish doctors and nurses headed to a Jerusalem hospital.[1343]

Haganah/IDF commanders hastened the outflow of the enemy population through psychological warfare.[1344] By circulating imaginary threats, the Jewish forces tricked many Arabs into running away.[1345] The non-lethal tactic shortened the war and probably saved many lives.

When the Arab Palestinians launched the war, they must have known many Arab and Jewish Palestinians would flee in fear.[1346] That common wartime phenomenon befell most of the 700,000 Arab Palestinians dislodged in the conflict.[1347] The Arab Palestinian exodus began with the Arab Palestinian upper and middle classes, who chose to wait out the

---

[1338] *Id.*; *See also* TESSLER, *supra* at 292.

[1339] ROZENMAN, *supra* at 227-28.

[1340] *Id.*

[1341] *Id.*

[1342] *Id.*

[1343] GILBERT, *supra* at 170.

[1344] TESSLER, *supra* at 296; SACHAR, *supra* at 334.

[1345] *Id.*

[1346] *See* LESCH, *supra* at 137; COLLLINS AND LAPIERRE, *supra* at 337 (1972).

[1347] *See* TESSLER, *supra* at 279, 294; *See also* MORRIS 1948, *supra* at 119; LESCH, *supra* at 137-38; and GILBERT, *supra* at 174.

war in neighboring countries.[1348] Those elites set an example of flight that the lower classes followed.[1349] The vast majority of Arab Palestinians fled from the war; they were not expelled.[1350] As the war turned against the Arabs, more Arab communities took flight. A few evacuations were ordered by local Arab leaders who deemed it treasonous for Arabs to live under Israeli rule.[1351]

By the time the Haganah/IDF commanders reached most Arab neighborhoods in Mandatory Palestine there was virtually no one left to expel.[1352] The few expulsions that did occur were compelled by Arab military threats.[1353] Had there been a policy of expulsion, Israel would not have permitted the internally located 160,000 Arabs to stay and become 20 percent of Israel's citizenry.[1354]

Despite the Arab onslaught, Israel's May 14, 1948 Proclamation of Independence appealed for inter-ethnic co-existence. The document urged Arabs to "preserve peace and participate in the upbuilding of the State on the basis of full and equal citizenship..."

After the war, Israel kept the armistice lines sealed primarily to deter Arab military infiltration. The fear was justified. For years after the signing of the armistice deals, Arab terrorists called *fedayeen* ("those

---

[1348] Morris Workshop, *supra*, p. 49.

[1349] *Id.*

[1350] *Id.*, pp. 49-50. For details, see MORRIS *BIRTH REVISITED*, *supra* at pp. 341, 505, and 598.

[1351] *Id.*, p. 50.

[1352] *Id.* For details, see MORRIS *BIRTH REVISITED*, *supra* at 265.

[1353] *Id.*

[1354] *Id.*

who sacrifice themselves") plagued Israel with thousands of attacks per year.[1355]

With the above background on the 1947-1948 war, we can assess the legality of the wartime conduct. To the limited extent the Haganah/IDF imposed expulsions, the actions did not violate treaty law or customary international law.

The intertemporal rule prohibits the retroactive application of an international law to events that occurred before the law took effect.[1356] At the time of the 1947-1948 war, there was no applicable treaty law prohibition against expulsions. None of the combatants had yet signed the Hague Resolutions, Israel had not yet signed the Fourth Convention or the International Covenant on Civil and Political Rights, and the Universal Declaration of Human Rights was not even considered a law.[1357] The term "ethnic cleaning" (the forced displacement of a group based on ethnicity) did not gain currency until the 1990's,[1358] and laws prohibiting the practice did not emerge until that decade.[1359]

[1355] GORDIS, *supra*, at 220.

[1356] Andrew Kent, *Evaluating the Palestinians' Claimed Right of Return*, 34.1 UNIVERSITY OF PENNSYLVANIA JOURNAL OF INTERNATIONAL LAW 149, 175 (2012) [hereinafter Kent], http://scholarship.law.upenn.edu/jil/vol34/iss1/3/. *See also* BROWNLIE, *supra* at 149.

[1357] Kent, *supra* at 179-198.

[1358] *See* Kent, *supra* at 217; *also see Ethnic Cleansing*, History.com, http://www.history.com/topics/ethnic-cleansing.

[1359] *See Practice Relating to Rule 129: the Act of Displacement, Section C. Ethnic Cleansing*, ICRC, https://ihl-databases.icrc.org/customary-ihl/eng/docs/v2_cha_chapter38_rule129_sectionc (last viewed August 12, 2017).

Customary international law as of 1948 prohibited expulsions only during armed occupations of foreign territory.[1360] It did not address situations like the 1947-1948 war, where Zionists expelled individuals to defend their own territory – or even disputed territory – from domestic or foreign attack. In the post-World War II era, expulsions to halt inter-ethnic bloodshed were lawful.[1361]

Consistent with the above guidance, the Nuremberg and Tokyo Tribunals prosecuted expulsions inflicted for criminal purposes and permitted expulsions based on "military necessity."[1362] Haganah and IDF commanders expelled Arab Palestinians based on acute military necessity. At risk was the survival of the entire Jewish population of Mandatory Palestine.

ii. The Palestinians have no right of return to Israel

The Palestinian argument for a right of return to Israel finds no valid basis in treaty law, customary law, or UN resolutions. The following provides details.

Palestinians theorize that the Zionist expulsions of Arab Palestinians during the 1947-1948 war, combined with Israel's continuing refusal to readmit the refugees, constitute a "continuing violation" that should be remedied under refugee laws in the treaties and customary norms of today, even though today's laws were not applicable during the War.

[1360] Kent, *supra* at 216.

[1361] *Id.* at 216-22.

[1362] *The Nuremberg Trial and the Tokyo War Crimes Trials (1945-1948)*, Office of the Historian, U.S. Department of State, https://history.state.gov/milestones/1945-1952/nuremberg.

That concept is groundless.[1363] The "continuing violations" theory, which made a few appearances in the tort law and employment law cases of certain countries, was widely deplored for its lack of predictable guidance, and it never appeared in international law.[1364] In addition, there can be no continuing violation where there is no initial violation.[1365] The Zionist expulsions and border closings of 1947-1948 were valid acts of self-defense.

Even if we could consider refugee laws in force after 1948, they would not assist Palestinians.[1366] The central treaty on refugees – namely, the Refugee Convention – does not even mention repatriation, much less establish a right of return.[1367] The thrust of the Convention prevents refugees from returning to their states of origin and guarantees their right to resettle in the destination states.[1368]

The Universal Declaration of Human Rights is a non-binding political statement that protects the right of an individual only to enter his own country. No Palestinian refugee can claim Israel is his own country if he is not a citizen of that state.[1369] The International Covenant on Political

---

[1363] Kent, *supra* at 176.

[1364] *Id.* at 176-77.

[1365] *Id.*

[1366] *Id.* at 178.

[1367] *Id.*

[1368] *Id.* at 194-95.

[1369] Marc Zell and Sonia Shnyder, *Palestinian Right of Return or Strategic Weapon: A Historical, Legal and Moral Political Analysis*, 8 NEXUS J. Op. 77, 99 (2003) [hereinafter Zell].

and Civil Rights is binding but is also limited to nationals of the given state.[1370]

The 1948 UN Resolution 194(III) was a non-binding political statement of the General Assembly that did not recognize any "rights"[1371] and which did not even attract any Arab votes. Moreover, the concept of repatriating Arab refugees, proposed in Paragraph 11, was only one element of a 15-paragraph "final settlement," which contained a condition of peaceful coexistence that most of the warring Arab states rejected.[1372] And the Paragraph 11 alternative of "resettlement" in Arab states was ignored by those states. Meanwhile, Israel feared that any return of Arab refugees without a final settlement would pose an intolerable national security risk.[1373] For these reasons, the UN proposal was stillborn.

iii. UN actions after Resolution 194(III) did not create a right of return

The many UN resolutions adopted after 1949, which reiterated the Palestinian "right" of return, were mere nonbinding political

---

[1370] *Id.* at 106.

[1371] Ruth Lapidoth, *Legal Aspects of the Palestinian Refugee Question*, Jerusalem Letter/Viewpoints, No. 485, Jerusalem Center for Public Affairs (Sept. 2002) [hereinafter Lapidoth Refugee Question, https://www.jcpa.org/jl/vp485.htm.

[1372] *Id. See* especially Resolution 194(III), paras. 1-6. The Resolution was formally opposed by Egypt, Lebanon, Syria, Iraq, Saudi Arabia, and Yemen. Ely Hertz, UN Resolution 194 and the "Right of Return," Myths and Facts (Oct. 8, 2012), http://www.mythsandfacts.org/article_view.asp?articleID=244.

[1373] TESSLER, *supra* at 311-15.

statements. Like Resolution 194(III), the duplicative resolutions supported both repatriation to Israel and "resettlement" in the Arab states. Regrettably, the Arab governments continued to ignore the resettlement option.

From the earliest days of the Refugee Convention, the prevailing solution for refugees was resettlement, not repatriation.[1374] Only in the late 20th Century did refugee experts begin to favor repatriation.[1375] Even then, the concept did not take hold. The UNHCR's 2014 Global Action Plan to End Statelessness urged states hosting refugees to (among other things) confer "nationality on their stateless residents,"[1376] and "grant nationality to stateless children born in their territory."[1377]

Again, in 2016, when the refugee agency issued a report lamenting the trend of forced displacement, it did not recommend the cure of repatriation but instead recognized "resettlement" as a "durable solution."[1378] Ironically, some of the same governments that vote for UN resolutions prodding Israel to repatriate Palestinians have opposed repatriation for refugees from their own countries.[1379]

[1374] Zell, *supra* at 109.

[1375] *Id.* at 111.

[1376] *Global Action Plan to End Statelessness, 2014-2024*, UNHCR (Nov. 2014), pp. 8-9, https://www.unhcr.org/en-us/protection/statelessness/54621bf49/global-action-plan-end-statelessness-2014-2024.html.

[1377] *Id.*, pp. 10-11.

[1378] *Global Trends, Forced Displacement in 2015*, pp. 25-26, UNHCR (June 20, 2016), http://www.unhcr.org/576408cd7.

[1379] Zell, *supra* at 111-112.

iv. **The Oslo Accords do not support a right of return**

The Oslo Accords do not endorse a right of return.[1380] They merely list the topic of "refugees" as an issue to be resolved in the Oslo final status negotiation.[1381] Until those talks are completed, Israel has the sovereign right to set its own immigration rules.

Israel has no obligation to compensate Arab Palestinian refugees.[1382] They and their Arab allies were the ones who caused the two wars that created the refugees.[1383]

The refugee issue to be negotiated under the Oslo Accords concerns both Arab and Jewish refugees.[1384] The Accords were designed to fulfill Security Council Resolution 242,[1385] and when Resolution 242 called for "a just settlement of the refugee problem," it addressed the rights of both Arab and Jewish refugees.[1386] All Arab states that disgorged Jewish inhabitants during and after the 1947-1948 War were co-belligerents in the war.[1387] Therefore any resolution of the refugee issue should compensate all Jewish refugees, regardless of which Arab territory they

---

[1380] Lapidoth Refugee Question, *supra.*

[1381] *Id.* (citing Oslo I, art. V.3).

[1382] *Id.* at section titled *A Right to Compensation?*

[1383] *Id.*

[1384] Telhami, *supra* at subtitle 4. Linkage with Jewish Refugees.

[1385] Oslo I, art. 1.

[1386] *Jewish Refugees from Arab Countries: The Case for Rights and Redress, Justice for Jews from Arab Countries, pp. 45 and 61 (Nov. 5, 2007),* http://www.justiceforjews.com/jjac.pdf.

[1387] Adi Schwartz, *What Can We Learn From the Exodus of Jews from Arab Countries?* in *Proceedings of an International Workshop, Hebrew University of Jerusalem Faculty of Law, 14-15 December, 2016,* 51(1) Israel Law Review 47, 90-93 (2018).

ran from.[1388] An Israeli government study found that Jewish refugees left behind over $150 billion of property in the Arab lands.[1389]

v. Palestinians vastly overstate the number of Palestinian refugees

In 1950, UNRWA established certain criteria to identify Palestinian refugees for the practical purpose of distributing relief services.[1390] But UNRWA never became a party to the more recent Oslo Accords, and the Accords did not define "refugee" for the legal purpose of negotiating that final status issue.[1391] In that final discussion, the Oslo signatories may negotiate the issue based on UNRWA's self-styled administrative designation or based on the treaty definition enshrined in the Refugee Convention. The difference would be enormous.

UNRWA serves millions of Palestinians who do not qualify as refugees under the Convention. Indeed, relocating all UNRWA beneficiaries to Israel would erase the democracy by converting the Jewish-majority state to an Arab-majority state.[1392] Accordingly, by honoring the globally recognized treaty definition of "refugee," the parties would ensure that

---

[1388] *Id.* at 92.

[1389] Dan Lavie, *Lost Jewish property in Arab countries estimated at $150 billion*, Israel Hayom (Dec. 16, 2019), https://www.israelhayom.com/2019/12/16/lost-jewish-property-in-arab-countries-estimated-at-150-billion/.

[1390] Lapidoth Refugee Question, *supra* at section titled "Who is a Refugee?"

[1391] *Id.*

[1392] *Id.*

their final status resolution of the topic is both legally defensible and realistic.[1393] The following shows how the treaty would apply.

The Refugee Convention defines a refugee as someone who:

> owing to well-founded fear of being persecuted for reasons of race, religion, [or] nationality... is outside the country of his nationality and is unable or, owing to such fear, is unwilling to avail himself of the protection of that country; or who, not having a nationality and being outside the country of his former habitual residence as a result of such events, is unable or, owing to such fear, is unwilling to return to it.[1394]

The above definition includes refugees but not their descendants.[1395] As of 2012, about 30,000 of the Arab Palestinians dislodged in 1948 were still alive.[1396] Those few surviving souls may qualify as refugees under the Oslo Accords. But extending Oslo to UNRWA's entire customer base would inflate the figure to as many as 5.4 million people, all due to UNRWA's anomalous policy of serving both refugees and their posterity. Nearly all members of that expanded class have never even seen Mandatory Palestine.

[1393] *See Id.*

[1394] Refugee Convention, art. I.A.(2).

[1395] Zell, *supra* at 109-110.

[1396] *US Senate dramatically scales down definition of Palestinian 'refugees',* The Times of Israel (May 25, 2012), http://www.timesofisrael.com/us-senate-dramatically-redefines-definition-of-palestinian-refugees/.

Notice that as the UNRWA-catered population swells through childbirth, Palestinians demand "justice" for a greater number of "refugees."[1397] Arab leaders admit they intend to flood the Jewish state with a rising tide of Arab humanity.[1398]

UNRWA departed further from the legal concept of "refugee" by aiding Arab Palestinians who never left their "country." Roughly 240,000 of the Arab Palestinians who abandoned their homes in 1948 merely traveled from Jewish-controlled western Mandatory Palestine to Jordanian-held eastern Mandatory Palestine (i.e. the West Bank).[1399] These internally displaced persons were never "outside the country of their habitual residence," as required for eligibility under the Refugee Convention.

Furthermore, UNRWA opened its doors to non-Palestinians. The relief organization assisted anyone "whose normal place of residence was Palestine during the period 1 June 1946 to 15 May 1948, and who lost both home and means of livelihood as a result of the 1948 conflict."[1400] The meagre two-year residency requirement gave UNRWA beneficiary status to tens of thousands of transient laborers from the Arab countries surrounding Mandatory Palestine.[1401]

[1397] Lapidoth Refugee Question, *supra* at section titled "Who is a Refugee?"

[1398] *See* Zell, *supra* at 91.

[1399] SACHAR, *supra* at 334.

[1400] *Who Are Palestine Refugees?* Palestine Refugees, UNRWA, https://www.unrwa.org/palestine-refugees.

[1401] *Israel, the Conflict and Peace: Answers to frequently asked questions,* Israel Ministry of Foreign

The treaty definition of "refugee" rules out many Palestinians based on their current citizenship. Article 1.C.3 of the Convention states that once a refugee "has acquired a new nationality, and enjoys the protection of his new nationality," the person is no longer a refugee.[1402] Under this clause, approximately 60% of Palestinians labeled "refugees" lost their refugee status after the 1947-1948 war, when they accepted Jordanian nationality.[1403]

Fewer than one-third of UNWRA-supported Palestinian refugees reside in refugee camps.[1404] The rest live in regular homes. Yet they all receive UNRWA welfare based on their "refugee" status, regardless of economic need.[1405] Hence, most Palestinians who call themselves refugees have in fact already resettled.[1406]

Affairs (Dec. 30, 2009),

http://mfa.gov.il/MFA/ForeignPolicy/Issues/Pages/FAQ_Peace_process_with_Palestinians_D ec_2009.aspx.

[1402] Refugee Convention, art. 1.C.3.

[1403] Lewis Saideman, *Do Palestinian Refugees Have a Right of Return to Israel? An Examination of the Scope of and Limitations on the Right of Return*, 44 Va. J. Int'l L. 829, 859-77 (Spring, 2004).

[1404] United Nations Relief and Works Agency for Palestine Refugees in the Near East, Where do Palestine Refugees Live? (2021), https://www.unrwa.org/palestine-refugees.

[1405] James G. Lindsay, *Fixing UNRWA: Repairing the UN's Troubled System of Aid to Palestinian Refugees*, Policy Analysis, Policy Focus 91, the Washington Institute (Jan. 2009), p. 24, https://www.washingtoninstitute.org/policy-analysis/view/fixing-unrwa-repairing-the-uns-troubled-system-of-aid-to-palestinian-refuge.

[1406] *Id.* at 53.

4.7: How should the parties maintain security?

Author's Prologue

International military experts believe one factor above all will decide the success of a Palestinian state: security.[1407] In their view, Israel and the prospective State of Palestine must build a security apparatus that permits Palestine to maintain internal security, ensures security for Israel, protects both entities from external threats, and earns related cooperation from regional powers.[1408]

The Oslo Accords were structured to transfer governmental power and territorial control from Israel to the Palestinians while maintaining security for Israel in a series of "trust-building" steps over a five-year "interim" period. By the end of the period, the rivals were to complete the permanent status negotiations needed to resolve the most contentious issues in dispute, including the matter of security.[1409]

The interim transfer of power was complex. In Gaza, the terms entitled the PA to govern about two thirds of the enclave and left the remaining one third in Israeli hands. Israel, meanwhile, was entitled to retain control over the area's land and settlements, as well as air and sea

---

[1407] Robert E. Hunter and Seth G. Jones, *Building a Successful Palestinian State: Security*, Rand Corporation (2006) [hereinafter Rand Security Report], https://www.rand.org/content/dam/rand/pubs/monographs/2006/RAND_MG146.2.pdf.

[1408] *Id.* 1-2.

[1409] Oslo I, art. V(3).

borders.[1410] Included in this authority was the power to continue patrolling the Philadelphi Route security corridor along Gaza's southern boundary.

The interim arrangement permitted Israel to control all civilian and security affairs of Jerusalem.

In the West Bank, the interim plan divided the region into three administrative districts. West Bank Area A represented the 18 percent of the West Bank that covered the six major Palestinian cities.[1411] In Area A, the PA was permitted to control both civil affairs and external security.[1412] Palestinians also controlled the 80% of Hebron that contained the Palestinian neighborhoods. This area was designated "H1." Israel retained the remaining sector, "H2," which featured a small Jewish community.

West Bank Area B, reflecting another 22% of the West Bank, reached the rural areas that surrounded the major Palestinian cities. In Area B, the PA controlled civil affairs and shared external security functions with Israel.

The communities of Areas A and B were noncontiguous. But together they hosted about 95% of the West Bank's Palestinian population.

[1410] Oslo II, art. XII.

[1411] The major cities were Jenin, Nablus, Tulkarm, Qalqilya, Ramallah, and Bethlehem. SMITH, *supra* at 447.

[1412] Oslo II, art. IX.

West Bank Area C covered the 60% of the West Bank not encompassed in Areas A and B. Area C covered the West Bank's entire Israeli population and about six percent of its Palestinians. There, Israel supervised both civil affairs and external security.

To ensure security during the interim period, Oslo required the PA to demilitarize but permitted the quasi-governmental entity to maintain a police force with light arms.[1413] Oslo obliged both sides to prevent acts of terrorism and other hostilities.[1414]

The Paris Protocol of 1994, incorporated as Annex IV to the Interim Agreement, established terms of cooperation to manage the intertwined Israeli/Palestinian economy during the interim period by establishing a joint economic zone. The terms of the Protocol governed issues such as taxation, labor, agriculture, industry, tourism, and insurance.[1415]

Meanwhile, the Jordan-Israel Peace Treaty of 1994 improved regional security by promoting cooperation between the two states on matters such as terrorism, drug trafficking, and illegal border crossings.[1416]

Pursuant to the Olso plan, the IDF began its assigned redeployments, and the Palestinians held elections to establish the PA. Through the late 1990's, various disputes and hostilities disrupted the interim process. In 1998, the parties signed the Wye River Memorandum, which clarified the obligations for Israeli withdrawal and Palestinian terrorist-control.

[1413] Oslo II, art. XIV.

[1414] *Id.*, art. XV.

[1415] Paris Protocol, arts. II-XI.

[1416] Rand Security Report, *supra*, p. 4.

After further recriminations, they signed the 1999 Sharm El-Sheik Memorandum. That document refined the timetable for the Israeli pull-out and scheduled the completion of a final status agreement by 2000.

The July, 2000 Camp David Summit aimed to expedite the fitful peace process by rushing straight to a final status agreement. Unfortunately, the ambitious approach failed to produce a deal. Further tensions triggered the five-year wave of Palestinian suicide bombings that characterized the Second Intifada.

Later that year, the protagonists regrouped in Washington, D.C. to discuss a US peace plan called "the Clinton Parameters." The Clinton Parameters outlined a middle ground position on each of the final status issues. Key to the security element of the compromise scheme was an international military force that would monitor the progress of the IDF's withdrawal from the Territories and remain in the Territories in place of the IDF until dismissed by mutual consent of the parties.[1417] Although the Clinton Parameters spawned intensive negotiations, they failed to break the deadlock. The US concluded that the Palestinians were unwilling to take the necessary risks for peace.[1418] The Palestinians complained the deal was unequal due to the inequality of the parties.[1419]

[1417] ROSS MISSING PEACE, *supra* at 752.

[1418] *Id.* at 756-58, 761, and 801-02.

[1419] Petter Bauch and Mohamed Omer, *The Oslo Accords fell well short of their goals*, Al Jazeera.com (Sept. 14, 2014) (arguing, among other things, that the Oslo final status talks wrongly elevated Israel's security needs above those of the Palestinians), https://www.aljazeera.com/indepth/opinion/2013/09/2013912114245222394.html.

The security equation changed when Israel unilaterally removed all troops and civilians from Gaza in 2005. In the wake of that "disengagement" a brief military clash between the PA and Hamas left Hamas as the de facto government of Gaza. Hamas soon began a campaign of rocket attacks against Israel, and Israel responded by erecting the Gaza Blockade.

In sum, the Oslo interim agreement produced elaborate security rules but witnessed widespread security breaches. Against this ambiguous backdrop, what terms of security should prevail at the final status stage?

A. The Palestinian Arguments

Summary of Arguments

The leading cause of insecurity in the Territories and region-wide is the Israeli occupation. Israel was supposed to end the occupation and withdraw to the Green Line through a series of military steps prescribed by the Oslo Accords. But instead, IDF soldiers continued to trample throughout the Territories and obstruct the free movement of Palestinians. Israel should have foreseen the inevitably violent blowback. At least, the occupying power should not have expected Palestinian police to help suppress the protests; that would have put the police in the traitorous position of supporting the protracted occupation.

The Palestinians have accepted the principle of making Palestine a non-militarized state with no ability to threaten Israel's security. That is all the parties need to meet Oslo's security goal. Israel's wish-list of additional security powers is merely a bid for continued occupation. A Palestinian state could not accept such affronts to its sovereignty.

Israel compounds the current security problem by inciting its people to hate and harm Palestinians. The signals of hostility emanate from the highest echelons of government and from the Israeli public. When Palestinians complain of the extremist attacks, Israeli authorities often turn a blind eye.

i. Achieving the Oslo goal of security requires an end to the occupation

The Israeli occupation is the primary cause of insecurity in the Territories and region-wide.[1420]

[1420] *Our Position: Security*, Palestine Liberation Organization, Negotiation Affairs Department [hereinafter PLO/NAD Position on Security], https://www.nad.ps/en/our-position/security.

Decades of life under occupation and exile have girded the Palestinian drive for freedom.[1421]

Israel never ended its occupation of the Territories, as envisioned by the Oslo Accords. It never completed its Oslo-required military withdrawal from those lands.[1422] The IDF should have withdrawn to the Green Line.[1423] That line of demarcation is generally recognized by the international community as the appropriate border between Israel and the future State of Palestine.

In the first stage of the planned Oslo withdrawal, Israel was required to pull its troops from 80 percent of the Gaza Strip and all of the Jericho area within two months, but the process actually took seven months.[1424] No matter how scrupulously the opposing teams of lawyers negotiated the scope and timing of the IDF redeployments, Israel repeatedly found excuses for delay.[1425] When the IDF did redeploy, it acted unilaterally, without seeking the Palestinians' prior consent.[1426]

[1421] *Id.*

[1422] *20 Years after Oslo*, Negotiation Affairs Department, PLO, State of Palestine [hereinafter PLO NAD 20 Years after Oslo], p. 6, http://www.nad.ps/en/publication-resources/publication/oslo-process-20-years. To clamp down the West Bank, Israel installed hundreds of checkpoints throughout the West Bank.

[1423] *See The Green Line is a Red Line: The 1967 Border and the Two State*, State of Palestine, Palestine Liberation Organization - Negotiations Affairs Department (June 27, 2011) [hereinafter The Green Line is a Red Line], https://www.nad.ps/en/publication-resources/factsheets/green-line-red-line-1967-border-and-two-state.

[1424] DOWTY, *supra* at 157.

[1425] *Id.*

[1426] *Id.*

During the Second Intifada of 2000 to 2005, the IDF violated Oslo II even more egregiously by re-occupying the West Bank Area A and B urban centers from which it had previously withdrawn.[1427] The troops acted as if Oslo I and II had never been signed.[1428] Even after the UN Security Council ordered Israel to cure its Oslo breaches, it continued to turn a deaf ear to these calls.[1429]

The Oslo Accords authorized the Palestinians to assemble a police force and assume responsibility for security in the Palestinian self-rule zones as the IDF withdrew from those places.[1430] During the withdrawal period, Israeli and Palestinian security forces were supposed to conduct joint security operations to prevent acts of terrorism and crime.[1431] The PA police and the IDF began the scheduled security cooperation in 1994, conducting joint patrols, fighting crime, and sharing intelligence.[1432] Over time, the PA forces saved Israel from several terrorist attacks, including suicide bombings.[1433]

However, the security cooperation faded in 1996, when Israel elected Prime Minister Benjamin Netanyahu.[1434] Decisions by the Netanyahu government to open an archeological excavation tunnel near the holy

---

[1427] SACHAR, *supra* at 1038, 1050, and 1054-55.

[1428] *Id.* at 1054.

[1429] *See* S.C. Res. 1435, U.N. Doc. S/RES/1435 (Sept. 24, 2002).

[1430] Gaza-Jericho Agreement, arts. VIII and XII; Oslo II, arts. XII, XIII, XIV and XV; Hebron Protocol, art. 4; Wye River Memorandum, art. II.

[1431] See *Id.* at arts. XIII and XV.

[1432] WATSON, *supra* at 212-13.

[1433] *Id.*

[1434] *Id.*

Haram/Temple Mount and construct housing in East Jerusalem provoked violent Palestinian protests that compelled the PA to discontinue the joint patrols in 1997.[1435]

The occupied people could not be expected to maintain security cooperation while Israel mocked the peace process.[1436] Despite the strain in bilateral relations triggered by Israel's actions, the PA resumed a cautious level of cooperation in 1998. This helped reduce the rate of suicide attacks.[1437] Sadly, no level of PA cooperation ever satisfied Israel.[1438]

In the bigger picture, Israel never appreciated the paradox of forming a Palestinian police force to maintain order while Palestinian armed resistance groups were struggling to overcome a belligerent occupation.[1439] The more the Palestinian police fulfilled their Oslo-mandated missions to dismantle terror networks, the more they frustrated the PLO's national movement to liberate Palestine.[1440]

Security cooperation broke down again in 2000, when Israeli political leader Ariel Sharon staged his provocative visit to the Haram/Temple

---

[1435] *Id.* at 213.

[1436] *Id.* at 213-14.

[1437] *Id.* at 214-217.

[1438] *Id.* at 216.

[1439] Alaa Tartir, *The Evolution and Reform of Palestinian Security Forces 1993-2013*, 4(1) Stability: International Journal of Security and Development, at subheading "Proliferation, Patronage and Corruption" (2015), http://www.stabilityjournal.org/articles/10.5334/sta.gi/.

[1440] *Id.*

Mount and thereby triggered the Second Intifada.[1441] In that war-like conflict, the PA security forces naturally fought on the Palestinian side.[1442] Israel's military then launched airstrikes against PA security targets, detained the Palestinian security personnel, and dismantled their security infrastructure.[1443] Ironically, Israel degraded the security apparatus that they had contractually agreed to help establish for their own protection.[1444]

From 2007 to 2013, the Palestinians rebuilt their security forces with financial assistance and training from the US and EU.[1445] The modernization effort showed the Palestinians remained credible partners for peace.[1446] During this period, the Palestinian police resumed their cooperation with the IDF and made further efforts to disarm the terror groups.[1447] But the initiative only revived unrealistic expectations that Palestinian authorities could restrain a resistance movement fighting for Palestinian statehood.[1448] Ultimately, the security cooperation engendered by Oslo wrongly criminalized the resistance and helped sustain the occupation.[1449]

[1441] *Id.* at subheading "Destroying and Reforming Palestinian Security Infrastructure."

[1442] *Id.*

[1443] *Id.*

[1444] *Id.*

[1445] *Id.* at subheading "The Fayyadism Phase: Re-Inventing Palestinian Security Forces (2007–2013)."

[1446] *Id.*

[1447] *Id.*

[1448] *Id.*

[1449] *Id.*

The occupation further eroded the bonds of security cooperation by breaching a related component of the Oslo Accords, namely, the guarantee of free movement between Gaza and the West Bank. Oslo I confirmed that the West Bank and Gaza comprised "a single territorial unit."[1450] The terms of "safe passage" between the two Territorial zones were embodied in the Protocol Concerning Safe Passage.[1451] In particular, the parties designated a 28-mile route to connect the Erez Crossing in Gaza to the West Bank town of Tarkumiya. Israel was responsible for issuing the safe passage permits. If Israeli security officials wanted to deny a permit, they were supposed to notify their Palestinian counterparts so the issue could be "discussed in the agreed channels."[1452] Safe passage was crucial to the success of the Oslo peace process.[1453] Connecting Gaza to the West Bank was needed to sustain the Palestinian economy and realize the vision of a Palestinian state.

In the 2000's, Israel eviscerated the Protocol Concerning Safe Passage by erecting its East Jerusalem/West Bank Barrier and Gaza Blockade. Ultimately, it became nearly impossible to move between the two Palestinian zones.[1454] Once the travel restrictions were installed, and the request for a travel permit was denied, there were no further discussions "in the agreed channels." In fact, Israel classified certain

---

[1450] Oslo I, art. IV.

[1451] United Nations Department of Political and Peacebuilding Affairs, United Nations Peacemaker, Protocol Concerning Safe Passage between the West Bank and the Gaza Strip (May 10, 1999) [hereinafter Protocol for Safe Passage], https://peacemaker.un.org/israelopt-safepassage99.

[1452] *Id.*, art. 6(C).

[1453] WATSON, *supra* at 143-44.

[1454] PLO NAD 20 Years after Oslo, *supra*, p. 7.

districts located east of the Green Line but west of the Barrier as "closed military zones," completely isolating Palestinians in enclosures that had previously served as robust crossroads for Palestinian travel and trade.[1455] Even the PA security forces became subject to travel restrictions.[1456] To this day, they need Israel's permission to move from one West Bank Area A town to another.[1457]

These frustrating conditions have, in rare cases, precipitated Palestinian police attacks on Israeli soldiers.[1458] But the problem with Israeli-Palestinian security cooperation is not Palestinian professionalism. It is the fundamental incompatibility between the occupation and the mission of cooperative policing.[1459] Palestinians view their security personnel as IDF subcontractors who help Israel prolong the occupation while showing a friendly face to foreign observers.[1460] No wonder that in a 2016 opinion poll, 70 percent of Palestinians said the security cooperation should end.[1461]

Solving the security problem will require Israel to withdraw all soldiers and civilians from the Territories and surrender complete control of the

---

[1455] *Id.*

[1456] Seth Binder, *What Palestinian-Israeli security cooperation?* Aljazeera, March 9, 2016, http://www.aljazeera.com/indepth/opinion/2016/03/palestinian-israeli-security-cooperation-160309091052648.html.

[1457] *Id.*

[1458] *See* Id.

[1459] *Id.*

[1460] *Id.*

[1461] *Id.*

area, including its airspace and territorial waters.[1462] Only when Israel takes these steps can the State of Palestine exercise its sovereign right to self-defense.[1463] Only then will Palestine be recognized as a sovereign state.[1464]

ii. Israel must withdraw its overreaching security demands

During negotiations on security, Israel made additional demands that would have significantly suppressed Palestinian independence.[1465] To begin with, Israeli negotiators insisted that Palestine should be a non-militarized state with no army or air force, no defense resources other than those needed for internal security and border control, no ability to threaten Israel, and no treaties with other states that would threaten Israel.[1466] Those are the only security terms Israel needed.[1467]

But Israel aggressively exceeded the above demands. In the final status negotiation at Camp David, Israel designed its security proposal to

---

[1462] PLO/NAD Position on Security, *supra.*

[1463] *Id.*

[1464] *Id.*

[1465] Omar Dajani, *No Security Without Law: Prospects for Implementing a Rights-Based Approach in Palestinian– Israeli Security Negotiations,* in INTERNATIONAL LAW AND THE ISRAELI-PALESTINIAN CONFLICT: A RIGHTS-BASED APPROACH TO MIDDLE EAST PEACE 192 (Susan Akram, Michael Dumper, Michael Lynk, and Iain Scobbie eds., 2011).

[1466] Arthur Hughes, *Security Challenges in a Two-State Solution: Is an International Role the Key?,* Middle East Institute (June 4, 2013) [hereinafter Hughes Security Challenges], https://www.mei.edu/publications/security-challenges-two-state-solution-international-role-key#_ftn2.

[1467] *Id.*

preserve vestiges of occupation.[1468] Israel demanded three early warning stations in the West Bank among the proposed security mechanisms.[1469] It also insisted on maintaining control of the Jordan Valley, which runs along the Jordanian border, purportedly to guard against enemy invasions using the new Palestinian state as an access route.[1470] Regardless of whether the accepted final status would produce Palestinian sovereignty in the Jordan Valley or not, Israel would retain control over the area for as long as six to 21 years.[1471]

There must be no ongoing IDF bases or other presence in the Territories beyond a brief transition period, which may be needed to evacuate Israeli settlers, and no right of emergency IDF deployment to the Territories.[1472] In the same vein, the IDF must not maintain early warning stations on Palestinian ground.[1473] Israel's push for IDF bases, emergency deployment rights, and warning stations in Palestine reflect the fanciful notion of a 'danger from the East.'[1474] The argument is concocted to justify Israeli military control over the Jordan Valley and

---

[1468] Jeremy Pressman, *Visions in Collision, What Happened At Camp David and Taba?* 28.2 International Security 5, 6 (Fall, 2003), https://www.researchgate.net/publication/ 265897546_Visions_in_Collision_What_Happened_at_Camp_David_and_Taba.

[1469] *Id.* at 16.

[1470] *Id.*

[1471] *Id.*

[1472] *Id.*

[1473] *Id.*

[1474] Akram Hanieh, *The Camp David Papers*, 30(2) Journal of Palestine Studies 75, 82-83 (Winter, 2001), https://www.jstor.org/stable/10.1525/jps.2001.30.2.75.

degrade Palestinian military might.[1475] But the purpose of the peace talks must be to end the occupation, not to legalize it.[1476]

Instead of giving the IDF residual control over the Territories, an international force should be deployed in the area, especially the Jordan Valley, to maintain security and operate any needed early warning stations.[1477] The international force could include an Israeli liaison officer to keep Israel informed on security issues and help resolve any disputes.[1478]

Standard international rules should apply to civilian aviation between the two countries, though special arrangements may be needed for military aircraft.[1479] Standard rules would also suffice to control the electromagnetic spectrum for purposes of radio communications, except in cases where Israel raises a legitimate security interest.[1480]

In his 2015 speech to the UN General Assembly, President Mahmoud Abbas requested the aid of an international peacekeeping force.[1481] Such a force might backfire by cementing the Israeli occupation.[1482] But the

---

[1475] *Id.*

[1476] *Id.*

[1477] Hughes Security Challenges, *supra.*

[1478] *Id.*

[1479] *Id.*

[1480] *Id.*

[1481] Diana Buttu and Nadia Hijab, *Why Palestinians Need an International Protection Force*, The Nation (October 22, 2015), https://www.thenation.com/article/archive/palestine-besieged/.

[1482] *Id.*

risk is outweighed by several factors.[1483] First, Palestinians need the security protection.[1484] IHL requires the occupying power to ensure the safety of the occupied population, but Israel has done just the opposite.[1485] Second, the Oslo Accords leaves the PA's own security forces in a compromised position where they must effectively protect Israel's military and the settlers.[1486] Third, an international force would help sideline the US, which continually pays lip service to the ideal of a two-state solution but continues to support Israel's military and uses its veto power in the UN to stymie efforts to end the occupation.[1487] A military guard against Israeli abuses may even help create the conditions needed to achieve a just and lasting peace.[1488]

iii. Israel must stop its incitements against Palestinians

Israel frequently poisons the existing security environment by flouting the Oslo II prohibition against incitement.[1489] The spiteful expressions attempt to deny Palestinians their right of self-determination, which is instrumental to prospects for a Palestinian state.[1490]

[1483] *Id.*

[1484] *Id.*

[1485] *Id.*

[1486] *Id.*

[1487] *Id.*

[1488] *Id.*

[1489] *See INCITEMENT: An Israeli Official Policy?* Palestine Liberation Organization, Negotiation Affairs Department (April, 2017) [hereinafter PLO/NAD Position on Incitement], p. 1, https://www.nad.ps/sites/default/files/25042017.pdf.

[1490] *Id.*

For example, Israeli extremists often call for "Death to Arabs."[1491] Messages on some social media sites have justified attacks on Palestinians.[1492] And Israeli officials have endorsed the use of lethal force against Palestinian assailants.[1493]

In Israel, incitement flows from the top. Prime Minister Benjamin Netanyahu made a remark during the March, 2015 election that fomented hatred towards Palestinians.[1494] Pleading with the supporters of his conservative administration he said:

> The right-wing government is in danger. Arab voters are heading to the polling stations in droves... Left-wing NGOs [i.e. non-governmental organizations] are bringing them in buses.[1495]

The racist incitement worked. Netanyahu's Likud party was re-elected by a wide margin.

[1491] *Diplomatic Quartet releases report on advancing two-state solution to Israel-Palestine conflict,* UN News Centre, pp. 3-4 (July 1, 2016) [hereinafter Quartet Report], http://www.un.org/apps/news/story.asp?NewsID=54379#.WLIiHeQzXbJ. The "Quartet" that produced this report was the same alliance of four leading international bodies – the UN, EU, US, and Russia – that authored the Israeli-Palestinian Roadmap for Peace in 2002.

[1492] *Id.*

[1493] *Id.*

[1494] *Binyamin Netanyahu, 'Arab voters are heading to the polling stations in droves,'* The Guardian, March 17, 2015, available at: https://www.theguardian.com/world/2015/mar/17/binyamin-netanyahu-israel-arab-election.

[1495] *Id.*

On another occasion, as the prime minister toured a security fence in Jordan, he spoke of surrounding Israel with fences and barriers "to defend ourselves against the wild beasts" in the neighborhood.[1496] The bigoted comment was an obvious reference to Palestinians and their regional supporters.

Yet another of the prime minister's incitements attempted to preclude full Palestinian sovereignty. He said:

> What I'm willing to give the Palestinians is not exactly a state with full authority, rather a state minus. This is why the Palestinians do not agree.[1497]

Similar assertions by other Israeli officials have threatened to annex the Jordan Valley and settlements in the West Bank.[1498]

Netanyahu is not the only Israeli official who resorts to incitement. In a 2015 interview broadcast on Israel's TV Channel 2, former Foreign Minister and Defense Minister Avigdor Lieberman remarked:

> There is no difference between the Communists, the Islamists and the Nasserists. What unites them is hatred

---

[1496] *Israel: Walled In*, Financial Times, June 29, 2016, available at: http://www.ft.com/cms/s/0/ccf4b532-3935-11e6-9a05-82a9b15a8ee7.html.

[1497] PLO/NAD Position on Incitement, *supra*, p. 2 (quoting a January, 2017 article in The Times of Israel).

[1498] *Id.*

of the State of Israel, and they represent the terrorist organizations in the Knesset.[1499]

Isaac Herzog, the former chairman of Israel's Labor Party, has also revealed racist views. In response to accusations that he was not strong enough as a leader, his party released a video interview in which someone from Herzog's military past remarked, "Herzog understands the Arab mentality... including through the crosshairs [of a gun]."[1500]

Anti-Arab racism pervades Israeli society. For example, the Beitar Jerusalem soccer club cultivates an ultra-nationalist fan base known for its anti-Arab, anti-Muslim chants.[1501] In the West Bank, radical right-wing Israeli youths commit acts of vandalism called "price tag" attacks on Palestinians.[1502] The extremists mostly burn cars, slash tires, destroy crops, and spray racist graffiti messages. But some of the hateful assaults have also resulted in murder.[1503] Often the perpetrators are not even arrested by Israeli police.[1504]

[1499] *In Israel's elections, racism is the winning ballot*, Adalah, The Legal Center for Arab Minority Rights in Israel (March 23, 2015), available at: http://www.adalah.org/en/content/view/8491.

[1500] *Id.*

[1501] "Unprecedented Israeli Action against Jerusalem Club's Anti-Arab/Muslim Racism," Huffington Post, July 9, 2016, available at: http://www.huffingtonpost.com/james-dorsey/unprecedented-israeli-act_b_7767344.html.

[1502] *'Price tag' attack strikes second Palestinian village inside Israel*, Middle East Eye (July 31, 2019), https://www.middleeasteye.net/news/settlers-price-tag-attacks-palestinian-village-inside-israel.

[1503] *See Id.*

[1504] *See* Jacob Magid, *Police arrest four Jewish teens for 'price tag' attack in northern Israel*, The Times of Israel (Dec. 12, 2918), https://www.timesofisrael.com/police-arrest-four-jewish-teens-for-price-tag-attack-in-northern-israel/.

Incidents like the ones described above demonstrate Israel's dismissive attitude toward the Palestinians. They reveal a political agenda of colonization, not mutual respect.[1505] They reflect a disregard for a two-state solution based on the 1967 lines, despite world support for such a peace plan.[1506] And they show how Israel consistently disregards its international law obligations.[1507]

In April of 2016, the PA proposed a resumption of meetings with an anti-incitement committee founded by the Wye River Memorandum.[1508] The purpose of the American-mediated committee, called the Tripartite Committee on Incitement, was to monitor Israeli and Palestinian media and school curricula for evidence of incitement. Few meetings were actually held. The Palestinian representatives were anxious to demonstrate their opposition to militancy and show the primary source of incitement was Israel. Unfortunately, Israel and the US rebuffed the overture.

In retaliation, Israel accuses the PA of "incitement" for paying salaries to Palestinian prisoners, and the families of Palestinian prisoners, arrested by Israeli security forces. However, the monthly payments are

---

[1505] PLO/NAD Position on Incitement, *supra*.

[1506] *Id.*

[1507] *Id.*

[1508] "Palestinian Authority accuses Israel of incitement," Al Monitor, April 26, 2016, http://www.al-monitor.com/pulse/originals/2016/04/palestine-authority-israel-committee-incitement-accusations.html.

a national, social, and humanitarian duty.[1509] When Palestinians sacrifice their freedom or life for their people, the least the PA can do is provide financial support for their families.[1510]

Fatah established the Martyr's Fund in 1967 to care for the widows and orphans of Palestinian guerrillas.[1511] Israelis called the individuals "terrorists," but they were really freedom fighters.[1512] The payments are not disbursed to members of Hamas or any other extremist group.[1513] Because Palestine has no army – only a police force with light weapons, as regulated by the Oslo Accords – the Palestinian people must do what they can to defend themselves from the cruelties of the occupation.[1514] When a fighter is arrested, tried, and/or convicted in Israeli courts, the result has no legal effect because Palestinians do not recognize the Israeli judiciary.[1515] Had the Arabs won the 1967 war, Israelis probably would have resorted to the same measures of resistance, and then Arabs would have enjoyed the privilege of outlawing the actions as "terrorist"

[1509] *Palestinians, Israelis dispute Tillerson on 'Martyrs' Fund'*, US News and World Report (June 14, 2017)(citing the Palestinian minister of prisoner affairs), https://www.usnews.com/news/world/articles/2017-06-14/palestinians-israelis-contest-tillerson-on-martyrs-fund.

[1510] *Id.*

[1511] The Palestinian Martyr's Fund Explained, Welcome to Palestine (June 24, 2017), https://www.welcometopalestine.com/article/the-palestinian-authority-martyrs-fund-explained/.

[1512] *Id.*

[1513] *Id.*

[1514] *Id.*

[1515] *Id.*

attacks.[1516] It is all a matter of perspective, military might, and the sympathies of the international media.[1517]

B. The Israeli Arguments

Summary of Arguments

Israel's troop withdrawals made good progress until the Palestinians exploited the vacated grounds to escalate their terrorist attacks. The assaults turned the Oslo peace process into a trail of carnage. For the parties to achieve security, Israel must withdraw to a secure border. Israel is not required to withdraw to the vulnerable Green Line.

If the final status arrangement produces a Palestinian state, Israel would also need safeguards against attacks by Palestinians or enemies to the east. The needed resources would help repel attacks originating from the ground, the air, and the radio airwaves.

Most important, the Palestinian leadership must replace its infrastructure of incitement with a culture of peace. Until the Palestinian people accept the existence of the Jewish state, the two societies will be doomed to perpetual strife.

---

i. The Oslo Accords entitle Israel to defensible borders

Throughout the Israeli-Palestinian face-off – even after the Oslo Accords were signed – the Palestinians have actively opposed the right of the

---

[1516] *Id.*

[1517] *Id.*

Jewish people to live in their own state in their ancestral homeland.[1518] Other regimes and militant groups have contributed to the eliminationist effort.[1519] This is the environment in which Israel must assess its security needs.

Israel is no bigger than New Jersey, or just 16,100 square miles,[1520] with a population of only eight million as of 2014.[1521] By contrast, the surrounding Arab states are 650 times larger by territory and over 37 times larger by population as of 2014.[1522] Also, consider the geographic dimensions of Israel and the Territories. Israel and the West Bank combined is only 40 miles wide.[1523] The distance from Israel's Mediterranean coast to the West Bank at its closest point is only nine

---

[1518] Moshe Yaalon, *Introduction: Restoring a Security-First Peace Policy*, in Israel's Critical Requirements for Defensible Borders, The Foundation for a Secure Peace, Jerusalem Center for Public Affairs (JCPA), p. 7 (2014) [hereinafter Yaalon], http://jcpa.org/requirements-for-defensible-borders/.

[1519] *Id.*

[1520] Uzi Dayan, *Defensible Borders to Ensure Israel's Future*, in Israel's Critical Requirements for Defensible Borders, The Foundation for a Secure Peace, Jerusalem Center for Public Affairs (JCPA), p. 35 (2014) [hereinafter Dayan], http://jcpa.org/requirements-for-defensible-borders/.

[1521] Yaakov Amidror, *The Risks of Foreign Peacekeeping Forces in the West Bank*, in Israel's Critical Requirements for Defensible Borders, The Foundation for a Secure Peace, Jerusalem Center for Public Affairs (JCPA), p. 68 (2014) [hereinafter Amidror], http://jcpa.org/requirements-for-defensible-borders/.

[1522] *Id.*

[1523] Amidror, *supra*, p. 68.

miles.[1524] And the hills of the West Bank overlook Israel's major population centers, including Jerusalem.[1525] An Arab military blitz from the West Bank hills along the narrow nine-mile "waist" could quickly sever Israel's northern region from the rest of the county.[1526] Militarily, these conditions leave Israel with a dire lack of "strategic depth."[1527]

The Oslo Accords required Israel to redeploy its West Bank troops, but the Accords did not mandate a withdrawal to the Green Line. The agreement called for the implementation of Resolution 242, which asked Israel and the Arab confrontation states to negotiate "secure and recognized boundaries free from threats or acts of force."[1528] In short, Israel is entitled to defensible borders. Consistent with that goal, Resolution 242 famously asked Israel to withdraw its armed forces from "territories" occupied in the Six-Day War, not "the territories" taken in the war.[1529] The deliberate omission of the word "the" left flexibility for the parties to negotiate borders other than the Green Line in consideration of Israel's security needs.[1530] Although Arab states lobbied against the omission, Egypt, Syria and Jordan ultimately accepted it.[1531]

[1524] Dore Gold, *Regional Overview: How Defensible Borders Remain vital for Israel*, in Israel's Critical Requirements for Defensible Borders, The Foundation for a Secure Peace, Jerusalem Center for Public Affairs (JCPA), p. 19 (2014) [hereinafter Gold Defensible Borders], http://jcpa.org/requirements-for-defensible-borders/.

[1525] Gold Defensible Borders, *supra*, pp. 35-36; Dayan, *supra*, p. 39.

[1526] Yaalon, *supra*, p. 13.

[1527] *See* Amidror, *supra*, p. 68.

[1528] Oslo I, art. I (citing Resolution 242).

[1529] Rostow, *supra* at 6-8.

[1530] *Id.*

[1531] TESSLER, *supra* at 419. Syria accepted Resolution 242 with no reservations about the wording after the 1973 War. *See* DOWTY, *supra* at 124.

The Green Line was never meant to be a border. When the Israeli-Jordanian Armistice Agreement of 1949 created the Green Line, the document expressly stipulated it was not a border.[1532] The intent was to let the adversaries change the line when transitioning from an armistice agreement to a peace treaty.[1533] Later, when the Armistice Agreement was replaced by the Israeli-Jordanian Peace Treaty of 1994, their Green Line legally disappeared.

Even if the Green Line still existed, it would not qualify as a secure border under Resolution 242, primarily because it would render Israel's main population centers vulnerable to close-range Palestinian attack. Even in the age of modern warfare, most wars are decided by ground forces.[1534] It would take Israel 48 hours just to call up its reserve ground forces in response to such an attack.[1535] The Green Line would also leave Israeli population centers vulnerable to mortars and short-range rocket fire. Ironically, such projectiles are even more difficult to repel than their long-range counterparts because they are more agile, easier to conceal, faster-acting, and cheap.[1536] With rockets alone, Palestinian terrorists positioned along the Green line could spread death, property destruction and panic throughout Israel continuously, just as Hamas

---

[1532] Yaalon, *supra*, p. 8.

[1533] Rostow, *supra* at 7-8.

[1534] Uzi Dayan, *supra*, p. 38.

[1535] Dore Gold, The Return of the Jordan Valley: American Withdrawal and the Future of Israeli Security, The American Interest (Oct. 16, 2019), https://www.the-american-interest.com/2019/10/16/american-withdrawal-and-the-future-of-israeli-security/.

[1536] Uzi Dayan, *supra*, p. 40.

already does – on a more limited scale – from its Gazan stronghold.[1537] Beyond the danger of these salvos, terror squads would likely infiltrate a Green Line border, or attempt to do so, on a frequent basis.[1538] Normal life for Israeli civilians would be all but impossible.[1539]

Accordingly, Israel deserves a border with more strategic depth than the Green Line affords.

Regardless of where the border is drawn, the IDF must maintain bases in the Territories, at least in East Jerusalem and the "Jordan Valley" corridor along the West Bank's Jordanian border.[1540] The Jordan Valley forms a barrier separating the West Bank from Jordan, thanks to the Eastern Samaria Mountain Range, which runs along the Valley's north-south route.

Without this defensive IDF presence, the prospective State of Palestine would likely devolve into another terrorist entity like Hamas and exploit the same freedom of military action that Hamas has wielded in Gaza ever since Israel withdrew from that domain in 2005.[1541] Worse still, Israel would face asymmetrical enemy threats on three fronts: Gaza, the West Bank, and the Hezbollah-controlled region of

---

[1537] *See* Armidror, *supra*, pp. 68-69.

[1538] *Id.*

[1539] *Id.*

[1540] Yaalon, *supra*, at 7-8 and 12-14.

[1541] Gershon Hacohen, *The West Bank's Area C: Israel's Eastern Line of Defense*, the Begin-Sadat Center for Strategic Studies, Bar-Ilan University, Mideast Security and Policy Studies No. 160 (April 19, 2019) [hereinafter Hacohen], p. 5, https://besacenter.org/mideast-security-and-policy-studies/west-bank-area-c-israel/.

Lebanon.[1542] Asymmetrical warfare, where terror groups use regular and irregular soldiers, fire a variety of projectiles at civilian targets, and fight in decentralized formations behind human shields, can inflict heavy losses on a conventional army and retard its progress indefinitely.[1543]

The above-described threats have grown more lethal as the terror groups have modernized their weapons.[1544] Those malevolent actors have used short-range and long-range rockets, armor-piercing missiles, shoulder-fired anti-aircraft missiles, attack tunnels,[1545] and unmanned aerial vehicles (drones)[1546] to inflict casualties and destruction.

If IDF troops are positioned in the Jordan Valley, they could help preserve Palestine's demilitarized status and root out incipient terror plots. The Israeli forces would also deter the smuggling of weapons from Jordan and discourage the build-up of foreign forces in that country.[1547] To the extent that Israel's sentries prevent Jordan from becoming a springboard for terrorist groups, they would lessen Jordan's security burden.[1548]

[1542] *Id.*, pp, 7 and 26.

[1543] *Id.*, p. 17-32.

[1544] Gold Defensible Borders, *supra* pp. 21-22.

[1545] *Id.*

[1546] Udi Dekel, *Control of Territorial Airspace and the Electromagnetic Spectrum*, in Israel's Critical Requirements for Defensible Borders, The Foundation for a Secure Peace, Jerusalem Center for Public Affairs, p. 87 (2014) [hereinafter Dekel], http://jcpa.org/requirements-for-defensible-borders/.

[1547] Dayan, *supra*, pp. 44-46.

[1548] *Id.*

The above monitoring functions must be accomplished by direct human involvement. Any attempt to monitor by remote control with high-tech devices could be foiled by enemies with similar high-tech skills.[1549]

Beyond the security challenges of the desired Palestinian state, Israel would face an overlapping set of threats orchestrated by Israel's archenemy, Iran, and its proxy militias in Iraq, Syria, Lebanon, and Gaza.[1550] The Iranian-backed fanatics already besiege Israelis with sporadic strikes. They feel emboldened by a strategic umbrella of Iranian ballistic missiles powerful enough to reach Israel.[1551] With further development in Iran's nuclear weapons program, the umbrella could become vastly more potent.[1552] This ominous specter is known as "the danger from the east."

Looking ahead, Israel must anticipate future dangers from the east. Arab states currently in disarray may eventually stabilize and rearm.[1553] Iraq is already rebuilding and amassing heavy modern weaponry in the process.[1554] Meanwhile, any number of the region's regimes may succumb to the global trend of Islamic extremism or otherwise regroup to confront Israel.[1555]

[1549] *Id.*, pp. 41-43.

[1550] Amidror, *supra*, p. 69.

[1551] *Id.*

[1552] *Id.*

[1553] Gold Defensible Borders, *supra*, p. 25.

[1554] *Id.*

[1555] *Id.*, p. 32

Experience has shown that Israel cannot rely on a mere exchange of security guarantees with the Palestinians.

During the five-year Oslo II period, Israel substantially completed its own security commitments by meeting its troop withdrawal benchmarks.[1556] However, the Palestinians disregarded their security promises.[1557] Oslo II had required the Palestinians to demilitarize[1558] and "prevent acts of terrorism."[1559] The Wye River Memorandum subsequently outlined a policy of "zero tolerance for terror" that required the systematic dismantling of terrorist organizations and their infrastructure.[1560]

Nevertheless, the more the IDF retreated from the major Palestinian cities, the more Palestinians exploited the vacated ground to attack Israelis.[1561] An unprecedented number of Israelis died in terror attacks during the Oslo interim period of 1994 to 1996.[1562] In fact, the Palestinians murdered more Israelis in the decade after the advent of

---

[1556] WATSON, *supra* at 105 and 114.

[1557] *See* Hacohen, *supra*, p. 38-39.

[1558] Oslo II, Art. XIV(3).

[1559] Oslo II, Art. XV(1).

[1560] Wye River Memorandum, Art. II.

[1561] *Question of the Violation of Human Rights in the Occupied Arab Territories, Including Palestine, note verbale dated 16 December 2002 from the Permanent Representative of Israel to the United Nations Office at Geneva addressed to the secretariat of the Commission of Human Rights,* Commission of Human Rights, fifty-ninth session, Economic and Social Council, E/CN.4/2003.G/21, (Dec. 23, 2002), p. 4, available at https://undocs.org/E/CN.4/2003/G/21.

[1562] GORDIS, *supra* at 366.

Oslo than in the decade before.[1563] Deeper disappointment accompanied the Second Intifada, when the Palestinian police assigned to combat Palestinian terrorism betrayed their writ and joined in the acts of terror. Clearly, the Oslo promise of "land for peace" needed stronger security safeguards.[1564]

The Palestinian assaults wreaked havoc on the IDF withdrawal. For example, a string of Palestinian suicide bombings in Hebron forced the IDF to suspend its scheduled pullback from that community.[1565]

To this day, the Palestinian security staff shirks its Oslo-codified duties. PA President Mahmoud Abbas uses the armed personnel mainly to retaliate against his political opponents and suppress public dissent.[1566] The squads also block Jews from visiting Joseph's Tomb in Nablus despite a provision in Oslo II that specifically guarantees Jewish access to West Bank holy sites such as Joseph's Tomb.[1567]

Palestinians attribute the security failures of the Oslo Accords to the hardships caused by Israel's alleged occupation of the Territories. They add that if Israel would end the occupation by withdrawing to the

---

[1563] For a catalog of terrorist attacks from September 13, 1993 (the signing of Oslo I) to September, 2000 (the start of the Second Intifada), see *Palestinian Terror and Incitement, Fatal Terrorist Attacks in Israel* (Sept. 1993 to 1999), Israel Ministry of Foreign Affairs, available at: http://www.mfa.gov.il/MFA/ForeignPolicy/Terrorism/Palestinian/Pages/Fatal%20Terrorist%20Attacks%20in%20Israel%20Since%20the%20DOP%20-S.aspx.

[1564] Yaalon, *supra*, p. 11.

[1565] See WATSON, *supra* at 42-47.

[1566] JONATHAN SCHANZER, STATE OF FAILURE 150-56 and 162-70 (2013).

[1567] Oslo II, Annex I, art. V and Appendix 4.

Green Line and recognizing it as a border, the motive for anti-Israel violence would subside. [1568]

This theory fails for two reasons. First, the supposed hardships of occupation could not have caused the breakdown of the Oslo Accords because the alleged antagonisms began long before the Accords were signed. Second, making the Green Line a border would not mitigate the passion of Palestinian terrorism. Terror groups like Hamas, the Palestinian Islamic Jihad, the Popular Front for the Liberation of Palestine, the Democratic Front for the Liberation of Palestine, and the Al-Aqsa Martyrs' Brigades refuse to recognize Israel within any borders.[1569] In 2005, when Israel retracted all troops and civilians to the Green Line outside Gaza, Hamas did not normalize relations with Israel; it bombarded much of Israel with various projectiles[1570] and sparked three wars over the next nine years.

A related misconception is that Israel's national security can be guaranteed by an International peacekeeping force.[1571] Such an armed unit failed to prevent Egypt from mobilizing troops to Israel's border and provoking war in 1967.[1572] Another international force did not stop PLO attacks from Lebanon in the 1980s or Hezbollah rocket attacks in

---

[1568] *See* Eric R. Mandel, *What Would Happen if Israel Withdrew from the West Bank and Ended the 'Siege' of Gaza*, The Jerusalem Post (Jan. 26, 2016), http://www.jpost.com/Opinion/What-would-happen-if-Israel-withdrew-from-the-West-Bank-and-ended-the-siege-of-Gaza 442855.

[1569] *See Id.*

[1570] Yaalon, *supra*, p. 11.

[1571] Hacohen, *supra*, pp. 40-43.

[1572] *Id.*

the 2000's.[1573] A single terrorist bombing of the US Marine barracks in Beirut, Lebanon precipitated an immediate US pullout from that country in 1983.[1574] And the multinational unit guarding the Sinai has done nothing to stem the smuggling of weapons to Hamas in Gaza or to disrupt the operations of jihadist terror groups among the Sinai Bedouin tribes.[1575] Israel's survival cannot be entrusted to the unreliable oaths of foreigners. Under Article 51 of the UN Charter, a nation has the right to defend itself with its own forces.[1576] Israel must be able to defend itself by itself.[1577]

[1573] *Id.*

[1574] *Id.*

[1575] *Id.*

[1576] Statement to the Knesset by Prime Minister Ben-Gurion on the situation along the Israel-Syrian frontier, in Foreign Policy, Israel Ministry of Foreign Affairs (April 10, 1962)(citing UN Charter, art. 51), http://www.israel.org/MFA/ForeignPolicy/MFADocuments/Yearbook1/Pages/3%20Statement%20to%20the%20Knesset%20by%20Prime%20Minister%20Ben-G.aspx.

[1577] *Netanyahu: 'Israel will defend itself, by itself, against any threat,'* Israel Hayom (Oct. 11, 2019), https://www.israelhayom.com/2019/10/10/netanyahu-israel-will-defend-itself-by-itself-against-any-threat.

ii. The final status must accommodate Israel's other vital security needs

To ensure peaceful coexistence between Israel and the proposed Palestinian state, Israel would require more than defensible borders and the strategic placement of IDF troops. It would also need:

1) authority to operate early warning stations in the Palestinian state;
2) a right of emergency IDF deployment in the new state;
3) priority management rights over Palestinian airspace; and
4) priority control over the shared electromagnetic spectrum.

Early warning systems would help detect any military mobilization on the Palestinian side of the border.[1578] These systems would be critical to offset Israel's lack of strategic depth.

The right of emergency deployment would let the IDF block the infiltration of enemy forces into the Palestinian state in violation of the final status agreement.[1579]

Control over Palestinian airspace would be essential to defend against aerial threats.[1580] An enemy combat aircraft could fly from anywhere in the West Bank to Jerusalem in under two minutes.[1581] The same aircraft

---

[1578] Amidror, *supra*, p. 77.

[1579] *Id.*

[1580] Dekel, *supra*, pp. 86-87.

[1581] *Id.*

could reach all the way to Israel's Mediterranean coast in just four minutes.[1582] Guarding against this scenario would demand fast reflexes. Israel would need time to identify the flight as suspicious, scramble an interceptor plane to engage the aircraft and determine whether it is hostile, and if necessary, shoot it down before it reaches Israeli territory.[1583] Variations on this protocol would address 9/11 style attacks and enemy drones.[1584] Israel could not simply fire anti-aircraft batteries and destroy airborne vehicles that look suspicious from the ground; a closer inspection would be required.[1585]

Palestinians repeatedly activate radio signal jammers to disrupt Israeli communications, including dialogs between airline pilots and the control tower at Israel's Ben Gurion Airport.[1586] From the high ground of the West Bank, an unauthorized transmission on a single channel can jam co-channel operations throughout Israel.[1587] Therefore Israel must reserve the right to monitor frequency operations on both sides of any permanent Israel/Palestine border and confiscate any radio devices that cause public harm.[1588]

[1582] *Id.*

[1583] *Id.*

[1584] *Id.*

[1585] *Id.*

[1586] *Id.*, pp. 91-92.

[1587] *Id.*

[1588] *Id.*

iii. **The Palestinians must stop their incitements against Israelis**

The cornerstone of a viable security plan would be a culture of peace.[1589]

Article XXII(1) of Oslo II required the parties to:

> abstain from incitement, including hostile propaganda, against each other... and take legal measures to prevent such incitement by any organizations, groups or individuals within their jurisdiction.[1590]

The Palestinians have violated this clause relentlessly.[1591] Less than a year after he signed Oslo I, PLO Chairman Yasser Arafat gave speeches pledging to disregard the agreement and resume the fight to "liberate" Palestine.[1592] To this day, Palestinian leaders constantly broadcast inflammatory Islamic rhetoric that incites their people to murder Israelis.[1593] The incitement is institutionalized not only in Palestinian government agencies but in their schools, mosques, and news media.[1594]

[1589] Yaalon, *supra*, p. 10.

[1590] Oslo II, art. XXII(1).

[1591] WATSON, *supra* at 217-223.

[1592] EFRAIM KARSH, ARAFAT'S WAR: THE MAN AND HIS BATTLE FOR ISRAELI CONQUEST 60-61 (2004) [hereinafter KARSH].

[1593] *Palestinian incitement and terrorism: Truth and lies, Behind the Headlines*, Israel Ministry of Foreign Affairs (Oct. 29, 2015), https://mfa.gov.il/MFA/ForeignPolicy/Issues/Pages/Palestinian-incitement-and-terrorism-Oct-2015.aspx.

[1594] CAROLINE GLICK, THE ISRAELI SOLUTION 8 (2014) [hereinafter GLICK].

Palestinian teachers and textbooks instruct students, as early as in the first grade, to hate Jews and "martyr" themselves for the cause of annihilating the "Zionist entity."[1595] The curriculum maintains that Israel is a myth and that "Palestine" encompasses all land from the Jordan River to the Mediterranean Sea.[1596] In Hamas's paramilitary training camps, thousands of children learn to shoot Kalashnikov rifles and make improvised explosive devices in preparation for the next war against the "Zionist enemy."[1597]

The Palestinian governments in both Gaza and Ramallah publicly support violent jihad against Israel.[1598] For example, in July of 2017, after three Arab Israeli terrorists shot and killed two Israeli police officers at the Temple Mount/Haram, and Israel installed metal detectors in the surrounding streets to prevent more shootings, senior Fatah officials called for a "Day of Rage," urging the Palestinian masses to riot against

---

[1595] *See* Eldad Pardo, *Palestinian Elementary School Curriculum 2016–17: Radicalization and Revival of the PLO Program*, IMPACT-se (April 2017) [hereinafter Pardo], http://www.impact-se.org/wp-content/uploads/PA-Curriculum-2017-Revised.pdf. *See also* KARSH, *supra* at 100-101.

[1596] Pardo, *supra*, pp. 12-14, 17-19, 26, 27, and 42.

[1597] *Here's What a Hamas Training Camp for Teens Looks Like*, Washington Post, Jan. 29, 2015, available at: https://www.washingtonpost.com/world/heres-what-a-hamas-training-camp-for-teens-looks-like/2015/01/29/ef0b4092-a33f-11e4-9f89-561284a573f8_story.html.

[1598] Quartet Report, *supra*, p. 3. *See also* Itamar Marcus & Barbara Crook, *Kill a Jew – Go to Heaven: The Perception of the Jew in Palestinian Society*, Jewish Pol. Stud. Rev., Fall, 2005, available at http://www.jcpa.org/phas/phas-marcus-crook-f05.htm.

Israelis for encroaching on an Islamic holy site.[1599] Three people died in the ensuing melee.

Palestinian religious leaders perpetuate the medieval "blood libel" that Jews kill non-Jewish children to use their blood in the Jewish Passover ritual.[1600] In one variation on this theme, Palestinian President Mahmoud Abbas falsely announced that a group of Israeli rabbis had demanded the mass murder of Palestinians by poisoning their water.[1601] At the start of the 2015-2016 Knife Intifada, a spate of knife attacks on Israelis by Palestinian youths, President Abbas delivered a televised speech announcing, "We welcome every drop of blood spilled in Jerusalem. This is pure blood, clean blood, blood on its way to Allah."[1602]

PA communications officials use social media sites to spread inflammatory falsehoods about Israelis and Jews that radicalize

---

[1599] Shlomi Eldar, *Fatah Officials Defy Abbas on Temple Mount Crisis*, Al Monitor (July 20, 2017), http://www.al-monitor.com/pulse/originals/2017/07/israel-palestinians-mahmoud-abbas-mahmoud-al-aloul-fatah-idf.html.

[1600] See KARSH, *supra* at 93-94; also see *Middle East Media Research Institute TV Monitor Project*, video of Hamas leader Salah Al-Bardawil claiming "Zionists . . . execute Palestinian children . . . and collect their blood . . . to knead it into the bread that is eaten on Passover," on AL-AQSA TV, (Nov. 26, 2015), available at http://www.memritv.org/clip/en/5187.htm.

[1601] *Palestinian president uses anti-Semitic trope against Israel in EU speech*, WASHINGTON POST, June 24, 2016, available at: https://www.washingtonpost.com/news/worldviews/wp/2016/06/24/palestinian-president-uses-anti-semitic-trope-against-israel-in-e-u-speech/.

[1602] *What Provoked Palestinian Knife Attacks in Israel*, THE NEW YORKER, October 23, 2015, available at http://www.newyorker.com/news/news-desk/what-provoked-palestinian-knife-attacks-in-israel.

Palestinian youth and encourage them to launch terror raids.[1603] One of the hateful messages was an instructional video titled "How to stab a Jew."[1604]

Under Palestinian law, the PA pays generous monthly salaries and benefits, via the PLO, to Palestinians convicted of terrorism and families of deceased terrorists.[1605] The payments, disbursed from the "Palestinian Martyr's Fund," scale to the length of the prison sentence. So the more the more heinous the crime, the greater the "reward."[1606] As of 2018, the PA has appropriated $403 million, amounting to seven percent of its budget, on these payouts.[1607] This government program offers a powerful incentive for Palestinians to murder Israelis.[1608]

Official Palestinian maps, like those in Palestinian classrooms, show the "State of Palestine" spanning all territory from the Mediterranean Sea

---

[1603] Hirsh Goodman, *The Knife and the Message: The First 100 Days of the New Palestinian Uprising (October 2015 – January 2016)*, JCPA (Feb. 29, 2016), http://jcpa.org/the-knife-and-the-message-the-roots-of-the-new-palestinian-uprising/the-knife-and-the-message-the-first-100-days-of-the-new-palestinian-uprising-october-2015-january-2016/.

[1604] *QUARTET REPORT*, *supra*, p. 3.

[1605] Brig.-Gen. (res.) Yossi Kuperwasser, *Incentivizing Terrorism: Palestinian Authority Allocations to Terrorists and their Families*, JCPA, at Introduction (Dec. 2016), http://jcpa.org/paying-salaries-terrorists-contradicts-palestinian-vows-peaceful-intentions/.

[1606] *Id.* at Ch. 1.

[1607] Lahav Harkov, *Palestinians Increase Payments to Terrorists to $403 Million*, JERUSALEM POST (March 6, 2018), http://www.jpost.com/Arab-Israeli-Conflict/Palestinians-increase-payments-to-terrorists-to-403-million-544343.

[1608] *Id.* at Conclusion.

to the Jordan River, in place of the State of Israel.[1609] The PA names streets, public squares and schools after Palestinians who die in "martyrdom operations."[1610]

Palestinian clergy preach that Jews evolved from "apes and pigs."[1611] Following such anti-Semitic sermons, the 2015 Knife Intifada disproportionately targeted Orthodox Jews, who were easily identified by their traditional clothing.[1612] A related attack set fire to the ancient Jewish holy site of Joseph's Tomb.[1613]

The PA-controlled Palestinian news media also incites against Israelis and Jews.[1614] For instance, on anniversaries of the 9/11 terrorist attack, a Palestinian columnist repeats the charge that the atrocity was an American Israeli plot.[1615]

[1609] *New Fatah Logo Eliminates Israel*, TIMES OF ISRAEL, Dec. 13, 2012, http://www.timesofisrael.com/new-fatah-logo-eliminates-israel/.

[1610] *QUARTET REPORT*, *supra*, p. 3.

[1611] GLICK, *supra* at 43; Kenneth Lasson, *Incitement in the Mosques: Testing the Limits of Free Speech and Religious Liberty*, 27 WHITTIER LAW REVIEW 3, 11, 20 (2005).

[1612] *Religious Jews Feel Targeted by Palestinian Attacks*, HUFFINGTON POST, Oct. 13, 2015, http://www.huffingtonpost.com/entry/religious-jews-palestinian-attacks_561d583de4b028dd7ea5680d.

[1613] *Palestinian rioters torch Jewish holy site Joseph's Tomb*, BBC NEWS, Oct. 15, 2015, http://www.bbc.com/news/world-middle-east-34547523.

[1614] Zenobia Ravji, *Facebook deactivates dozens of accounts of Palestinian journalists and activists*, MIDDLE EAST EYE (May, 2020), https://www.middleeasteye.net/news/facebook-deactivates-accounts-dozens-palestinian-journalists-and-activists.

[1615] *Palestinian Columnist: 9/11, An American-Israeli Plot*, THE MIDDLE EAST MEDIA RESEARCH INSTITUTE, Special Dispatch No. 4940 (Sept. 10, 2012), https://www.memri.org/reports/palestinian-columnist-911-%E2%80%93-american-israeli-plot.

Until Palestinians embrace the concept of co-existence with the Jewish state, the peace process cannot succeed.[1616]

[1616] Yaalon, *supra*, p. 10.

CHAPTER 5:
CONCLUSION

This study, invited you to be the judge of the Israeli-Palestinian dispute. You have now heard the major legal arguments of both sides. What do you think?

Maybe now, even partisan readers may appreciate the fairness of the opposing point of view.[1617] Then again, some readers may feel more ambivalent than ever. The legal issues are unusually complex and contentious. And equitable considerations weigh heavily on both sides.

Others may conclude that no amount of legal insight can resolve the conflict, that clever lawyers will spin the law however they want, and that peace can be achieved only through political compromise. Maybe so. But how likely is it that two peoples with divergent political outlooks, deadlocked in a century of violence, will break the impasse through politics alone?

Humanity has developed a wealth of international jurisprudence, a body of law that represents our common values. That shared baseline of agreement has not replaced political leadership. But it has given

---

[1617] *See* James A. Baker, III, *Lawyers as Leaders: Being a Lawyer Prepared Me For Diplomacy on the World Stage*, 81 TEX. B.J. 94 (Feb. 2018), https://editions.mydigitalpublication.com/publication/?i=470180&article_id=2991646&view=articleBrowser&ver=html5.

leaders crucial guidance when managing international conflicts, including wars.

As for the Israeli-Palestinian controversy, none of the component issues is devoid of legal precedent. Lawyers have previously helped enemies draw permanent borders, steward religious landmarks, decide the fate of settlements, free refugees from statelessness, and protect national security. In fact, these were just the types of issues resolved by the Egypt-Israel Peace Treaty of 1979 and the Jordan-Israel Peace Treaty of 1994.

True, the war in the Holy Land is intractable partly because the land is considered holy. But political divides based on religion have been bridged. The Good Friday Agreement of 1998 resolved decades of ethno-nationalist violence between the Catholics and Protestants of Northern Ireland. More relevant to the instant study, Israel and Azerbaijan have maintained solid ties ever since the Muslim state declared independence in 1991, despite the traditional antipathy of the Muslim world towards Israel. Azerbaijan is known for its religious tolerance and openness to relations with the West. In 2020, Israel and four Muslim countries – the United Arab Emirates, Bahrain, Sudan, and Morocco – surprised the world with their normalization pact called the Abraham Accords.

Even when international conflicts are settled by war, the former combatants may form partnerships forged in law. The US followed that pattern with Great Britain, Mexico, Spain, Germany, Japan, and Vietnam.

Taking a legal approach to international problem-solving does not per se turn enemies into friends. A peace treaty ideally requires meaningful participation by both antagonists. That may explain why many peace plans failed to solve the Israeli-Palestinian conflict. The UN Partition Plan, the Arab Peace Initiative, the Quartet Plan, and the Peace to Prosperity Plan lacked input from one or both of the affected parties.

Another essential ingredient in the peacemaking recipe is public acceptance. If the warring leaders cannot convince their respective clients that the drafted resolution is fair, the deal may never succeed. The recalibration of public opinion may be more difficult than the work at the negotiating table. Still, every human bias that can be learned can be unlearned. Israelis and Palestinians can find hope in these principles of conflict resolution.

Peaceful coexistence for many Israelis and Palestinians is already a fact of life. As many as 200,000 Palestinians work at jobs in Israel.[1618] Trade between the Israeli and Palestinian economies exceeds $900 million.[1619] Israeli-Palestinian business ventures collaborate on projects in renewable energy and digital healthcare.[1620] A nonprofit organization orchestrates classes for Israeli and Palestinian high school students to develop their high-tech skills and form social bonds.[1621]

[1618] *Grassroots partnership aims to boost Israeli–Palestinian business ties*, JERUSALEM POST (Feb. 21, 2019), https://www.jpost.com/israel-news/grassroots-partnership-aims-to-boost-israeli-palestinian-business-ties-581260.

[1619] *See Id.*

[1620] *Id.*

[1621] *Palestinian and Israeli Teenagers Meet to Shape Their Future with Tech*, FORBES (March 18, 2018), https://www.forbes.com/sites/samarmarwan/2018/03/18/palestinian-and-israeli-teenagers-meet-to-shape-their-future-with-tech/?sh=4992298e27f7.

Israelis and Palestinians have all the tools they need to build a stable, trusting relationship. With the right mindset and a common respect for law, they could quickly bring a century of bloodshed to a mutually agreeable end.

With the above principles in mind, how should the Israeli-Palestinian conflict be resolved? What should be the number, size, and shape of the resulting territorial possessions? Who should maintain what rights of control? Maybe all these factors must yield to a higher priority.

Above all else, any mutually acceptable solution must permit all participants to say, "This land is ours."

APPENDIX: MAPS

MAP	DATE	DESCRIPTION
1	Prehistoric	The Levant
2	1,020 B.C.E.	Ancient Kingdom of Israel
3	750 C.E.	Arab Muslim Empire
4	636-1880	Jews Under Foreign Rule
5	1683	Ottoman Empire
6	1683-1917	The Ottoman Levant
7	1881-1914	Major Arab and Jewish Settlements
8	1922	British Mandate Palestine
9	1922	Creation of Transjordan
10	1937	Peel Commission Partition Plan
11	1944	Land in Jewish Possession
12	1947	UN Partition Plan
13	1949	Armistice Lines
14	1948, 1967	Depopulated Palestinian Villages
15	1947-1948	Jewish Communities Lost in 1947-1948 War
16	1949-1967	Division of Jerusalem
17	2003	Palestinian Refugee Camps
18	1969	Israel, Arab States and OIC States

Have something to say?
Please take a second to leave me a review on
AMAZON.COM

And as promised, you can download a compilation of these maps in PDF format (helpful especially if your book version is black and white):

www.bit.ly/ajm-appendix

ABOUT THE AUTHOR

Joel M. Margolis is a senior corporate counsel in an international telecommunications company. As a telecom lawyer, he has worked for decades in government affairs, including international matters.

He is also a certified information privacy professional (CIPP-US), a former registered lobbyist, and former holder of a top-secret security clearance. He has never represented a party with an interest in the Israeli-Palestinian dispute.